ROUGH WEATHER SEAMANSHIP

for SAIL AND POWER

DESIGN, GEAR, AND TACTICS FOR COASTAL AND OFFSHORE WATERS

ROGER MARSHALL

INTERNATIONAL MARINE/McGRAW-HILL
CAMDEN, MAINE · NEW YORK · CHICAGO · SAN FRANCISCO ·
LISBON · LONDON · MADRID · MEXICO CITY · MILAN · NEW DELHI ·
SAN JUAN · SEOUL · SINGAPORE · SYDNEY · TORONTO

The McGraw·Hill Companies

Visit us at: www.internationalmarine.com

1 2 3 4 5 6 7 8 9 DOC DOC 9 8 7 6

Library of Congress Cataloging-in-Publication Data
Marshall, Roger.
Rough weather seamanship for sail and power : design, gear, and tactics for coastal and offshore waters / Roger Marshall.
p.   cm.
Includes index.
ISBN 0–07–139870–8 (hardcover : alk. paper)
1. Boats and boating.   2. Sailing.   3. Heavy weather seamanship.
I. Title.
GV777.5.M37 2006
797.1—dc22   2006000750

Questions regarding the content of this book should be addressed to
International Marine
P.O. Box 220
Camden, ME 04843
www.internationalmarine.com

Questions regarding the ordering of this book should be addressed to
The McGraw-Hill Companies
Customer Service Department
P.O. Box 547
Blacklick, OH 43004
Retail customers: 1–800–262–4729
Bookstores: 1–800–722–4726

Photos and illustrations by the author unless otherwise noted.

Other books by Roger Marshall:

All About Powerboats
Essential Sailing
The Complete Guide to Choosing a Cruising Sailboat
Sail Better
Marshall's Marine Sourcebook

Contents

Introduction

Most mariners, be they sailors or powerboaters, fear a storm at sea. They worry that their vessel isn't capable of handling the conditions or that, out of ignorance, they may put their boat and themselves in a dangerous situation. Good books have been written to address such fears with concrete information and advice, but most such books focus on the worst-case scenario: a severe storm encountered far at sea.

This book, by contrast, treats the worst-case scenario as the far end of a continuum that begins in more familiar territory, closer to home: the squall you encounter in a local bay; the storm that buffets your boat at its mooring or in its marina slip; the steep seas that spring from nowhere when a frontal breeze blows against a tidal or ocean current; or the gale that disrupts a short ocean passage with drenching spray, seasickness, and exhaustion but poses no real threat provided you know what to do. Most of us encounter a gale sooner or later, but few of us will ever face a severe storm at sea. Use a fresh 20-knot breeze to help you prepare for 25. Use your first 35-knot gale to prepare for 45. And use this book to help the learning process along.

The first two chapters will help you understand when rough conditions are imminent and under what circumstances you can expect dangerous seas. Sailors once used to put out to sea no matter what the weather. They watched the clouds and the barometer, and were knowledgeable about the kinds of conditions that give rise to dangerous weather. Today, television and Internet forecasts predict the weather as far as five days in advance, and radio broadcasts tell you what to expect over your location in the nearer term. Chapter 1 shows you how to augment this information with your own "deck-level" observations. If you pick your weather carefully and are not at sea for extended passages, you may never have to confront a full-blown storm. Chapter 2 explains how waves and wave patterns evolve, and how they can become dangerous.

Unfortunately, until you have been out in a storm or two, it is hard to know what to do and where to go. In fact, you might not even know whether your boat is suitable to face a storm. Chapters 3, 4, and 5 address this concern, showing you how to choose a sail- or power-boat that will weather a storm and how to adapt your present boat to cope with rough weather at sea. These chapters discuss gear and installation options for sail- and powerboats, and tell you what is best. My opinions often differ from conventional wisdom, but they are based on 40 years of sailing in all kinds of weather, the testing I have carried out on a range of gear and equipment, and the feedback I have gleaned from other experienced sailors on what works and what doesn't.

More often than not, during a storm your boat will be in harbor—where it should be—tied to a marina or lying to a mooring. While you are safe ashore, your boat is taking the brunt of the heavy weather. Have you taken every precaution to ensure that it is protected properly? Chapter 6 will give you the necessary guidance.

In chapters 7 and 8 we meet rough weather at sea. As it approaches we make our preparations (Chapter 7), and when it hits (Chapter 8), we respond flexibly with tactics we've thought through and practiced beforehand—tactics adapted to our boat, our crew, and our situation. We might even change those tactics as a storm progresses, and Chapter 8 describes how to do this.

In Chapter 9 we look at gear and techniques that will keep our crew members safe in rough weather at sea. The focus is on safety aboard, since it's rare that a boat must be abandoned. But it's prudent to know beforehand what you would do if you were to lose your boat in a worst-case scenario, so we also discuss gear and techniques that will help you survive in a life raft.

In Chapter 10 we explore the sort of ingenuity and creativity that a skipper needs to make emergency repairs to a storm-damaged boat, and in Chapter 11 we discuss how to make an emergency distress call and what to expect from search-and-rescue personnel.

I have added a number of heavy-weather scenarios throughout the book—both real and fictional—to illustrate the sort of thinking you should do when the going gets tough. Trying to decide where a storm is going to go, and whether you are in its path, is one example of such thinking. Old-time mariners, without the benefit of modern weather forecasts and radio communications, used certain rules of thumb to help make these kinds of decisions and many of these rules still apply today. Of course, they are not perfect, but neither is the science of weather prediction or the techniques of storm sailing. Hopefully, this book will help you make smart decisions, and give you peace of mind in heavy weather.

In short, this book is intended to give you the confidence to face rough weather—whether that means a garden-variety afternoon blow or a major storm. By making this book's techniques and checklists a part of your sailing repertoire, you will be able to sail anywhere with complete confidence in your abilities.

One

Understanding the Weather

You are heading out to sea over a glassy swell on a bright sunny morning. There is barely a cloud in the sky. The wind is light—about 8–10 knots from the south—and it looks as if you are in for a beautiful day. A few hours later, however, dark clouds race in from the north. Within minutes rain pelts down, beating the sea flat and killing the wind while lightning flashes in the distance. An hour later, the wind is cold and blowing a gusty 25 knots out of the north. Clouds scud across the sky bringing short, sharp showers. What happened to the weather?

Quite simply, a cold front passed through and ruined your sunny day. A front is the demarcation line between two moving air masses and can cause a variety of weather changes. It can also be fairly easy to identify by looking at the clouds, a weather map, or a barometer. Unfortunately, according to a survey by England's Royal National Lifeboat Institution, more than 80 percent of the recreational sailors in UK waters do not look at a weather map or obtain an up-to-date forecast before heading out, and in all likelihood a similar situation exists in America and elsewhere.

Here's a comforting thought: in most cases, the bigger the storm, the more warning you will have of its approach. While far from perfect, modern meteorology is more than capable of providing advance warning of extreme weather events like hurricanes or powerful nontropical storms. With today's communications, including the Internet, weatherfax, satellite phones, weather radio, and your television set, there's no excuse for getting caught on the water by a big storm (unless you're far at sea).

More likely challenges include the garden-variety depression that was forecast to give 25 knots of wind but intensifies to 35 instead; the strong breeze made even stronger by local topography or effects of heating and cooling; the 4-foot seas turned into steep, bone-jarring, 8-foot brutes by shoal water or opposing currents; or the sudden squall or microburst not foretold by regional weather reports. All these conditions can be scary and uncomfortable, but none need threaten your boat or your crew.

It takes some effort and experience to understand the weather, but you can easily learn the difference between a warm front, a cold front, and an occluded front—along with the weather conditions each might bring. You can also learn to recognize cloud types and the weather they might herald. This chapter is an overview of the factors that brew up rough weather and the tools you can use to predict what's coming. We'll aim to reduce a complex subject to useful, straightforward components, organized around the following subtopics:

1. **Sources of weather information.** The best storm tactic is to avoid storms altogether; modern weather forecasting makes this more feasible than ever.
2. **Highs, lows, and weather fronts.** These systems control the weather in the middle latitudes (roughly between 30 and 60 degrees north and south), so we'll look at their causes, behaviors, and characteristic indicators. We'll also examine atmospheric patterns and instabilities.
3. **Clouds.** There are messages in the clouds. Learning to read what the clouds say can enhance your boating pleasure.
4. **Deck-level Forecasting.** Using information covered in the previous topics, we'll discuss some simple forecasting techniques.
5. **Nontropical Rotational Storms.** These "weather bombs," typified by east coast extreme low-pressure systems, deserve special mention. We'll discuss how they develop and grow.
6. **Thunderstorms.** A thunderstorm is usually a call to abandon the day's sailing and head for shore. Here you learn about the dangers of lightning, microbursts, and downbursts.
7. **Tropical storms.** The principal weather-makers of the tropics (roughly between 23 degrees north and south). When they become hurricanes they are the most dangerous storms of all.

Sources of Weather Information

Before heading out on the water, you should certainly obtain a local forecast and then update it onboard if and when you can. Your own deck-level observations are also important, but your earliest indications of what lies ahead will come from official weather forecasts. The best source of regional weather information is a professional meteorologist, who draws upon satellite imagery, extensive synoptic weather observations, data both at ground level and in the upper atmosphere, and computer modeling to construct a reliable forecast.

Most of us have access to forecasts on local radio and TV channels, and also on The Weather Channel (cable TV or weather.com). Weather maps and forecasts also appear in local newspapers and most newspaper websites and other online sites. Most such forecasts in the United States are developed from National Weather Service (NWS) data. (The NWS is a division of NOAA, the National Oceanic and Atmospheric Administration.) Forecasts are also available directly from the NWS internet site at www.nws.noaa.gov or by monitoring NOAA Weather Radio, which also broadcasts local forecasts—including marine forecasts—on VHF radio frequencies. VHF radio is the most

These cumulus clouds promise mild, sunny weather. (Photo courtesy NOAA/NWS)

convenient and dependable source of weather information for boaters in U.S. coastal waters.

Environment Canada provides marine forecasts for Canadian waters at www.weather office.ec.gc.ca/marine. The Met Office gives forecasts for British waters at www.met office.com, as does the BBC (www.bbc.co.uk/ weather). In Australia, the Bureau of Meteorology forecasts appear at www.bom.gov.au. Worldwide forecasts are also available from commercial sources and can be found by searching the web.

Boats offshore can receive forecasts via high-frequency (shortwave) radio, either as voice broadcasts or as text messages for fax or monitor via a modem. NOAA's Ocean Prediction Center (OPC) provides forecasts for the high seas from 65 degrees north to 15 degrees south (except the Indian Ocean) via radiofacsimile and shortwave radio, and the U.S. Coast Guard provides radio forecasts in both voice and text on high and medium frequency bands.

The United States Coast Guard (USCG) also supports NAVTEX, which provides medium frequency coastal forecasts to onboard text receivers out to about 250 miles. See www.navcen.uscg.gov for details. Commercial forecast services are also available to offshore boaters, most by subscription.

In short, there is little excuse for leaving shore without an up-to-date forecast. The precise path of a low-pressure center and the influences of local topography and conditions might still bring you milder or more severe conditions than a regional weather forecast has led you to expect, but the official forecast is the place to start.

Highs, Lows, and Fronts

All the information that a meteorologist needs to construct a middle-latitude weather forecast is shown on a weather map, which includes areas of high and low pressure, wind direction, and cloud coverage, as well as an abundance of other information. The weather maps used by professional meteorologists are much more complex than the weather map shown in your local newspaper or on your TV. But for the purposes of a weekend sail, the newspaper map is adequate. It will give you a good idea of what weather to expect over the next few hours and (with decreasing confidence) the next day, two days, and beyond.

To understand what weather maps are telling us, let's look briefly at the elements of middle-latitude weather. Much of the material that follows is adapted, with permission, from Bob Sweet's excellent *Onboard Weather Forecasting: A Captain's Quick Guide* (International Marine, 2005).

What Makes the Weather?

Air is normally densest at sea level, where it weighs just over an ounce per cubic foot, but it becomes less dense with altitude. Above 50 miles in altitude, in the *thermosphere*, the density of air can scarcely be measured. It varies with temperature, cold air having a greater density than warm. The density of air is also affected by its moisture content. Water molecules weigh less than the molecules of nitrogen and oxygen they displace in moist air, so moist air is less dense than dry air and tends to rise. Moisture content has far less effect than temperature on air density, however.

Three-quarters of the mass of air is concentrated in the bottom 5–10 miles of the atmosphere (known as the *troposphere*). As a result, virtually all of the world's weather takes place in this bottom layer. Only rarely does a thunderstorm build through the *tropopause*, the layer of rapid temperature change separating the troposphere from the *stratosphere* above it. As cold air is denser than warm air, the tropopause can be as little as 3–5 miles high at the poles, but it hovers at 10 miles or even higher over the equator. For similar reasons, the

troposphere in general is lower during the night than during the day.

The ultimate engine that drives the earth's weather is the unequal distribution of heat over the planet's surface. Simply put, the tropics receive more heat energy from the sun than the poles, and the result is a continual poleward transport of heated air and heated water (in the form of ocean currents) from the equatorial regions. Heated air rises in a broad band called the *doldrums*, roughly between 15 degrees north and 15 degrees south—an area of light and baffling winds punctuated by violent thunderstorms—and when it reaches the upper troposphere it flows poleward, both north and south. At roughly 30 degrees north and south, some of the air has cooled enough to subside, forming a band of high pressure and light and variable winds known as the *horse latitudes*. (These latitudes are so called because this was usually the area where a seaman worked off his dead horse—the advance pay or "horse" he received upon signing on for the voyage.) The rest of the upper-atmosphere air from the tropics continues poleward, subsiding over arctic and Antarctic areas.

This poleward movement of air aloft is balanced by an equatorward movement of air at the earth's surface. Part of the air that sinks at around 30 degrees north and south flows back toward the tropics to replace what has risen aloft there. In the Northern Hemisphere this north-to-south surface flow is deflected to the right by the spinning of the earth, and in the Southern Hemisphere the south-to-north movement is deflected to the left. The result is the northeast and southeast trade winds, respectively.

The rest of the air that sinks at 30 degrees north and south flows poleward at the surface, and is deflected to the right in the Northern Hemisphere and to the left in the Southern Hemisphere to form the prevailing westerlies that characterize the circulation patterns of the middle latitudes.

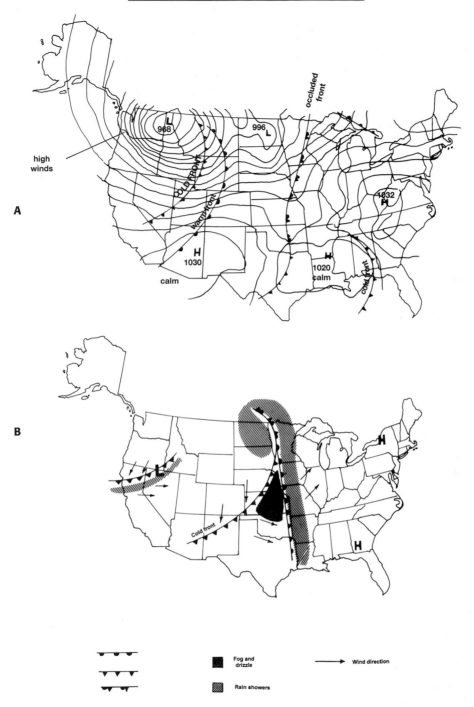

A weather map may include wind direction and speed, isobars, high- and low-pressure areas, cloud coverage and a lot more. A full weather map can be very cluttered, so many forecasters separate a surface analysis map (A)—showing highs, lows, isobars, etc.—from a map (B) showing cloud cover, areas of rain, and other features. The latter map shows how fog and rain often develop in front of a cold front and behind a warm front.

Along the polar fronts, at about 60 degrees north and south, the prevailing westerlies run into high-latitude easterlies flowing from the poles toward lower latitudes, which forces the comparatively warm, moist air of the westerlies aloft. Rising air always causes instability—this is why bad weather is associated with low pressure—so it comes as no surprise that the polar front is a zone marked by frequent, severe storms.

This, then, is the fundamental atmospheric circulation pattern for the earth. The various bands just described migrate north during the northern summer and south during the northern winter, and there are geographic effects as well. The prevailing westerlies of the Southern Hemisphere, for example, circle the globe virtually unimpeded by landmasses, giving rise to the *Roaring Forties* and *Furious Fifties* of sailing legend. But this is the basic pattern. Now let's focus on the middle latitudes. This, after all, is where most of us spend our time.

The Middle Latitudes

In the temperate regions, roughly between 30 and 60 degrees north and south—that is, between the horse latitudes and the polar front—weather systems generally move west to east, steered by the prevailing westerlies at the surface and by east-flowing jet streams aloft.

These upper-atmosphere jet streams average speeds of more than 50 knots and can reach 200 knots or more. They are concentrated around 30 degrees north and south (the *subtropical jet stream*), where air is sinking, and over the polar fronts around 60 degrees north and

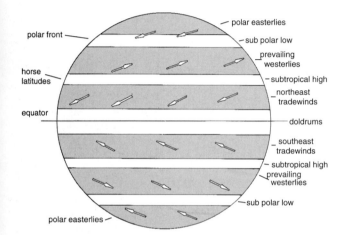

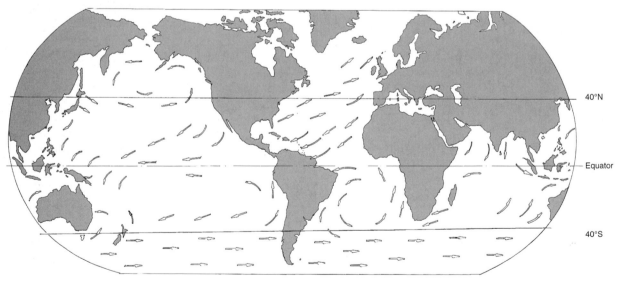

World atmospheric circulation cells. The drawing at top shows how the wind bands would establish themselves if there were no land. The drawing above shows how land tends to deflect the wind. Only in the region of the Southern Ocean can the wind go around the globe unimpeded.

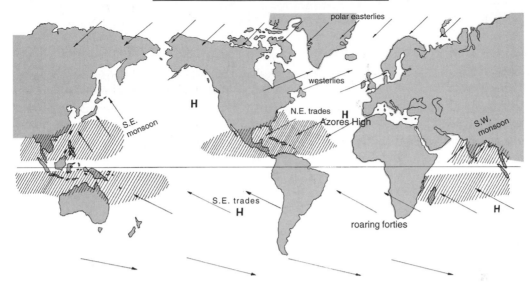

The major wind bands of the world for July. The semipermanent high-pressure areas (H) are in their typical locations for this time of year. The shaded areas show where tropical storms (hurricanes or cyclones) are most likely to occur. More than half of all Atlantic hurricanes start near the Azores as if they were spinning off the tropical lower portion of the Azores high-pressure that dominates the North Atlantic weather systems during summer. They develop as they move across the tropical areas of the Atlantic and often come ashore on the East and Southeast coasts of the United States. Other hurricanes originate in the Caribbean and head toward Mexico and the U.S. Gulf Coast.

south (the *polar jet stream*), where air is rising. These boundary zones in the planetary atmospheric circulation are regions of rapid horizontal temperature change, and it is horizontal temperature gradients that cause wind—both aloft and on the surface. The jet streams migrate with the seasons, either poleward or equatorward. In the northern winter, for example, the subtropical jet stream may disappear entirely from North American weather maps, while the polar jet stream dips far south, sometimes steering arctic air all the way to Florida.

Highs and Lows

Middle-latitude weather is dynamic and constantly changing, dominated by an endless, generally west-to-east parade of high- and low-pressure systems. For the purposes of this book we'll put aside the complex atmospheric mechanics that form these systems and just accept their existence, so familiar to all mariners.

Air pressure is a function of the weight or mass of the atmosphere above us. At sea level the air pressure is approximately 14.7 pounds per square inch, 1,000 millibars, or 760 mm of mercury at 0°C (32°F). We call 14.7 psi *one atmosphere* of pressure. On weather maps or *synoptic charts*, areas of low and high pressure are delineated by *isobars*, roughly concentric circles that connect points of equal atmospheric pressure and show how air masses are moving. Air masses move as the atmosphere tries to equalize differences in horizontal pressure, with the air in high-pressure areas flowing toward low-pressure areas—thus creating wind.

The *highs* denote areas where air is sinking, which is why barometric pressures are higher there. Since air warms as it sinks, and warm air can hold more moisture than cold air, high-pressure cells are areas of clear, stable weather, and often of light surface winds as well.

Storm Warnings and Small Craft Advisories and Warnings: What They Mean

Storm Warnings

You go down to your yacht to get your boat ready for a sail. Halfway through rigging your boat you notice that flying from the yardarm of the signal mast at your marina are two square red flags with a black square at the center of each. Ignore them at your peril. They are hurricane warning flags. One square flag means that a gale is approaching. This flag system originated in the seventeenth century and has been refined ever since. The current flag system in the United States goes back to 1958, when a single triangular red pennant came to mean a small craft advisory. However, in 1989 the National Weather Service suspended its coastal warning display network, so you are only likely to see these signals displayed at Coast Guard stations, yacht clubs, and other private institutions today. Two triangular red pennants mean a gale is expected. A single square flag with a square black center means a strong gale is expected and two square red flags with black centers mean that a hurricane is approaching. I can't resist adding that no mast (and possibly no yacht club) means the hurricane has already gone by.

At night these signals are replaced by a red light over a white light for small craft warnings, white over red for a gale warning, two red lights for a strong gale, and white over red over white for a hurricane.

Small Craft Advisories and Warnings

Small craft advisories and warnings are issued by the National Weather Service.

- **Small Craft Advisory.** A small craft advisory simply means that strong winds of more than two hours' duration are expected. There is no legal definition of a small boat, nor is there a blanket definition of wind strength. Wind strength can vary according to the area in which it's predicted but is around 20 to 33 knots.
- **Gale Warning.** A gale warning indicates that a gale with winds between 34 and 47 knots is approaching the forecast area.
- **Storm Warning.** A storm warning indicates that wind strengths will be higher than 48 knots.
- **Hurricane Warning.** A hurricane warning is issued when winds are above 64 knots.

In America the forecast area is usually given between recognizable points, such as Cape Cod to Watch Hill in New England. In Britain, the forecast is given according to the sea areas depicted on the shipping forecast. The shipping forecast areas have names such as Biscay, Plymouth, Portland, and Wight and can be found on the BBC's website at www.BBC.co.uk.

The *lows* denote areas where air is rising, which is why barometric pressures are lower there. Since rising air will cool and will eventually become supersaturated, low-pressure cells are areas of instability marked by precipitation and often by strong winds.

Isobars are usually more closely spaced around lows than highs, denoting stronger winds in the lows. A high might be a thousand or more miles across, while a low tends to be more tightly coiled—typically 400 or fewer miles across. Simply put, good weather is associated with highs, bad weather with lows.

Surface winds spiral inward toward the center of a low, counterclockwise in the Northern Hemisphere and clockwise in the Southern

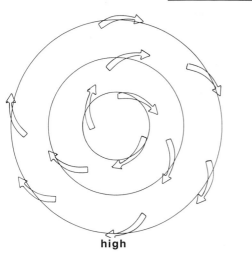

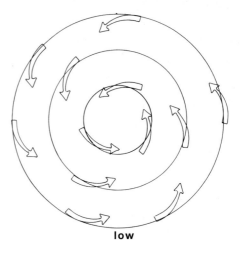

Wind patterns around a Northern Hemisphere high and low.

Hemisphere. The winds spiral outward from a high, clockwise in the Northern Hemisphere and counterclockwise in the Southern Hemisphere. The characteristics of highs and lows are summarized in Table 1–1.

If a low is to your west, your local weather is likely to deteriorate as the low approaches. If a low is to your east, your local weather is likely to improve as the low moves away. Use Buys

Ballot's Law to find the direction of a nearby low, as follows: face the wind and extend your right arm to your right. The low will be centered about 15 degrees behind your outstretched arm over water, or about 30 degrees behind it over land. (The difference is due to the greater frictional effect on wind of land versus water.)

In practice, we listen to what the weather forecaster tells us, but we must also weigh this

Table 1–1. Characteristics of Mid-Latitude High- and Low-Pressure Systems.

	High	Low
Weather	Generally fair	Stormy, precipitation
Temperature	Stable—long periods	Cool to warm changing to colder
Motion (avg) [~West to East]	Winter: 565 nm/day Summer: 390 nm/day	Winter: 600 nm/day Summer: 430 nm/day
Winds	Moderate, rising near edge	Strong and changing with possible high seas
Pressure [Typical]	Rapid rise on approach, slow decline on retreat	Rapid fall on approach, slow rise on retreat
Clouds	Sparse, near periphery	Wide variety, all altitudes

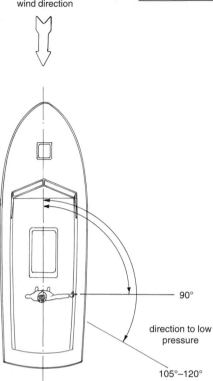

wind direction

90°

direction to low pressure

105°–120°

Using Buys Ballot's Law to detect the center of a low in the northern hemisphere. (In the southern hemisphere you would use your left arm rather than your right.)

information with local circumstances, since local conditions can often vary dramatically from those indicated by the "big picture." For example, on Narragansett Bay, Rhode Island, on a clear sunny day the thermal winds are southerly and blow from the cold ocean to the warm shore as warm air onshore rises. These winds are often called onshore breezes. Even if a cold front has just passed through and the regional winds are from the north, the local breeze might muscle its way in, resulting in a northerly at the north end of the bay, a flat calm at the south end, and a southerly a mile or so offshore. The distance the southerly penetrates northward will depend on the temperature differential over sea and land. At night the opposite phenomenon occurs in that the land may cool more than the sea and the breeze blows seaward or offshore.

In early summer, the southerly at Newport, Rhode Island, will come in around noon or 1 P.M. and will stay until 8 or 9 P.M. Planning to set sail earlier than noon means that a boat will have to motor to its destination. But because the air-water temperature differential is quite large (the land may be 80°F when the water temperature is only 45 or 50°F), the southerly may be blowing

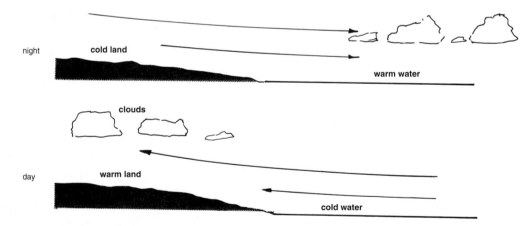

night

cold land

warm water

clouds

day

warm land

cold water

Onshore breezes are caused when sun- or city-warmed air rises over land, sucking in more air at ground level from the surrounding area. Sea (or lake) water takes longer to warm up, so cool air almost always flows from the cool sea to the warm land, causing onshore breezes. At night the land may cool to a lower temperature than the sea, and an offshore breeze may develop. The strength of such a breeze is determined by the temperature differential between land and sea.

25 knots by 5 P.M. Learning local conditions can make your boating much easier and safer.

Fronts

The lows that drive our middle-latitude weather form along the boundaries between adjacent air masses—for example, between the cold, dry air mass that persists over Canada and the warm, moist air mass that recurs over the southern United States. A low is born when a kink forms along one of these boundaries and begins a counterclockwise rotation. East of the kink, southerly warm air starts to override colder air to the north and east, while to the west, northerly cold air pushes south and east, displacing the warmer air ahead of it. The resultant frontal boundaries (called *fronts*) separating regions of cool or colder air from warm air assume the shape of an inverted V, with the low at its apex.

The newly formed system migrates eastward, steered by the overhead jet stream that follows and defines the air mass boundary, until the low dissipates several days later. The isobars

surrounding the low show distinct bends along fronts, marking abrupt shifts in wind direction.

A front is named for the relative temperature of the advancing air behind it. A warm front denotes warm air overriding cooler air ahead, while a cold front marks cold air overtaking warmer air ahead.

The weather sequence you experience with the passage of a low depends in large measure on whether the low passes to your north or south. When a low passes poleward of you (to your north in the Northern Hemisphere), both fronts are likely to pass overhead. In the accompanying illustration, as the system moves overhead along the lower dashed line, you can visualize the corresponding change in pressure by observing the isobars that pass by. The arrows indicate wind direction at each location, with the wind shifts clearly visible. The characteristic progressions of cloud types heralding the approach of each type of front are also labeled. If the low is moving to your south (as in the upper dashed line), you may have a period of rain without distinct fronts.

Cold fronts move faster than warm fronts, and as a result the cold front associated with a mature low (one that is several days old) will overtake the warm front, lifting the warmer air off the ground and forming an *occluded front* (often shown as a purple line on weather maps) of moderating weather characteristics. The occluded front will usually dissipate within a day or so, and the low itself may dissipate soon afterward, having traveled several thousand miles since its birth.

On a weather map, the red half circles along a warm front and the blue triangles on a cold front point toward the front's direction of advance. Occasionally two fronts meet and oppose each other, forming a *stationary front*, depicted by alternating segments of cold and warm front symbols.

Here are the typical conditions you will experience as a low passes by:

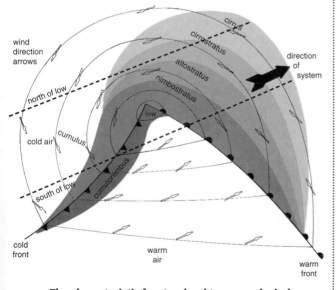

The characteristic fronts, cloud types, and wind directions you might expect as a low moves by you to the north or south. Follow the appropriate dashed line through this illustration to see what you might experience.

Advancing Warm Front

In a warm front, the overtaking warm air rises gradually up and over the cold air, forming a long wedge or incline. When a Northern Hemisphere low is passing north of you, you will see high *cirrus* clouds as much as 24 hours or 600 miles ahead of the warm front, followed by *cirrostratus*. The barometer will begin to fall. Up to half a day later, the winds will *back* (change in a counterclockwise direction) from south to southeast, and *altostratus* clouds will begin to move in under the cirrostratus. As the ground-level warm front continues its approach, the clouds will steadily become lower and thicker while the barometer continues a steady fall. Precipitation will begin as much as 200 miles or more ahead of the front. As the front passes, the temperature will rise and the winds will *veer* (change in a clockwise direction) from southeast to southwest. Within the warm sector, the wind direction will be fairly steady from the southwest (in the Northern Hemisphere) while the barometer will be somewhat steady. The skies may clear and the temperature will remain mild.

Advancing Cold Front

The interval of relative stability within the warm sector will end with the approach of the cold front. Unlike the slow transition of a warm front, the cold air behind a cold front abruptly forces the overtaken warmer air aloft. This rising warm air cools and can no longer hold all its moisture, becoming highly unstable. Dangerous squall lines can develop 100 miles or more (several hours) in advance of the front. High storm clouds will pile up, leading to gusty winds, squalls, and possibly thunderstorms as the front approaches. The barometer may fall immediately ahead of the cold front, perhaps rapidly—due to the narrow band of rising air. The period of rain will be brief but could be severe. As the cold front passes, the winds will veer from southwest

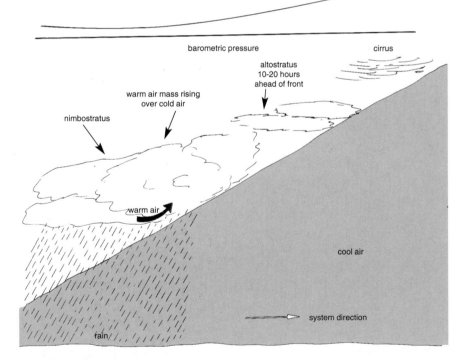

A vertical section through an idealized warm front, showing the characteristic signs of its approach.

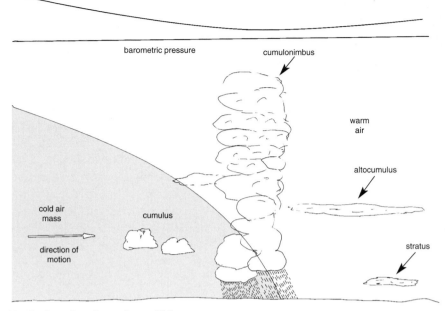

barometric pressure

cumulonimbus

warm air

altocumulus

cold air mass

cumulus

direction of motion

stratus

Vertical section through a cold front.

to northwest with gusts, and the temperature will drop. *Cumulonimbus* clouds will give way to *nimbostratus*, followed by clearing. Pressures will rise quickly. Clear, cool, dry weather is the norm behind the front, but those northwest winds can continue gusting. An assortment of clear-weather *cumulus* clouds may be seen.

North (Northern Hemisphere) or South (Southern Hemisphere) of the Low

If you are poleward of an approaching low, you will not experience a warm or cold front. Instead, there will be an indistinct transition between the cool air ahead of the low and the colder air behind it, a zone characterized by nimbostratus clouds and steady rain, especially close to the low. The approaching low will cause changes similar to those that characterize an approaching warm front, except that—in the northern hemisphere—the winds will back from east to northeast (rather than veering into the southwest) as the low passes to the south, and there will be no warm sector. Barometric

pressures will fall gradually with the approach, then rise as the low moves off, while the winds gradually back into the northwest. The infamous *nor'easters* of the northeastern United States result when a low stalls near the coast. The northeast winds north of the low dump moisture picked up from the sea during their counterclockwise circuit.

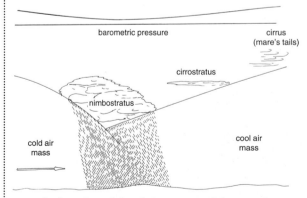

barometric pressure

cirrus (mare's tails)

cirrostratus

nimbostratus

cold air mass

cool air mass

A vertical section of the changes you might experience as a low passes to your south in the Northern Hemisphere.

Clouds

Clouds can tell boaters a lot about what is happening in the atmosphere. Sometimes their message is obvious, but at others it is more subtle and can provide information regarding the weather to come hours or even days ahead.

Cloud Types

We've all watched high cumulus clouds develop on a summer's day. They are usually harbingers of warm comfortable weather, which is likely to remain for a few days. But if the cumulus clouds climb higher and a circulation develops within them, their bases may darken and the good weather can very quickly turn into a nasty thunderstorm with rain, hail, lightning, or even a tornado. By keeping a weather eye open, as old-time sailors would say, you can head for port to avoid the worst of bad weather.

In order to learn what clouds are telling you, you need to recognize cloud types and understand what is happening in the sky around you. If you see one weather omen, look for a second to confirm your assessment. For example, if you awaken on a summer's morning to fog and a heavy dew that burns off before noon, you will know that fair weather is likely to continue. If, at the same time, the barometer remains steady, then you have further confirmation that the good weather is likely to remain. If clouds thicken into heavy cumulus and darken in the afternoon, you may see a heavy thunderstorm before dark. If the evening stays clear and the sun sets in a blaze of red, you might not see much wind, but the weather will be fine the following day. Under these conditions the sailor should look for thermal-generated onshore breezes (sea breezes), as the overlying system is too weak to overcome them.

Meteorologists have divided clouds into three categories that are found at various levels in the atmosphere: high, medium, and low.

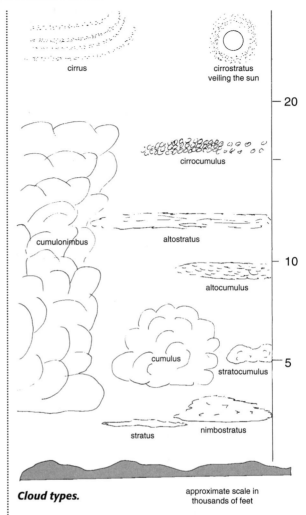

Cloud types.

approximate scale in
thousands of feet

High Clouds

High clouds generally exist above 20,000 feet (6,100 m) and can rise as high as 30,000 feet (9,150 m). They appear wispy and insubstantial because water droplets become ice crystals at altitudes above 20,000 feet. There are three kinds. All include the root name *cirro-* or *cirrus,* and often they accompany the leading edge of a frontal system. Cirrus clouds, sometimes called "mares' tales," are long, fibrous, strand-like clouds that usually presage the arrival of a warm front and unsettled weather, perhaps within 24

High clouds include cirrus (top), cirrostratus (center), and cirrocumulus (above). (Photos by NOAA/NWS [top] and Bob Sweet)

hours. They are often seen alongside jet contrails, and if seen in thick bands high in the sky, may well be embedded in the jet stream.

If cirrus clouds stay high in the sky and don't increase, bad weather is still some distance away, but when they begin to form thick clumps and to lower, and either give way to or are undercut by altostratus, the front is closer, and it may rain within hours. This may also be true when cirrus clouds develop curls or hooks in their ends, but curls usually mean that the low pressure will pass to your south (in the northern hemisphere.). It's also important to note the speed at which cirrus clouds move across the sky. In general, if they move fast, a front is likely to be approaching fast and the wind strength will be higher. A slow movement usually indicates the opposite, although this may not always be true.

Cirrostratus clouds are also high clouds, but in contrast to cirrus clouds they are flat, not wispy. When they stretch in a continuous thin sheet or veil across the sky, the coming warm front may be 12–24 hours away—closer to 12 if the lower surface of the cirrostratus is well defined. When cirrostratus are not increasing and are not continuous, the low will probably pass equatorward of you, and you are unlikely to see stormy weather.

The third type of high-level cloud is cirrocumulus. These

thin, puffy, globular clouds sometimes form lanes in the sky, known as a "mackerel sky" for its scaly appearance. Lower than cirrostratus, they are usually seen in winter, and indicate fair but cold weather.

Mid-Level Clouds

Medium- or mid-level clouds are found between 6,500 and 20,000 feet (2,000 and 6,100 m). The names of mid-level clouds are given the prefix *alto-*, as in altostratus or altocumulus. Altostratus clouds are grayish or blue-gray, and may be composed of water or ice, depending on the air temperature. They usually signal the approach of stormy weather, and when they thicken, long-lasting precipitation may follow.

Altocumulus clouds are usually made of water droplets and also show the approach of bad weather. If they form in bands or rows, a warm front is passing. If they start to climb high in the sky, they usually signal the onset of thunderstorms.

Midlevel clouds include altostratus (top) and altocumulus (above).

Low Clouds

Low clouds, which generally stay below 6,500 feet (2,000 m), include nimbostratus, stratus, cumulonimbus, and cumulus clouds. Nimbostratus and cumulonimbus are the true precipitation clouds and may be accompanied by rain, gusty winds, snow, or hail. Nimbostratus are thick, heavy clouds that block out the sun and bring with them almost continuous precipitation. They may be accompanied by low-flying scud, or *pannus*, which hurries across the sky below a raging storm and occasionally moves in a direction different from the higher-level clouds. Nimbostratus clouds often accompany the passage of a warm front.

Stratus clouds, like nimbostratus, are low and gray, but they may descend to form fog or may lift and disappear.

Stratocumulus clouds are low-level altocumulus-like clouds that you see at the end of a gale or storm. They usually fall apart or disappear as the weather improves. These are the clouds you will see when weather forecasters tell you to expect gradual clearing with some sunny breaks.

Cumulus clouds are the ones you see on a sunny day. They look like huge, puffy balls that gradually rise in the sky. When they stay flat on the top, expect fair weather to continue. If they rise very high, and the base darkens and stays flat, expect gusty winds and showers. If they turn into cumulonimbus, expect a thunderstorm with rain, possibly hail, lightning, and strong, gusty winds. You may even see a tornado or waterspout. Avoid these clouds if possible.

Deck-Level Forecasting

You can synthesize what we've covered so far to create your own deck-level forecasts, either to confirm or modify what the region-wide forecasts are telling you. Table 1–3 summarizes the signs of stable and changing weather.

Low-level clouds include cumulus (top); stratocumulus rain clouds that often portend an imminent clearing (middle); and stratus, which often bring steady but light rain (above). (Courtesy NOAA/NWS)

Table 1–2. Characteristics of Frontal Systems

Warm Front

What happens? Warm air replaces cold air.

	24 hours ahead	Leading edge	Passing overhead	Trailing edge
Cloud Formation				
High	cirrus with hooks		cirrostratus	
Medium		altostratus	stratus	
Low				stratocumulus
Weather	dry	heavy rain	rain stops	fog or drizzle
Wind	light	increasing	veering (clockwise)	steady winds
Visibility	clear	decreasing in rain	poor	Poor
Barometer	falling	steady	rising	rising
Wave conditions	calm	swell	confused	increasing

Cold Front

What happens? Cold air replaces warm air.

	24 hours ahead	Leading edge	Passing overhead	Trailing edge
Cloud Formation				
High	cirrus			
Medium		alstostratus	cumulonimbus	
Low		nimbostratus		clearing
Weather	maybe rain	heavy rain	maybe a shower	clears
Wind	increasing	becoming gusty	veering (clockwise)	strong and gusty
Visibility	poor	poor during rain	clearing	very good
Barometer	falling slowly	falling	reaches bottom	rising
Wave conditions	increasing	flattened by rain	confused	lumpy, increasing

Occluded Front

What happens? Colder air replaces cold air and warm air is forced aloft, this is not unlike a warm front.

	24 hours ahead	Leading edge	Passing overhead	Trailing edge
Cloud Formation				
High	cirrus	cirrostratus		
Medium		altostratus		
Low		stratus	stratus	
Weather	light rain	heavy rain	rain	clearing
Wind	calm			
Visibility	moderate	poor	poor	improving
Barometer	steady/may fall	steady/may fall	steady/may rise	rising

Stationary Front

What happens? Front is not moving and all conditions remain the same.

Table 1–3. Signs of Stable and Changing Weather in the Middle Latitudes

	Continuing Good Weather	Indicators of a Change
Skies	Clear, light to dark blue, bright moon, contrails dissipate	Hazy, halo (sun or moon) thick lingering jet contrails
Clouds	Few, puffy cumulus, or high thin clouds, higher the better	Veil of clouds, clouds at multiple layers & directions, cirrus
Winds and seas	Generally steady, little change over day; sea swells same direction	Strong winds in early morning, wind shift to S; seas confused, varying directions
Temperature	Stable: heavy dew or frost at night	Marked changes; increase in humidity
Dew point	Marked spread between dew point & temperature = no fog	Close spread: probable fog if temperature drops
Barometer	Steady, rising slowly	Falling slowly
Sunrise	Gray sky at dawn or sun rising from clear horizon	Red sky, sun rises above horizon due to cloud cover
Sunset	Red sky, sun 'ball of fire' or sets on a clear horizon	Sun sets high above horizon color color purplish or pale yellow

Here's how to refine a regional forecast with your own observations:

Approaching Low

Clouds: high cirrus, gradually lowering and thickening

Wind: backing to southeast and possibly increasing

Barometer: begins to fall (2–10 mb in three hours)

Offshore swell: increases, with decreasing period

Rain: within 15–24 hours

Fronts: if low is west to northwest and passing to your north, you will see fronts; if low is west to southwest and passing to your south, you will not see distinct fronts

Approaching Warm Front

Clouds: cirrus or "mackerel" clouds—front is more than 24 hours away; lowering and thickening (altostratus, nimbostratus)—front is less than 24 hours away

Rain: begins lightly, then becomes steady and persistent

Barometer: falls steadily; a faster fall indicates stronger winds

A northern hemisphere low-pressure system on which the locations of the low's center, the warm front, and the cold front have been superimposed, together with the axis of the overhead jet stream that steers the surface low. (Courtesy NOAA/NWS)

Winds: increase steadily, staying in the southeast
Visibility: deteriorates, especially in rain

Passing Warm Front

Sky: lightens toward western horizon
Rain: breaks
Wind: veers from south to southwest and may decrease
Barometer: stops falling
Temperature: rises

Within Warm Sector

Wind: steady, typically from the southwest, strengthening ahead of cold front
Barometer: steady—may drop shortly ahead of cold front
Precipitation: mist, possible drizzle

Approaching Cold Front

Wind: southwesterly and increasing; line squalls possible 100 miles or more ahead of front
Barometer: begins brief fall, could be rapid
Clouds: cumulonimbus builds to the west
Temperature: steady
Rain: begins and intensifies, but duration short (typically 1–2 hours)

Passing Cold Front

Wind: veers rapidly to northwest, gusty behind front
Barometer: begins to rise, often quickly
Clouds: cumulonimbus, then nimbostratus, then clearing
Temperature: drops suddenly, then slow decline
Rain: ends, gives way to rapidly clearing skies, possibly with leftover altocumulus

Nontropical Rotational Storms

In the area from Cape Hatteras, North Carolina to Cape Sable, Nova Scotia, they are known as nor'easters. In the English Channel they are known as Channel gales or storms. In other parts of the world they have other names. They are nontropical rotational storms that can produce winds of more than 85 knots, and have been known to generate waves as high as 90 feet (from offshore data buoy information). Nontropical storms are difficult to predict in intensity and duration. In winter they may generate white-out conditions as snow is driven horizontally. In late summer they can destroy boats and property. Fortunately they don't often occur during the summer sailing season, but if you have to deliver a boat out of season you could be caught at sea by one.

Nor'easters are spawned along the east coast of the United States when one or more lows move off the coast and encounter warm, moisture-laden air from the Gulf Stream. The greater the difference in temperature between the two air masses, the more chance there is of a storm. As its counterclockwise rotation deepens, the northern sector of the low or lows draws more moist air in from the ocean, and the storm feeds itself, expanding further, much like a hurricane. The storm can intensify extremely quickly, lashing the coast and off-lying waters with intense gales and heavy precipitation. (A drop of 24 millibars in 24 hours is called a "bomb" by forecasters.) But the storm can collapse just as quickly.

Quite often winds will exceed 50 knots and be accompanied by snow, heavy rain, and hail. Though the circulation around the low is rotary, this is not a tropical storm, but it can be powerful nevertheless; the so-called "Perfect Storm" of October 1991 was one such nor'easter. The season for nor'easters is from October to April, while the North Atlantic hurricane season is from May to October, so the two types of storm rarely prowl at the same time. In late October 2005, however, a nor'easter and a hurricane delivered a one-two punch to shipping in the western North Atlantic: hurricane Wilma—having devastated Cancun, battered Cuba, and walloped South Florida—charged northeast into the North Atlantic at an extraordinary 50 knots (try dodging that storm in a 6-knot boat!), packing winds up to 120 knots. Meanwhile, inshore from Wilma, two lows combined off the coast to develop a nor'easter that dumped several inches of rain and developed gusts up to 60 knots between New Jersey and Maine. The outer bands of this storm entrained moisture and energy from Wilma—a tropical storm and an extra-tropical storm interacting—showing that nature is forever ignoring the descriptive boxes we create.

Thunderstorms

You hear a far-off rumble and look around. In the distance you see a dark-bottomed cumulus cloud, and as you watch, a flash of lightning hits the sea. You start timing, and 19 seconds later you hear the thunderclap. Divide 19 by five, since sound travels at a speed of about 1 mile every 5 seconds over sea. (Light travels at 186,000 miles per second, so you see the lightning flash essentially as it happens.) The storm is almost 4 miles away, and it could be moving toward you at 25 knots, which gives you about 8 minutes to prepare. Of course, since lightning can strike as far as 15 miles from a thunderstorm cloud, you may already be in the danger zone. Thunderstorms are usually accompanied by strong winds, sometimes hail, and occasionally intense microbursts. The most intense thunderstorms can even generate tornadoes or waterspouts.

Preparation for thunderstorms should start when you are still ashore. Before you go out on the water, listen to your local TV weather forecast or look on the web. See if a cold front is likely to come through the area where you are sailing. The chances are good that a frontal system will trigger thunderstorms. As you are preparing to cast off lines, listen to the NOAA weather channel on your VHF radio. This too

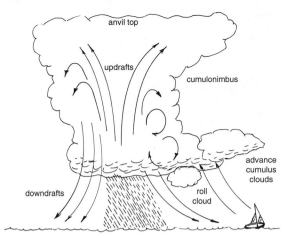

Cross section through a thunderstorm. This is a young storm, and could become larger and more powerful as it matures.

will warn of approaching weather. Understand what the terms mean. A *thunderstorm watch* means that the conditions are right for a thunderstorm in your area. A *thunderstorm warning* means that thunderstorm activity is already occurring and may be approaching your area. A *severe thunderstorm watch* or *warning* tells you that severe winds (more than 50 knots) and hail are likely to develop or have already developed and are coming your way.

Thunderstorms are of two origins: air mass or frontal. A warm, humid day is often the precursor to the former sort, as water-laden warm air rises to 20,000–30,000 feet (6,100–9,100 m) forming huge cumulus clouds with anvil tops, often called *thunderheads*. These storms may consist of single cells, as often happens near the Gulf Stream.

Frontal thunderstorms are associated with the near-vertical wall of cold air in an advancing cold front, which forces warm, moisture-laden air aloft at a rapid rate. Such storms often come in groups, sometimes stretched out a hundred miles or more along the front.

If you hear a report of a thunderstorm warning or severe thunderstorm watch, don't take your boat out if there is any likelihood the storm will hit you. Stay ashore and stay safe. If you are already on the water and too far from land to reach home, you need to take precautions.

First among these is to ascertain the direction from which the storm is coming. This is not always as easy as it sounds, given the extent of air pollution along the coast. Look for tall cumulus clouds with flat, anvil-like tops. Quite often they will have dark gray or black underbellies.

If you see clouds like this, you need to get everyone into life jackets, close hatches, and reduce sail. While you are doing so, listen to the NOAA weather radio to find out just how severe the thunderstorm is. You can ride out a thunderstorm with moderate rain and winds, but a severe one may seriously tax your skills.

In a severe thunderstorm with strong winds of more than 50 knots, you will need to reduce the boat's windage. If you have time, remove any roller-furling headsail and stow it below. If the storm is already almost on top of you, roll up the sail with two or three turns of the sheet around the furler, maybe set a storm jib, and remove or reef the mainsail down to the second or third reef. Remove the bimini top and any lee cloths or laundry. Close and dog down the hatches and insert the washboards. If you are towing an inflatable dinghy, you might want to deflate it and stow it in a locker. Put small children below or under the dodger, where they will not get hurt by hail or heavy rain. Have your VHF handy and preset it to channel 16. Have a plan worked out should you get hit by lightning, and set a course to take you away from the darkest part of the cloud, since this is usually where the winds are highest, the rain heaviest, and the hail largest.

As the storm approaches the wind will usually die, so turn on the engine to ensure that you retain maneuverability. With the engine running you will also be able to turn into the wind, making it that much easier to get the sails down in heavy winds. Another reason to keep moving is that lightning rarely strikes a moving boat.

The first part of the storm you will feel is the gust front, a cool blast of wind moving along the leading edge. This wind will feel cooler and could be extremely strong—a few such gusts have been clocked at more than 85 knots. It may also arrive from a completely different direction from the wind you have been sailing in. Shortly thereafter you will experience rain, possibly hail, lightning, and lots of thunder. Steer directly into the wind under power.

In a powerboat, moderate your power so that you don't crash through the waves and slam hard. In a sailboat, motor into the storm or sail on a close reach to pass through the bad weather as quickly as possible. The waves will be short and steep and could be very choppy. The idea is to get through the thunderstorm quickly and into the cooler air directly behind it. As the storm progresses the wind will continue to shift, often moving from southerly to northerly as it approaches and passes.

Generally, thunderstorms don't last long, so if you can get through the leading edge of the storm successfully, you will probably be OK. As a rule, the higher the winds in the storm, the faster it will blow past.

Microbursts and Downbursts

A severe thunderstorm may include a microburst (less than 2 miles in diameter) or a downburst (larger). These events occur when localized heating produces a cloud mass of great vertical development that cools and collapses suddenly. The descending air may be dry at ground level if its moisture evaporates during descent, or it may be associated with rain. A downburst is often seen as a roll cloud—a low, horizontal, tubular-shaped cloud associated with the leading edge of a thunderstorm. Still, the winds generated by a downburst should not be confused with the more general gust front of an approaching thunderstorm. The winds of

A downburst might be signaled by a roll cloud like the one shown here. But whether or not it is associated with a downburst, a roll cloud always indicates strong gusts and squall lines with sudden wind shifts. A squall line might precede a cold front by a hundred miles or more, or it might accompany the passage of the front. (Photo courtesy of NOAA/NWS)

a downburst may last 5–30 minutes. A microburst is shorter, but its winds can be hurricane strength or greater (some have been clocked at more than 100 knots). The winds arrive as a bulging downward vortex, rather like a big fist coming out of a cloud to smash the ocean surface. Microbursts have enough power to overwhelm most boats and have downed airplanes, and should be avoided at all costs.

This rainshaft is being hurled from the bottom of the cumulonimbus cloud by a microburst. The rain might be accompanied by gusts of more than 50 knots. (Photo courtesy of NOAA/NWS)

Waterspouts

A waterspout is essentially a small tornado occurring over water, and should always be considered dangerous (though small ones may not be) and avoided. Fortunately, waterspouts are not as violent as the tornadoes that form over land. They are often associated with thunderstorm cells, and are sometimes spawned in the outer bands of a hurricane or along the northern edge of the Gulf Stream.

Hail

Hail also appears during thunderstorms when the moisture precipitated out of the clouds is lifted to even greater heights, where it passes through colder air and freezes. If this precipitation is supported aloft for a long time by the thunderstorm, the hail stones can grow extremely large before their own weight causes them to drop to the ground.

A waterspout. (NOAA photo by Dr. Joseph A. Golden, 1969)

Lightning

In Florida, which has more lightning strikes than any other state, lightning kills more than 100 people a year. A lightning bolt can carry 50,000 volts of electricity and can generate a temperature hotter than the sun's surface. While you're reading these few sentences there will be more than 100 lightning strikes worldwide. Sounds awe-inspiring, doesn't it? Lightning has been a problem ever since boats went to sea, and with their tall metal masts sticking up above everything else, sailors in particular seem to be asking for a lightning strike.

Today, however, we think we understand what causes lightning and how we can prevent it from hitting a boat. This is important, because in an electrical storm your boat might be carrying your family and friends, not to mention thousands of dollars' worth of electrical equipment that can be cooked in a split second.

What Causes Lightning?

Lightning is basically a spark jumping across a gap between negatively charged clouds and a positively charged object. The positively charged object may be inside another part of the same cloud, or another cloud. It may be the ground, a boat at sea, or the sea itself.

As moisture circulates in the cloud, there is a buildup of negatively charged ions. According to current theory, negatively charged ions tend to collect at the bottom of a cloud, while positively charged ions collect at the top. This polarization can only be discharged when it has enough power to overcome the resistance of air to the passage of electricity. When it is raining, moisture saturates the gap between a cloud and the ground, and the lightning needs less charge to leap across the gap than in dry air. Also, because the gap between a cloud and the ground is reduced by the height of a sailboat's mast or a powerboat's bridge, it makes sense that these structures are likely to attract a strike first. Fortunately for those at sea, experience has shown that a moving boat, even a sailboat, is less likely to be struck by lightning than a boat at a dock or a mooring. This phenomenon has been attributed to the fact that a moving sailboat's masthead or a powerboat's flying bridge may be dissipating ions as it moves back and forth.

How to Protect Your Boat

There are two main schools of thought regarding the best way to protect your boat. The first contends that you should install a *lightning protection rod* that will safely channel lightning into the water without damaging your boat. The second contends that you should make your boat less conducive to lightning strikes by installing an *ion dissipater* at your masthead or tuna tower. The dissipater, which looks like a hairy metal bottle brush, creates a continuous ion path to the water and thus, according to manufacturers, prevents the build-up of static electricity that attracts lightning.

Proponents of fitting a lightning rod at the masthead say that it provides a "cone of protection" around the boat, inside which lightning does not strike. The tip of the cone must be very sharp in order to concentrate energy and draw a lightning strike to it. A copper conductor then runs from the rod to the keel to provide a path for the discharge of electricity. The copper conductor should be tightly bolted to a keel bolt so that the keel will act as a conductor between the boat and the ocean. The conductor should be made of No. 6 or No. 8 AWG uncoated wire, and bends should have a turning radius of no less than 8 inches (20 cm).

The problem with this scenario is that any bolted joints in the connection between masthead and keel are likely to create a high-resistance path when thousands of volts are applied to the circuit. A high-resistance path will typically get very hot and melt metal, much as an electric arc welder would. Another problem comes when the keel is coated with fairing

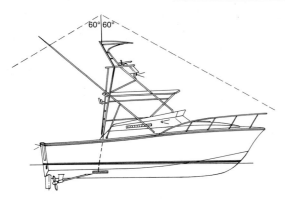

The cone of protection for a powerboat. No. 6 AWG wire is led down the tower and directly to a plate in the hull. Do not paint over the ground plate, which should be at least 1 square foot (0.09 sq m) in area. On this boat the outrigger extends outside the cone of protection and should therefore be grounded.

compound and antifouling. It no longer has direct metal-to-seawater contact, and the build-up of electricity can do strange things. I have seen keels on boats struck by lightning from which all the fairing compound and antifouling was blown off by the force of a lightning strike.

The best way to set up a lightning protection rod is to run the copper wire or strip directly from the mast to a plate in the hull that has not been antifouled. This will direct a lightning strike directly into the water (and will, most probably, blow the plate out of the hull!) It is also possible to terminate the copper strip at deck level. When a storm threatens, a secondary conductor wire is attached to the strip from the masthead with a crocodile clip, and the other end of the secondary conductor is draped over the side and into the water, where it terminates in a plate. But lightning does not follow sharp turns well as it flashes through the boat, so any lightning protection scheme must be as straight as possible from masthead to water.

How to Protect Yourself

The best protection in a lightning storm is to get off your boat and into a building. If you can't do that, however, the main thing to remember is to stay away from any metal fittings that might attract lightning on your boat, since side flashes can split off from the main flash and pass through anything nearby. That means staying about 6 feet away from a sailboat's mast, standing rigging, and steering wheel, or a powerboat's tuna tower.

Other than that there is not a lot you can do to protect yourself or your boat from lightning strikes, although I've heard it suggested that you can try parking your boat next to a bridge or a boat with a taller mast and hope the lightning strikes these other objects first.

Electronics and Lightning

Most electronics work with circuitry that uses a few micro- or milliamps. When a lightning surge slams through the boat, many of these circuits will be ruptured and destroyed. The only possible repair is to replace the circuit boards, usually at considerable cost.

To protect your instruments from lightning, you should either install some form of surge protection in the circuits that power your electronics or physically disconnect your boat's electronics in a thunderstorm. The latter course may seem inconvenient but is a small price to pay if you want to avoid the loss of hundreds of dollars worth of gear in a split second.

Tropical Storms

Tropical weather systems form near the equator, in the low-pressure area known as the Intertropical Convergence Zone, or ITZ, and in latitudes as high as $22\frac{1}{2}$ degrees north and south. Heated ocean water is the "fuel" of all tropical systems. There are several categories, ranked by increasing order of severity.

Table 1–4: The Beaufort Scale

This scale was originally devised by Admiral Sir Francis Beaufort (Royal Navy) in 1808 and is still used in many parts of the world. It has been revised many times.

U.S. Weather Forecast Equivalent	Beaufort Scale Number	Seaman's Estimate	Wind Speed (Knots)
Light	0	Calm	Less than 1
	1	Light	2 to 3
	2	Breeze	5
Gentle	3	Gentle breeze	6–9
Moderate	4	Moderate breeze	10–13
Fresh	5	Fresh breeze	14–18
Strong	6	Strong breeze	19–24
	7	Moderate gale	25–30
Gale	8	Gale	31–36
	9	Strong gale	37–44
Heavy gale	10	Heavy gale	45–55
Storm	11	Heavy gale	56–62
Hurricane	12	Hurricane	65 +

A *tropical disturbance*, the weakest tropical system, shows organized convection over a diameter of 100–300 miles and may be accompanied by thunderstorms and rain but not by strong sustained winds. It poses little direct threat. It may or may not have a rotary circulation pattern, and may never develop into anything more serious. But if ocean water temperatures are suitable—above about 80°F—it can develop into a tropical depression, a tropical storm, or even a hurricane, so any tropical disturbance during hurricane season should be cause for concern, especially if you are about to commence a bluewater passage. If the disturbance develops an organized rotary circulation and sustained winds of less than 35 knots, it is considered a *tropical depression*, and bears close watching. There may be heavy rain, and there may be gusts substantially above 35 knots, but well-found boats over 35 feet should be able to handle what comes.

Occasionally a depression will soak up enough heat from the warm waters beneath it and encounter just the right upper atmospheric conditions to intensify into a *tropical storm*, with winds between 35 and 64 knots. At that point it is given a name. Already extremely dangerous, and with the potential to become worse, it is tracked even more closely by forecasters and mariners as described below. You want to be safely in port long before a tropical storm passes anywhere near.

Most tropical storms intensify no further, but again, when conditions are just right, one will develop winds of more than 65 knots in a closed, rotational, intense circulation. At this point it is termed a *hurricane* in the Atlantic and eastern Pacific, a *cyclone* in the western Pacific, and a *typhoon* in the Indian Ocean.

Hurricane forecasters still do not know all the ingredients that are needed in the alchemy of a major hurricane, but they include warm

Table 1–5. The Saffir/Simpson Hurricane Scale

	Central Pressure in Inches	Wind Strength	Storm Surge	Damage above Normal
Category 1	over 28.94	64–82 knots	up to 5 ft (1.5 m)	minimal
Category 2	28.5–28.93	83–96 knots	up to 8 ft (2.4m)	moderate
Category 3	27.9–28.49	97–113 knots	up to 12 ft (3.6 m)	extensive
Category 4	27.17–27.9	114–134 knots	up to 18 ft (5.5 m)	extreme
Category 5	less than 27.17	over 134 knots	over 18 ft (5.5 m)	catastrophic

ocean waters (80°F [27°C] or higher) to a mixed depth of 200 feet, moist air in the middle troposphere, a thunderstorm complex to build a heated column into the upper atmosphere, light winds and lack of wind shear along that column, and a strong upper-atmosphere flow above the system in order to "exhaust" the moist, heated air rising through the column. Finally, the storm must be above 5 degrees of latitude to meet sufficient Coriolis force to spin it into a hurricane.

The rotation is counterclockwise in the northern hemisphere, clockwise in the southern hemisphere. A Category 5 hurricane is one of the most powerful forces on earth, and there are simply no storm tactics adequate to cope with it. Your primary object, therefore, is always to avoid hurricanes at sea, preferably on land too!

Hurricane Tracking

Well before a hurricane arrives in North America, the National Weather Service will issue a *hurricane watch*, which tells you that a designated area is in danger of being hit by the storm. At this time you should be ready to move quickly in case the situation deteriorates further. A hurricane watch is upgraded to a *hurricane warning* if it is determined that the hurricane is likely to hit an area within 24 hours. Hopefully, by this time, your boat will have been hauled or safely moored and you will either be ready for the storm surge or have evacuated to higher ground.

You should never set a hard and fast passagemaking schedule during hurricane season, which extends from May through November in the North Atlantic. Always be prepared to modify your departure date due to the weather. If a tropical disturbance were to appear just before your departure, you would be wise to delay for a few days to see how the system develops. Most bluewater cruisers evacuate the hurricane zones altogether during hurricane and cyclone season, either by heading south to Trinidad and points on the South American coast if they are in the Caribbean, or by waiting out the season in temperate waters (such as New Zealand's) if they are in the western Pacific.

Being at sea in a small boat in a wind of hurricane strength is not something you want to experience. The waves are huge, white-capped foaming breakers, and it is almost impossible to look to windward, because rain and saltwater spray sting your eyes so badly. If you are aboard a sailboat, your smallest sails aren't small enough, and you may have to run off under bare poles. If you are aboard a powerboat, it's almost impossible to fight the waves, and even in the best-found boat your survival is in doubt. You may have no idea how long these conditions will last, and you will become extremely fatigued. All you want to do is sleep, but even that is impossible because the boat's movement is so violent. With satellite monitoring of storm systems and early broadcasts by television, you should be able to avoid being at sea during extremely heavy weather as long as you stay flexible on your departure date.

But suppose you're unlucky or careless enough to find yourself in the path of an approaching storm? What then? The first mention you'll hear of a tropical storm in the Atlantic is when it's a mere tropical wave or disturbance somewhere in the middle of the ocean. The majority of such disturbances never develop into storms, and the majority of tropical storms do not become hurricanes. But if, as days pass, a disturbance does develop into a tropical storm and then a hurricane, you should pay closer and closer attention. If there's any chance the storm could come your way, you should start plotting its reported positions. The storm may still be 1,000 miles away and give every indication of passing well east or west of your location, but you should still plot its positions to develop an idea of its track. Your goal at this point should be to avoid fresh gale winds—that is, winds of more than 34 knots. National Hurricane Center (NHC) forecast discussions will include the radii of 34-knot winds around a hurricane center (see below).

Be attuned to the early-warning signs. For example, swell periods in the Atlantic basin are typically 6–9 seconds. A period of 9–12 seconds in the tropical or subtropical Atlantic during hurricane season indicates that a storm might be approaching, and if it increases to 12–15 seconds, you can be reasonably certain there's a storm out there. If you see swell periods like that in the more enclosed waters of the Caribbean Sea or Gulf of Mexico, you can be absolutely sure.

Similarly, if you see a drop in barometric pressure below 1010 millibars in tropical or subtropical sea areas during hurricane season (normal pressure there being 1012–1020 mb), you should suspect the approach of a storm. Small but perceptible rises and falls in the barometric pressure superimposed on a general decline will confirm that a storm is approaching. This pump-ing action is due to alternating gusts and updrafts in the outer bands of a hurricane system.

More generally speaking, no matter what ocean you're in, you need to plot the storm's position and make sure that you can sail to the weakest side of it or away from it as the cyclone or typhoon develops. Remember, too, that tropical cyclones in the Southern Hemisphere rotate clockwise, the opposite direction to those in the Northern Hemisphere. By plotting the predicted course of the storm you should, in theory at least, be able to avoid it. In reality, however, hurricanes are highly unpredictable, and when plotting a storm you should provide for a wide margin of error. Traditionally, mariners have plotted an arc of at least 20 degrees to either side of the storm's course and tried to avoid being anywhere in that 40-degree cone. (That's not a bad practice even today, but the method shown on page 149 is slightly more refined.)

When plotting possible storm tracks on a map, first mark the storm's center, then draw a circle around that location with a radius equal to the radius of 34-knot winds as given in the NHC's wind radii discussions. This radius could be as small as 50 or as large as 200 nautical miles, depending on the power of the storm.

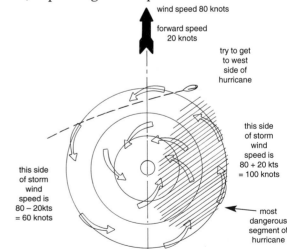

wind speed 80 knots

forward speed 20 knots

try to get to west side of hurricane

this side of storm wind speed is 80 + 20 kts = 100 knots

this side of storm wind speed is 80 – 20kts = 60 knots

most dangerous segment of hurricane

An anatomy of the dangerous and so-called navigable semicircles in a northern hemisphere hurricane. (The term "navigable" as used here is strictly relative.)

(The radius of hurricane-force winds around the eye can be 25 miles for a small hurricane and 150 miles for a large one.) The rationale for this conservatism is that boat handling is difficult in 34 knots of wind, and a hard-to-manage boat will have a difficult time escaping the edges of the storm. At wind speeds of more than 34 knots, seas can become large enough to damage even large vessels. (Here we're assuming a uniform radius around the storm's plotted center, but in fact the 34-knot radii will vary according to the quadrant of the storm—something to remember if you're ever caught out there.)

The next step is to add another 20 miles of radius to account for the possible error in the fix, as stated by the NHC. Then plot similar circles around the hurricane's predicted position in 12, 24, 36, and 48 hours, but increase the radius of each circle to account for the forecast error radius of approximately 100 miles per day. Thus, the plotted circle at 12 hours will have a radius 50 miles greater than the current position, the 24-hour radius will be 100 miles greater than the current plot, and so on. The result is a danger cone centered on the forecast track—the best picture you can make of where the storm is likely to go in the next 48 hours. Notice how large the area that you have plotted has become. Nevertheless, this danger cone is substantially narrower than the 40-degree cone mariners have traditionally used, and should be regarded as a minimum avoidance plot. If you can get outside that 40-degree cone, by all means do so.

You should attempt to take your boat out of this zone if possible. If it is impossible to get clear of the area, set your course to take you to the left side of a northern hemisphere hurricane or to the right side of a southern hemisphere typhoon.

You can find out more about hurricanes at http://www.aoml.noaa.gov or on the National Hurricane Center website at http://www.nhc.noaa.gov. Table 1–6 is a summary of hurricane

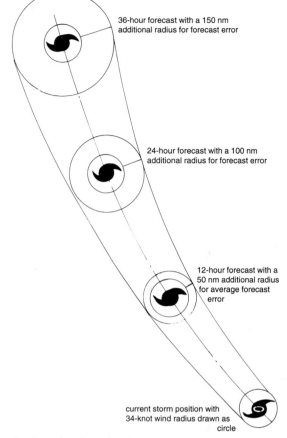

36-hour forecast with a 150 nm additional radius for forecast error

24-hour forecast with a 100 nm additional radius for forecast error

12-hour forecast with a 50 nm additional radius for average forecast error

current storm position with 34-knot wind radius drawn as circle

Plotting a hurricane's advance.

forecast products available to Atlantic mariners. This is taken from the *Mariner's Guide for Hurricane Awareness in the North Atlantic Basin*, by Eric Holweig, published by NOAA and the National Weather Service. To find out more about southern hemisphere typhoons and tropical cyclones, go to http://www.bom.gov.au/climate.

If in spite of tracking a hurricane, in spite of sailing hell for leather toward port, you are caught at sea, there are some steps you can take to reduce the severity of the storm. If the storm, in the northern hemisphere, is heading directly northward at 20 miles an hour, winds on its west side (because of its counter-clockwise direction) will be lower than winds on its east side. The area from the storm's one o'clock

Table 1–6. Summary of Tropical Weather Products

Product	Title/File or Chart Name	Description
Atlantic Tropical Weather Discussion	AXNT20 KNHC or MIATWDAT	Covers tropical & subtropical Atlantic discussing & describing significant synoptic weather features while tracking easterly tropical waves through the Atlantic Basin.
Atlantic Tropical Weather Outlook	ABNT20 KNHC or MIATWOAT	Covers tropical & subtropical Atlantic discussing areas of disturbed weather and their potential for development out to 48 hours.
Atlantic Tropical Cyclone Forecast/ Advisory	WTNT2x KNHC or MIATCMATX where X is active storm number 1 through 5	Issued for every tropical cyclone in the Atlantic Basin. Contains forecast through 72 hours for as long as the system remains a tropical cyclone.
Atlantic Tropical Cyclone Discussion	WTNT4X KNHC or MIATCDATX where X is the active storm number 1 through 5	Issued in conjunction with the Tropical Cyclone Forecast/ Advisory to explain the forecasters reasoning behind analysis and forecast of the Tropical Cyclone.
Special Tropical Disturbance Statement	WONT41 KNHC or MIADSAAT	Issued to provide information on strong, formative, non-depression systems focusing on the major threats associated with the disturbance.
Atlantic High Seas Forecast (North Atlantic from 7N to 67NW of 35W)	FZNT01 KWBC or NFDHSFAT1	Provides analysis & forecast information on wind & sea conditions in the region out to 48 hours. During periods with active tropical cyclones in the basin, this product will include latest initial position/intensity along with the 36-, 48-, & 72-hour forecast positions/intensities taken from the TCM. Tropical Cyclone position/intensity at the 12- & 24-hour forecast periods will only be included if expected to be upgraded/downgraded.
Atlantic High Seas Forecast (Atlantic S of 31NW of 35W including the Gulf of Mexico & Caribbean Sea)	FZNT02 KNHC or MIAHSFAT2	Provides analysis & forecast information on wind & sea conditions in the region out to 48 hours. During periods with active tropical cyclones in the basin, this product will include latest intial position/intensity along with the 36-, 48-, & 72-hour forecast positions/intensitites taken from the TCM. Tropical Cyclone position/intensity at the 12- & 24-hour forecast periods will only be included if expected to be upgraded/downgraded.
Offshore Forecasts	FZNT21 KWBC or NFDOFFNT1 FZNT22 KWBC or NFDOFFNT2 FZNT23 KNHC or MIAOFFNT3 FZNT24 KNHC or MIAOFFNT4	Provides analysis & forecast information on wind and sea conditions to mariners operating mainly a day or more from safe harbor. 3- to 5-day outlook for the region is included at the end of this product.

Table 1–6. *(continued)*

Type	Issue Time (UTC unless noted)	Distribution	Notes
Text	0005, 0605, 1205, 1805	INTERNET FTP MAIL	Only issued from June 1 to Nov 30.
Text	0530, 1130, 1730, 2230 Eastern Local Time	INTERNET FTP MAIL MF VOICE	
Text	0300, 0900, 1500, 2100	INTERNET FTP MAIL HF VOICE MF VOICE	Forecast/Advisories on subtropical cyclones will use the same WMO/AFOS headers with the actual advisory labelled SUBTROPICAL. Special Forecast/Advisories can be issued at intermediate times as conditions warrant. These will use the same header as the scheduled forecast/advisory.
Text	0300, 0900, 1500, 2100	INTERNET FTP MAIL	
Text	As required	INTERNET FTP MAIL	
Text	0300, 0900, 1500, 2100	INTERNET FTP MAIL HF VOICE MF VOICE	Forecast commences at latest previous synoptic time from the time product is issued. Therefore forecasts commence at 0000, 0600, 1200, 1800 UTC. This product is the combined Atlantic, Gulf of Mexico, & Caribbean Sea forecasts. This product is directed toward the largest oceangoing vessels.
Text	0430, 1030, 1630, 2230	INTERNET FTP MAIL HFFAX WWV HF VOICE HF SITOR HF VOICE INMARSAT-C	Forecast commences at latest previous synoptic time from the time product is issued. Therefore forecasts commence at 0000, 0600, 1200, 1800 UTC. This product is directed toward the largest oceangoing vessels.
Text	430 AM, 1030 AM, 430 PM, 1030 PM Local Standard time. (Remember to add 1 hour during Daylight Savings Time)	INTERNET FTP MAIL HF VOICE MF VOICE NAVTEX NOAA WEATHER RADIO (in Select Locations)	There are four headers for this product depending on geographic location of forecast. New England waters are FZNT21. West Central North Atlantic are FZNT22. SW North Atlantic and Caribbean Sea is FZNT23. Gulf of Mexico is FZNT24. Availability of this product on NOAA Weather Radio is based on transmitter availability. Contact nearest NWS Forecast Office to see if this product is transmitted via NOAA weather radio in your area.

Table 1–6. *(continued)*

Product	Title/File or Chart Name	Description
Coastal Forecasts	VARIOUS **See Notes for further information	Provides analysis & forecast information on wind & sea conditions to Mariners operating in the near shore environment. 3- to 5-day outlook for the region is included at the end of this product.
Tropical Surface Analysis	Fax Chart Name: PYEA8X where X is 6 for the 000 UTC analysis, 7 for the 0600 UTC chart, 5 for the 1200 UTC, and 8 for the 1800 UTC	Analysis of the Atlantic Basin from 5N to 35N including the Gulf of Mexico and Caribbean Sea. These charts include current position, intensity, and motion of any active tropical cyclone in the basin when applicable. Additionally, this chart shows the trough axis of any easterly tropical wave being tracked by the Tropical Prediction Center.
Wind/Wave Chart	Fax Chart Name: For NOWCAST/12 HR chart file name is PYEA9X where X is: for the chart valid 0000/1200 UTC, 7 for chart valid 0600/1800 UTC, 8 for chart valid 1200/0000 UTC, and 9 for chart valid 1800/0600 UTC. For 24 HR/36 HR chart file name is PWED9X where X is 8 for the chart valid 000/1200 UTC, and 9 for chart valid 1200/000 UTC.	Issued in 2 forms. The first is a NOWCAST/12 HR forecast issued four times daily. The second is a 24 HR/36 HR forecast issued 2 times daily. These charts include latest forecast position and intensity of any active tropical cyclone in the basin. Analyzed and forecasted combined sea heights are also found on this chart.
Marine Prediction Center Graphical Products	Various Chart Headers. See the BOSTON HF Fax schedule or visit the MPC web site for details on product availability.	Graphical surface analysis charts. Forecast surface charts our to 96 hours. Forecast 500 MB charts out to 96 hours. See height analysis. Satellite imagery.
Strike Probabilities	WTNT71-75 or MIASPFAT1-5	Gives the percentage chance of a tropical/subtropical cyclone passing within 75 nm to the right or within 50 nm to the left of a specified point, looking in the direction of cyclone motion.

Table 1–6. *(continued)*

Type	Issue Time (UTC unless noted)	Distribution	Notes
Text	430 AM, 1030 AM, 430 PM, 1030 PM Local Standard time. (Remember to add 1 hour during Daylight Savings Time)	INTERNET MF VOICE USCG VHF VOICE NOAA WEATHER RADIO	File names and product headers are determined by the National Weather Service Forecast Office issuing the product. For particular file name and header information for a particular coastal forecast contact the nearest NWS Forecast Office.
Graphic	As soon as completed after the synoptic times of 0000, 0600, 1200, 1800 UTC	INTERNET FTP MAIL HF FAX	
Graphic	For the NOW/ 12 HR product is issued by 0055, 0655, 1255, 1855. For the 24/36 HR product is issued by 0000, 1200.	INTERNET FTP MAIL HF FAX	
Graphic	Various	INTERNET FTP MAIL HF FAX	Products focused on area of the Atlantic from 31N-67N including portions of the Gulf of Mexico. Format and content of products is similar to those issued from the Tropical Prediction Center. Web Site Address for MPC: http://www.mpc.ncep.noaa.gov/
Text	0300, 0900, 1500, 2100	INTERNET	Probabilities are given for 0-24, 24-36, 36-48, & 48-72 hours, with 0-72 hour given by adding the individual probabilities together.

to the storm's seven o'clock is where you will encounter the strongest winds. If the winds are 75 miles an hour they will be increased by the forward speed of the storm to around 95 miles an hour. On the west side the opposite is true: winds will be decreased. Therefore, when caught at sea in a hurricane always head for the west side of the storm. This often means that as you cross the top of the storm you will have following winds driving your boat close to its fastest speeds, which will require some careful helming.

It's worth repeating that, even if you plot the storm's center and listen to National Hurricane Center predictions, there is no guarantee the storm will follow the predicted path. A check of the NHC website suggests that for a 72-hour prediction a storm can be as far as 300 miles off. As the prediction time increases, the distance error also increases.

The NHC suggests that you read its booklet on hurricane prediction. It is available for download (52 pages) at http://www.nhc .noaa.gov/marinersguide.pdf, or you can go to http://www.nhc.noaa.gov/HAW2/english/ marinesafety.html for safety information. Chapter 3 of the NHC booklet gives you all the radio, internet, and other sources that offer information on hurricanes in the North Atlantic basin.

There are so many influences on the direction and strength of hurricanes that it is impossible, even with today's technology, to predict exactly where a hurricane is going to go. It is also difficult to predict how intense the storm is going to be. A hurricane feeds off the energy in warm ocean water, and an area of warmer water can increase a hurricane's intensity dramatically in a few hours. This is precisely what happened to Hurricane Katrina just before it hit New Orleans in 2005. When a hurricane passes over cooler waters, however, it loses intensity. As a result, many hurricanes are downgraded as they pass over cooler coastal waters just before making landfall.

In another example, Hurricane Charley, in August 2004, intensified from a Category 1 storm to Category 4 in the last few hours before making landfall over Ft. Myers, Florida, missing its predicted landfall by almost 60 miles and carving a swath of destruction across the state. Nevertheless, there are enough data to suggest certain general tracks and probabilities for each month of the North Atlantic hurricane season. The information for other areas of the world may not be as extensive, but wherever you may be, you should gather all that's available.

The NHC booklet suggests that you check forecasts four times a day when you're at sea in an area subject to hurricane threat. The hurricane advisory includes graphs suggesting that vessels avoid certain areas during hurricane months. Charts assembled by hurricane researchers show that certain tracks within the anticipated hurricane strike area experience a higher-than-normal incidence of strikes by major storms.

The booklet also proposes the "1–2–3 Rule" for hurricane avoidance, which is derived from 10-year average forecast errors for North Atlantic hurricanes. The method is exactly as outlined above, except that the plot is carried out

This satellite photo of Hurricane Mitch as it approached Honduras on October 26, 1998, gives a sense of the power unleashed by a Category 5 hurricane. (Photo courtesy Laboratory for Atmospheres, NASA Goddard Space Flight Center)

one, two, and three days ahead, rather than to a maximum of 48 hours.

As a hurricane gets closer, you should continue to plot its position while narrowing the margin of error as appropriate. If you're at sea, continue your efforts to get as far out on the safe side of the advancing storm as possible.

You should never leave harbor in an effort to "slip past" a storm or just skim through its edges, since you might very well end up facing its full fury. Once caught in the edge of a storm, you can quickly find yourself being drawn in even deeper, since the winds spiral in toward the center. Leave harbor *only* if you are confident that you can *completely* avoid the hurricane. Otherwise, your best bet when a storm is forecast is to try to get your boat hauled and secured ashore where it will be safest, or at least make sure it is securely moored. After that, you need to get yourself to higher ground. We'll discuss hurricane preparations further in Chapter 6.

STORM SCENARIO

What to Do if You Are Caught in a Storm or Hurricane

How do you decide when to run off from a storm, when to broad reach or close-fetch toward it, or when to stream warps? Here are a few general guidelines.

First, you need to know how much sea room you have. Figure that you need at least 50–60 miles to leeward if you intend to heave-to. If you decide to run before a storm, you might sail as much as 250 miles in a 24-hour period.

Second, if you are about to be enveloped by an Atlantic or Caribbean hurricane, head for its left-hand side (to the west side of a storm traveling north or the south side of a storm traveling west). On this side, the forward velocity of the storm system will decrease the effective wind speed within the system. Conversely, on the right-hand side of the storm, the storm's speed of travel will increase the wind speed. If the storm is traveling at 15 knots, the difference in sustained wind speeds from one side to the other of its track will be 30 knots, which is considerable. In the Southern Hemisphere, the safe side will be to the right of the storm's direction of travel.

You should also have a good idea of the track and diameter of the storm, which will help you decide which way to head to get away from it and how long you will be in it. The radii of hurricane- and storm force (47-knot) winds are usually given in National Hurricane Center advisories. Tracking the direction of the storm is important. I know of one instance in which two boats making a passage in company encountered a storm. One skipper failed to track the storm's direction, and he and his crew ran off before it. They spent nearly 48 hours in very bad weather. The other boat tracked the storm, tacked over, and was out of the bad weather 12 hours later.

Suppose you are at sea and hear that a storm is coming. You've been tracking the storm's path from the Caribbean and have weather predictions showing it crossing between you and mainland America. You plot the predicted course of the storm and the time it will take you to reach the nearest port. Your options are to head east and out to sea, to head southwest for Bermuda in the hope that you will be able to get into the harbor as the storm builds, or to head in a westerly direction toward the East Coast in the hope that a rescue helicopter will be able reach you if your boat runs into trouble. What would you do?

Studying your charts and plots, you realize that heading west would put you closer to the storm's predicted track and in its strongest (right-hand) sector—the worst place to be. Should the storm veer to the east as it approaches, you might be trapped there for a

continued

long time. Heading east would put you well out of range of rescue forces, but would give you about 400 miles of sea room and take you away from the heart of the storm unless it veers to the northeast. The final option, heading toward Bermuda, would, at your present speed, put you off St. David's Light about the time the wind there reaches hurricane force. Given the reefs around the island, entering the main channel to Hamilton Harbor in heavy weather is not to be recommended.

Experienced sailors who have confidence in their boats would probably head east, hoping to avoid the storm. Even if they had to heave to and their boat made 200 or 300 miles of leeway during the storm, they would have plenty of sea room, and if the storm headed toward shore, they might miss it altogether.

A powerboat's tactics might be very different. Given its greater speed, it might well be able to beat the storm to Bermuda and be safely docked before the blow hits. If there were no possibility of making Bermuda, however, heading east to avoid as much of the storm as possible would be the favored route. This presupposes, of course, that only a seaworthy powerboat with plenty of fuel capacity would be that far offshore to begin with.

Two

Waves

On a calm day there are no wind-driven waves, and the sea looks flat. All you may see is an underlying swell, which may come from a storm a thousand miles away. For sailboats, it is the worst of times. For powerboats, it is the best: a fast ride on a smooth sea.

Much like radio waves moving through the air, waves in the ocean represent energy radiating outward from a disturbance. In non-breaking waves, the water itself does not move except in small orbital rotations that return each water parcel nearly to its point of origin after the wave passes by. Even these small oscillations decrease rapidly with depth, ultimately disappearing at a depth that depends on wave height.

The vast majority of wave systems are generated by wind blowing across the water's surface. But there are other wave sources as well. For example, a boat moving through water creates pressure waves, and tidal races can create standing waves similar to those in whitewater rivers.

Underwater volcanoes, earthquakes, or landslides can also generate waves. These tidal waves, or *tsunamis*, can strike a shore with devastating effect, as was vividly and tragically demonstrated by the one that swept ashore on much of the Thai, Sri Lankan, southern Indian, and Sumatran coastlines on December 26, 2004. This so-called Boxing Day Tsunami was triggered by a magnitude 9.15 earthquake under the Indian Ocean that lasted close to 10 minutes (in contrast with the usual few seconds) and was powerful enough to vibrate the entire planet a few centimeters in its orbit. But tidal waves are rarely felt by mariners unless their boats are close to shore.

What mariners routinely encounter are wind-driven waves, sometimes arriving from more than one direction at once. Add to these waves a ground swell, the occasional boat wake, and such local effects as tide races, wave trains bending around islands and headlands, waves steepening in shoal water, or waves reflecting back to sea from breakwaters or steep shorelines, and things can get interesting—even on a pleasant day with an ordinary fresh breeze. Crank the wind up to gale force so that some of those waves start breaking, and it's easy to see why waves can be a bigger challenge than winds in rough weather.

Wind-Generated Waves

Let's say you are out in a boat on a windless day, surrounded by mirror-smooth water. (In truth the surface of the restless sea is never entirely still. There is always some slight movement: a low ground swell, perhaps almost imperceptible; a leftover sea from a wind that died long since; or the wake from a distant boat.) Then a gentle breeze springs up, and ripples immediately begin to form on the sea surface. These ripples, or *capillary waves*, result from the friction of moving air on the water's surface, and once formed they give the wind something to push against, so they tend to grow.

At Beaufort Force 1 (1–3 knots of wind speed), however, they remain tiny scales without crests. A sailor looks at these ripples and sighs, for this is not enough wind to get anywhere. Often, sailors will notice a streaky wind pattern as the breeze struggles to overcome the sea's inherent surface tension. At Force 2 (4–6 knots), this surface tension breaks down and the ripples build to small wavelets, and as the wind speed increases to Force 3 (7–10 knots), the wavelets increase to a maximum height of 2 feet and begin to crest with small whitecaps. (Note, however, that a Force 3 breeze must blow at least 8 hours over a fetch of at least 25 miles to build 2-foot waves. We'll discuss the concepts of wind duration and fetch below.) For a sailboat helmsman these are signs that the wind is coming, and the boat starts to gather way. Aboard most powerboats, the ride is still smooth, but increasing winds warn of rougher conditions on the way.

At Force 4 (11–16 knots) the wavelets build to waves, which provide increased resistance to the wind's passage. This leads to a further increase in wave height and numerous whitecaps, or "white horses." The waves at this stage are short and steep but less than 4 feet high and fairly regular, and sailboats over 30 feet will have little problem with them. Smaller sailboats, however, might find it hard to drive into this chop, especially when the waves travel at an angle of up to 30 degrees from the wind direction, putting them almost dead ahead on one tack. This sometimes happens close to land when the breeze bends around a headland or shifts direction as it builds.

A sea breeze in Rhode Island Sound, for example, often comes in from around 160–170 degrees early in the afternoon, but veers to around 220 degrees as the afternoon wears on and the breeze builds. This creates a change in the wave configuration, which often results in lumpy seas. Small sailboats trying to beat into these choppy head seas can be stopped dead when they hit some of these waves, and powerboats with shallow-deadrise hulls (less than 8 degrees at the transom) will start to slam if driven too hard into the seas.

At Force 5 (17–21 knots), the waves build further, to a height of 4–8 feet, but they can't get any steeper without breaking, so they must also lengthen. These longer, higher waves may or may not be harder to negotiate than the shorter chop of a Force 4 breeze, depending on the boat. The whitecaps will begin to be blown off into spray, and most sailboats will change

Wave Terminology

Breaker—a coastal breaking wave. As a wave approaches shore, quite often at speeds of 15 or 20 miles per hour, water depth decreases until, at a depth roughly equal to 1.3 times the wave's height (or to put it another way, when the wave's height is about 80 percent of the water depth), the particles of water within the wave can no longer complete their oscillations. At that point the wave breaks, its crest falling forward into the trough ahead, and the kinetic energy of the oscillating wave is released in a rushing mass of surf. When the water shoals gradually the wave will also break gradually, and the result is a *spilling breaker*. When the water shoals abruptly the break is more abrupt and violent, and the result is called a *plunging breaker*.

Breaking wave—a wave at sea that becomes so steep that wind, an intersection with another wave, an encounter with a tidal or ocean current, or some combination of these factors causes it to lose stability. At that point the crest moves more rapidly than the water beneath it and it collapses forward, dissipating much of the wave's energy in a headlong rush and fall of foaming water. Breaking waves represent the single biggest danger to boats caught in storms.

Deepwater waves—waves that inhabit a depth of more than half their own wavelength.

Fetch—the distance of open water—unimpeded by landmass—over which the wind blows.

Frequency (F)—the number of waves per second that pass a fixed point. A wave with a period (see below) of 10 seconds has a frequency of 0.1.

Fully developed seas—when wind-driven waves are as large as they can be for the given strength of wind—that is, when the wind has blown over a sufficient time and fetch to build the waves to the maximum extent of its capability—the seas are said to be fully developed.

Height (H)—the vertical distance from a wave's trough to its crest.

Length (L)—the distance from one wave crest to the next, which in an ideal deepwater wave is related to its period by the formula: L (in feet) = 5.12 P^2, with P measured in seconds.

Period (P)—the time in seconds taken for one wave (crest to crest) to pass a fixed point. In an ideal deepwater wave, period is related to wavelength by the formula: $P = 0.443 \times \sqrt{L}$, where L is the wave length in feet.

Rogue wave—a transitory wave much higher than surrounding waves and much higher than the significant wave height. Though a rogue wave seems to come from nowhere, it is in fact the superimposition of two or more wave crests. For example, two 20-foot waves could, in theory, combine to produce a 40-footer of brief duration, which will break if the combined height makes the wave unstable. Rogue waves are sometimes called *freak waves*.

Sea state—prevailing wave conditions for the locale in question, often expressed in terms of direction of wave train or trains and significant wave height.

Shallow-water wave—a wave that exists in water that is less than ¹⁄₂₀ of its wavelength.

Significant wave height—the average height of the highest one-third of the waves in a system. (The highest waves may be twice as high as this average.) Sea state forecasts are often expressed in terms of significant wave height.

Steepness—the ratio of wave height to wave length. Any ratio higher than 1:7 (stated another way, any *crest angle* less than 120 degrees) makes the wave unstable and causes it to break.

Swell—a wave that has moved well beyond the gale or storm from which it originated. For example, a hurricane north of Bermuda may generate a swell on the coast of New England.

Transitional waves—waves that are neither deep- nor shallow-water waves.

Velocity (C)—the speed at which waves move past a fixed point. A deepwater wave's velocity (in knots) can be estimated by multiplying its period (in seconds) by 3. When the wave moves into shallow water and begins to "feel" the bottom, it slows down because of friction from the seabed, and in very shallow water (relative to wave length) its speed in knots becomes $3.1 \times \sqrt{depth}$ (in feet).

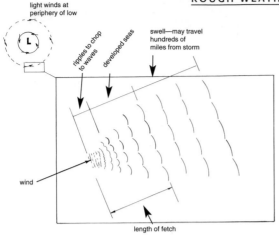

The life cycle of wind-driven waves. (Adapted from Waves and Beaches, by Willard Bascom)

to a smaller jib and tuck a reef or even two in the mainsail. A powerboat with steep deadrise and a fine bow will give a much easier ride in this kind of sea than one with a flatter bottom or blunter bow.

It might seem surprising that an increase of wind velocity from Force 4 to Force 5 can double the wave height, but in part this is because the force of the wind increases twice as fast as its velocity. Thus, when the wind increases from Force 5 to Force 6 (22–27 knots) the seas build from 8 to a maximum of 13 feet, given enough time and fetch for the wind, and whitecaps are everywhere. Force 7 (28–33 knots), is a moderate gale. Now the seas heap up and white foam is blown in streaks along the axis of the wind. If the breeze keeps on building to a fresh gale, Force 8 (34–40 knots), the waves are higher and

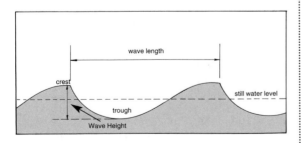

The anatomy of a wave.

longer still, and the foam that was blown from the crests by the Force 7 gale is now visible everywhere; the white streaks on the water, moving in the direction of the wind, are known as *spindrift*. A sailboat, depending on its size, will carry three reefs in its mainsail and a No. 3 or No. 4 headsail or perhaps a storm jib. Its motion close-hauled will be labored, with the bow slamming and throwing water to leeward in powerful bursts. Waves might wash into the jib on a sailboat with low-cut sails, possibly damaging the sail. Unless the boat is racing or has no sea room to leeward, it's probably time to bear off and stop fighting the seas. Going downwind will be a pleasure as the apparent wind shifts aft and becomes much lighter, but steering in these seas will require constant watchfulness, as discussed in Chapter 8.

Aboard a powerboat, the helmsman will have reduced speed upwind and will be taking some hard slams on the bow. Water will frequently break over the bow, and spray will blow back inboard. A powerboater in a small boat should be heading downwind on a course for shore (zigzagging to keep the wave on the quarter if necessary), especially if the wind is forecast to keep on increasing. He will in all likelihood wish he'd listened more carefully to the weather forecast before heading out and will resolve always to do so in the future. Powering downwind in a following sea will require alertness, but should not be too difficult if the boat is not prone to broaching. We'll discuss this in Chapter 8.

In winds of Force 6 and stronger, the wave crests are anything but regular. The system you see from your boat as a series of crests is more likely the aggregate of a number of wave trains, each with its own period, height, and direction. When two or more intersecting wave trains are temporarily in phase so that the crests of one reinforce the crests of another, this *constructive interference* causes especially steep, high peaks. Conversely, when wave trains get out of phase you want to avoid tacking when the wave trains are in phase.

Force 9 (41–47 knots) is a strong gale, and if it blows for more than 25 hours over a fetch of more than 280 miles, it can build seas as high as 40 feet. If these intersect another wave train or are steepened by an opposing current—as in the Gulf Stream—the results can be even more dramatic. Waves more than 75 feet high have been recorded in these conditions. By Force 9 even the largest, most well-found sailboats have given up all pretense of progress to weather and are engaged in storm tactics as discussed in Chapter 8. Hopefully, you have listened to the weather forecast and are safely ashore well before a strong gale hits.

In Force 10 conditions, with wind speeds of 48–55 knots, the waves will be very high, with dense streaks of foam along the sea surface coloring the water surface white. Fully developed seas can be as high as 30 feet on average, with substantially higher ones reported. The noise will be horrendous as the wind howls through the rigging. The boat's deck will be continually soaked with green water coming aboard.

The wind is blowing at about 25 knots. This 100-foot sailboat has a single reef in the main and three rolls in the jib, but a smaller boat would need a second reef and a smaller headsail.

so that the troughs of one coincide with the crests of another, they cancel each other out in what is called *destructive interference*. That is why sailors and boaters who have experienced large waves often say the biggest ones come in groups of three. The groups may or may not be threes, but the phases of strengthening and weakening are real.

An observant sailor can take advantage of these phases when the time comes to tack in heavy seas simply by waiting until the wave trains are temporarily out of phase and their crests and troughs are partially canceling each other out. Of course, the opposite is also true—

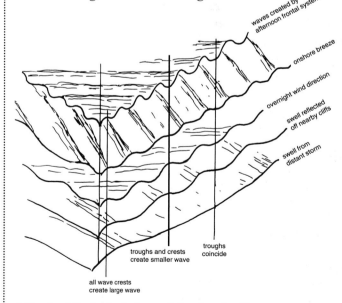

waves created by
afternoon frontal system

onshore breeze

overnight wind direction

swell reflected
off nearby cliffs

swell from
distant storm

troughs and crests
create smaller wave

troughs
coincide

all wave crests
create large wave

A "laminate" of a typical sea state, showing the several wave trains of which it is composed.

Table 2–1. Characteristics of Swell in Deep Water

Period (seconds)	Wave length (feet)	Speed (knots)	Water depth to feel bottom (feet)
6	184	18	92
8	326	24	163
10	512	30	256
12	738	36	369
14	1000	42	500
16	1310	48	655

Adapted from Bascom, Waves and Beaches *(Anchor Books, 1964)*

Sooner or later the wind stops blowing, but the waves that have been created travel onward until they either become imperceptible or collide with the shore as surf. Without the ongoing force of the wind, storm wave crests become lower, longer, more rounded, and more symmetrical, their sectional shapes approaching an ideal sine curve of uniform period (often 6–9 seconds) and height. These waves, known as *swell*, can travel thousands of miles with little loss of energy. Table 2–1, adapted from Willard Bascom's wonderful 1964 book *Waves and Beaches: The Dynamics of the Ocean Surface,* shows the characteristics of ocean swell. The last column is the water depth in feet at which swell of the given length becomes a shallow-water wave and starts to feel the bottom. At that point it will begin to steepen in its approach to shore. Note that any swell period longer than ten seconds probably results from a major storm or hurricane.

Rough-Weather Seas

As we've seen, the arrival of wind brings into play three factors that affect waves—the length of time the wind blows, the distance or fetch over which it blows, and the strength of the wind. All these factors play a part in the height and length of the wave. Moderate winds blowing for a long time over a great distance can generate longer and larger waves than much stronger winds blowing for only a short period of time over a short stretch of water. The results can be awe-inspiring when a strong wind blows uninterrupted over an essentially unlimited fetch, as in the Southern Ocean, where westerly winds circle the globe unimpeded by any landmass.

Bernard Moitessier, in his book *The Long Way,* describes these Southern Ocean "greybeards," often 40 or 50 feet high, with something approaching reverence. Table 2–2, again adapted from Willard Bascom's *Waves and Beaches,* summarizes the characteristics of fully developed seas (those unlimited by fetch or du-

As waves move away from the point where they were generated, they become longer and lower. This swell can travel thousands of miles with little further loss of energy.

Table 2–2. Fully Developed Seas Resulting from Winds Unlimited by Fetch or Duration

Wind speed (knots)	Fetch (nautical miles)	Duration of wind (hours)	Average height (feet)	Significant height (feet)	Average height of highest 10% (feet)
10	10	2.4	0.9	1.4	1.8
15	34	6	2.5	3.5	5
20	75	10	5	8	10
25	160	16	9	14	18
30	280	23	14	22	28
40	710	42	28	44	57
50	1420	69	48	78	99

Adapted from Bascom, Waves and Beaches *(Anchor Books, 1964)*

ration of wind) for various wind speeds. Remember that significant height means the average height of the tallest one-third of the waves. But note that Bascom's highest wave heights for wind speeds of 40 and 50 knots are higher than those reported elsewhere, and in any event it is extremely rare for gale-force winds not to be limited either by duration or fetch.

You might ask how a boat can survive the fully developed seas of a Force 8, 9, or 10 gale, but remember that waves become unstable when their ratio of height to length exceeds 1 to 7. Thus the higher waves in a fully developed sea are also longer, and as long as the wave is not breaking, the water itself is not moving, and the boat will float up over the wave successfully. The crest angle in a wave at its maximum steepness (1:7) is 120 degrees, and a little geometry tells us that a boat's heel angle on such a crest, ignoring other factors for the moment, would be 30 degrees—uncomfortable perhaps, but hardly life threatening. Wave height in itself is not the chief danger. The danger comes from breaking seas.

Breaking Seas

Deepwater breaking seas differ from breaking surf in fundamental respects. Surf is caused when a shoaling seabed slows the wave through frictional drag. Eventually the crest of the wave outruns its base, and the wave collapses forward in the familiar plunging or spilling breakers that we admire at the beach.

Seas that break in deep water have not been slowed by friction and thus are moving at higher velocities. Donald Jordan, developer of the Jordan Series Drogue (See Chapter 8), has done a lot of thinking, wave tank work, and analysis to characterize breaking waves in open water, and he concludes that they are caused in three ways:

1. Storm waves may break when slowed and steepened by an opposing ocean current. This happens—notoriously—when northerly gales run into the north-flowing Gulf Stream off the east coast of the United States.
2. A storm can be strong enough to build high seas so rapidly that the seas do not develop a matching increase in length and speed. Such seas become too steep to be stable, and they break, eventually forming longer seas. This explains why the steep seas encountered in the early stages of a storm may be more problematic than the longer, more mature seas later in the storm.

3. Two or more seas can intersect, or one can overtake another, and the sum of their crests creates a wave too high to be stable.

Jordan believes that most breaking seas result from a combination of the second and third factors. What's more, he believes that the third factor is more likely to arise when one wave overtakes another than when two waves from different directions intersect. He suggests that waves intersecting at something approaching a right angle are more likely to peak up and collapse in place than to create a breaking crest with great forward velocity in its tumbling mass of turbulent white water.

In Jordan's description, and in Table 2–2, a storm wind generates waves of various heights distributed around an average height that depends on the strength of the wind, its duration, and its fetch. All the waves move in the direction of the wind, but the larger waves have greater velocity than the smaller and therefore overtake and "consume" them. In this way a big wave gets bigger until its height becomes unstable, at which point it collapses in a breaking wave, the white water from its crest tumbling down the wave front with a roaring noise that gives a breaking wave its other name, "growler."

These breaking waves are the biggest threats to boats, as was vividly demonstrated in the 1979 Fastnet Race and the 1998 Sydney-Hobart Race discussed later in this book. Imagine thousands of tons of foaming water rushing and falling toward your boat at speeds approaching, or even exceeding 40 knots, and you'll see why this is so. As we'll see in Chapter 8, the Jordan Series Drogue is designed to help in exactly this situation.

Rogue Waves

Mariners have a special name for the biggest of these breaking seas; they are called *rogue waves*. The largest reliably reported wave was estimated at 112 feet (34 m) high from the deck of the USS *Ramapo* in 1933. The *Queen Elizabeth II* encountered a 29-meter (95-ft.) wave during a North Atlantic hurricane in 1995, and the Draupner oil production platform in the comparatively shallow North Sea measured a 26-meter (85-ft.) wave in a January 1, 1995 storm. Radar evidence from the *Goma* North Sea oil field records more than 450 rogue waves in a 12-year period. Sea buoy measurements suggest that both average and extreme North Atlantic wave heights have been increasing in recent decades, for reasons that are still unclear, but monsters of 80 or 90 feet (24 or 27 m) and higher remain mercifully rare worldwide.

On the other hand, breaking seas of 50 feet (15 m) and higher were reported from the 1979 Fastnet Race, the 1998 Sydney-Hobart Race, and in a number of other mariners' accounts—enough to convince us that rogue waves of that size are not rare. The European Space Agency reported in June 2004 a study using satellite-based synthetic aperture radars that found more than 25 giant waves over 25 meters (82 feet) in height around the globe in one radar sweep, suggesting that such waves occur much more frequently than was previously believed. This study suggests that most rogue waves occur in areas where ordinary waves encounter strong currents and eddies, for example, the Agulhas Current off South Africa.

A boat located to the right of the path of a northbound hurricane in the North Atlantic might first feel an underlying swell moving to the north-northwest, after which it will experience light winds out of the south or southeast. These winds will in turn induce small waves on top of the swell, which becomes shorter and steeper. As the storm approaches from the south, the wind will continue to veer and build in intensity, creating larger waves from the southeast, which can build to a large height. If the storm passes to the west, the wind will veer into the southwest, superimposing southwesterly waves on the existing southeasterly waves,

The "Queen's Birthday Storm" swept the Pacific north of New Zealand in early June 1994, battering a fleet of cruising sailboats with wind speeds as high as 90 knots and waves that one merchant captain reported as high as 100 feet. Bill and Robyn Forbes were forced to abandon their 38-foot catamaran, Ramtha, and are shown here being hauled through raging seas in a helicopter harness to the New Zealand Navy ship Monowai. The breaking sea in the background looks well over 50 feet. (Photo by CPO AHS Lindsay Turvey, Royal New Zealand Navy)

resulting in steep, confused seas. If the storm is a slow mover, the result can be especially chaotic, with large and small waves jostling about from different directions in one area—a breeding ground for rogue waves.

When Hurricane Ivan, a Category 4 storm, roared north through the Gulf of Mexico in May 2004, a moored buoy measured a significant wave height of 50 feet (15 m) ahead of the storm. Unfortunately the buoy broke loose before the hurricane's eyewall arrived, but this was the second largest significant wave height measured to date, exceeded (by a few tenths of a meter) only by one measurement from the North Pacific. When the average of the highest third of the waves (which is what significant wave height represents) is 50 feet, much bigger

individual waves can be expected, and indeed this happened. An array of wave/tide gauges, moored at depths ranging from 195 to 295 feet (60 to 90 m), measured a wave 91 feet (28 m) high, one of a group of waves of approximately 10-second periods that included several 66-footers (20 m). These waves were not in the eyewall, but extrapolation from wind data suggest that wave heights in the eyewall may have exceeded 130 feet (40 m).

Elsewhere, large tankers moving in the Agulhas Current off the coast of South Africa have encountered extremely large rogue waves that were big enough to smash portions of their hulls. The horizontal shear of the current has been shown to be strong enough to refract storm waves that run counter to the current,

A freak storm struck the 1998 Sydney-Hobart Race fleet with winds of more than 80 knots, piling seas as high as 80 feet or more against the currents of the Bass Strait. In this photo taken from a helicopter, the crew of the 41-foot Stand Aside, already rolled and dismasted, await rescue. This breaking sea, which looks between 60 and 80 feet high, almost rolled the boat again. (Photo by Peter Sinclair)

focusing the energy of the waves on certain locations.

Wise sailors steer clear of the Agulhas Current if possible, and they venture into hurricane waters in hurricane season only with extreme caution. They listen to weather forecasts and stay put whenever a tropical disturbance is reported to be tracking anywhere near the planned passage. They leave port warily, like a pedestrian stepping off a Manhattan curb.

Other Wave Factors

Pressure Waves
Waves caused by the passage of a boat through the water are called *pressure waves,* and are only found on the water's surface. Submarines, for example, do not create large pressure waves. At maximum speed a ship creates waves both at its bow and at its stern, and while these wave crests rarely achieve much height, they can travel a long way, depending on conditions. Pressure waves can become dangerous when a large ship passes nearby at high speed, and the waves in the ship's wake interact with the existing sea state to form especially large or steep waves. Depending on the proximity of the vessel, pressure waves can be short, very steep, and move very fast. Once I was sailing a dinghy in the English Channel when a megayacht doing more than 30 knots passed nearby. A short time later the dinghy was subjected to waves 5–8 feet high, even though the other boat was more than a mile away.

Interference, Refraction, and Reflection

As we noted earlier, when two wave trains with different periods, wavelengths, and/or directions meet, the result is interference. The meeting waves can combine to generate extra-high crests (constructive interference) or cancel each other out where a wave trough and a crest meet to create low spots (destructive interference).

Refraction occurs when a wave moves toward the shore at an angle. The end of the wave nearest the shore slows down more than the end in deeper water, so the wave bends until it is almost parallel to the shore. This bending and redirection, when combined with interference, can cause some strange results. Waves refracted around an island, for example, may cause a confused sea with an almost checkerboard pattern on the leeward side.

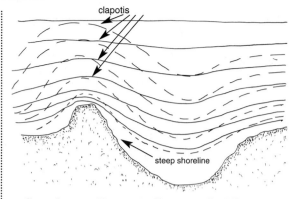

Reflected waves "bounce" off a seawall, cliff, or steep shoreline and form destructive or constructive crests with incoming waves. These standing waves are called clapotis.

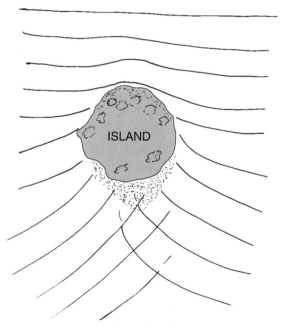

Refracted waves are "bent" as the wave makes contact with the seabed. This effect causes the wave to refract or bend until it is almost parallel to the shoreline. In the lee of an island the effect can be seen as a series of diamond-shaped waves, and often a sandy beach on the lee side of the island.

Reflected waves occur when a wave hits a breakwater, cliff, or steep shore. The wave energy is reflected back against the incoming waves, sometimes coinciding with them to produce standing waves, or *clapotis*.

All these phenomena—as well as the steepening of waves that occurs in shallow water and when wind opposes a tidal current—can complicate conditions in an inlet. Many inlets present difficult, challenging conditions for boaters, and should not be attempted without local knowledge except at slack tides and in settled conditions.

Storm Surge

Not only is the sea surface in the low-pressure center of a hurricane or extra-tropical storm slightly higher than the surrounding water, but the storm itself will also push a wall of water ahead of its dangerous semicircle as it plows its way across an ocean. The surge ahead of a Category 1 hurricane (wind speeds of 64–82 knots) might be 4–5 feet above normal sea level; it can rise to 18 feet ahead of a Category 4 storm and 23 feet or more ahead of a Category 5 hurricane. Storm waves then ride atop this surge, which is why storm surges are responsible for much of the major coastline damage in a major storm, whether of tropical or extra-tropical origin.

A North Sea storm in the winter of 1953 caused a storm surge of more than 10 feet (3 m) against the dikes on the Dutch coast. Storm waves rode in on top of the surge, topping the dikes, eroding their inner foundations, and ultimately breaching them. More than 800,000 acres of Holland's low country were flooded, and 1,783 people died.

A storm surge coinciding with the top of a high tide can raise the sea level to heights unseen in many decades. On the island where I live, a storm surge can cut the island into three parts, making it almost impossible to evacuate. If you live near the coast, you need to be aware of such events when a storm is about to occur so that you will be sure to evacuate in a timely manner. When leaving your boat in a marina or slip, you need to make sure that the docks will not be submerged or float off the tops of pilings when the storm surge hits. You should also make sure that your boat has mooring lines with enough slack in them to ride out the storm surge.

Storm surge damage. This is the Jamestown, Rhode Island, waterfront during a hurricane high tide. The street is flooded, and the boats in the background have been washed ashore. (Photo courtesy Jeff McDonough, the Jamestown Press)

Tsunamis

Most sailors at sea will never feel a tsunami. They are rare, occurring at the rate of about one per year worldwide. Even if you do encounter one, in deep water the wave's energy will pass right under the boat with barely a ripple, because its wavelength is extraordinarily long. It is coastal dwellers who will feel the effects of a tsunami, when it comes on shore. Shoaling water causes it to build to tremendous heights. The trough of the wave can actually empty a bay of water, but its crest can surge many miles inland, which is probably why tsunami are also called tidal waves.

These waves are caused by underwater disturbances such as a volcanic eruption or underwater landslide on a massive scale. The wavelength of a tsunami can be extremely long, up to several miles, so it will lose energy very slowly and can travel great distances. A tsunami's velocity can be very high; waves moving at more than 350 knots have been noted in the Pacific. Like other waves, tsunamis can be refracted and reflected, which can cause even more devastation when the wave hits shore.

The trough of a tsunami usually precedes the crest, and boats in a harbor are left high and dry as the water is sucked out. Then a large, devastating wave crest follows, often high and powerful enough to move several miles inshore over flat land. A tsunami that hit Chile in 1868 left ships 2 miles inland.

Ocean Currents

Around the world, giant ocean currents move seawater vast distances. The Gulf Stream may be the best known, but there are many others. Mariners can take advantage of these currents to make faster transits when the current is moving in the same direction as the boat. But ocean currents can also be extremely dangerous. For example, when a cold front with strong northerly winds sweeps seaward off the coast of Florida, seas in the north-flowing Gulf Stream

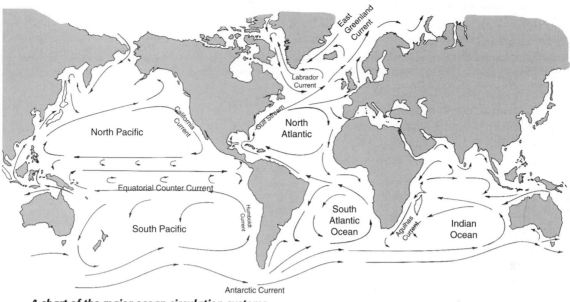

A chart of the major ocean circulation systems.

not only grow large, they are also short and steep. Described by some mariners as resembling moving walls, they can cause a lot of problems, especially for smaller boats.

We have already mentioned the rogue waves that have damaged and destroyed large ships in the Agulhas Current off South Africa—a phenomenon that appears to result from the current focusing wave trains by refraction on certain hard-to-predict places. Similar phenomena could happen elsewhere. Whenever the wind direction opposes the direction of a tidal stream or ocean current, mariners should avoid sailing in the stream axis. Try to get out to the edges, where the seas are likely to be considerably smaller.

Strategies for Big Waves

When you encounter big breaking seas close to shore, you should probably turn on the engine and either power or motorsail out of there. If you reach off to gain speed in a sailboat, you may get caught by a wave and rolled over. But if you try to sail closehauled or on a close reach, you may not be able to build up enough speed to drive through the crests and make it out. In this case, turning on the engine may be your only choice.

Out at sea, you may opt to reach off and try to drive the boat through large waves in the hope that you will sail into calmer seas in a short while. If you have sea room to leeward, you might want to look for a flat spot and turn the boat to run at an angle to the seas. Eventually, you should find calmer waters that will enable you to turn back on course.

In a powerboat at sea, as long as you have enough fuel you should be able to power or "jog" directly into the wind until you are through the worst of the seas. Your only limit on how much jogging you can stand may be the endurance of your crew. Things might get rough, however, if your boat gets in sync with the waves. Accelerations and slamming will increase, and your only option may be to decrease speed until the boat gets out of phase with the waves, meanwhile trying not to lose steerageway. We'll discuss these strategies in greater depth in Chapter 8. Offwind, a wave train may be moving at 22–26 knots, and to keep a boat in a single wave would mean traveling at insane speeds in strong winds. Many powerboaters use a drogue to keep the flat transom of the boat facing into the seas while the boat is powered at a reduced speed directly downwind. A drogue stops the stern from being pushed off course by the waves and causing a broach. Again, we'll cover these strategies in Chapter 8.

Rolling

Heavy rolling can be most uncomfortable in a boat in a seaway. It occurs when a boat heads across a large sea, and can easily be reduced by a slight change in course. On larger powerboats, stabilizers (discussed elsewhere in this book) can help reduce rolling. Although sails will tend to reduce the amount a sailboat rolls, getting beam-on to large seas is to be avoided. If you find yourself beam-on to breaking seas, make a course change immediately or you could get rolled over. If you have reduced sail or are under

bare poles, the inertia of the mast mercifully makes it harder for a sailboat to develop the same type of quick roll that occurs on powerboats.

Pitching

Pitching occurs when the boat drives into a head sea. If pitching becomes too bad, the boat will get wet decks, and the engine may overstrain when the propeller comes out of the water and races. Heavy pitching can be reduced by changing course and taking the seas at an angle, or by slowing down. Pitching can also create situations where the bow slams heavily into oncoming waves.

Heaving

Heaving is the motion of the entire boat being raised and lowered by oncoming seas. If heaving is not coupled with heavy pitching or rolling, it does not do a lot of harm to the boat and does not seem to upset the crew unless the motion is extreme.

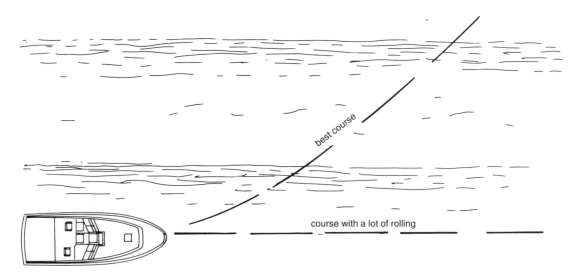

Changing course is the easiest method to reduce rolling. A boat sailing or powering beam-on to the seas will roll heavily, but roll can be reduced by changing course as shown. This will also reduce the chances of being rolled completely over. Some pitching will result, but this is far preferable to a deep roll.

Slamming

When the bows of a sail- or powerboat crash into a head sea, the boat may stop completely or be slowed down. The energy driving the boat is either absorbed by the sea or transferred to the structure of the hull. The component absorbed by the hull causes hull plating to deflect, and enough deflections can cause a structural failure to occur. From a designer's standpoint, a boat requires adequate reinforcement in the forward portions if it is to be used in heavy seas.

Heavy slamming can affect the crew as the boat accelerates and slows. Not only can they lose balance and possibly fall, but the "off" watch may find it difficult to sleep. In the long term this can cause undue crew fatigue.

The effect of almost all of the motions outlined above can be mitigated if the boat is slowed down or turned to a new course, which in turn affects the ability of the boat and crew to handle the vessel and make rational decisions.

Three

Confidence Starts with a Good Boat

The storm strengthens as lightning briefly illuminates white-crested waves towering over your boat. Your storm jib and trysail drive the boat forward, plowing through the waves like a subway train in a flooded tunnel. Green water cascades across the deck. You steer by feel through the black night, its darkness broken only by flashes of lightning and your instrument lights. Seething waves loom to windward, while rain and wind lash your face, making it hard to see. The wind indicator at the masthead gyrates wildly. You stagger, putting a foot on the rail, and briefly check your harness tether as the boat heels momentarily to 50 degrees. Another foam-crested wave passes under the boat. You pray the boat is strong enough to withstand the wild slalom down each wave's back. Every four or five minutes a hull-jarring crash shakes the rig as the boat sails off the top of a wave, finding nothing behind it. How many such 30-foot drops can the boat take? You have already been in this storm for several hours, and there's no sign of relief from its stinging assault.

Although many mariners never experience a storm at sea as severe as this, the chances are good that, if you go to sea regularly, at some point you will encounter rough weather. *Heavy weather* is a relative term. The impact of weather depends on several factors, including a boat's size. Smaller boats, by virtue of their lighter weight, have a much harder time than larger boats in gale-force winds and seas. A prolonged 30-knot blow with 15-foot seas, for example, can be a real test for a 30-footer but only moderately uncomfortable for a strong 45-footer. The smaller boat will also sail more slowly and will spend longer in the storm before it can get back home. The boat's stormworthiness is another factor. For instance, if a sailboat has a bridge deck between the cockpit and the companionway, large waves that flood the cockpit cannot get below. Without this fundamental safety feature, it could be sunk by a boarding wave or a knockdown.

Finally, the kind of weather that you consider "heavy" will depend greatly on the experience and skills of your crew. If you have never been out in heavy winds and seas before, your first encounter may seem like a nightmare. But gradually, as you gain more know-how, you will build confidence, and your definition of "heavy weather" will move up a notch or two.

Few people intend to sail in bad conditions, but such conditions can intrude on the best-laid plans. On one particular Sunday, for example, I watched a cold front blow through our local harbor. The day had started out sunny and warm with a light southerly breeze. It was a perfect day for sailing, and many people headed out to nearby islands. Then, around two o'clock in the afternoon, the skies darkened and the wind died. Within an hour a cold front had turned the conditions into a cold, blustery, rainy afternoon with a gusty northerly wind blowing at more than 25 knots. Many of the boats had to slog through some pretty dirty weather in order to get back to port. If this story sounds familiar, that's because it happens so often.

In this chapter you'll take the first step toward building peace of mind in bad weather by making sure you have a boat that merits confidence. There are many features to look for in a

---

Offshore and Off Soundings

Throughout this book we refer to "going *offshore*," by which, in general, we mean out of sight of land. Before the advent of electronics, when depth soundings were taken with lead lines, the hundred-fathom line (600 feet) was the practical limit at which depth could be measured. Beyond that depth a boat was *off soundings*. As used in this book, the terms have the same meaning.

---

boat that will be able to handle rough conditions, from adequately sized cockpit drains to sturdy windows that can withstand being slammed by a sea, to numerous handholds below deck and securely fastened lockers. Many such features, but not all, can be readily retrofitted, as we'll see in the next chapter. But the basic parameters of a hull's design and construction are especially hard, if not impossible, to retrofit. Those parameters are the focus of this chapter.

Hull Construction

Before we discuss the specific features of seaworthy sailboats and powerboats, we should address one or two construction features that are common to both. The first of these is access to plumbing, wiring, and fasteners. Most fiberglass boats are built on production lines, with the hull molded separately from the interior liner. Often the interior liner is completely fitted out before it is dropped into the hull. The electrical-wiring conduits, plumbing fixtures, and refrigerator and freezer connections are all sealed from view between the hull and liner. All the deck hardware, down to the stanchion backing plates, and all the electrical wiring and other gear may be installed on the deck's underside before it is mated to the cabin overhead liner. Only after the interior fittings have been finished is the deck dropped onto the hull and bolted in place.

The result is that it may be difficult—or impossible—for the boatowner to get at these fixtures later if they need to be serviced or replaced. You can't really blame builders, who struggle to keep their boats affordable. But what can you do about this access issue? I suggest that when shopping for a new boat you make *ease of access* one of your criteria for selection. If you already own a boat, go through it carefully and figure out how to access critical areas. If you need to cut access panels, do so while you have the time and leisure to make a nice hatch cover, rather than when water is flowing through an inaccessible hole in the hull.

All replacement wiring installed behind the liner should be run in conduits so that it can easily be removed and replaced. Similarly, plumbing should be run in conduits or otherwise be easy to remove. Check the steering system to make sure you can access every part of it. It is critical that you be able to access every part of the hull interior, because, as Murphy's Law tells us, the one part you cannot get near will be the part that is holed.

Watertight compartments are another important issue. The question is, are they needed at all? On a small boat, installing watertight compartments can make access difficult in many areas. On larger offshore boats, however, they almost certainly should be fitted. For boats that compete in round-the-world races, watertight compartments are required. At what point do they become essential? I would say that the answer lies not in the size of the boat you sail, but in the distance you intend to go offshore.

Consider first what a watertight compartment must do. In its meanest form it needs to keep the vessel afloat long enough for rescuers to arrive. That means the boat must be large enough to be fitted with a watertight compartment that will support the entire immersed weight of the boat and provide unflooded space in which the crew can survive while rescuers get organized. The amount of space required for the crew is difficult to determine. For example, my boat design company once had a client who wanted a steel-hulled boat with watertight compartments. After crunching the numbers, we divided the boat into three compartments, each with a watertight bulkhead. If one compartment were holed, the boat would stay afloat with about 2 feet (60 cm) of freeboard, but if water penetrated a second compartment the boat would have less than 6 inches (15 cm) of remaining freeboard—not enough to shelter the crew. If this design were to be built of lighter materials, however, it would have floated with plenty of space for the crew.

Bear in mind, too, that a watertight bulkhead may not be totally watertight. It may have holes for wiring and plumbing, and there may be small leaks around the door. Naval warship builders use glands between watertight bulkheads and they pressure-test compartments to ensure that they will stay watertight, but yacht builders rarely do so, and water can seep through a boat's so-called watertight bulkheads. Designers call this factor *permeability*, and most yachts are assumed to have a permeability factor in the 80th or 90th percentile. Such a yacht will sink eventually, and a "watertight compartment" should be looked upon merely as a feature that will give the crew time to cover a hole and pump the compartment dry or be rescued. Think of it as water-resistant, not waterproof, and you'll be on the right track.

Heavy-Weather Hulls: Sailboats

What hull features are best for a sailboat that might be caught in heavy weather? So few boats sail consistently in bad conditions that there isn't a large body of information on this question. But we can start by outlining a few basic characteristics that make obvious differences in a boat's heavy-weather ability. Then we will look at each part of the boat to establish the kind of cruising hull that should be at home in stronger winds and seas.

Displacement

All other things being equal, a heavy or moderately high-displacement boat has an easier motion through the water and is less fatiguing on the crew than its lighter counterparts, and a less fatigued crew makes better decisions and fewer mistakes. Film footage of the storm-racked 1998 Sydney-Hobart Race clearly shows how lighter boats were pushed around by waves and how jerky their motion seemed, even from a helicopter hovering overhead. This is exactly the type of motion that quickly leads to crew fatigue.

Since a boat's weight also depends on its size, the best way to consider displacement is in relation to length, using a displacement/length ratio. Most production boats have a displacement/length ratio between 150 and 250, but in a serious storm you would be more comfortable and confident in a boat at the 200–250 end of the range. For instance, the Valiant 42 has a displacement/length ratio of 256, the Hunter 34 has a ratio of 210, and the Freedom 40 a ratio of 245. Displacement, however, is not the only indicator of a stormworthy boat. Its engineering and construction are more important. A heavily built boat might be poorly engineered, while a lighter boat may be superbly engineered and therefore stronger.

Length

Just before my ninth Bermuda Race I was told by the late Jeffrey C. Foster—a great sailor and yacht broker—that I needed to pay more attention to the length of the boat I sailed on. "Choose a boat with at least a foot of length for every year of your age," Jeff advised me. "Bigger is better. It gets you there faster, and your trip is much more fun." He subsequently refined his formula to a foot of *waterline* length for every year of age.

Of course, he was right. The bigger the boat, the faster you sail and the shorter the time

A boat's displacement/length ratio is determined by the following equation:

$$\frac{\text{Displacement in pounds}/2{,}240}{(\text{LWL}/100)^3}$$

you spend at sea where storms can find you. Plus, the bigger the boat the more comfortable an offshore voyage becomes, even if you don't experience heavy weather. Small boats can survive dirty weather, but the ride is bouncier and wetter. And as we mentioned earlier, the crew gets more fatigued and the boat takes longer to reach a safe haven. In a full-blown storm these negative factors are magnified. A small boat is also much more likely to be capsized by breaking waves than a large boat.

The influence of size was clearly demonstrated to me on a transatlantic race, when the 100-foot boat I was aboard roared past a 31-foot cruising sailboat. The wind was blowing 30–35 knots, and we had a single roll in our roller-furled headsail but no reef in the main. We were sailing on a close reach and hitting 12 to 14 knots. The 31-footer was carrying a No. 3 or 4 headsail and two reefs in the main. The crew looked thoroughly wet and uncomfortable as spray broke over the bow and flew back into the cockpit. Shortly after we passed the smaller boat, the wind increased and swung farther ahead. We beat to windward for the next seven days until we reached Falmouth, England. The 31-footer probably took another week, and the ride must have been miserable. The boat was undoubtedly still at sea when a subsequent gale hit. The point here is not that you shouldn't cruise in a small boat. Some epic trips have been made this way. But if you go sailing in a small boat you need to take extra care about selecting the right weather window and preparing your heavy-weather inventory.

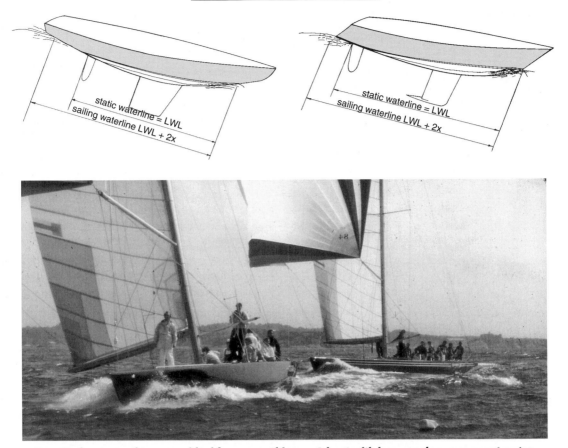

Top: Moderate overhangs are ideal for seaworthiness. A boat with long overhangs may get water on deck continuously, while a boat with short overhangs may tend to "dive" through waves rather than climbing over them. But note that the overhangs of a sailboat will be shorter when it is heeled than when the boat is upright. The boat on the left might pitch excessively under power with its long overhangs, but its heeled waterline is much longer, and its heeled overhangs much shorter, so the boat will pitch less under a press of sail. Bottom: These twelve-meters show how overhangs increase the effective waterline under sail.

People who sail smaller boats say that they are easier to handle, the gear is easier to use, and sail changes are easier—and all this is certainly true. On the other hand, with today's sail-handling gear, most people can handle a larger boat, and an increasing number—including many full-time cruising couples—choose to do so.

Just as length is important, so is the ratio between length overall and length on the waterline. A boat with a short waterline and long bow and stern overhangs carries a lot of weight in its ends, including anchors, bow rollers, a windlass, a chain locker, and the stemhead fitting at the bow; and quite possibly a lazarette filled with heavy gear in the stern. The result is a buoyant midsection and heavy ends, which increases the potential for hobby-horsing.

To reduce pitching, overhangs should be moderate, between 12 and 25 percent of the length of the boat. But overhangs that are less than 12 percent of the boat's length do not give enough reserve buoyancy to lift the bow over

Planing boards had to be fitted on this round-the-world racer to prevent the boat from diving into waves.

approaching waves. Consequently the boat will have a tendency to plow into waves such that green water comes crashing down the deck.

The Shape of the Bow

The bow of a cruising boat serves as a platform from which to operate the anchor-handling equipment, tie up the boat, and set or remove headsails. In a storm, it is the space from which you might launch a sea anchor (See Chapter 8). Usually it has cleats for mooring the boat, as well as attachment points for additional sails or roller-furling gear. The bow, then, contains a lot of gear in a confined space. In order to support the weight of this gear, a stormworthy boat needs plenty of buoyancy forward.

A U-shaped bow does not possess a large reserve of buoyancy and may tend to drive into waves instead of rising over them. It also makes the foredeck uncomfortably narrow for handling the anchor and sails. The same can be said for the nearly plumb bows that are appearing more and more on performance cruising boats in imitation of the racing designs that have been spawned by the IMS (International Measurement System) racing rule. A V-shaped bow, on the other hand, gains buoyancy as it submerges, making it a good shape for heavy weather. It also provides a respectable deck surface on which to perform anchor- or sail-handling tasks. Its principal drawback is the large, flat panels in the bow, which can flex and vibrate as the bow hammers into a sea. On occasion this has led to panel failure, but the problem can be solved by using slightly rounded panels for rigidity. This type of bow is usually developed with medium overhangs and has plenty of deck area. It gives a boat an older, somewhat dated look, and has fallen out of favor, but it might be the best shape for a boat that encounters heavy weather.

Note that the bow, no matter what its shape, can have a bowsprit to increase the base of the sail plan or a bow platform to increase the working space forward. Both features, however, make it harder to work the foredeck in bad weather. Without a roller furler for the headsail, crew may have to venture out to the end of the sprit to get sails down, exposing them to greater accelerations (and occasional dunkings) and making it harder to hang on and work. Not for nothing were bowsprits in the age of working sail known as widow-makers!

The Shape of the Stern

For heavy weather, a boat also needs a buoyant stern—a stern that will lift as a wave passes under it, not one that allows water to come aboard. This means that it should have some volume above the waterline. In most cases, it

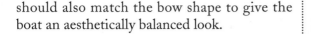

should also match the bow shape to give the boat an aesthetically balanced look.

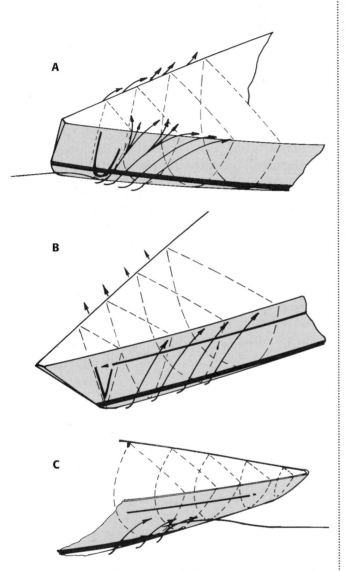

A U-shaped bow (A) has little reserve buoyancy and can submerge as it plows into a sea, especially when, as here, it is almost plumb and has little overhang. A V-shaped bow (B) provides reserve buoyancy, but its flat panels may reverberate as the boat hammers into a seaway. This one also has no overhang, which is a recipe for green water on deck. A V-shaped bow with slightly rounded panels and moderate overhang (C) has more form rigidity than the shape in B and may be stronger in bad weather.

The stern shape is critical to the boat's behavior. A boat with a large, fat stern and fine bow will tend to sail bow-down as it heels, which can cause the rudder to lift out of the water slightly and become less efficient. The boat may also be more prone to broaching in heavy weather, as we'll see in Chapter 8. On the other hand, a fat-bodied, fine-sterned boat may not have the power to dampen pitching, since it has minimal buoyancy in the ends. A moderately beamy stern—on the order of 65 to 85 percent of the maximum beam of the hull— and a combined bow/stern overhang of 15 to 20 percent of LOA seems to make the most effective stern shape for rough weather.

It is important that the hull lines run aft without distortions that could have a negative effect on sailing performance in extreme conditions. In the early to mid-1970s, for example, the International Offshore Rating rule (IOR) led designers to develop boats with a large *bustle* or *kicker*—a bloated hull section just in front of the rudder that was intended to make the water "think" the boat was longer than it actually was. Just aft of the bustle the buttock lines turned sharply upward to squeeze the boat into its rating girth station. This shape caused considerable turbulence over the rudder blade in strong winds, to the point where many boats were almost incapable of being steered. Avoid buying an older used boat with an IOR bustle. A clean shape aft helps to maintain clean water flow across the rudder and decreases the likelihood of broaching.

Beam

Beam plays a large part in the tendency of a boat to capsize, according to the *Safety From Capsizing* report published by the United States Yacht Racing Union (USYRU—now known as the United States Sailing Association, USSA) and the Society of Naval Architects and Marine Engineers (SNAME) in June 1985. Other things being equal, boats that are narrow rela-

A

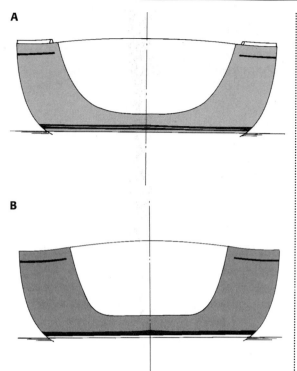

B

A moderately beamy stern shape seems the most effective compromise for cruising sailboats (A). If the buttock lines are pulled down slightly, the transom can be made slightly flatter, as in (B), which makes it easier to build in a stern platform and step.

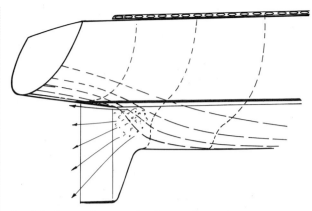

On older boats the stern is often sucked up around the rudderstock, creating turbulence near the top of the rudder blade. At speed, this turbulence may spread down across the blade, making the boat hard to steer.

tive to their length are less prone to capsize than beamy boats, and are quicker to reright if they do go over. On the other hand, lots of beam gives a boat more interior space and more sail-carrying ability, especially if the beam is carried to the waterline. Extra beam can also help position crew outboard, where their weight contributes more to the boat's righting arm, although most cruising sailors don't like to sit on the rail.

So what do you look for? Once again, moderation is the best option, with the length-to-beam ratio being a good indicator of whether a boat is excessively narrow or wide. A ratio of around 2.75 to 3 is most popular in the smaller boats, and a ratio of 2.3 to about 2.8 is the

norm for larger boats. My own preference in a larger boat is the 2.5 to 2.75 range. Note that because length can be manipulated by adding a bowsprit or changing the slope of the transom, most designers use either length on deck (LOD) or waterline length (LWL) relative to maximum beam or waterline beam for a more reliable result.

The Hull Bottom

Another indication of a good hull for heavy weather is the depth and shape of its bottom. In general, flat-bottomed boats, while highly efficient when sailing to windward, are uncomfortable or even dangerous in heavy weather. For one thing, the shallow bilges cannot contain even a small amount of water without it spreading everywhere in a seaway. Also, a flat-bottomed hull usually means a light hull with a lot of pounding and motion (heave and pitch) in heavy weather, which can be extremely fatiguing for the crew. Finally, a fairly light, flat-bottomed boat with a lot of beam needs to be sailed at a small angle of heel, but in strong winds it may heel excessively, putting both the keel and the rudder close to the water's surface and reducing their effectiveness.

A hull for offshore work should be slightly V-shaped, as here, to keep the bilge water in the bilge and to give the boat better handling in a seaway.

A better hull shape for heavy weather cruising is a boat with a moderate displacement and deeper bilges. In other words, the hull sections should be slightly V-shaped. This helps to keep water in the bilges, alleviates or even stops pounding, makes the motion easier for the crew, and keeps the keel and rudder well below the water's surface.

Stability

Stability is a quality that you need in just the right amount. If a sailboat has enough stability and is carrying the appropriate amount of sail, it will be able to punch through waves and keep driving. A boat with inadequate stability will have to shorten sail earlier and may not have the power to drive into a head sea. In bad weather, such a boat might require its engine to make headway against the sea.

But too much stability causes problems of its own. A boat with extra-high stability wants to come back upright quickly after each puff of wind. This gives it a jerky, quick motion, which can be extremely fatiguing for the crew. A powerboat with too much stability provides a jerky ride which, *in extremis,* can toss people off their feet. We'll explore the subject of stability in greater detail later in the chapter, after covering the basics of stormworthy sailboat and powerboat hull design.

The depth of the keel plays two major roles in a boat's resistance to capsizing, according to the USYRU/SNAME report mentioned earlier. First, a deep-draft keel increases the boat's righting moment and stability, making it harder to capsize. Second, a keel with plenty of lateral area has to displace a large amount of water in order for the boat to capsize. This "trapped" water provides both a certain amount of resistance to heeling and a damping effect when the boat is subjected to a beam-on wave strike.

Another consideration is that both deep draft and high lateral plane—the area of the boat hull, keel, and rudder when viewed from the side—make it easier for a boat to heave-to in moderately heavy weather. Modern racing boats with minimal wetted surface are usually not able to heave-to and must take an active approach to handling heavy weather, as we'll see in Chapter 8.

Table 3–1 includes four metrics that bear directly on a cruising sailboat's suitability for heavy weather.

Heavy-Weather Hulls: Powerboats

High-speed powerboats have one advantage over sailboats when it comes to heavy weather. While most sailboats travel at speeds of less than 10 knots, planing powerboats are capable of 20 knots or more. A 30-knot powerboat 40 miles from shore can make its way to a safe harbor within an hour and a half, whereas a sailboat would take at least four hours and probably longer. Provided the crew keeps an eye on the weather, most powerboats can be safely tied up at the dock before a storm hits.

Unfortunately, the speed of a powerboat can also be its undoing. Going too fast in heavy weather a boat can fly off a wave, then break up or capsize. Speed can also be a problem if the boat is powered into a head sea at a speed that establishes synchronous motion. When this happens, the boat's natural heave and pitch periods coincide with the wave period, exaggerating the motion. Green water may come across the deck and the motion may even result in severe structural damage.

In heavy weather it is always prudent to slow down, and in extreme conditions you may be able to make only 1 or 2 knots of headway. Great care must be taken at such speeds, however, since a large wave can momentarily stop the boat or even force it to go astern. If this happens, steerage will be lost and the boat is liable to turn beam-on to the seas. For this reason, powerboats that go offshore should carry a drogue, since in some conditions it may actually be better to power downwind while trailing a drogue to keep the boat's stern pointed toward the overtaking seas. We'll explore this further in Chapter 8.

The features that make for a stormworthy hull depend on the type of boat. In general, there are three distinct styles of powerboat that feature some rough-weather ability in their designs: high-speed, deep-V craft that travel at

(text continues on page 68)

Table 3–1. What Sailboat Ratios Tell Us

The important thing about ratios—such as the displacement/length ratio, or the sail area-to-wetted surface ratio—is that they are non-dimensional. They show the relationship between two measurements on a boat, not the measurements themselves. As a result, ratios allow meaningful comparisons between boats of different sizes.

This table shows key ratios for a number of modern cruisers. The best boats for sailing in heavy weather are those with a displacement/length ratio of more than 175 or 200 and a sail area/displacement ratio that is as low as possible while still providing adequate power. Bear in mind, however, that a high displacement/length ratio and a low sail area/displacement ratio make for a slow boat that will spend longer at sea and may not be able to evade an approaching storm. This table shows another metric that gives some idea about a boat's ability to sail offshore in heavy weather. Known as the *capsize factor*, it tries to predict how a boat will respond in extreme waves. According to the formula, more seaworthy boats have a capsize factor of less than 2.

(continued on page 64)

Table 3–1. *(cont.)*

Sailboat	LOA or LOD	LWL	Beam	Draft Keel (Dp)	Draft (Wing or Shallow) Centerboard Up/Down		Displacement lbs	Ballast lbs	Sail Area Main and 100% Foretriangle
Baltic 40	39.37	32.73	12.73	7.25		5.7/5.25	14990	6173	780.87
Baltic 43	43.34	35.76	13.78	8		6.1	19750	8487	901.39
Baltic 47	47.74	39.5	14.4	8.7	6.8	5.9/9.9	24692	10141	1174.08
Baltic 52	52.5	43.14	15.4	9.2			31967	13228	1310.41
Baltic 58	58.5	47.57	16.6	10.5			41888	18078	1624.96
Baltic 60	60.5	52	16.4	9.8			41888	16314	1792.05
Baltic 64	64	51.5	17.3	11			56218	24652	1971.13
Baltic 67	67	59	17.7	11.9			40786	15653	2179.94
Baltic 70	70.5	59.1	16	12.5			39249	21936	2120.88
Beneteau Oceanis 36cc	36.42	31.2	12.5	5.2			13382	4155	551.25
Beneteau Oceanis 40cc	41	36.75	12.75	5.58		5.58	18740	5300	687.17
Beneteau Oceanis 411	41.66	36.08	13	5.58		4.75	17196	5500	695.04
Beneteau Oceanis 44cc	44.58	36.75	14			5.75	20944	6835	835.11
Beneteau First 40.7	39.25	35.1	12.25	7.84		6.16	15200	5950	806.14
Beneteau First 42s7	42.5	35.75	13.5	7.58		5.5	18220		771.85
Cabo Rico 36	34	26.66	11	4.84		4.16	15500	5800	611.29
Cabo Rico 38	38	29.25	11.5	5			21000	7800	930.74
Cabo Rico 40	40.25	32	12.66	5.25			26800	10400	930.74
Cabo Rico 45	45.5	35	13.16	6.5		5.5	35600	13500	1136.09
Cambria 40	41.5	32.5	12.25	7.25		4.92	22200	7500	821
Cambria 44/46	45.86	36.25	13.48			5	28600	11500	1009.46
Caliber 35LRC	33.84	29.84	11.33	4.5			13100	6100	563.38
Caliber 40LRC	39.1	32.5	12.66	5.1			21600	9500	738.66
Caliber 47LRC	48.58	39.5	13.16	5.16			33000	13000	1014.17
Catalina 36 MkII	36.33	30.25	11.92	5.84		4.42	13500	6000	653.41
Catalina C380	38.42	32.42	12.33	7		5.33	19000	6800	761.2114
Catalina 400	40.5	36.5	13.5	6.75		5.5	19700	7250	810.25
Catalina 42 MkII	41.84	36	13.84	6		4.84	20500	8300	842.8825
Catalina 470	46.5	42	14	7.84		5.5	27000	8800	1010.125
Hunter 376	37.25	32	12.58	6.5			15000	4950	683.71
Hunter 410	40.66	37.84	13.84	6.42			19500	6700	822.99
Hunter 42	42.5	38	14	4.92			24000	7700	816
Hunter 430	42.5	38	14	4.92			23800	7700	837.5
Hunter 450	44.25	38.58	14	5.5			26000	9500	907.00
Island Packet 37	38.5	31	12.16	4.5			18500	8200	928.03
Island Packet 40	39.33	39.33	12.92	4.66		3.84	22800	10000	774.34
Island Packet 45	45.25	37.58	13.33	4.84			28400	12500	928.03
J/120	40	35	12	7			13900	6000	779.98
J/130	42.8	38.2	12.8	8.5			15000	6350	955.88
J/160	52.7	47.5	14.5	8.8			31000	11000	1375.06
J/42	42	35.1	12.2	6.6			19700	7000	789.68

Engine hp	I	P	E	J	Ratios and Coefficients		Capsize Factor	Displ/ hp	Overhangs (LOA-LWL)/ LOA	Beam/ Length Ratio
					SA/ Disp	Displ/ Length				
43	53.81	47.9	15.63	15.11	20.56	190.86	2.07	348.60	0.169	2.96
43	57.97	51.67	15.75	17.06	19.75	192.81	2.04	459.30	0.175	2.98
62	65.29	57.41	20.01	18.37	22.16	178.86	1.98	398.26	0.173	3.15
88	70.14	61.81	19.32	20.34	20.82	177.75	1.94	363.26	0.178	3.22
100	76.6	68.4	23.1	21.8	21.57	173.72	1.92	418.88	0.187	3.29
100	80.38	72.34	24.1	22.9	23.78	132.99	1.89	418.88	0.140	3.64
120	86.19	78.1	23.66	24.3	21.50	183.74	1.81	468.48	0.195	3.42
140	87.6	79.3	26.7	25.6	29.45	88.66	2.06	291.33	0.119	3.83
140	78.1	81.8	29.8	23.1	29.39	84.88	1.89	280.35	0.162	4.25
27	42.32	35.76	14.44	13.85	15.65	196.70	2.11	495.63	0.143	2.87
48	48.23	41.96	15.65	14.88	15.59	168.56	1.92	390.42	0.104	3.31
42	47.67	41.5	14.83	16.25	16.70	163.45	2.02	409.43	0.134	3.19
85	46.13	52.4	16.31	17.68	17.59	188.38	2.04	246.40	0.176	3.02
30	51.60	48.85	17.72	14.47	1.35	156.92	1.98	506.67	0.106	3.29
48	50.86	47.41	17.22	14.3	17.84	178.02	2.06	379.58	0.159	3.04
27	41.5	36	15.17	16.3	15.74	365.18	1.77	574.07	0.216	2.79
50	52.42	46.25	17.58	20	19.57	374.62	1.67	420.00	0.230	2.92
62	52.42	46.25	17.58	20	16.64	365.12	1.70	432.26	0.205	2.91
75	57.25	51	21.17	20.83	16.80	370.68	1.60	474.67	0.231	3.06
50	55.75	50	15	16	16.64	288.71	1.75	444.00	0.217	3.05
62	62	56	16.5	17.66	17.28	268.04	1.77	461.29	0.210	3.09
27	43	39.25	12	15.25	16.23	220.10	1.93	485.19	0.118	3.03
50	50.5	45.75	13.25	17.25	15.24	280.90	1.82	432.00	0.169	2.95
75	54.5	47.83	18	21.42	15.78	239.04	1.64	440.00	0.187	3.45
30	46.75	41	13	14.33	18.45	217.73	2.01	450.00	0.167	2.92
42	54	47.92	15.66	14.66	17.11	248.92	1.85	452.38	0.156	3.02
42	52.66	47	17	15.5	17.78	180.86	2.00	469.05	0.099	3.11
50	53	46.75	15.6	16.42	18.01	196.15	2.03	410.00	0.140	2.99
55	58.25	51.5	20	17	17.97	162.69	1.87	490.91	0.097	3.45
36	48	49	15.25	12.92	17.99	204.36	2.04	416.67	0.141	2.92
50	47.75	45.42	19.25	16.16	18.18	160.67	2.06	390.00	0.069	3.14
62	55.5	48	15.5	16	15.70	195.26	1.95	387.10	0.106	3.12
50	50	50	17.75	15.75	16.20	193.63	1.95	476.00	0.106	3.12
59	55.46	49.33	17.75	16.92	16.54	202.13	1.89	440.68	0.128	3.17
38	54.92	47.5	17.5	18.66	21.24	277.23	1.84	486.84	0.195	2.93
50	49.84	42.84	15.5	17.75	15.41	167.31	1.83	456.00	0.000	3.50
62	54.92	47.5	17.5	18.66	15.96	238.89	1.75	458.06	0.170	3.24
38	50.5	46.5	17.8	14.5	21.59	144.73	2.00	365.79	0.125	3.35
47	57	52.5	18.5	16.5	25.15	120.13	2.08	319.15	0.107	3.43
88	66.5	62	24.16	18.83	22.30	129.13	1.85	352.27	0.099	3.77
47	50.5	46.5	18	14.7	17.33	203.37	1.81	419.15	0.164	3.31

(continued on page 66)

Table 3–1. *(cont.)*

Sailboat	LOA or LOD	LWL	Beam	Draft Keel (Dp)	Draft (Wing or Shallow) Centerboard Up/Down	Displacement lbs	Ballast lbs	Sail Area Main and 100% Foretriangle
Jeanneau 36.2	36.1	30.5	12.42	6.25		12320	3410	512.8027
Jeanneau 40	40	33.33	12.92	6.33	4.92	16094	5291	682.3975
Jeanneau 42.2	42	33.32	13.46	5.42		18519	5754	703.045
Jeanneau 42cc	42.1	33.32	13.46	5.42		18920	5742	734.39125
Jeanneau 45.2	45.25	38.42	14.66	6.58		20570	7110	795.0125
Jeanneau 52.2	50.5	41.66	15.1	5.92		33000	12320	993.6078
Morgan 38	38.5	32.5	12.33	7	5.33	19000	6800	700.2778
Morgan 45	45.25	37.84	13.9	6.5	5.58	25225	8975	816.375
Pacific Seacraft 37V	36.92	27.75	10.84	5.5	4.42	16000	6200	618.46125
Pacific Seacraft 40V	40.33	31.25	12.42	6.1	5.16	24500	8600	853.65
Pacific Seacraft 44V	44.1	33.65	12.8	6.25	5.3	27500	9400	976.4352
Sabre 362	36.16	30.5	12	5.52		13800	5520	634.869
Sabre 402	40.2	34	13.33	7.33		19000	7400	822.25
Sabre 452	45.2	38.33	14.1	6.75		26500	10200	1027.005
Santa Cruz 52	53	46.5	14	9		21000	9850	1216.975
Shannon 39	38.58	32.84	12	5.5		18700	6900	748.375
Tartan 3500	35.21	30	11.75	6.5	4.84	11400	4200	615.3125
Tartan 3800	38	31	12.42	6.84	5.33	16000	6500	664.9282
Tartan 4100	41.25	35.75	13.5	7	5.33	19000	6400	810.875
Tartan 4600	46.2	39.58	14.33	8.92 5.5	4.84/9	24000	8500	1014
Taswell 44	44	35.25	13.66	6.25	5.25	23500	9600	855.1
Taswell 49	48.84	41.92	15	7	5.5	40000	11500	1066.5
Taswell 56	55.84	46.75	16.5	7.5	6	48500	17750	1389.5
Taswell 58	58	47.92	16.1	6.25		65000	19600	1441.88
Trintella 42	42	35.75	13.78	5.9		29750	12122	982.725
Trintella 47	47.25	37.84	14.76	6.45		35264		1085.08105
Valiant 42	39.9	34.5	12.33	6	5.5	24500	9500	808.3825
Valiant 50	50.00	40.250	13.840	6.250		35500	11000	
Westerly Oceanlord 41	40.50	35.250	13.500	5.500		20878	8000	764.25
Westerly Ocean 43	43.50	35.920	13.900	5.750		29767	12123	950.1125
Westerly Ocean 49	48.58	42.160	15.160	7.160		28940	11680	1009.7143
X-Yachts X-362	36.10	30.500	11.400	6.200	5.000	11440	4960	589.03275
X-Yachts X-382	37.70	31.800	12.200	6.600	5.500	14333	6174	703.0234
X-Yachts X-412	42.30	32.400	12.800	6.500		16314	7716	797.1753
X-Yachts X-442	44.30	36.700	13.600	7.500		21300	9480	956.06455
X-Yachts X-482	48.00	41.000	14.100	8.200	7.200	26455	11023	1148.4605
X-Yachts X-612	60.00	52.100	16.700	9.500	6.500	47400	20060	1735.65

Engine hp	I	P	E	J	Ratios and Coefficients SA/ Disp	Disp/ Length	Capsize Factor	Displ/ hp	Overhangs (LOA-LWL)/ LOA	Beam/ Length Ratio
27	42.33	36.25	14.42	11.88	15.39	193.85	2.15	456.30	0.155	2.82
60	50	43.25	15.66	13.75	17.13	194.05	2.05	268.23	0.167	2.97
62	50.88	45.58	15.5	13.75	16.08	223.49	2.04	298.69	0.207	2.85
62	50.83	44.75	15.5	15.25	16.56	228.33	2.02	305.16	0.209	2.85
62	51.14	46	16.5	16.25	16.95	161.93	2.14	331.77	0.151	3.01
88	58.58	51.16	17.66	18.5	15.46	203.75	1.89	375.00	0.175	3.17
42	50.5	42.16	15.66	14.66	15.74	247.09	1.85	452.38	0.156	3.03
50	52.75	46	16	17	15.19	207.84	1.90	504.50	0.164	3.13
51	44	38.17	14.25	15.75	15.59	334.26	1.72	313.73	0.248	2.94
51	49.5	44.25	18	18.4	16.20	358.40	1.71	480.39	0.225	2.89
51	58.88	50.92	16	19.33	17.15	322.20	1.70	539.22	0.237	3.02
32	48.5	41.6	14.83	13.46	17.66	217.14	2.00	431.25	0.157	2.92
50	54	47.5	17	15.5	18.48	215.81	2.00	380.00	0.154	2.93
76	59.5	52.5	19.2	17.58	18.49	210.08	1.90	348.68	0.152	3.12
62	64.55	57.5	21	19	25.59	93.24	2.03	338.71	0.123	3.82
50	52	47	15.25	15	17.00	235.71	1.81	374.00	0.149	3.15
27	46.75	41.25	14.25	13.75	19.44	188.49	2.09	422.22	0.148	2.93
38	49.75	43.33	14.33	14.25	16.76	239.77	1.98	421.05	0.184	2.87
47	54	47.75	17	15	18.23	185.64	2.03	404.26	0.133	3.04
62	59.5	53.5	19	17	19.51	172.80	1.99	387.10	0.143	3.17
50	55	49	16	16.84	16.68	239.52	1.91	470.00	0.199	2.97
75	60	53.5	18	19.5	14.60	242.41	1.76	533.33	0.142	3.21
110	69.5	62.5	20	22	16.72	211.91	1.81	440.91	0.163	3.26
140	69.5	61.58	22	22	14.28	263.70	1.61	464.29	0.174	3.42
50	60.1	56.76	18.3	15.42	16.38	290.68	1.78	595.00	0.149	2.98
62	62	58.33	18.37	17.72	16.15	290.56	1.80	568.77	0.199	2.95
42	50.33	45	13	20.5	15.34	266.35	1.70	583.33	0.135	3.22
63	53.5	53	16	20	0.00	243.04	1.69	563.49	0.195	3.34
40	51.51	45.5	15.48	16	16.13	212.80	1.96	521.95	0.130	3.00
50	58	53.5	18.27	15.91	15.83	286.73	1.80	595.34	0.174	2.97
78	60.37	52.98	17.72	17.9	17.15	172.40	1.98	371.03	0.132	3.20
20	46.75	40.68	14.1	12.93	18.57	180.00	2.03	572.00	0.155	3.08
28	50.4	43.97	14.44	15.3	19.07	198.98	2.01	511.89	0.156	3.00
38	54.13	47.58	15.42	15.9	19.84	214.13	2.02	429.32	0.234	2.91
59	59.39	52.17	16.73	17.5	19.92	192.37	1.97	361.02	0.172	3.10
75	65.13	57.7	18.7	18.7	20.70	171.36	1.90	352.73	0.146	3.34
110.000	79	71	23.3	23	21.21	149.63	1.85	430.91	0.132	3.59

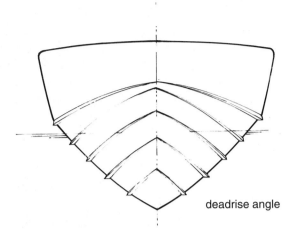

deadrise angle

The deadrise angle affects a boat's performance in heavy seas. This boat carries steep deadrise back at least to the midsection, and will give a comparatively soft ride in a chop.

Bow and stern photos of the same boat show a fairly constant deadrise carried from the forefoot back to the transom. This deep-V boat will have better seakeeping ability in a heavy sea than a planing hull with flat stern sections.

more than 40 knots and have a high *deadrise*—the transverse angle that the hull bottom makes with the horizontal—at the transom; moderately fast, semiplaning boats (often sportfishing boats) with a moderate transom deadrise (between 12 and 18 degrees) and a speed potential of around 20–30 knots; and low-speed cruising or trawler-style yachts with either a moderate deadrise (around 10–14 degrees) or a round-bottomed hull with a keel or skeg. The style of powerboat to avoid for offshore work is one with a high-speed, low-deadrise or flat-bottomed hull, especially if it is combined with low freeboard forward.

The boat's length also plays a part in its stormworthiness. In general, the longer the powerboat, the less it will be affected by waves and wind. A 22-footer can be flipped by a sea as small as 5 feet high, while a 66-footer in the same sea may experience no more than a little pitching. A larger boat can also handle the short, steep seas of a rising storm or those kicked up by strong winds blowing over shallow water much better than a smaller boat.

Powerboat Ratios

A few simple ratios can tell you a lot about a powerboat's ability to handle heavy weather. Among the most useful of these are the displacement/length ratio, the freeboard/length

Harmonic Motion

If the interval between seas coincides with a boat's natural harmonic period of pitch, the boat's pitch amplitude will increase with each successive wave. The only solution in this case is to slow down enough to take the boat out of sync with the waves.

ratio, the length/beam ratio, and the speed/length ratio.

Displacement/Length Ratio

The displacement/length ratio is found in the same way as for sailboats, with the ideal range for a powerboat depending on the style of boat. For high-speed deep-V craft, for example, the safe range is 130 to 160, for sportfishing boats it is 175 to 275, and for slow-speed, displacement-hulled boats it is 250 to 350. Lower ratios are more likely on fiberglass boats and higher ratios—sometimes as high as 400—are possible on steel-hulled boats. In general, faster boats handle better with low displacement/length ratios; a boat combining a high displacement/length ratio with a high speed/length ratio is likely to pitch in heavy weather.

Freeboard/Length Ratio

Powerboats, especially slow-speed boats, need relatively high freeboard to keep water off the deck. Designers use the freeboard/length ratio to compare hulls. The freeboard can be measured at one, two, or three places, then divided by the length to get the ratio. Typically, bow, midship, and stern freeboards are taken and either averaged or used in three separate ratios. On boats with extremely variable freeboard, such as sportfishing boats (high bow, low stern), the three values should be listed separately. On a boat with relatively consistent fore-and-aft freeboard, such as a trawler-style yacht, they may be averaged.

Length/Beam Ratio

In general, the wider the beam relative to length, the less the boat will roll in heavy weather, although the shape of the hull also affects performance. On boats with a length/beam ratio of 3 or less, a round-bottomed hull seems to work better in a seaway. When the length/beam ratio is higher than 3, a chine hull performs better. The German Navy found this to be true in World War II when its round-bottomed, high-powered E-boats experienced better performance in a seaway than the chined hull shapes of the British and American motor gun boats and torpedo boats. In general, displacement powerboats have length/beam ratios similar to those of sailboats, whereas faster boats are beamier.

Speed/Length Ratio

The speed/length ratio tells us a lot more about the way a powerboat is likely to perform in heavy winds than most other criteria.

Displacement powerboats, those that cruise at speed/length ratios of 1.5 or less, are incapable of planing and generally perform similarly to sailboats in heavy weather, with one critical difference: sailboat masts have a damping effect on the rolling of the boat, whereas a powerboat without a mast may roll much more.

Boats with a speed/length ratio between 1.5 and 3 operate in the intermediate zone between displacement and planing speeds and are considered semiplaning. These hulls generate some hydrodynamic lift at higher speeds and can partially climb out of "the hole in the water" that traps displacement hulls at slower speeds. To do this they require a wider waterline beam than a displacement boat and flatter bottom sections, especially aft. Boats that can reach a speed/length ratio higher than 3 are considered true planing boats; at such speeds most of the weight of the hull is supported by hydrodynamic lift rather than buoyancy.

The great advantage of a planing or semiplaning boat over a displacement hull is in its

---

A boat's speed/length ratio is determined by the following equation:

$$\frac{\text{boatspeed (in knots)}}{\sqrt{\text{LWL (in feet)}}}$$

ability to outrun heavy weather. Once overtaken by a storm, however, any powerboat will be forced to slow down to displacement speeds, and at that point a displacement hull with its moderate waterline beam, deep sections, greater displacement/length ratio, and comparatively fine ends will have the most comfortable motion, with a longer roll period and less extreme accelerations. At the other end of the spectrum, a wide, light planing boat with shallow bilges and flat bottom will subject its occupants to snap rolls, sudden accelerations, pounding, and slamming.

Even in a fair-weather chop, boats that run at a speed/length ratio higher than 5 can experience significant accelerations and will slam into head seas. These accelerations may get as high as 2g, imposing a dramatic load on the hull bottom between 30 and 50 percent aft of the bow. One way of mitigating these loads is to make the deadrise angle quite high, as in deep-V powerboats, and in fact, some high-speed deep-V powercraft carry deadrise angles of more than 22 degrees aft to the transom to minimize loads as they slam into a head sea. High deadrise angles make the landing softer

Table 3-2. Powerboat Seaworthiness Factors

	Most Efficient Hull	Fastest Hull	Inshore Fishing	Trawler-Style Yacht	Inshore Cruiser
Boat speed	Low to moderate	Highest	Low to moderate	Low	Moderate
Sea states	Flat water	Flat water	Moderate seas	Moderate to large seas	Moderate to large seas
Wave height	0–1 feet	None	0–2 feet	Sea heights to 30% of length	Sea heights to 20% of length
Hull shape	Round hull	3-point hydro	Vee or round	Round or vee	Round or vee
Hull length	Long	Moderate	Moderate seas	Moderate to long	Moderate to long
Draft	Shallow	Low	Shallow	Moderate to deep	Moderate to deep
Waterline length	Long	Low	Moderate	Moderate to heavy	Moderate
Beam	Narrow	Wide for stability	Moderate	Proportional to length	Proportional to length
Displacement	Light	As light as possible	Light to medium	Moderate to heavy	Moderate to heavy
Horsepower	Low or very low	Very high	Low to moderate	Low to moderate	Low to moderate
Bow height	Low to moderate	Low	Low to moderate	High	Low to moderate
Bow fineness	Fine to moderate	Fine	Fine to moderate	Moderate to full	Moderate to full
Bow flare	Moderate	None	Minimal	Moderate to high	Low to moderate
Deadrise angle	Low	Moderate	0–5 degrees	5–12 degrees	5–12 degrees
Seaworthiness	Limited	Limited	Limited	Good	Good
Comfort when stopped	Tendency to roll	None	Moderate	Some roll	Some roll
Comfort at cruising speed	Comfortable	None	Moderate	Comfortable	Good
Comfort at full speed	Comfortable	None	Moderate	Comfortable	Good
Range	Moderate	Limited	Limited	Extensive	Moderate
Construction costs	Moderate to high	Very high	Moderate	Moderate to high	Moderate
Suitable for Use on:					
Estuaries/salt marshes	Yes	No	Yes	No	Yes
Small ponds/small lakes	Yes	No	Yes	Yes	Yes
Large lakes	Select optimum conditions	Select optimum conditions	Select optimum conditions	Yes	Select good conditions
Coastal shorelines	Select optimum conditions	Select optimum conditions	Select optimum conditions	Yes	Select good conditions
Open ocean	Select optimum conditions	No	Select optimum conditions	Select good conditions	Select optimum conditions

and enable the boat to keep going longer in heavy seas.

Still, heavy seas can destroy any boat that tries to power through them at too high a speed. If a racing boat drives into the back of a large wave (a mishap known as "stuffing it"), the entire bow section can disintegrate. Be slow and careful when you power into large waves.

High-Speed Craft

In general, the only high-speed craft that face occasional heavy weather are deep-V offshore racers. While these boats are dynamically sta-ble at speed, they roll heavily when powering slowly in a seaway. Consequently, they should avoid heavy weather if possible. Typically, a performance deep-V can travel at 50–70 knots or more, which puts it within an hour of a safe port in most cases. If a boat like this does get caught in a sudden storm, the crew's best option is to power slowly into the wind or at a slight angle to it until the front blows through. Usually this style of boat will take more abuse than its crew can, so the crew will slow the boat long before hull failure occurs.

Offshore Cruiser	Offshore Sportfisherman	Inshore Racer	Offshore Racer	Inshore Catamaran	Offshore Catamaran
Moderate	High	Very high	Very high	Moderate to high	Very high
Moderate to large seas	Moderate to large seas	Moderate seas	Moderate to large seas	Moderate seas	Moderate to large seas
Sea heights to 30% of length	Sea heights to 30% of length	Sea heights to 20% of length	Sea heights to 30% of length	Sea heights to 20% of length	Sea heights to 30% of length
Round or vee	Vee hull	Vee hull	Vee hull or catamaran	Round or vee	Mostly vee
Moderate to long	Moderate	Long	Long	Long	Long
Moderate to deep	Moderate	Low to moderate	Low to moderate	Low	Low
Moderate to heavy	Moderate	Long	Long	Long	Long
Proportional to length	Proportional to length	Proportional to length	Narrow for length	Narrow hulls/wide overall	Narrow hulls/wide overall
Moderate to heavy	Moderate	Light to moderate	Light to moderate	Light to moderate	Light to moderate
Moderate	Moderate to high	High	High	Moderate to high	Moderate to high
High	Moderate to high	Low	Low	Moderate	Moderate
Moderate to full	Moderate	Fine to moderate	Fine to moderate	Moderate	Moderate
Low to moderate	High	Minimum	Minimum	Moderate	Moderate
8–15 degrees	10–18 degrees	8–20 degrees	15–25 degrees	10–20 degrees	15–25 degrees
Excellent	Good to excellent	Limited	Moderate to excellent	Good	Good
Some roll	Good	Some roll	Some roll	Good	Good
Excellent	Good to excellent	Good	Moderate	Good	Good
Excellent	Good to excellent	Good	Good	Good	Good
Extensive	Good	Limited	Good	Low to moderate	High
Moderate to high	Moderate to high	High	Moderate to high	Moderate to high	Moderate to high
No	No	No	No	No	No
Yes	Yes	No	No	Yes	No
Yes	Yes	Yes	Yes	Yes	Yes
Yes	Yes	Yes	Yes	Yes	Yes
Yes	Yes	Select best conditions	Yes	Select optimum conditions	Yes

This said, however, I once sea-trialed a 40-foot deep-V powerboat in winds of 30 knots. As the boat cleared the harbor and headed out, the full force of the wind hit us, and we found ourselves facing seas as high as 5–8 feet. The factory representative cranked the throttles forward and we gained speed, starting to bounce from one wave top to another. Then the companionway door flew off its tracks, after which a lighting rack below decks shattered and crashed to the cabin sole. We were hanging on but taking a pounding. With each crash something else broke inside the boat. Finally, when I thought my kidneys could stand it no longer,

Running at high speed, this fleet of deep-V Wellcraft Scarabs can get into harbor before bad weather hits. (Photo courtesy Wellcraft Marine)

the factory rep slowed down before we totaled the interior.

Then the rolling started. This type of hull is very narrow for its length, and when not moving at high speed it tends to roll badly. When running downwind in heavy winds, however, accelerations and impacts are much lower and less likely to damage both the boat and its occupants.

Under no circumstances should a high-speed boat get beam-on to steep seas at slow speeds. Getting beam-on in a boat that rolls heavily puts the boat at risk of being rolled completely over, especially when the seas are breaking.

Medium-Speed or Semi-Planing Powerboats

Semi-planing boats (usually sportfishing-style craft) typically have V-shaped hulls, but the deadrise angle at the transom is usually in the 12- to 18-degree range. The hull shape may be a constant deadrise—that is, with the same deadrise angle from the middle sections of the hull aft to the transom—or it may have a variable deadrise angle that is deep at the midsection but decreases to the 12- to 18-degree range at the transom. In general, a variable deadrise hull provides a better ride in heavy seas, thanks to its deeper forebody sections.

Typically, sportfishermen using this style of hull travel longer distances—often to the outer edges of the continental shelf, 40–100 miles offshore, in search of gamefish. Their tactics in heavy weather, if they cannot get to port, are usually to power into the wind or at a slight angle to it at a speed that allows the boat to minimize slamming and avoid synchronous pitching. Alternatively, when a safe harbor is located downwind, they will power downsea, bearing in mind that in heavy weather a harbor entrance can be a real problem. Trying to run an inlet in heavy weather has been the downfall of many powerboats. If you cannot make it into an inlet, go somewhere that has an easier approach. If you aren't sure you can negotiate an inlet, don't try.

Unlike sailboats, which can sail across the waves at a slight angle, powerboats have only two heavy-weather tactical options: they can either motor gently into the teeth of the storm, or at a slight angle to it (a tactic that commercial fishermen call *jogging*), or they can run away from it, keeping the waves at a slight angle to the stern. The hull shape of a boat intended to confront heavy weather needs to be suited for one or the other of these two tactics, or both. When powering into head seas, for example, the bow should be high enough and have enough reserve buoyancy to climb over most waves, but not so high that waves and wind can blow the bow around. The forefoot should be deep enough to soften the ride and grip the seas (but not so deep that the boat trips over it when running downsea, as this could cause a broach). For either tactic, the midship sections should have enough beam to give the boat good transverse stability. And for running downsea, the stern should be high enough to prevent breaking seas from coming aboard, or the cockpit should have large freeing ports or scuppers to get rid of water fast, or both.

Bow Flare

The reserve buoyancy needed in the bow of a boat that takes heavy weather head on is best provided by flaring the bow, as in many mid-sized sportfishing boats. The Carolina-style sportfishing designs of Buddy Davis and others, with their dramatically flared bows, are able to head into short, steep seas offshore or into breaking inlets and still stay dry. Boats with less flare, such as those designed by Ray Hunt, tend to be wetter and allow more spray on deck. In extreme conditions, the Hunt design will probably be quite wet, but its small deck area will allow it to punch through a

The pronounced bow flare on a boat like this Luhrs 400C sportfisherman can help keep the foredeck dry in tough going. Note the low sides aft, needed for working a fish. To counter this vulnerability, the cockpit sole is above the waterline and there are large freeing ports on either side of the transom. Still, this boat will handle heavy seas bow-to rather than stern-to. (Photo courtesy Luhrs Marine)

wave quickly. The Davis design will probably stay fairly dry until a wave breaks over the bow, but then it might stop dead. Most Carolina-style boats are quite large, however, and the chances of a wave breaking over the boat are fairly remote. A boat with a lot of interior volume forward, like a Cabo, will provide plenty of buoyancy forward and is also unlikely to stuff the bow into a wave in heavy going, though its full bow sections may make a rougher ride in a head sea.

The Midship Section

Considerations other than stormworthiness typically dictate the midbody shape of a sportfishing boat. Still, a boat with more deadrise amidships will provide a softer ride than a boat with a flatter bottom. This kind of boat will also be able to butt into waves in heavy weather without major slamming impacts. For this reason, a variable deadrise hull will have better seakeeping ability than a constant deadrise hull.

This Wellcraft 270 has a full bow that will provide reserve buoyancy, if not a smooth ride, in rough weather. Inside the cabin, those full sections forward make for a comfortable layout. (Photo courtesy Wellcraft Marine)

Most moderate-speed powerboats have a relatively wide beam between the chines to ease the transition from displacement to planing mode. These boats are usually dynamically stable at speed—that is, the hull is well supported on a planing surface, which helps prevent it from rolling or capsizing.

The Stern Section

A boat with a beamier stern is less prone to broaching in following seas than a boat with a comparatively fine stern, deep forefoot, and full bow sections. But a beamy stern with a low deadrise angle provides a harder ride in a seaway.

Trim Angle

When powerboats operate at moderate to high speed/length ratios, their trim angle contributes significantly to the impact forces on the bottom of the hull. A boat's trim angle is its fore-and-aft attitude—the angle between its at-rest waterline and its waterline underway—and in general, a lower trim angle (a more bow-down attitude) results in lower impact forces on the hull bottom. Some hulls with variable deadrise angles run naturally at lower trim angles in a seaway and therefore have better performance and lower impact levels than constant-deadrise hulls. On the other hand, a boat running at too low a trim angle is in danger of stuffing its bow into a head sea. In this case it is necessary to retrim for heavy weather by moving heavy gear, such as anchors and anchor chain, aft.

Low-Speed Powerboats

Low-speed powerboats such as cruisers and trawler-style motor yachts are usually displacement boats, which means that they are simply incapable of speeds much more than 1.5 times the square root of waterline length. For a trawler yacht with a 36-foot waterline, this means a top speed of 9 knots or less.

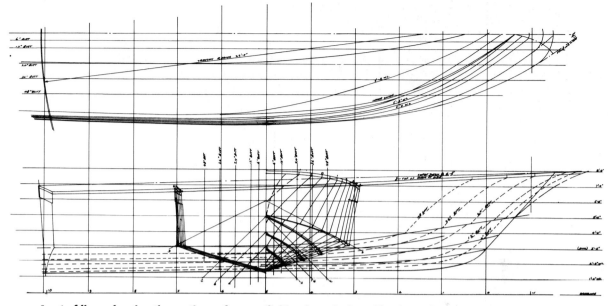

A set of lines showing the sections of a sportfishing boat designed by the author. Note the flared topsides forward. The deadrise is fairly constant from transom to midsection, making this a constant-deadrise hull. The bow sections are not deeply veed, so the boat may pound somewhat in a seaway, but it has ample buoyancy and room for accommodations forward. In the profile view, the buttock lines (dashed) run out straight and flat aft and meet the transom at right angles, indicating that the hull has enough bearing aft to plane, if fitted with the right power package. Indeed, this boat achieved 36 knots in sea trials.

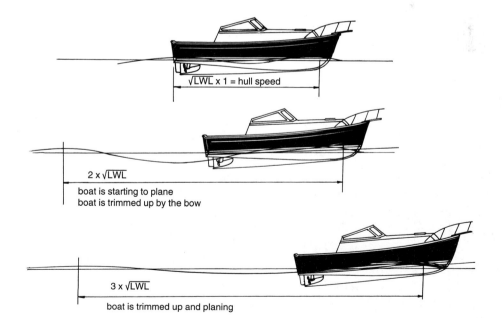

√LWL x 1 = hull speed

2 x √LWL

boat is starting to plane
boat is trimmed up by the bow

3 x √LWL

boat is trimmed up and planing

As a boat makes the transition from displacement to planing speeds, its trim angle increases. At higher planing speeds the bow should once again drop down.

Bilge keels run along the side of this hull (behind the staging to the left of the picture) to reduce rolling in a seaway. (Photo courtesy Interlux)

Such a boat is more likely to be caught out in heavy weather than a faster boat and should therefore be designed to handle it. Many boats of this type have a lot of top-hamper (masts, stacks, and boats stowed on the upper deck level), which raises their center of gravity and causes them to roll heavily. To reduce rolling, bilge keels—long, flat keels on either side of the hull running parallel to the centerline—are often fitted. These appendages add wetted surface but cut down on rolling by a half to one-third, depending on the boat. This is a good example of a feature that may not be important during a cruise across the bay but can make a large difference in heavy weather.

Underway, both wind and sea may act upon a low-speed hull, and it may have to take a lot of punishment from heavy weather before it can make port. The hull structure should be especially strong, and the boat must have plenty of stability.

The Bow

The bow of a displacement powerboat should be slightly rounded below the water, with some flare above. The rounded sections reduce slamming, while the flare provides a reserve of buoyancy that comes into play when the bow is pressed into a wave. Many low-speed powerboats have spray rails above the waterline to throw spray clear of the hull in moderate seas. Such a spray rail should be shaped so that it does not restrain the bow from rising over a sea in heavy weather.

The Midship Section

The midship section on a low-speed powerboat might be round or chine. In general, round bilges confer better seakeeping ability, especially when combined with a large keel or a pair of bilge keels. A chine hull with relatively low deadrise may have a tendency to pound in a head sea.

The Stern Shape

Some displacement boats have canoe- or cruiser-style sterns, much like a double-ended sailboat. Also known as a lifeboat stern, this style developed in wood-planked boats because planking fastened to a sternpost made for a stronger construction than plank ends landing on a transom. This stern was ideal for lifeboats, which were often rowed through heavy surf and required a tapered stern for easier handling. With the development of powerful engines,

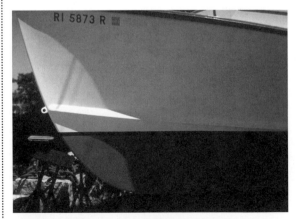

A spray rail like this should help prevent the bow diving into a wave and reduce the suction of water climbing up the bow of the boat.

however, the canoe stern was largely replaced by transom sterns and is now seldom seen. A transom stern is less likely to "squat" when the engine or engines are turning at high rpm, and it also allows more volume in the stern sections, where the owner's stateroom is often located.

What you won't see on most displacement hulls, however, is the large, flat transom of many planing designs. In profile, a planing boat's transom typically meets the hull bottom at something close to right angles, making a clean exit for passing water at planing speeds

Most higher speed boats have a sharply cut off stern, known as a transom or destroyer stern. This allows the water flow to separate from the hull quite cleanly when the boat is moving at speed. When the boat is moving at slower speeds, the large, flat stern can get slammed by heavy seas approaching from aft. (Photo courtesy Wellcraft Marine)

but creating a lot of turbulence and drag at displacement speeds. The deeper stern sections of a displacement boat typically sweep up toward the transom when viewed in profile, so that less of the transom is immersed to create drag at displacement speeds.

Sailboat and Powerboat Stability

Transverse stability, a vessel's resistance to heeling, is derived from two sources: waterline beam and vertical center of gravity. The beamier a boat, the harder it is to tip over, just as it is hard to tip over a pyramid standing on its wide, flat base. In contrast, a narrow-beamed boat, such as a canoe, will turn over easily.

When a canoe is fitted with a counterbalance such as an outrigger, we increase the width of its base and can stop it from turning over. Adding beam to a sailboat gives a similar if less dramatic result. As an alternative to increasing the width of a boat, we can add weight in the form of a keel to lower its center of gravity (G). In either case (increasing the beam or adding ballast), what we are doing is affecting the relative positions of the *center of gravity*, the *center of buoyancy* (B), and the *metacentric height* (M) to give the boat more stability. The center of buoyancy is the center of the immersed volume of the hull, while the metacentric height can be imagined as the center around which a boat rotates when heeled. Making a boat wider has the effect of raising M.

If you calculate the vector sum of the longitudinal and vertical centers of gravity of every object on a boat, including its hull and keel, you will eventually locate the vessel's overall center of gravity, both fore-and-aft (longitudinally) and vertically. Typically, the vertical CG is near or just above the waterline, and the longitudinal CG on a sailboat is around 52–58 percent of the waterline length aft of the bow. On a powerboat, the weight of the engines may move the longitudinal CG farther aft. In order to lower the vertical CG as much as possible, sailboat designers can make the keel deeper or install a lead bulb at the bottom of the keel. Placement of ground tackle, batteries, tanks, and other heavy objects will also affect the CG, as will deck stowage of a dinghy or making a mast, say, five feet taller. Powerboat designers can add ballast or locate heavy gear lower in the hull.

In big-ship architecture, the true measure of tenderness or stiffness is the time taken for a ship to roll from one side to the other—known as the *period of roll*. But for small boats the righting moment (defined below) is the accepted standard of stability. A boat with a low righting moment is tender, while a boat with the opposite characteristic is stiff. The movement of a tender boat is a quick response to a puff of wind—a readiness to heel—while a stiff boat has a jerky motion and resists heeling. Again, too much of either tendency is bad.

The Stability Curve

When a designer calculates stability, he includes the shape and area of the waterline plane, the weight of the ballast, and the height of the boat's center of gravity in the calculation. The result is known as the *restoring* or *righting moment*—that is, the moment acting to restore the boat from heeled to upright condition. Mathematically, the righting moment is the product of the righting arm, the boat's displacement,

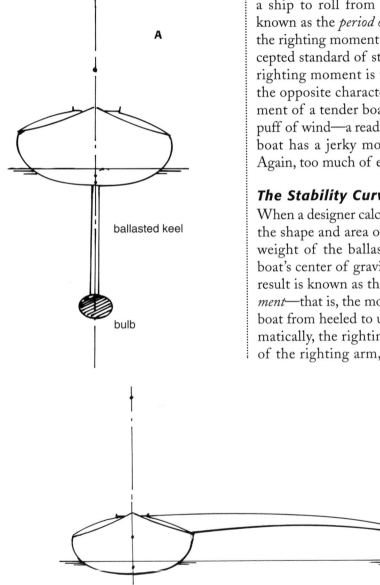

A

ballasted keel

bulb

B

A narrow-hulled vessel such as a canoe can be made more stable with properly positioned crew weight, a ballasted keel (A), or an outrigger (B). Added beam (in this case the outrigger) confers stability by increasing the metacentric height of a vessel, whereas adding a keel lowers a boat's center of gravity.

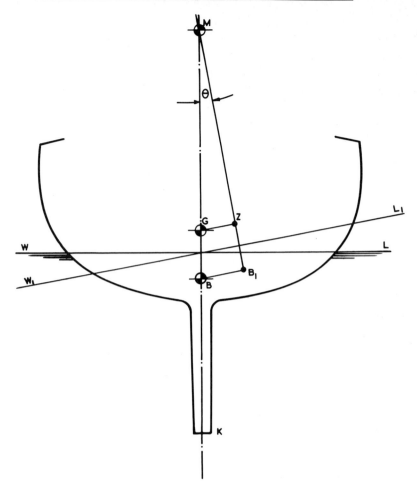

The locations of various centers used in the stability calculations. G is the vertical center of gravity, B is the vertical center of buoyancy, and M is the metacentric height. When a boat is heeled (naval architecture convention shows the waterline heeled) B moves to B1 and the metacentric height stays in approximately the same place. The resultant righting moment (the force acting to return the boat to an even keel) will be proportional to the distance from G to Z, which is called the righting arm or righting lever. Raising M (by adding beam) or lowering G (by adding keel ballast) will increase the righting arm length.

and the force of gravity. As the boat heels, the shape of the waterplane changes, causing a change in the location of the center of buoyancy and the length of the righting arm. For each angle of heel a new restoring moment can be calculated. The results form a curve of static stability, as shown in the illustration of a 35-foot boat (next page), calculated using the ProSurf yacht design computer program. Each point on the curve is the righting or restoring moment at that angle of heel. The overall curve shows to what degree a boat will resist being rolled over by wind or sea. The curve for a multihull is steeper than that of a monohull. The multihull's great beam gives it greater initial stability, but that stability vanishes quickly at heel angles greater than 80 to 90 degrees, due to the lack of a ballast keel. To make matters worse, the multihull is much more stable in the inverted position than the monohull, which is much more likely to come back upright after a capsize.

Fortunately, most powerboats operate in the first 15 degrees of the stability curve, and most sailboats in the first 30 to 35 degrees. Only rarely do boats heel more than 30 degrees.

Generating a stability curve in this manner requires that a boat's design parameters are

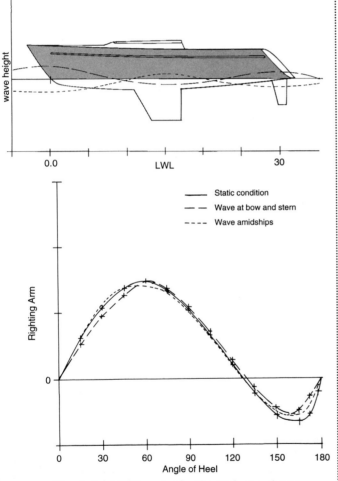

The static stability curve for the 35-footer shown above as predicted by the ProSurf Yacht Design Program (from New Wave Systems) for three conditions: in flat water, with a wave amidships, and with waves at bow and stern. The heel angle of vanishing stability is 122 degrees for this boat.

known precisely, and this is only possible with a computer-generated design. Alternatively, on a boat afloat, the righting moment can be found using an inclining test, in which a heavy weight is placed on the end of a spar swung outboard at 90 degrees to the boat's centerline. This weight heels the boat by a measured amount. When the weight, its distance from the centerline, and the heel angle are all known, the static stability can be calculated.

Designers often reference a design stability curve to the edge of the deck and assume that the deck is flat across the boat. This is easier than adding the cabintop to the lines plan drawing, but bear in mind that the curve is slightly lower than it would be if the cabintop were included.

How Hull Shape Affects Stability

As we have seen, all other things being equal, a narrow boat has less stability than a beamier vessel. Yet two boats of equal waterline beam having identical centers of gravity can display quite different transverse stabilities. This is due to the impact of the shape of the waterplane. On a planing powerboat hull, the additional beam aft increases the volume of displacement and often changes the vertical location of B. In the figure on page 82, B is higher on powerboat X than it is on sailboat Y. If the distance from B to M for both boats is the same, the position of M for the powerboat will be higher. This will increase GM and hence increase initial stability.

The depth of the hull is another factor influencing a vessel's stability. For example, if B is lower in the hull, then the distance from B to B_1 (see the figure on page 79) is likely to be larger, making GZ longer, and GZ multiplied by displacement gives the righting moment.

The Center of Gravity

Lowering the vertical CG is probably the easiest method of increasing a boat's stability. On a powerboat, an owner can place lead ingots in

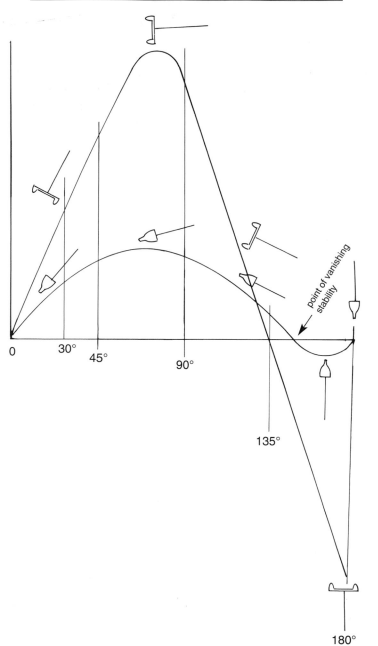

0   30°   45°   90°   point of vanishing stability   135°   180°

Static stability curves for a monohull and multihull of similar lengths. For this monohull the point of vanishing stability is about 140 degrees, but for some sailboats it can be as low as 105 degrees. The multihull is impressively stable up to a heel angle of 90 degrees, but its stability then drops rapidly, disappearing altogether at 135 degrees. For powerboats the point of vanishing stability is often between 90 and 120 degrees. Only rarely, however, do boats heel beyond 30 degrees or so.

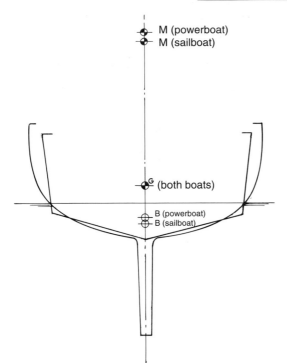

The midsections of a powerboat and a sailboat of equal length. If the vertical center of gravity is the same in both boats, the powerboat will have greater initial stability because its center of buoyancy and metacentric height are higher. The sailboat's keel, however, will give it greater ultimate stability.

the bilge to increase stability, although it is difficult to do much more than that, except to lighten the topsides by removing heavy gear. Adding lead ingots also increases the weight of the boat and may influence its speed and handling. You should not try to change the CG of a boat without consulting a naval architect or qualified boat designer.

On a sailboat, the easiest method of increasing stability is to lower the CG of the keel. This can be done by installing a new bulbed keel. When we did this on one of our designs it lowered the CG by 7 inches (18 cm) and increased the righting moment by about 12 percent. Note that if you decide to change the CG of your keel, you may have to increase

the size of your boat's rigging and mast. Again, this should be done in consultation with the vessel's designer or a good boatyard that can also give you a cost estimate for the change.

Stability in Waves

Several other factors affect a boat's stability when it is at sea. One of these is waves. Another, which we'll look at later, is free surface. Waves passing under a boat can momentarily increase or decrease its stability. Take another look at the boat shown on page 80. The diagram shows a 3-foot (1 m) wave—as would be found in winds of about 15 to 20 knots—passing under a 35-foot (11 m) boat, and the graph shows the change in stability the boat suffers due to this relatively small wave.

The solid curve shows the boat in design condition, equivalent to flat water. The curve with long dashes shows how the stability changes when 3-foot waves are under the bow and stern, and the curve with short dashes shows the result when a 3-foot wave is amidships. The changes are subtle in this small sea, but will be much more pronounced in 8- to 10-foot seas or higher—so much so that the boat might have virtually no stability under certain momentary conditions.

Note that in this example, we've assumed all conditions to be static, as if the wave were frozen in place. We make this assumption because dynamic conditions are so difficult to measure, but we know that stability can vary wildly in dynamic situations. For example, a sailboat in heavy weather might find itself sailing across the slope of an approaching wave. Under static conditions the boat would have adequate stability to resist capsize, but now the boat is being forced sideways by the sheer power of the breaking wave crest. In these conditions the lee rail might dig in and the boat might pivot over its rail, in which case a lot of stability may be of little use.

Deep-V powerboats suffer some loss of stability as they transition from displacement to planing mode. According to Peter Du Cane, in his book, *High Speed Small Craft*, a flat-bottomed boat transitioning from displacement to planing mode can expect an increase in stability nearly proportional to the square of its speed, but the opposite occurs with a deep-V or round bilge hull. As the hull rises out of the water, the static righting arm is substantially reduced.

Once on a plane, however, dynamic stability comes into play. The boat is supported by lifting forces all along its bottom, much as an airplane wing is supported. These forces tend to increase the vessel's overall stability, despite the loss of static stability. The actual contribution of hydrodynamic lift to stability depends on the boat's speed, the shape of its bottom, and other factors.

Vanishing Angle of Stability

Let's return for a moment to the concept of the vanishing angle of stability, as illustrated by the graphs on page 81. In extreme circumstances a boat might be heeled to 90 degrees (known as a *knock-down*). Usually a boat will recover from this situation and the crew will continue to sail (albeit white-faced and high on adrenaline). From experience, I can tell you that, after you have put the spreaders in the water, you sail a lot more moderately!

Real trouble begins when the boat is heeled beyond 90 degrees. For a boat like the Beneteau 390, the *vanishing angle of stability* (VAS)—the point at which the righting moment curve crosses the base line—is 109 degrees. That's a rather low VAS for a monohull sailboat. If the boat is heeled beyond that angle, it will continue to roll over. Typically, a boat with a low VAS tends to stay inverted longer and is slower to reright itself than a boat with a larger VAS.

How often is a boat likely to get knocked over that far? Not often. But when we consider the static effects of waves and the dynamic effects of waves and the boat's own motion, we're forced to recognize that in fleeting moments, the VAS might drop as much as 20 degrees or more below its nominal value; moments later it might be 20 degrees of more above that nominal value. Should the boat be overpowered during the few seconds that the VAS is low, a spectacular capsize might result. Due to the unpredictable location of the vanishing angle of stability in waves, a higher initial value is better.

Tender and Stiff Boats

As we have seen, stability in moderation is good, but too much initial stability, like too much of most things, is bad. A sailboat with a lot of initial stability has a jerky motion that is likely to tire the crew. A stiff boat will also need a heavier mast than a similar but less-stable vessel, because the mast and rigging sizes are determined from the righting moment. The rigging will need to be heavier too, as will the sail materials.

A powerboat with high initial stability will heel when the wind or seas increase, but the boat will try to return to the upright position as soon as possible. The vessel's motion will be jerky as it tries to stay upright, a condition known as a *snap-roll*. This motion can be violent enough to cause injury to the crew. The only cure is to raise the CG of the boat until the motion becomes easier.

Tender sailboats tend to heel more quickly. If a boat is extremely tender, it will require a reduction of sail area even in moderate winds, quite possibly leaving it without adequate power to drive through a head sea. As we noted earlier, adding lead in the bilge or redesigning the keel is one of the easiest fixes. Another solution is to remove the aluminum alloy mast and install a lighter, carbon-fiber spar. Changing to a carbon mast can increase stability by as much as 10 percent. The good news is that very few sailboats these days are designed outside the optimum range of stability.

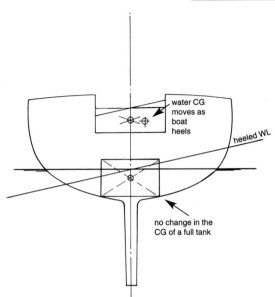

Free surface reduces stability when a sailboat's cockpit is filled with water. The boat's stability drops dramatically until the water is allowed to flow out.

An overly tender powerboat will roll onto its chine and stay heeled in that attitude until the next wave, a sharp turn, or a shift of weight triggers it to flop over onto the other chine. This condition, known as *chine walking,* can be quite frightening and is certainly undesirable, especially if it occurs as the boat slides down the back of a wave and into a broach. It should be corrected by putting additional lead in the bilge or in the bilge keels and by removing heavy items from positions high in the boat.

The Effect of Free Surface

A free-surface effect develops when a water or fuel tank is half filled and the boat heels. The liquid flows to the lowest part of the tank, and if the tank is large enough, this can influence the vessel's CG.

If you've ever tried to sail a boat after the cockpit has filled with water, or tried to move around in a swamped dinghy, you will have experienced the effect of free surface firsthand.

Simply put, the effect accentuates any motion of the boat, and it increases a boat's tendency to capsize. The effect is negligible for boats with small tanks, but can be significant for a boat with a very large fuel or water tank.

Powerboat Stabilizers

Without a mast to damp its rolling, a powerboat can roll horrendously, but there are several ways to slow and even stop this. Most methods of stabilizing require the vessel to be underway to work effectively, but anti-roll tanks work whether the boat is underway or not. A gyroscope incorporated into an anti-rolling system is now part of most stabilizing systems and will prevent rolling even while a boat is at anchor.

There are two main methods of stabilization. The older method, *passive stabilization,* developed around 1874, involves two tanks placed reasonably high on the boat and makes use of the free surface effect mentioned above. If these tanks are half filled with water and connected by a narrow pipe, they become an effective roll reducer. The theory is simple. As the boat rolls, water in the higher tank wants to move to the lower tank. But the connecting pipe is of small diameter, so the movement of the water lags the roll period of the vessel by about 90 degrees and effectively damps the roll. Making sure that the diameter of the connecting pipe and that the consequent movement of the water matches the roll period is critical. If the ship and the water flow between tanks get out of phase, the roll might actually increase enough to capsize the vessel.

A better method, *active stabilization,* uses twin stabilizer fins (similar to rudder blades) that protrude from the sides of the boat below the waterline and ideally within its maximum beam. When the vessel is underway, the fins move so as to reduce roll. For example, if the boat rolls to port, the starboard fin turns downward to drive the starboard side of the boat down, while the port fin turns upward to try to drive the port side up. The first patent for these fins was issued to John Thornycroft in 1889 in Britain. It wasn't until gyroscopes were incorporated into the design of these stabilizers, however, that they became really successful. Today, most large motor yachts have some form of anti-roll device.

Designing for Heavy Weather Below Deck

You have been on watch for two hours (about all you could stand in the high winds), and now you go below. Here you can hardly tell that a storm is raging. It is uncannily calm apart from the motion, which causes you to look for a handhold as you walk through the cabin. The cook is in the galley, braced against the bulkhead, and wearing a harness hooked to an overhead pad eye. He offers you a half-full cup of hot soup, and you gratefully accept. You are glad to get out of the keening wind, with its eerie whining through the shrouds. How is it possible that everything is so calm below, while on deck a major storm is howling in the rigging, throwing tons of seething green water at the boat?

One reason is that the skipper paid attention to stormworthy features long before the boat got into severe weather. Everything is organized and functional. He checked that the companionway ladder was usable in heavy weather, that the seacocks were solidly mounted, and that there were enough handholds throughout the boat—all features that are critical to comfort and security during a storm at sea.

The Companionway Hatch or Door

Doors and hatches are notoriously vulnerable to direct hits by heavy waves. On commercial fishing boats that are built for heavy weather, doors to the weather decks are made of steel and are watertight. But on most recreational powerboats they are made of glass and set in wood or alloy frames. These doors are not seaworthy

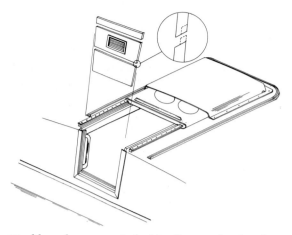

Washboards are easy to fashion for your boat and can be a real lifesaver in heavy weather. Note how the washboards (inset) are made with an overlap to stop water coming into the boat.

and are certainly not stormworthy, even though they are functional and attractive for the other 99 percent of the time the boat is in use. For that 1 percent of rough-weather conditions, however, the skipper should have a backup, perhaps a sheet of plywood kept under a bunk that can be screwed or bolted over the door when required. On a sailboat, the companionway hatch is usually kept closed in heavy wind and seas, which can make for stifling conditions below deck. To provide some ventilation in heavy

A soft dodger can keep a lot of spray and rain off the cockpit crew in moderately bad weather.

The dodger on this boat is strongly fabricated from fiberglass and is ready for the Southern Ocean. There is no need for a dodger of this nature unless you intend to cross oceans under sail.

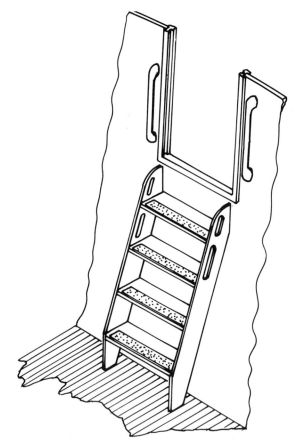

A companionway ladder should have nonskid on the steps and handholds, as shown here.

weather, washboards are made in several parts, so that just two out of three boards can be inserted to let some air below. In moderately heavy weather a canvas dodger can help shield the hatchway, but in severe weather it can get blown away, leaving the hatch with little protection. Some cruising boats are equipped with a hard dodger to provide good protection in heavy winds and seas, although this could be a difficult retrofit for a boat that is not already so equipped.

Ladders

The most dangerous aspect of a sailboat's companionway is the ladder. A good companionway ladder has non-skid treads and handholds on both sides. It may also have treads that are angled at either end to make passage up or down easier when the boat is heeled. A flybridge ladder should have the same features. Ideally, a ladder should also have both overhead and side handholds.

Seacocks

Seacocks on all boats going offshore should be bolted through the hull. I am not a fan of the latest style of plastic or Marelon through-hulls that are simply screwed and caulked in place. When I go to sea in a boat that might face severe weather, I prefer to have old-fashioned bronze through-hulls and seacocks that are bolted through the hull skin. Even then, I tie a wooden bung or plug near each seacock. Should the seacock fail and water start flooding into the boat, I can hammer the

Through-Hulls and Seacocks

The terms seacock and through-hull are used pretty much interchangeably today. But in the past, "through-hull" referred to the metal fitting that went through the hull, while "seacock" referred to the valve that turned the water flow off and on.

bung into the hole. Note that this kind of operation requires enough space to swing a hammer. I like to see plenty of access room around seacocks.

In order to minimize the number of through-hulls in one of my designs, I installed a manifold (*sea chest*) from which all the intakes were led, limiting our through-hull openings to two large intakes with strainers, one on either side of the keel. Should one intake get blocked, the other is large enough to handle the load. Should a pipe fail inside the boat, the owner can either turn off the two seacocks or the valve leading to that specific line.

Handholds

Handholds are important, both when a boat is upright and when it is heeled. When you are thinking of buying a boat, walk through the cabin to see if the handholds fall naturally to hand. Then check again when the boat is under sail or power. If you have to lunge across an open space to reach the next one, see if you can fit another in the gap. Make sure each handhold is sturdy. In heavy weather, if a sea hits the boat as you are moving across it, one handhold may have to support your entire weight while you gyrate around the cabin.

Bunks

If you are at sea in heavy weather, you might find yourself spending a fair amount of time in your bunk—not necessarily because you want to try to sleep through the storm, but because a bunk is often the safest place on the boat. In fact, there may be so much motion in the cabin that moving around without injury is impossible. As a result, the location of your bunk inside the hull is critical to comfort. If it is in the forepeak, you won't sleep, since the boat's motion is most pronounced there. You may not even be able to stay in a forepeak berth, as the accelerations will launch you out of it. The ideal place for a storm bunk is usually

just aft of the center of buoyancy of the hull, where pitching is lowest.

Another problem with a bunk in heavy weather is that an average-sized berth is too large. You may suddenly find yourself airborne as a boat flies off a wave. Also, any projections along the edge of a bunk can give you a nasty bruise if you land on one. To remedy this situation, try stuffing a sail bag, a kitbag, or other gear in the bunk with you to stop yourself from moving around. Don't overdo it though; there's no point in piling gear into a bunk if it takes you 15 minutes to get out.

Be aware that many boats today have bunks where you lie with your head lower than your feet when the boat is underway. Also, many bunks are laid out in odd places with no leecloths. These bunks are designed for sleeping in port, not sleeping in heavy weather. We'll have more to say about leecloths in Chapter 4.

If you intend to roam far offshore, before you buy your next sail or powerboat, climb into

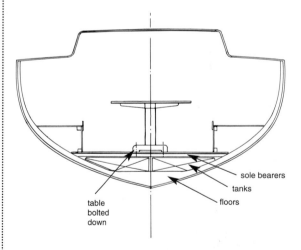

Sole bearers are the pieces of dimensional wood that support the cabin sole. They are not the floors of the boat unless the boat has an extremely shallow draft and the cabin sole is mounted directly onto the floors. A dining table should be bolted through the sole bearers to ensure that it won't collapse in high seas if a crew member falls against it.

the bunk and see if it is comfortable. If it is, try getting into it during the sea trial to confirm your first impressions.

Dining Table Fastenings

The cabin table is one of the most vulnerable pieces of gear on the boat. In heavy weather it is typically used as a handhold, as a leaning post, and as a place to wedge your feet as you try to stay on one side of the boat or the other. It should be strongly bolted to the underlying beams or sole bearers, rather than just to the cabin sole itself. Only in this fashion will it stand up to heavy loads like those that might be imposed on it by falling crew.

Designing for Heavy Weather On Deck

During a severe storm, being on deck can be a taxing experience. As your boat fights the waves, a welter of spray will continually pour into the cockpit. On some occasions the entire bow may disappear into a roiling, seething mass of green sea water.

In severe weather a canvas dodger is not much use. As we mentioned earlier, it will get blown away as the storm builds, so it must be stowed. Even a powerboat windshield is not very effective in extremely heavy weather. As a result, without an inside steering station the crew is exposed to the elements, which can be both fatiguing and severely limiting in terms of visibility. How can you minimize your exposure and make sure that you stay safe while on deck in severe weather?

Cabintops and Sides

The major problem with the cabintop on a sailboat is its height, the steepness of its sides, and the watertight integrity of the ports or hatches. If a cabintop is too high the helmsman will have difficulty seeing over it. If the helmsman's seat is raised in order to increase visibility, he is

placed in a position where he is more vulnerable to a boarding sea.

The angle of the cabin sides can also pose major problems for crew walking around on deck. In general, when working on a new design, I specify that cabin sides have an angle of no more than 30 degrees from the vertical. This helps prevent crew members from inadvertently stepping on the side and breaking or straining their ankles. Of course, when the boat heels, the orientation of the cabin side changes, which poses another set of problems. Typically, builders will place non-skid on the cabintop, but rarely do they put it on the side of the cabin, which can become a slippery walking surface when the boat is heeled.

Another problem with a cabin side is that it is relatively vulnerable to impact force. If you look at past sail- and powerboat failures, you'll often find that the cabin windows on the lee side were stove in when a boat was tossed onto its beam ends. Indeed, I've heard of some wooden boats in which the entire cabin side collapsed, leaving the boat open to boarding seas. This is exactly the situation that occurred aboard *Sword of Orion*, one of the older wooden boats competing in the 1998 Sydney-Hobart Race.

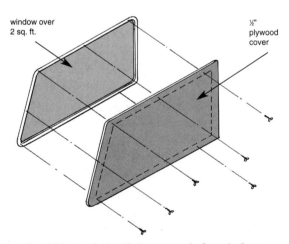

window over 2 sq. ft.

½" plywood cover

You should have plywood covers made for windows larger than 2 square feet if you are going out to play in rough weather.

Cabin Windows and Hatches

On a powerboat, the biggest problem is often the sheer size of the cabin windows. If a wave hits a large window, it is likely to blow the glass out unless the unit has been strongly installed. This is especially true of windows on the forward face of the cabin. If you routinely go out in heavy weather, you should carry plywood boards capable of covering a blown-out window.

The fashionable "sun-shade" overhang on the forward face of some cabins can be another problem area, since heavy seas coming over the bow can wash across the deck and slam against the underside of this overhang. In some cases (mostly on older wooden boats), seas have peeled back this overhang, leaving the cabin open.

The watertight integrity of deck hatches is always suspect. I once found by experiment that a 1-pound weight hung from the bottom flange of a large opening hatch was enough to distort it. A bolt can exert many times that amount of force, so the slightest unevenness of the hatch boss can give rise to a leak. Companionway

hatches are also liable to leak when subjected to a direct jet of water. Consequently, they should be fitted where they can best be shielded from massive jets of water.

Hatches should also be installed so that a wave coming aboard will slam them shut, rather than opening them and letting water below. In my opinion, the fact that the large foredeck

Morning Cloud *in happier times. Note the large foredeck hatch, which was always difficult to close.*

STORM SCENARIO

The Loss of *Morning Cloud*

When Sir Edward Heath was Prime Minister of England, he raced *Morning Cloud*, a Sparkman & Stephens-designed 43-foot sailboat. I worked at Sparkman & Stephens when the boat was designed, so I spent a fair amount of time working on the design of the deck layout in conjunction with Owen Parker, the boat's skipper, and the other members of the crew.

The boat had a cockpit of the maximum size allowed by the rating rule, and a large foredeck hatch secured by two barrel bolts. As I remember, the hatch itself was tightly gasketed and

could only be closed firmly if a crewman stood on it while the bolts were shot home. The hatch increased the speed of sail handling, but according to survivor reports it might have sprung open and taken in water when the boat was lost off the Owers Lanby, a few miles east of the Isle of Wight on England's south coast, in September 1973. (A lanby is a "Large Automatic Navigational Buoy"—this one had replaced the Owers lightship a few years earlier.)

We had raced the boat in gales several times that summer and experienced no problems, but when returning from Burnham Race Week the boat got into serious trouble and sank, with the loss of two crew members. I had left the boat to return to the S & S office in New York by that time, but I believe the storm trysail was in the locker in Hamble marina before the boat left for Burnham.

continued

According to newspaper reports, the boat was sailing under reefed mainsail just east of the Owers Lanby, and wind strengths were in the 45- to 50-knot range. The Owers ledge area is well known among sailors for the heavy overfalls created by a westerly gale, and should be left on the starboard hand in these conditions by any yacht heading west. Another yacht, the Swan 43 *Casse Tete*, was making the same trip and altered course out to sea when it became apparent that the Owers light was to the southwest of them, fine on the port bow, also according to newspaper reports. Once around the Owers light the boat would have been in the lee of the Isle of Wight and almost in the relatively safe waters of the Solent.

Under mainsail only, *Morning Cloud* would have been making a large amount of leeway, and it is understandable that the skipper would not want to stand out to sea on starboard tack again. Had he done so he would probably have been sailing almost directly toward France, and the tidal stream would have been sweeping him back toward Dover.

As the boat neared the overfalls of the Owers ledge, it was rolled by a gigantic wave and thrown onto its beam ends. According to reports, the crew had not put the washboards in place because the companionway hatch cover was keeping most of the water out. There was no bridge deck on the boat because the halyard working platform in the hatch was designed to be part of the working cockpit. The cockpit itself had a winch pedestal and was designed to have partitions under the mainsheet track to cut down on the amount of water that could flow forward at any one time. These partitions were never installed, and a prudent seaman would have kept the lower washboard in place in case the cockpit got filled.

At the time of the knockdown, two crewmen wearing harnesses and tethers were tossed into the water. One of the men, Gardner Sorum, was recovered, but the other, Nigel Cumming, was lost when his rope tether broke. The boat turned around and went back to look for Cumming. At that time, the skipper went below and found about a foot of water above the cabin sole, possibly from the large forehatch—which may have opened—or from the cockpit after the knockdown. The boat passed the point at which Cumming was lost and tacked again to come back onto the original course.

As the boat neared the point of the first knockdown, it was thrown over again, putting the mast into the water and twisting the spreaders. At this time, crewmember Christopher Chadd had just come on deck wearing a life jacket without a harness, and when the wave hit he was swept over the side and lost. Now there were only two uninjured crewmen left aboard the boat, and the decision was made to get into the life raft. The men in the life raft got seasick but made it to shore. A fishing trawler dragged up the remains of the boat two weeks later.

hatch opened forward and could not be fastened properly was a contributing factor in the loss of British Prime Minister Edward Heath's 43-foot *Morning Cloud* in 1973.

Vents and Other Openings

Other vents will need to be closed in heavy weather. On one cruising boat of my acquaintance the dorade-style vents had cowls that stood 18 inches high. When green water poured across the deck, these cowls acted like giant scoops and shot amazing amounts of water below deck. Since that time, I have recommended that boatowners buy the highest cowls they can comfortably fit on the boat, turn them backwards to draw air from the interior, and replace them with deckplates in storm conditions. I have yet to find a dorade or any other style of vent that didn't leak in heavy winds. To prevent the air from becoming stifling below decks, you'll need to fit a couple of small fans that can run off the battery.

Mushroom vents, hatch vents, clamshells, and just about any other type of vent should also be closed in heavy winds. If you plan on running the engine or generator, however, make some provision to vent the cabin from someplace other than the cockpit. There have been instances where carbon monoxide from engine exhaust has been pulled below to cause serious problems for the off-watch crew.

Sailboat Cockpits

The cockpit on an offshore sailboat should be relatively small if the boat has conventional cockpit drains, but it can be larger if the boat has transom openings designed to quickly dump out any water. For years the Bermuda Race committee specified how large a cockpit should be on participating boats, but that specification has become increasingly irrelevant in recent years, as cockpits have become larger and larger while relying on open transoms to drain water overboard.

Many cruising sailors feel a sense of insecurity if the cockpit is open at the back, a sense that is perfectly valid: open-stern cockpits can be insecure, especially if you have children on board. But with the right helmsman's seat and a removable panel under the seat the feeling of

---

How Much Water Can a Cockpit Hold?

Let's assume that the cockpit shown here is filled to the level of the seats. The total volume of water is 24 cubic feet (0.7 cu m), weighing 1,536 pounds (700 kg). That's about three quarters of a ton of additional weight in the aft end of the boat. If the cockpit were filled to the top of the coamings, it would hold 92 cubic feet (2.6 cu m) or 5,888 pounds (2670 kg)—almost three tons—of seawater. Imagine your boat with a swamped cockpit, trying to recover before the next wave hits. It will need fairly large cockpit drains, and, as we saw earlier in the chapter, the free surface effect of this water affects the stability of the boat.

If we assume that the cockpit has a pair of 3-inch drains, we can calculate the drain area and the amount of water that will pass through it. For example, drain B in the accompanying figure has a footprint area of about 10.6 square inches or .74 square feet, but the strainer bars across it reduce this area to .63 square feet. (The effective area of drain A, with

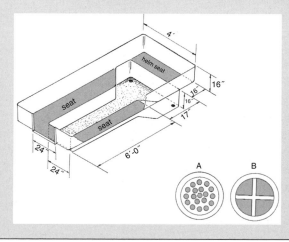

continued

strainer, is less than half the footprint area.) If we assume that the water level in the cockpit is three feet above the surrounding ocean (it may be less if the boat has a full cockpit) it will drain at a rate of about 0.12 cubic feet per second. Our calculation shows that it will take 3.33 minutes to drain the cockpit when filled to seat level.

According to current wisdom, three minutes is an acceptable length of time for a cockpit to drain. If the cockpit is filled to the coaming top, it will take about 12 minutes to drain. If the cockpit swamping puts the stern drain within one foot of sea level, it could take as long as 25 minutes to drain. In order to make this cockpit drain a lot faster, it would be easier to run two 3-inch-diameter pipes out to the transom rather than have them go through seacocks under the cockpit.

Note that this calculation is made for the boat in a static, upright condition. In dynamic conditions water may be thrown out of the boat as it wallows. The low point of the cockpit will be at the main hatch, which will also allow about half the water to go below rather than drain overboard.

insecurity becomes manageable. On a closed-stern cruising sailboat, the cockpit can also be reasonably large, if it has efficient drains. I prefer a cockpit that drains aft to the transom, where large cutouts will allow water to run away fast.

All seagoing cockpits—large or small—should also have a bridge deck at the forward end and high coamings. The bridge deck will stop water from going below, while the high coamings offer comfort and raise the tops of winches to a level where they are easy to use. The accompanying sidebar shows how much water it takes to fill an average cockpit, and how much time a single 3-inch-diameter drain takes to empty the cockpit.

Transoms and Transom Ladders

Having sailed on many, many boats, and having tried to get aboard boats from the water on a number of occasions, I have become a fan of open transoms for cruising sailboats—not the completely open transoms found on racing boats, but transoms that allow a sailor to climb back aboard easily. A large open space under the helmseat also makes room for a life raft, either under the seat or in a transom locker. This makes the raft much easier to launch in an emergency.

Although many boaters don't realize it, getting back aboard a boat after you have fallen off can be extremely difficult—even a death sentence—because it can be so difficult to climb a boat's slippery topsides. In fact, a boat was once found sailing unmanned in the Mediterranean Sea because the crew had gone swimming, and the last man over the side had forgotten to lower the swim ladder. Steps on the transom, especially when combined with a ladder, make the task of getting back on deck as simple as

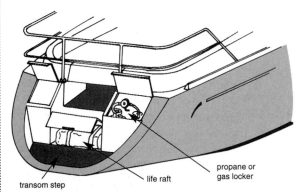

transom step — life raft — propane or gas locker

If the transom is shaped properly, it can become a lifesaver when a crew goes overboard. A stepped transom with a swim ladder (not shown) makes climbing back aboard easy. On this design, the life raft is hidden under a step. The gas locker is also placed well aft, where any leakage can drain over the side. On one of our designs we added a freshwater shower, plus a locker (left) for snorkel equipment.

putting the ladder in the water and climbing aboard. In fact, an open transom, which can be blocked off with a removable board, allows many potential lifesaving features to be added.

Whether you own a sailboat or a powerboat, a transom or side ladder is essential. The best types are those that fold inboard and have three or four steps so that larger people can easily climb aboard from the water. Some ladders are much too short to be used by anyone other than a child. A side or transom ladder (and the latter option is my preference), should extend well into the water—if you fall off the boat you may have to climb back aboard unaided.

The Garelick Eez-In ladder (see page 112) is the best that I have seen. It folds away into the transom when not in use, but if a person falls overboard, he or she can easily swim to the ladder fitting, pull the fastpin release, slide the ladder out, and climb back aboard.

Pulpits, Pushpits, and Lifelines

In rough going, strong lifelines with a sturdy bow pulpit and stern pushpit (also called a sternrail) are a real godsend on a sailboat. If you slip, you will probably fetch up against the lifelines and remain aboard the boat, provided the lifelines are high enough and are paired with a prominent toerail or bulwark. Both the pulpit and the pushpit should be strongly bolted through the deck, and they can serve multiple tasks. For example, a pulpit on a sailboat serves as a place to clip halyards, to sit while working on the headsail, to carry the navigation lights as high as possible on the bow, and to keep the foredeck crew onboard. On a powerboat a pulpit provides a handhold on what is often otherwise a bare foredeck.

The pushpit can be designed with built-in seats, life ring holders, the stern light, a barbecue holder, an outboard bracket, and a stern gate for transom steps.

The best pulpits are at least 24 inches (60 cm) high, and on cruising sailboats over 35 feet (11 m) long they should be 27 inches (68 cm) high. A yacht of over 60 feet (18 m) LOA might want a pulpit and lifelines that are 30 inches (76 cm) high. The lower the lifelines and pulpits, the more likely they are to catch you just behind the knees and send you overboard. Lifeline stanchions are commonly spaced no more than 7 feet (2 m) apart, the maximum distance allowed by offshore racing rules. If you have a gate in your lifeline, make sure it can be securely fastened, and tape over the clip when you're offshore so that it cannot open inadvertently.

Powerboat Cockpits

On powerboats, cockpits should be reasonably small, but this often poses a problem on sportfishing boats where you need to be close to the water to reach fish and leaders, and you also need room—a circle about 10 feet (3 m) in diameter—to operate a fighting chair. The result is a large cockpit with low freeboard and a relatively low cockpit sole, a situation that can be made even less seaworthy by fitting the cockpit drains only a few inches above the waterline. If the boat has large fuel tanks aft, filling those tanks can put the drains lower still. Add the weight of several anglers and a large fish, and those drains may actually sink below the waterline and let water into the cockpit. Consequently, it is vital to make sure that all cockpit sole hatches are watertight and dogged down. Boats have sunk when the cockpit flooded and the cockpit hatches were not watertight. When buying a new boat, this is a major point to check. You should also check that the transom door can be opened outward in an emergency to drain water overboard.

"Underway, the cockpit of a large sportfishing boat usually affords passengers the best chance to stay dry," notes Dean Clarke, executive editor of *Sport Fishing* magazine, who has spent hundreds of hours in the cockpits of sportfishing boats. But he adds that when fighting a large fish, many boats back down as fast as possible to regain line the fish has taken off the reel. Often, a wall of water pushed by the blunt transom rises up high enough to come over the transom coaming and into the cockpit.

> Once, while fishing off Palm Beach, Florida, at the height of sailfish season, we got more than we bargained for on a brand-new 55-footer. Sailfish season in Florida runs from about December to March. And, as luck would have it, the best fishing happens in the worst weather. In a strong north wind, when a cold front meets the Gulf Stream flowing from the south, the seas seem to stand straight up, about as tall as a two-story house. We started backing up after a pair of hooked sailfish, and the skipper got a little too much momentum going for the conditions. Two waves, one after the other, broke directly into the cockpit. The mate immediately popped open the transom door, and at the same time the skipper gunned the engines ahead.
>
> We figured afterward that in a 10-foot by 12-foot by 3.5-foot cockpit, the amount of seawater that filled us totaled 420 cubic feet. At 64 pounds per cubic foot of seawater, we instantly gained 26,880 pounds, more than the weight of a smaller boat. Had the deck hatches on our boat not been watertight, the bilges most certainly would have filled, and our problems would have become far graver.

Pilothouses, Bridges, Cabins, and Cabintops

For heavy-weather sailing, a pilothouse can be a godsend. Sitting where it is warm and dry while the storm rages outside can boost morale and cut fatigue tremendously. Some boats even have the navigation station and a bunk in the pilothouse, which enables the skipper to be ready in an instant if an emergency develops.

The problem with a pilothouse, however, is the size, material, and bedding of the windows, and the fact that these structures can be vulnerable to the elements. Heavy-duty rein-forced glass bedded in strong metal frames is a lot better than regular reinforced glass bedded in rubber. If you have such windows on your boat, be sure to have plywood panels with which to cover them in bad weather, as we noted earlier.

An exposed powerboat bridge is one of the worst places to be in heavy weather, but it is the area where everything can be seen easily, so at least a part of the crew will have to spend time there. A hard dodger over the top of the windshield can make life far more pleasant for a crew member who has to drive the boat to the nearest port. A dodger will also cover instruments that may take a beating in heavy weather.

On boats that routinely go into heavy weather, builders will sometimes install a watertight cabin that is high enough and contains enough volume so that the boat will be self-righting. On British RNLI lifeboats, for example, the cabin is designed so that a capsized boat can self-right again within minutes. However, I know of no recreational powerboat that offers such a safety feature.

Tuna Towers and T-tops

Although tuna towers and T-tops aboard powerboats are extremely helpful, both for seeing fish and for getting a better perspective when looking for navigation lights at night along the shore, they can also be a real source of danger, especially in heavy weather. Too many people up high in a boat can result in a dangerous amount of instability, and there's always the possibility of a crew member falling from the ladder. In heavy seas it's not a good idea to operate the boat from the tower, due to the violent motions there.

T-tops are a good idea for smaller boats as long as you don't try to sit or stand on them while looking for fish. They lower stability slightly, but they provide shelter and a place for electronic gear and life jacket stowage.

The Mast and Rigging

Recent research has shown that mast inertia—the resistance of a mast to moving or rolling—is critical in helping to prevent a capsize. In heavy seas a heavier mast will damp the effect of a wave strike because it does not want to roll with the boat until a second or two after the wave hits. The heavier the mast, the longer the delay in the roll, so owners of cruising boats shouldn't worry too much about how large their mast is; rather they should avoid a spaghetti-thin mast that has four or five sets of spreaders and multiple wires to hold it up. This type of mast is hard to tune, hard to keep in column, and reacts faster to a wave strike. (A mast is said to be *in column* when it is perfectly straight or slightly curved in one direction. It is *out of column* when it has an "S" shape or is bent in two directions.)

Standing rigging is another area where high-tech solutions might not necessarily be the best choice for a heavy-weather cruiser. In my first Bermuda race, the fleet got pounded by the tail end of a tropical depression. The 55-foot *Zephyros*, aboard which I was sailing, was about 60 miles off Bermuda when the storm hit, with no chance of getting into a harbor. When the storm—which packed gusts of more than 70 knots—finally waned some 40 hours later, we inspected the boat and discovered a fist-sized dent in the mainmast, caused by compression in the spar. We were fortunate that the mast stayed in the boat. After further analysis we realized that the backstay had been cranked down tight for the entire storm, and with no "give" in the structure, rigging loads had probably caused the dent. (We also cracked the main bulkhead away from the hull in way of the shrouds, split a 3/4-inch plywood bulkhead just abaft the shrouds clean across, and did a great deal of other damage.)

Since that event, I prefer to leave a little "give" in the rig to absorb some of the shock loads imposed by sailing off the top of a wave.

Consequently, in a cruising boat design, while I generally specify a rod headstay or roller furling, I prefer discontinuous rod or wire upper shrouds with 1 × 19 wire lowers and backstay, since wire provides just a little give. It is the owner's choice whether to use a wire or rod backstay.

Most sailboats today use some form of roller furling. But while perfectly acceptable for inshore sailing and even for use by singlehanders going around the world, most experts don't consider it particularly seaworthy in heavy conditions. All round-the-world racers who use roller furling have a second headstay on which they can hank storm sails when the going gets rough. The problem with roller furling is that, as the sail is reefed, the top and bottom parts of the sail revolve with the stay, while the middle part distorts slightly. This makes the sail very full for heavy-weather conditions. A sail that is too full tends to heel the boat more, making it slower and more liable to broach. In heavy conditions, a flatter sail allows the boat to stand up better, sail faster, and respond to the helm better. We discuss other options for heavy-weather rigs in Chapter 5.

The Engine Compartment

There is a large difference between sail- and powerboat engine compartments. A sailboat can sail its way out of trouble and need only use its engine if it cannot sail for some reason. A powerboat, on the other hand, must rely on its engine to go anywhere. Ideally, in severe weather, the powerboat will have two engines running in case one of them should fail.

The Powerboat Engine

In a heavy sea, a powerboat must keep its engines running, or it will be nearly helpless before the wind and waves. The biggest problem in heavy weather is that the boat is subjected to a lot of movement, which stirs up the fuel and raises sediment that normally lies on the bottom of the tank. Too much sediment can block fuel filters and lines and eventually stop the engine. At the height of the storm, you may lose an engine just when you need it most. Fortunately, a twin-engine boat can keep going under one engine while the filters are changed. But if one filter is clogged and both engines are drawing from the same tank, it is likely that the filters on the other engine will soon be blocked too.

A boat that may be expected to see heavy conditions should have twin engines that not only draw fuel from separate tanks, but are also able to switch between tanks. It should also carry a supply of spare fuel filter elements and have all the filters located where they can easily be changed underway.

Each engine's electrical system should ideally be separate from the other engine, although it should be possible to switch over in an emergency. This ensures redundancy should one engine's electrical system fail. Remember that while a diesel engine will keep running without electrical power, a gas engine will stop. If two gas engines are wired into the same circuit, you could lose both engines in an instant.

The engines should also be mounted on heavier than normal mountings on rigid engine bearers. As the boat heaves and pitches, the engine—the heaviest object in the boat—tends to move. This movement increases wear on shafts, bearings, and shaft logs. Eventually, it can lead to failure in these parts.

A little engine movement is unavoidable, no matter how carefully the power unit is secured, so fuel lines should be connected via flexible hoses. And remember that a copper pipe connection will eventually work-harden and crack or break. Fuel tanks should be rigidly mounted so that they cannot move inside the hull, and fuel lines should be mounted at the top of the tank, so that if they break, fuel cannot drain out of the tank and into the bilge. Tank breather pipes should be raised to the highest possible point to prevent the ingress of water.

Prop shafts should be properly bolted in place and carefully aligned with the engine. As with fuel lines, a flexible coupling between the shaft and the engine is a good idea, since the engine will move around to some extent no matter how securely it is fastened. The bolts in each shaft should be wired so they can't come undone. There have been cases where the entire shaft has dropped out of a boat, letting water in through the shaft log.

Another vulnerable point in the engine compartment is the air intakes. Aspirated diesel engines require a lot of air, and after-cooled and turbocharged engines require even more, so the air intakes must be quite large. For example, a 400-horsepower turbocharged engine requires an opening of 44 square inches or more to admit enough air. That means a 10- by 4.4-inch (approximately 25 cm by 11 cm) hole must be cut in the hull or superstructure for each engine. That's a minimum requirement, but to aid in cooling the engine compartment, the hole should be about a third to half again as large. With these kinds of holes in the hull, water is going to get in no matter how good the baffle system, so all air intakes should be as high as possible and well baffled to keep water from getting into the engine room.

The Sailboat Engine

All of the comments regarding fuel cleanliness, filters, movement, and air requirements for a powerboat engine also apply, to slightly less extent, to a sailboat engine. The big difference is that a sailboat engine is only used in heavy weather if the mast or rig cannot be used or if they prove insufficient. Very often, sailboat engines are just too small to be of any use in heavy conditions, and this is a serious problem. Remember, the larger the engine, the easier it will be to power into a heavy sea and to get home safely. When buying a boat, make sure the engine is at least as large and preferably larger than the recommended minimum.

The Prop Shaft and Propeller Strut

One of the biggest dangers in heavy weather is a line tangling in the prop or rudder. When the wind is high there is virtually no possibility of going over the side to cut the line loose, which leaves a mariner with few options.

If you do snag a line on the prop shaft, stop the engines. That will help you determine which shaft the line is on and whether you can get it off. But be careful. Often, when the engines are set to idle, the shaft will continue to revolve slowly, making the problem worse. You can try putting the engine astern to unwrap the tangle, although in my experience, it's a tactic that almost never works. In lighter conditions you can put a person in a dinghy or over the side to cut the line. If you put a person in the water, however, be absolutely certain that the engines remain stopped. Under moderate conditions you may be able to reach the shaft or prop with a knife tied to the boathook. But be careful not to saw into your hull, your prop, your prop shaft,

This line cutter is available from Spurs Marine. You should check to see that line cutters such as these are legal in your state. (Photo courtesy Spurs Marine)

or yourself. In heavier conditions, it is inadvisable to put anyone over the side. You may have to deploy a drogue or storm anchor to keep the bow into the wind while you wait for more favorable conditions to untangle the prop shaft.

STORM SCENARIO

Fishing for a Fright

You have been fishing with friends nearly 24 miles offshore from your normal port, and you are packing up to head home. It's been a successful day. You have some choice fish to sell, which will help pay for your outing, but the extra weight has put the boat deep in the water, and now the cockpit sole is just above the waterline.

Until now the wind has been blowing from the south, light to moderate. But the sky is dark to the northwest, and you realize that a front is moving through the area. You tune in to the weather radio and learn that, sure enough, a severe weather front will be on you within the hour. Winds are forecast at 40–50 knots, with golf-ball sized hail, thunder, and lightning. The boat has a top speed of 34 knots. There is another port within 16 miles, but your car and your usual fish buyer will not be there. What should you do?

Your options are:

1. Open her up and try to get as near to your home harbor as possible.
2. Run farther offshore and hope that the front will abate before it hits you.
3. Head for the nearer harbor and hope you can ride out the storm there before proceeding to your home port.

(continued on next page)

Option 1: You certainly should hightail it out of there as soon as possible. Getting close to shore will make it easier and faster for rescue services to reach you in case of trouble, but this is no time to be fixated on your home harbor.

Option 2: This is not a good idea, since running farther offshore puts you farther from rescue services, and there is no guarantee that the front will abate.

Option 3: Head for the nearest harbor as fast as conditions permit. Hopefully you will be able to ride out the storm there, then make it to your home harbor after the weather system has passed through.

In this scenario, Option 3 is by far the best. Option 1 is the next best, but only if you can get close to your harbor before the severe weather strikes. Avoid Option 2.

Perhaps the best way to solve this problem is to avoid it in the first place by having a line cutter fitted to your prop shaft. (Spurs Marine makes one of the leading brands.) This is a particularly good idea if you routinely go to sea in areas heavily infested with lobster pots or fishing nets, but you should find out whether line cutters are legal in your state before installing one. You might also want to fit an appendage on the propeller strut to keep lines out of the prop or even fit a prop guard or cage around the prop itself.

One relatively recent development is the Ring Prop, which has an outer ring around the blade tips. Ring Props rarely tangle or snag lines, pushing them aside instead. While a Ring Prop will knock a knot or two off your top speed, it gives peace of mind when powering through a field of lobster pots.

The Steering System

The steering system is the most important part of a boat. Without it you can neither control the boat, nor get it to safety. On a sailboat, there is usually only one rudder, but a powerboat often has two. Sailboat rudders usually provide some feedback to let the helmsman sense the load on the blade and its orientation. The loads on powerboat rudder blades, on the other hand, may be so high that they could overpower the helmsman. To prevent this, the typical power-boat steering system is so highly leveraged that it provides little feedback from the rudder.

Sailboat Rudders

In heavy weather, sailboat rudders should be large enough to give the helmsman total control of the boat, bearing in mind that sail area should be reduced to help steering control. Two types of rudder are desirable for offshore work: a skegged, or skeg-hung rudder and a balanced rudder. In general, a skegged rudder gives better directional control, is slower to turn the boat, and is easier on the helmsman in heavy weather than a balanced rudder. On the other hand, a balanced rudder feels more sensitive to the helmsman, which allows him to make faster corrections when starting to lose control. It is also easier to repair in the event of damage.

For a heavy-weather boat sailed by a couple, I would recommend a skegged or half-skeg rudder simply because it is more forgiving, while a fully crewed racing boat will find it easier to steer using a balanced rudder. But the racing crew may have to steer by hand in heavy weather rather than let the autopilot do the work because balanced rudders are so sensitive. This may affect their ability to do other work or to make intelligent decisions during a storm.

The major parts of the steering system are the rudder blade, the rudderstock, the quadrant, and the steering controls. The steering controls may be hydraulic, geared, wire, or cable. Each poses slightly different problems in heavy weather.

Handling Abilities

Rudder design can impact the way a sailboat steers. For example, some older boats have a lot of sweepback on the rudderstock, which puts load on the rudder blade when the helm is turned. Consequently, a good helmsman must be able to differentiate between rudder blade loading and weather helm, since in heavy seas, loading on the rudder blade cannot be eliminated by reducing sail area. The only solution to this problem is to redesign the rudder blade with a more vertical stock.

The helm will also feel heavy if the entire rudder blade is behind the rudderstock, which will again result in increased blade loading. To eliminate this effect, some additional area needs to be built up along the leading edge of the blade to "balance" it.

A balanced rudder carries between 10 and 33 percent of its area in front of the rudder stock. The smaller the area, the greater the pressure trying to force the rudder blade to follow the course of the yacht. Balancing the rudder makes the steering more sensitive and less tiring. This is not an issue with a skeg-hung rudder, since the skeg acts as a wing and directs water over the rudder blade. A skegged rudder is less sensitive, however, and can be more prone to stalling if lift is destroyed along the line between the skeg and the rudder blade.

If the helm gets too heavy as a result of excessive loading, your autopilot may have problems controlling the boat. At the very least it will use excessive amounts of power and "hunt" a lot—that is, make continual corrections—as it tries to maintain a steady course in rough seas. Balance the helm to operate as lightly as possible and the autopilot will steer the boat without much effort at all. One client asked us to redesign his boat's rudder because it wore out the autopilot battery in light winds and could not hold the boat on course in heavy winds. After we transferred some of the rudder blade area

STORM SCENARIO

Rudder Failure

You are steering your 35-foot sailboat some 20 miles from shore when there is a bang from under your feet and the steering turns to mush in your hands. What do you do?

The first step is to find out if the boat has been holed. Bring the boat head to wind and let the sheets run, then go below and check for hull damage. If the skeg has been torn off, the steering will turn to mush *and* you could have a large hole in the hull. If you find no damage below deck, check the lazarette or the locker in which the steering gear is located. If the quadrant is still moving when you turn the steering gear, the cables are okay. If the quadrant and the steering wheel turn in different directions, the problem lies in the steering cables, and you will need to figure out how to reinstall the cables or fix anything that is broken.

If you have followed the advice in this chapter, you will have a separate quadrant for your autopilot and will simply turn it on to guide you home. If the rudder blade is broken, there may be enough remaining to get you home, or you may need to call a towing service. In this case, you should let the Coast Guard know what has happened and contact your towing-service provider.

Whatever the case, unless the boat is certain to sink, do not launch your life raft, and do not climb into it or the dinghy as a precaution. If you do and the wind picks up, you may find that your boat sails away without you.

in front of the stock, made the entire blade more vertical, and filled in an IOR-induced hollow in the hull, the rudder gave fingertip control of this 40-footer, and the autopilot handled the load with ease. The owner was delighted. By changing the shape of the rudder blade, we had transformed the boat.

Consider installing an autopilot with its own quadrant on the rudderstock. That way, you'll have a back-up system if your primary steering system fails.

Dual Rudders

Dual rudders pose their own problems for the cruising sailor. Usually they are only fitted on boats with very wide transoms, wide enough to lift the windward blade out of the water when the boat is heeled. The blade that remains in the water is vertical and therefore very efficient, but the linkage between both blades and the helm station can cause a lot of additional friction.

Powerboat Rudders

It seems that more and more powerboats are being built with small rudders. While these boats are controllable at speed, if the boat has to slow down in heavy going, the rudder may be too small to be effective, which puts the crew in jeopardy. Another problem with powerboat rudders is the location of the stock on the blade. Putting some blade area ahead of the rudder stock lightens the load on the rudder cables or hydraulic rams, but too much area in front of the stock can make the boat difficult to control in rough weather.

Twin or Single Rudder?

On a powerboat, a single rudder is usually placed on centerline in the wake stream of the single propeller. This is both efficient and cost effective. Twin rudders work in the prop stream of a twin-engine boat, and may be toed—or angled—one or two degrees outboard to increase their effectiveness. Powerboat rudders can be small and re-main effective because they are in the prop stream. As we mentioned earlier, however, at slow speeds when there is not a lot of prop stream, the boat may exhibit control problems. The good news is that twin rudders give you a spare to get you home if one blade is sheared off.

Hydraulic Steering

The hydraulic steering used on powerboats and large sailing yachts can be somewhat limiting, since it offers little or no feedback to the helmsman. Before heading to sea, check the reservoirs to ensure that they are topped off. Also check the fittings to which the rams are attached. Hydraulic steering can exert a force strong enough to tear the rams from a bulkhead or frame. Make sure the rams are well lubricated and move easily.

Geared Steering

Geared steering can take many forms. The simplest consists of a quadrant bolted to the head of the rudderstock and a pinion on the steering wheel. This type is still used in some older-style sailing vessels, but it lacks feedback, and the gears tend to wear in the middle of the quadrant after long use.

In another style, the entire linkage between the wheel and the rudderstock consists of gears. Any misalignment in the system is hard to correct, but there is good feedback to the helmsman.

A geared steering system incorporates universal joints at each directional change, so it is often more reliable in heavy going than a wire-cable steering system. I have sailed a boat with geared steering extensively and only experienced one gear failure, when a mounting for a universal joint ripped its bolts right through the bulkhead. An incident like that shows just how much force is exerted on a steering system.

Pull-Pull Cable Steering

Cable steering is commonly used on sailboats. It consists of wires leading from the quadrant via turning blocks to the steering pedestal. The cable ends mate to the two ends of a chain within the pedestal, and the chain runs over a sprocket on the wheel shaft. As the wheel is turned, the chain pulls one cable or the other, which turns the quadrant. This system provides a lot of feedback to the helm, but heavy pressure on the mechanism can cause the wire to stretch and conceivably drop off a sheave if guards are not placed correctly. Sometimes, too, turning blocks are inadequately anchored. They should be strongly bolted in place with backing plates and adequate reinforcement. The steering system is highly loaded in heavy weather, and failure can lead to catastrophe.

Push-Pull Cable Steering

Generally reserved for smaller boats, push-pull cable steering consists of a cable sliding in a housing. Turning the steering wheel moves an arm at the wheel, pulling or pushing the cable through the housing, which in turn moves a quadrant arm to turn the rudder. This is not a

STORM SCENARIO

Dream Catcher's Rudder Failure (as Reported by Denny Thompson)

"We left Hawaii late, after waiting a few days to see what was going to happen to a developing storm off Mexico. We reached north for eight days looking for the westerlies to give us a comfortable ride to Seattle. The Pacific High seemed permanently stuck in one spot, and we did not have enough fuel to power through it. When we noticed a deep low approaching from behind us, we could do nothing except wait for it to hit. As it butted against the high, we watched the wind rise. It finally peaked with sustained winds over 50 knots for about 24 hours.

"We were sailing downwind with just a storm jib and the wheel locked off, basically hove-to downwind, with the crew all below. *Dream Catcher* was behaving well for the conditions, with the seas running between 15 and 18 feet. At 1400 we took a drastic roll and seemed to fall off a wave. My best guess is that the boat rolled 60 or 70 degrees to port, crashing in the trough, but came right back up. The crew looked at each other with amazement. Then we started looking for water, but found none. I decided to keep a deck watch after that,

but even had I been on deck earlier, I doubt I would have seen the wave that knocked us down. It seemed to come from nowhere.

"We had sailed another 30 hours when the helmsman called me out of a deep sleep, saying that he couldn't feel anything. A quick check over the side showed that the rudder wasn't turning. I told the crew we would keep normal watches but would just drift through the night. The wind and waves had calmed considerably, and at first light I went over the side to survey the damage. I found that the rudder had fractured both vertically and horizontally. There was no chance of saving it. We spent the next couple of hours fashioning an emergency rudder out of the spinnaker pole and some plywood that was under the vee-berth. With this jury rig we set sail again and taught ourselves how to steer with the sails and our awkward steering pole. For the next 14 days we sailed this way toward the Washington coast. As we refined the design, we were able to get our 24-hour averages back up to 120 miles.

"We were approaching the Washington coast when the weather started to deteriorate again. At that point I decided to call the U.S. Coast Guard and declare a *Sécurité* due to the difficulty of steering and the fact that we were approaching the shipping lanes. The coast guard declared the voyage 'manifestly unsafe,' leaving us with little control over our future choices. The Coast Guard wanted us to heave

(continued next page)

to and drift until they arrived, but I decided that it would be better to close the distance toward them and the coast and to continue to sail as best we could. The weather deteriorated further, and it took them 20 hours to reach us.

"Once there, they rigged a towline with our help around the mast and through the chocks on the bow. We didn't have any chafing gear, so they provided blankets to wrap around the bridle. With no rudder we had been streaming a drogue about 300 feet behind us in the gale, but that had done nothing to stop the yawing. We were transferred to the cutter with the seas running 8–10 feet, and the tow commenced at about 8 knots, even though *Dream Catcher*'s hull speed was 6.75. The bridle only lasted about five hours before it broke. As it did, it snaked over the deck, ripping off everything in its way: bow pulpit, lifelines, and deck hardware. Because it was too dark to launch their tender, the Coast Guard decided to let *Dream Catcher* drift for the night.

"The next morning we went back aboard *Dream Catcher* to rig a new bridle. All the Coast Guard had left were steel cables that were too short for the job, so for the rest of the tow the cables ground into the hull. When we finally reached Neah Bay, Washington, *Dream Catcher* was brought to the dock and we got a look at the damage. The rudder damage was less then 15 percent of the repair costs. The Coast Guard had done the rest.

"My crew and I were grateful for their help, but I still believe the damage and aggravation could have been avoided had the Coast Guard allowed us to proceed under our jury-rigged steering."

good steering system for heavy weather, when the loads become extremely high. These loads impose a lot of friction, slowing response times, and system failure is not unusual.

The Rudder Stock

There have been a number of heavy-weather rudder failures on boats where the rudder stock did not extend to the bottom of the rudder blade. For example, on Denny Thompson's *Dream Catcher*, a Pearson 40 returning from Hawaii in heavy seas, the rudder blade snapped off just below the skeg because the stock only went halfway down the rudder. If you are purchasing a boat that will be going to sea in heavy winds, you should make sure not only that the rudderstock extends to the bottom of the rudder, but that there is a knock-out hole in the trailing edge of the blade, enabling you to rig a steering line should the quadrant or any internal part of the steering gear break.

We'll return to the question of how to cope with steering failure in Chapter 10.

Four

Stormproofing Your Boat

Before Tom Rodenhouse—an auto-body shop owner in Grand Rapids, Michigan—sailed his Valiant 40, *Morning Winds*, around the world, he worked with the Valiant factory team to check every system and make sure every piece of gear was functional and would work in all conditions. He also carried spares and gear specifically intended for sailing in heavy weather, having learned that preparation was the secret to success. Finally, he made an arrangement with Valiant Yachts to ship him gear if anything broke or went wrong.

Preparation can take many forms and can be done at any time. For instance, you might check your boat's entire electrical system during the winter, reasoning that if electrical gear works in cold, damp weather it's more likely to work in a gale at sea. In the spring you might inspect your fuel tanks to make sure they are clean, so that dirt will not clog filters and stop fuel flowing to the engine at a critical time. You can do many preparation chores in the fall or over the winter when you take the boat out of the water.

In this chapter we'll look at how to make an existing boat more suitable for cruising in heavy weather. Of course, most of the recommendations in this chapter are intended primarily for offshore cruisers, whether sail or power. But many of the less critical items—such as a non-skid mat in the galley—can easily be incorporated into any boat and might make a great

A Valiant 40 similar to Morning Winds, *the one Tom Rodenhouse sailed around the world. (Photo courtesy Valiant Yachts)*

difference if you ever go out for an afternoon cruise and find yourself facing an unexpected summer squall.

Preparing the Deck and Deck Equipment

Nothing good can come of loose gear on deck when bad weather hits, whether you are sailing around the world or around the harbor. At best it is apt to simply disappear over the side. At worst it might fly through a window or hatch and cause a severe breach in your defenses from boarding seas. All gear on deck should either be removed or tied securely in place with strong lines. Round-the-world sailor Chris Bouzaid of Autoprop, in Newport, Rhode Island, recommends carrying high-tech Spectra line for lashing, since it's light, strong, and can be used almost anywhere. According to Bouzaid, "Quite often a light Dacron or nylon line or sail tie isn't strong enough to stand the force of heavy seas coming aboard."

Anchors

Once I was helping to deliver a 52-foot cruising ketch when we ran into a stiff head sea. We were near the coast, and the short, steep waves were superimposed on a heavy swell from a storm offshore, plus other reflected waves from the nearby rocky shoreline made the seas unusually hard to predict. As a result, the trip rapidly became miserable and wet as solid green water rolled over the bow and slammed into the cabin windows. The two anchor rollers on the bow held a 60-pound (27 kg) Bruce and a 100-pound (45 kg) CQR (plow) anchor. Both were securely tied down—*or so we thought.*

At one point we pitched into a particularly vicious wave, and the plow anchor simply burst its lashing, flying upward and smashing the underside of the pulpit, bending the 1-inch (2.5 cm) diameter stainless steel tubing several inches. Fortunately, the anchor didn't come down on the deck, where it might have done serious damage, but it did disappear over the side, where, suspended from a short length of chain, it slammed against the hull repeatedly. In the terrible sea conditions and at considerable danger to fingers and toes, it took two men quite some time to get the hook back aboard and secured tightly.

The lesson is obvious: we thought we were prepared, but obviously our preparations were not sufficient. Our lashing around the anchor was nowhere near strong enough—hardly a surprise when you consider that water and waves have been known to move houses, vehicles, and large chunks of shoreline. When preparing for

(continued on page 106)

An anchor stowed on a powerboat that does not expect to face heavy weather.

Storage on a bow roller with a sturdy steel restraining band.

In this photo, the boat looks salty enough with two anchors on a bow roller, but neither anchor is pinned in place, and when they bounce off the roller they will swing right back into the hull.

Three anchors, with the two plows pinned in place. To gain more options, this skipper should consider stowing the Danforth, which seems to be a light lunch hook, in place of the plow on the second bow roller.

An example of stormproof stowage for a Bruce anchor on a powerboat. There is no way this anchor is going to break loose.

There are many ways to stow an anchor for casual use, but few to stow it properly for heavy weather.

rough weather, ask yourself what would happen if a piece of gear were to get loose. Even a can of baked beans can cause considerable damage when tossed around at high speed inside a boat.

It might seem like a good idea to stow all anchors below in case the going gets heavy, but close to shore you want an anchor or anchors on the bow with chain attached. Anchors deployed in timely fashion have saved boats and even large ships from being driven ashore by winds and seas. If, however, you are a long way out at sea, it makes sense to stow anchors in the bilge. Doing so will keep weight off the bow, contribute to the boat's stability by lowering its center of gravity, and confine those heavy lumps of metal where the motion is less violent.

A steel pin inserted right through the anchor is the best way to restrain it on a bow roller. Even this is no guarantee unless the pin is sturdy. After encountering heavy seas on one boat, we found that a half-inch stainless steel pin restraining a plow anchor had bent so severely we had to hammer it out of the bow roller. Don't forget to secure the inboard end of the anchor as well, since it will bang on the deck if not lashed down. Wrapping the end of the anchor in rags and securing it with a piece of line may be the best way to prevent this problem. Also make sure the anchor chain is cinched tightly with a chain stopper, a *devil's claw*, or a turnbuckle to prevent it from running out if it gets loose. Below deck, anchor pads with strong lanyards should be glassed or bolted to the hull structure to ensure that a stowed hook cannot move.

Next, you will want to find a way to plug the hawsehole to the chain locker. Most hawseholes are covered with a metal cap that is slotted to fit over the chain, but these covers inevitably allow water to leak below. Experienced skippers stuff sponges or rags around the chain and duct tape the mess in place. The result is not pretty, but it works. If you don't want to tape rags and sponges around your fitting, you'll end

A chain stopper on the inboard end of the anchor chain takes the load off the windlass and stops the chain from moving.

up pumping the bilges a lot—green water on the foredeck *will* find its way below.

While up in the bow you might also want to find a way to secure the chain in the hawsepipe—the conduit from the chain locker to the hawsehole. Otherwise it will rattle and bang as the boat lurches and pounds into a seaway, to the point of keeping the off-watch awake just when they need rest the most. A good way to reduce this noise is to seize a rope to the chain with light line and feed both into the hawsepipe together, so that the chain is constricted.

Finally, if you have an anchor well or locker on the foredeck, as many boats do, you might want to seal its edges with duct tape. No matter how good the gaskets are, water will get by them and into the locker—possibly faster than the scupper with which the locker *should* be equipped can drain it. I once found that filling the anchor locker on a 24-foot (7 m) boat with water depressed the bow 4 inches (10 cm). Even a larger boat can lose 1 or 2 inches (2.5 or 5 cm) of freeboard when its anchor locker is filled with water. Think about how much more pitching and hobbyhorsing your boat would do with that much additional weight in its bow—enough to bury the foredeck endlessly in each successive head sea. Another minor point to remember is that the anchor and chain should be cleaned before they are put in a locker. Dirt can soon block the locker drain.

Sea Anchors and Drogues

Both sea anchors and drogues are trailed from a boat to keep it from turning broadside to dangerously steep and breaking seas, but they are distinctly different devices. A sea anchor—often in the form of a parachute with a large surface area—is deployed from the bow. It is intended to hold the bow into the seas. A drogue—which is smaller than a sea anchor and might be a tire, a cone, a smaller parachute, a timber structure, or some other object—is deployed from the stern. It is intended to slow the boat to a safe speed and to hold its stern into the seas.

Moderately heavy long-keeled cruisers may lie to a sea anchor successfully, but today's fin-keeled and balanced-rudder sailing yachts may not be able to do so in heavy seas. (They also may not lie ahull in heavy seas, but we'll save that discussion for Chapter 8.) They simply do not have the weight or the underwater lateral profile to balance the pressure of gale force winds on the rig and topsides. With the wind pressure concentrated forward of amidships, and the underwater profile concentrated aft of amidships, you can do nothing to keep the boat from yawing, often violently, or the bow from falling off the wind and exposing the side of the boat to breaking seas. For such a boat the dynamic approach outlined in Chapter 8 is the best way to get through heavy weather.

On a moderate- to long-keeled boat, a sea anchor can work wonders, allowing the boat to ride out an open-ocean storm with its bow tucked safely (if not exactly comfortably) into the seas. Deep-sea commercial fishing boats have ridden out storms in similar fashion, motoring slowly ahead—*jogging*—to relieve the load on the sea anchor line.

If you want to find out how your boat will lie to a sea anchor, watch it on a mooring or set

A chain locker should seal tightly to prevent water ingress in heavy seas. Note the gasketing around the edge of the locker, and the dogs to make sure the lid is firmly sealed.

your anchor on a windy day and see if the boat will lie peacefully to it. If your boat yaws and swings around on its ground tackle, there is a good possibility that it will exhibit the same behavior when lying to a sea anchor.

Bear in mind also that a boat lying to a sea anchor is moving backward at one or two knots, depending on the size of the anchor. That movement puts a lot of load on your rudder and its bearings. Lashing the rudder on centerline seems to be the best way of handling this situation, although even that method may not be strong enough for some balanced rudders. For this reason, too, a long-keeled boat with an attached rudder fares better on a sea anchor.

A drogue, on the other hand, should be aboard virtually every modern cruising boat, sail or power, that intends to go offshore and therefore may be caught in high seas and strong winds. Drogues are so important that a large part of Chapter 8 is devoted to their use.

Bridge Decks

A bridge deck, as described in Chapter 3, is basically a raised portion of the sole between the cockpit and the cabin that provides a barrier to keep water from pouring below if the cockpit is swamped. If your sailboat already has a bridge deck, you are in good shape. But what if it doesn't?

You have several options. First, at least aboard a sailboat, you can use washboards to help cover the companionway. They will leak a little if the cockpit is completely filled, but they will keep most of the water out. One drawback with washboards is that they may float out of their grooves if the boat is knocked down or capsized. To eliminate this possibility you should install a catch or bolt to hold each washboard in place.

If your boat has only one large washboard to block the companionway, it's a good idea to cut it in half and install a lip on the inside face of the lower board to help prevent water ingress.

That way in bad weather you can put the lower half in place and close the hatch cover. The small gap left at the top will allow air to circulate without letting a lot of rain below. In severe weather you can install all the boards and even tape the insides of the seams to prevent water from getting in. Do *not* join both boards together with hinges, or you will find as you sail along that the hinged boards bang together and keep everyone awake. Another option—far less satisfactory—is to block the companionway with an icebox or hamper in the forward end of the cockpit. The crew will have to step over it, but at least it will provide some measure of protection from downflooding.

On most powerboats, the cockpit sides are high enough to block most seas, and bridge decks are not required. If waves large and steep enough to flood the cockpit are ever encountered, the boat should face them, hopefully with a high and buoyant bow and perhaps with a sea anchor streaming from the bow (see Chapter 8). Still, it is important to ensure that a powerboat's cockpit is self-draining. The cockpit sole must be safely above the waterline, and freeing ports or large scuppers must be fitted to quickly return water into the ocean, where it belongs. A flooded cockpit weighs down the back of the boat, making it more likely that even more water will come aboard. Also, water in the cockpit can easily lead to catastrophic interior flooding through poorly gasketed hatches in the sole. Finally, as Dean Clarke, executive editor of *Sport Fishing* and *Marlin* magazines, points out, electrical wiring under the cockpit sole or rail could be short circuited or even deliver electrical shocks to cockpit occupants.

Jacklines

On a sailboat in heavy weather you will probably have to go forward on deck at some point, and it is essential that you wear a safety harness and tether and have a safety- or jackline rigged on the side deck to which you can attach it. The jackline should be flat wire or flat webbing (which will not roll underfoot) fastened to a shackle or a cleat at each end. (Do not use a lashing to hold the line in place. It can chafe and break.) Use the carabiner clip on the end of your harness tether to hook onto the jackline before you leave the safety of the cockpit. When moving around on deck use two tethers, clipping one on before you unclip the other, so that you stay connected at all times. A typical clip is illustrated in Chapter 9.

If a webbing line is fastened to a cleat, take up on it occasionally to remove the stretch. A wire line should be shackled to a pad eye and be fitted with turnbuckles to ensure that it is kept fairly taut. Frankly, I've sailed on boats with webbing jacklines and I don't trust them. Manufacturers take special precautions to ensure that harness tethers (which are made of webbing) meet certain specifications, but no such specifications exist for webbing jacklines, and they can degrade through neglect and from exposure to ultraviolet light, salt water, and chafe. If you use one, replace it every second or third season. My preference is for a stainless steel wire shackled between two pad eyes or strongly bolted deck blocks.

Be sure that all jacklines are in place *before* you leave port. If you wait until you are at sea, you may find that an essential part is missing, or you might forget about it until a storm hits. Trying to put out a safety line in bad weather is like walking a tightrope without a net. Sometimes you'll succeed, sometimes you won't.

When rigging a side-deck jackline, make sure it's within reach of the cockpit so that you can hook your safety harness tether onto the line without unhooking from the cockpit safety line or strongpoint. Terminate your jacklines 6 or 7 feet (1.8 or 2.1 m) forward of the transom, so that if you go overboard and are dragged along at the full stretch of your tether you will still be within reach of the transom, where your fellow crew can reach you and haul you back aboard. This may seem an insignificant detail but it is very important. Sailors have drowned while being dragged through the water at the end of a perfectly good safety harness and tether.

Never go on deck in bad weather without wearing a harness, or even better, a harness with an inflatable life jacket. In our testing (discussed in Chapter 9) we found that it was impossible for a person in the water to drag him- or herself forward, or for the crew to drag that person to the boat, if the vessel was moving at more than 4 knots.

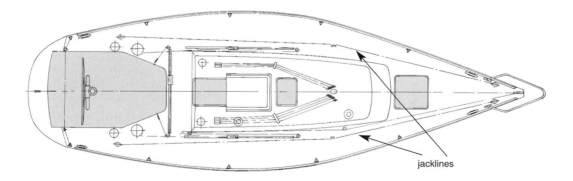

jacklines

Jacklines should run from bow to stern and end about 6 feet (1.8 m) forward of the transom. A crew should be able to clip on before leaving the cockpit and reach the mast or foredeck without unclipping.

A short tether keeps an overboard crewmember close enough to the boat to reach the rail and possibly pull him- or herself back aboard. (Photo courtesy Lirakis Harnesses)

Powerboats present a different set of circumstances. Without headsails or mainmast controls to worry about, powerboat crew members are less likely to have to go forward in heavy weather. This is an advantage because the narrow side decks and bulky pilothouse of a powerboat typically make this a precarious enterprise. And a tethered crew unfortunate enough to fall off a powerboat would stand a fair chance of being sucked into the prop or props. For this reason I don't recommend jacklines for powerboats unless one can be secured along the centerline of the boat and the harness tethers are short enough to prevent crew from falling over the side.

If you set a sea anchor from a powerboat, of course, someone's going to have to venture out on the foredeck. To minimize exposure, lay out the sea anchor and its warp in the cockpit, tether yourself to the boat, and take only the bitter end of the sea anchor warp forward. Pass this *under* the bow rail from outside in and through the chocks, so that the warp will not pass over the pulpit when paid out, then cleat the end off. Go aft again, then launch the sea anchor from the relative safety of the cockpit, perhaps while the boat jogs slowly ahead to help hold the bow up and relieve the strain. Alternatively, if you can reach the bow cleats from a foredeck hatch and the foredeck isn't being continuously swept by green water, make your way forward inside the boat and work from the relative safety of the open hatch. But again, wear a harness cleated to a strongpoint inside the boat.

Heaving Line

Another type of safety line that every sailor and powerboater should have on board is a throwing or heaving line. This line has a *monkey's fist* or loop in one end to provide extra weight when it's heaved over the side. There are also some commercially made rocket-launched safety lines on the market. If a crew goes overboard or you need to take a boat under tow, having one aboard could be a godsend. Tossing a throwing line long distances is an art that many mariners no longer possess. Practice at home on the lawn so that you will know what you are doing in an emergency. See also the discussion of Crew Overboard Modules in Chapter 9.

Handholds and Strongpoints

There should be handholds all around a boat, both inside and on deck, which can be easily used whether the boat is upright or heeled. Installing a number of strong points or pad eyes is also a good idea, since these will allow you to hook on when you are likely to be in one spot for a while.

Strobes and Spotlights

A masthead strobe light can help a rescue helicopter find you but should never be used to summon the harbor launch or to let people on shore know where you are. It is a recognized safety signal and could trigger a search and rescue (SAR) operation, which you may have to pay for unless you are in real trouble.

Spotlights can help you find a mooring at night, locate a dock or a crew overboard, and serve myriad other uses. In rescue situations a vertical spotlight beam can help a helicopter find you.

The DistresS.O.S. light from ACR Electronics could also be helpful as an alternative to a flare pack. This light sends out a Morse code SOS signal when turned on, and its beam is reputed to be visible for up to 18 miles. The battery lasts a long time and the light can be directed at a potential rescue vessel, so it is probably more effective than a flare. In my opinion, it is certainly more effective than the Coast Guard-approved flare packs offered by some manufacturers.

In my experiments with these flares, I have found that they burn quickly, drop lots of hot slag, and may not burn at all when wet. SO-LAS-approved flares are preferable, but even these can have problems. In high winds the flare may not stay airborne for long, and in low cloud conditions (as in many storms) the flare may go off in the cloud. The SOS light solves many of these problems. It is usable over a long period of time—you can aim it directly at a potential rescuer and keep it going for five or ten minutes or more—and it is unaffected by low clouds or high winds, although you might bounce the light flashes off the clouds to get more range. The only advantage of a flare is that it gets the light higher into the air for a few minutes, but if the rescuer is not looking in that direction when the flare goes off he may not see it.

Another emergency idea from ACR Electronics is the Rapid Fire PFD strobe light.

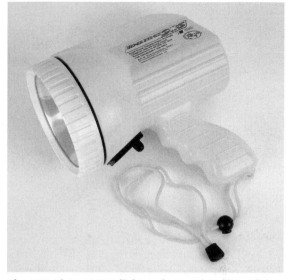

The ACR DistresS.O.S. light and several strobes of the sort that should be aboard your boat. (Photo courtesy ACR Electronics.)

With one of these pinned to your personal flotation device (PFD), you will be seen if you fall off your boat during the night. ACR makes several varieties. Just remember not to pin the strobe through an inflatable life vest! Remember, too, to ship plenty of batteries onboard for flashlights and spare bulbs for navigation lights and flashlights. We'll talk more about strobes and flares in Chapter 9.

Watertight Hatches

You *will* get green water across the deck of your boat in heavy weather, and if it is deep enough it will flood your ventilators and put your hatches under considerable pressure. Remember that hatches are often a boat's weak point in its battle with the elements. With this in mind, cut plywood boards to fit any hatch opening larger than 2 square feet (about 0.2 square meters) and devise some method of installing them. If a hatch gets blown out during a storm, you have something to fill the hole.

Speaking of offshore hatches, I have lived with many and prefer the heavy-duty type made by Goiot and by Atkins and Hoyle, although the hatch dogs tend to poke you in the kidneys when you climb past. Lewmar hatches do not have any protruding hatch fittings, which cuts down on bruises when you have to climb through them. Yet it seems that almost all hatches leak at one time or another, due less to defective construction than to imperfect mating with the boss on which they sit. Hatches need to be bolted to a perfectly flat fiberglass hatch boss in order to be leak-free, but on many production boats the bosses are not flat.

Ladders

In English sailing circles it used to be said that the three things you should never take aboard a boat are a wheelbarrow, a naval officer, and a ladder. A wheelbarrow has no use on a boat unless it is to dump tea in Boston Harbor, and a naval officer was thought to be too rigid in his thinking for the easygoing ways of a sailboat (although I have sailed with some highly competent naval officers, both active and retired). As for ladders, your boat may already have one or more on board—one in the companionway, perhaps another on the transom, or one to get

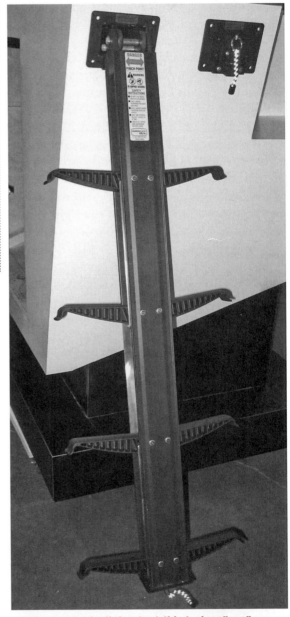

The Garelick Eez-In ladder can be up to five feet long. When stowed, all that is visible is the 6" x 6" plate on the boat's transom (left). When the pin is pulled, the ladder slides out and down to provide a quick and easy way back aboard (right).

you to your powerboat's flybridge. I for one find them extremely useful.

Unfortunately, one feature you'll rarely see near a transom ladder is a harness strong point, which is too bad. What if you have to pull an overboard crew back on deck? You will probably need both hands for lifting, and a pair of harness strong points will enable you to clip on and keep your hands free.

Strong points aside, a transom ladder should always extend deeply into the water when deployed, since quite often a crew member in the water doesn't have the arm strength to hold onto a short ladder and hoist himself aboard without a deep foothold. A fold-up ladder with rungs that extend below the waist of a person in the water makes his or her recovery much easier. Powerboaters should consider fitting an Armstrong ladder or a fold-down ladder to enable anybody in the water to get out quickly. This can be critical when the water temperature is low enough to cause the rapid onset of hypothermia (see Chapter 9). I recommend the Garelick Eez-In ladder for all powerboats. It can be stowed almost invisibly in a vessel's transom, yet a person overboard can swim around to the stern, pull the Fastpin from the stowed ladder, lower the ladder, and climb back aboard easily.

All interior ladders should have plenty of handholds on either side and should have nonskid on each tread. If there are bulkheads or overheads near the ladder, it's a good idea to fit extra handrails there as well for extra security.

A mast ladder can be helpful if you regularly sail singlehanded, but I dislike them because they put extra weight aloft, can snag sails, and are too easy to slip from in a seaway. Still, I can see that they would be very useful if you had to make a repair to a halyard sheave box or spreader while sailing shorthanded or in other such circumstances.

Inclinometer

A minor item, but one that will make it easier for you to handle your sailboat, is an inclinome-

An inclinometer can help you determine when the boat should be reefed. This one is glued to the hatch casing for visibility from the helm.

ter, available from Davis Instruments and other sources. This simple device will tell you when your boat is heeled too far, so you will know when it's time to reef. Be sure you install your inclinometer where it is easy to see from the helm position.

Nonskid

Even something as seemingly minor as the nonskid on the deck of your boat should be looked at carefully, since it can make a huge difference in heavy weather. If the deck is slippery, you can easily slide over the side. If your nonskid is losing its grip you may need to reapply it. Keep it in top shape.

There are several options for renewing nonskid. One is to buy paint with nonskid compound in it, such as Interlux's Interdeck paint. Another is to paint the deck, sprinkle a nonskid compound over the wet paint, and then apply a second layer. More specifically, you can apply a one- or two-part polyurethane paint, sprinkle it with sand or ground walnut shells or a commercial nonskid, and then apply the second coat. If you use sand, make sure it's clean—beach sand might contain salt, which will degrade the paint. Sand has two disadvantages: it can work like sandpaper on your foul-weather gear, very quickly wearing it away;

also it does not absorb paint and tends to break out of the paint layer after moderate use. For these reasons some yards prefer ground walnut shells, even though they tend to impart a brownish cast to the paint. Interlux recommends using a polymeric compound, which is clear, doesn't affect paint color, has good paint absorption, and can be used with any single- or two-part polyurethane or varnish. You can either mix it with the paint and then apply it directly, or punch holes in the top of the can and sprinkle it on a wet coat of paint or varnish.

If you use Pettit's Easypoxy (a topside and deck enamel paint) on your deck, you need to add Pettit 9900 Skidless Compound before applying it. Stir the paint often to keep the nonskid particles in suspension. Pettit recommends two coats.

Another manufacturer of nonskid paint is Trend Coatings. Its Captain's Choice Deck Grip paint is acrylic-based with white quartz, pumice, and epoxy in the formulation. You should first apply a primer over your present nonskid after scraping off any loose paint and thoroughly cleaning the surface. When the primer is dry, apply the Deck Grip using a $\frac{1}{8}$-inch nap nylon roller for best results. Make sure the paint is well stirred and apply the nonskid by working out from a center spot rather than rolling the paint in one direction and then at right angles as you normally would. To protect it from wear, apply a sealer after the paint layer is dry. Another option—one often used by boatbuilders—is to apply a layer of gelcoat with a high-nap roller. One professional painter at Jamestown Boatyard recommends the use of a $\frac{3}{16}$-inch-nap nylon roller over carefully masked-off areas when applying gelcoat, which provides a rough surface to ensure good footing even in severe conditions.

If you only have a small area to cover, you might use 3M's Safety Walk as an alternative to paint or gelcoat. This product, sold in strips $\frac{3}{4}$ inch to 6 inches wide and rolls 60 feet long,

The nonskid portions of a deck painted by the Jamestown Boatyard in Rhode Island.

comprises abrasive mineral particles bonded to a durable polymer film with a pressure-sensitive adhesive on its underside. You simply cut the desired length from the roll, peel off the protective liner, and press the strip into place. To improve the look and to prevent corners from peeling upward after a season or two of use, round off each corner before pressing the tape down. 3M Safety Walk is particularly useful on ladders, narrow steps, and Plexiglas or acrylic hatch covers that are likely to be walked on.

Two other good products are TBS (from Wichard, in Portsmouth, RI) and Treadmaster M. Both maintain their nonskid properties even when submerged. TBS looks more like sandpaper and comes in sheets of various bright colors, while Treadmaster M comes in 47- by 35-inch sheets about ⅛ inch thick. You permanently glue both materials down where you would normally paint non-skid. Treadmaster M is available in white sand, gray, teak, and sport white colors.

Preparing the Rig

What does a sailboat's rig experience in heavy weather? The mast is hammered by high winds, and the masttop accelerates violently back and forth. It may even get buried in a wave. Your primary concern is that the rig does not fail. This means that you need to make a number of careful checks during the off-season.

The Mast

In recent years, I've noticed that many boatowners leave their mast in the boat over the winter in an effort to save money. That, however, is a sure way to wear it out quickly. When pounded by a summer storm, a boat will slide sideways on its mooring or heel slightly, easing the shock of the wind on the mast. But a boat stored on stands or in a cradle cannot move, so the mast has to absorb the full force of the wind. The mast will vibrate and flex and the wind will also strain the rig and the stands supporting the boat. If your boat has overwintered with its mast stepped, take extra care to ensure that the spar is in sound shape before you head offshore.

Here are some hints for inspecting any rig, whether left in place overwinter or stored in a spar shed. There are some additional suggestions in the sidebar on page 117.

- Before launching, carefully check your entire rig, starting at the masthead, where you should make sure that the electronic wind indicator arm is firmly bolted in place and that all wiring sockets get a fresh shot of an electrical spray such as CRC to prevent corrosion. Check the masthead light, if your boat has one. It's good practice to fit a new bulb each spring, even if the old one has not yet burned out, and to spray the socket with a corrosion preventative. If you have a Windex or mechanical wind indicator, it should be properly oriented and firmly seated. (It's a good idea to carry a spare Windex, or at least spare arms, in case the one at the masthead is damaged or lost in a blow.) Make sure the yard does not damage the Windex and electronics vane when they are installing the mast.

- Examine all the halyard sheave boxes in the masthead crane, and check the blocks and their surrounding areas for signs of chafe, corrosion, or other damage. Damaged sheaves can cut halyards. If you have a three-halyard masthead crane, replace the chafing pieces on either side of the exit boxes. A low-chafe halyard box can only be fitted when a new spar is ordered, but replacing chafing pieces and end-for-ending your halyards regularly can help reduce chafe. On a long cruise, chafe needs to be watched carefully. Some skippers send a crew to the masthead every other day just to check on halyard and sail chafe.

- Carefully check the terminals of all rigging. Look for bent pins, signs of elongation around holes, cracks in swaged fittings, and loose or missing pins. Any damaged parts should be replaced immediately.

- Look, too, at *both* ends of all spreaders. The inboard ends should not be split at the weldings, as often happens when the mast works in a seaway, and there should be no signs of stress around the pins. I once went to the masthead just before a 200-mile race to align the wind instrument arm on a boat fresh from the boatyard. Checking the rig on my way down, I found that the inboard ends of both spreader tangs (the metal pieces welded to the mast to hold the spreaders in place) were cracked clear across. The damage probably came from poor handling in the boatyard. We decided to abort the race and return to the yard rather than run the risk of dismasting.

- If you have winches on the mast, they should be stripped and cleaned from time to time—ideally every year. Winches can and do get soaked by breaking seas, and salt water may combine with winch grease to form a solid mass that renders a winch inoperable.

- Before stepping the mast, inspect its base for corrosion. (Quite often, bubbling in the paint layer is the first sign of spar corrosion.)

The mast should be pulled out of the boat regularly and carefully checked before you go offshore.

- Finally, look at all mast wiring to be sure there are no breakages or poor connections. Try to ensure that no electrical connections exit the mast in the bilge, where they can easily get wet. Ideally, they should exit just under the deck.

- After the mast is in the boat, check the wedges to make sure they have been installed properly and haven't worked loose. You don't want mast wedges to drop out unexpectedly, destabilizing the spar in a seaway. Install the mast boot and cover to keep water out of the boat.

Shrouds and Stays

Shrouds and stays need to be maintained, just like the rest of the rig. Before the season starts, remove any shroud protectors and check the toggles, pins, and fittings for signs of wear, bending, cracking, or corrosion. Check the chainplate holes for signs of elongation too. Replace damaged parts as necessary. In general, chainplates and shrouds are sized to provide a safety factor about two or three times the breaking strength of the wire rigging, but that should not prevent you from replacing damaged gear.

Halyards

A worn or chafed halyard may survive years of ordinary use, but the first heavy weather will probably break it, at which point the sail it was carrying will usually blow over the side. It will need hauling back aboard by crew working in harm's way. To avoid such a risk to the crew you should perform routine maintenance on all halyards, sheets, and guys during the winter. If you opt to leave the mast in the boat for the winter, pull each halyard for complete inspection using a messenger line.

Once out of the mast, all halyards should be scrubbed and rinsed to remove salt and other contaminants. Check the halyard shackles for bent pins and damage. When ordering a new halyard, always ask for eye splices at both ends.

Spar Check

Inspect your spar while it is out of the boat so that you don't have to go aloft when the boat is afloat. Here's what to look for:

- Make sure halyards are replaced if they show signs of chafe.
- Check light fittings and replace bulbs if required. Make sure all light fittings are watertight. (Tip: paint seams with clear fingernail varnish to seal them.)
- Check all antennas at the masthead. Before the boat is launched, make sure you install and adjust the wind indicator and antennas so that you don't have to go aloft (then hope the yard doesn't mash them when they put the mast in your boat).
- Check both ends of the spreaders before the mast is installed.
- Look over all the standing rigging. Check for meat hooks, cracks in swage fittings, corrosion, and bent fittings. Replace as required.
- Check each sheave box carefully. Make sure the sheave rotates easily and that its edges are not broken or cracked. Replace a sheave if you find signs of wear.
- If you have a three- or four-halyard masthead, why not remove one halyard and run a messenger instead? A messenger is a ⅛-inch-diameter (3 mm) line that stays in the mast and can be used to feed a new halyard up through the mast should an existing halyard break. If you have to reeve a new line you will need a weight on the end, known as a mouse. You need to make sure the mouse will fit through the sheave box. (Check it while the mast is in the yard.) Until that day comes, the messenger saves weight aloft. Without one, if you ever need to rig a new halyard at sea, you will have to go aloft and reeve it externally. I've used 40-pound test fishing line as a temporary messenger, but it will abrade and fail if left in the mast for a long time. For a more permanent messenger, use nylon or Dacron line. Check all wiring in the mast. Look for abraded coverings where wiring passes through the mast.
- Beware of putting too many wires and rope halyards in your mast. Halyards can get tangled around each other inside the spar. If possible, check that screws driven into the mast cannot snag halyards inside. Cut screws short if need be.
- Check the mainsail track for loose screws, bent track, and corrosion.
- Check your roller-furling gear and make sure that everything works properly. I like to spray luff grooves with Teflon to make it easier for sails to go up and down. Wear a mask—Teflon can harm your lungs.
- Check insulators on the backstay, if fitted. Make sure they are not cracked or corroded.

That way you can easily end for end the halyard and it will last twice as long.

Sheets

At the end of each season take your sheets and guys home and wash them with warm, soapy water. Check them carefully for *herniations* (places where the inside core has erupted through the exterior cover) or abrasions (where the cover has worn away, leaving a hole). If you find damaged spots, fit a new sheet. (Note: do not use old Dacron sheets and guys as docklines—they don't stretch sufficiently to absorb shock loads. Nylon is a better choice.) Check the splices and any shackles on the lines and replace them if they are damaged.

Sheets and guys in good condition should handle heavy going without problems, but one or two sets of heavier-weight sheets and guys could also be useful. For example, if you have

½-inch (12 mm) sheets you might want to carry a pair of ¾-inch (18 mm) sheets as a backup for heavier conditions.

Preparing Engines and Mechanical Gear

On a powerboat the engines are the only source of motive power, and it behooves you to make sure they will function properly in all conditions, not just storms. Still, there are steps you can take to ensure that your engines are particularly well suited for heavy conditions.

For example, boats with twin engines should have separate fuel lines, filters, and fuel return lines for each engine, running to separate tanks. This reduces the chances that dirty fuel will contaminate both engines at the same time. By the same token, wiring the engines from separate battery banks will reduce the chances that an electrical problem will stop both engines—although builders do not often do this.

Also check that all piping leading to the engine either incorporates a flexible section or is itself made of a flexible material. All engine piping should be Coast Guard–approved and suitable for its application. High-pressure fuel line hoses connected by compression fittings to engines, filter-separators, tanks, and fuel manifolds are a better choice than soft rubber hoses connected with hose clamps. Copper tubing should not be used in conjunction with high-pressure hose, since the continual flexing to which it is subjected by engine movement and vibration will eventually work-harden and break it.

Fuel Tanks

According to the American Bureau of Shipping (ABS) and the American Boat and Yacht Council (ABYC), fuel tanks should be made of materials that resist corrosion and attack by fuel or oil. Stainless steel (preferably grade 316L or 304L), aluminized steel, aluminum, or copper are recommended. Galvanized steel and food-grade plastic (polyurethane or polyethylene) tanks can be used for fresh water but not for fuel; it will react with the zinc coating on galvanized steel and can eat through some plastics. If you are building a steel-hulled boat, you can build in a steel tank provided it is sandblasted, primed, and painted with an epoxy-based paint.

Stainless steel tanks have been used in Europe for many years and have high reliability. The manager of the Jamestown Boatyard prefers to use stainless steel for fuel tanks. "They are reliable and don't corrode as readily as aluminum," he says. "With a plastic or aluminum tank under the cabin sole, a carpenter could penetrate the tank when screwing the sole bearers down, but it is a lot more difficult to penetrate a stainless tank."

Most small powerboats use an aluminum tank, sprayed with an epoxy-based paint and often foamed in place. These tanks are usually placed in a tank well under the cockpit sole. Aluminum tanks are also used in any boat built of aluminum, but they can create an unwanted battery if you run a copper line (plumbing or wiring) through the bilge and let some water into the bilge.

Some yachts these days use molded fiberglass tanks for fuel and water. These tanks work well provided the tank is well made. However, fiberglass tanks tend to be about 30 percent heavier than aluminum. My own feeling is that fuels are solvents and should not be put in a fiberglass tank, although this material is satisfactory for water tanks.

All joints on metal tanks should be welded, and in fact, the ABYC provides its member builders with specific recommendations regarding welding methods for different tank materials. Note that stainless steel is harder to weld and more prone to weld failure than other metals. If you encounter a leak in a gasoline tank, pull the tank, discard it, and replace it with a new one. Do not attempt to reweld a leaky gas tank. The resulting bang can make your eyes water!

Check that all tanks are securely fastened. Imagine putting 200 gallons (760 L) of fuel in a tank and powering out to sea. If you hit a big wave and the tank breaks free of its mountings or tabbings, you now have more than 1,500 pounds (670 kg) of fuel plus the weight of the tank moving around in the bottom of your boat. A large tank flying across the inside of the hull can severely damage or even sink your boat. But the tank should also be removable from the interior in case it ever has to be replaced.

Smaller outboard craft may have plastic tanks that sit in the cockpit. If your boat has this type of tank, make sure it is fastened down with straps and is Coast Guard–approved. A 50-gallon (190 L) tank can weigh more than 300 pounds (136 kg) when filled, and you don't want it moving around in the boat.

If you have tanks to port and starboard they will probably be linked with a crossover pipe to allow the transfer of fuel. Check that this pipe has a working shut-off valve. On a powerboat with separate fuel lines from each tank, the crossover line would normally stay closed, to be opened only if one tank runs out of fuel. Keeping a crossover line closed is especially important on a sailboat to prevent fuel from draining to the lower tank when the boat is heeled.

The fuel fill cap should be clearly marked with the type of fuel—gasoline or diesel—and you should use different-sized fittings on the fuel and freshwater caps so the two cannot be inadvertently swapped. There should be a coarse fuel filter in the fill line to prevent large particles from reaching the tank, and all fuel fills should seal tightly to keep out water. Ideally, the area immediately around the tank fill should be raised an inch or so above the surrounding deck level. That way a minor water spill cannot find its way into the fuel opening.

Filters

Carry multiple spare filters for all your systems. As mentioned earlier, the shaking a boat is subjected to during heavy weather can stir up fuel and move sediment from the bottom of the tank. When filling tanks from an unknown source, use a filter funnel to help prevent dirt from getting into the tanks. It may be a little slower, but it's good insurance.

Bilge Pumps

No matter how well you prepare your boat, water will find its way below in heavy weather. Typically, both cruising sailboats and powerboats are equipped with a high-output engine-driven bilge pump for emergencies and an automatic battery-operated pump of lesser capacity—often activated by a float switch—to keep the bilge dry when nobody is aboard. Engine-operated pumps move a lot of water as long as the engine is running, and battery-operated pumps save labor as long as there's life in the battery. Ocean-racing sailboats are required to carry two hand-operated bilge pumps, and any prudent seaman will want to have at least one hand-operated backup pump as well as a big bucket or two when all else fails. Ideally you should mount the largest possible manual pump in the cockpit with its pick-up hose in the bilge. An Edson Bone Dry 30 gallon-per-minute (109 L) or a Whale 10 pump is ideal for this application. In an emergency it puts the user in the cockpit, not belowdecks where flooding might make the pump hard to reach. On a powerboat, a large Edson or Whale pump can be mounted in the wheelhouse or anywhere accessible from deck.

Your automatic bilge pump should be wired directly to the battery rather than through the battery isolation switch. The latter arrangement will deactivate the pump if you turn off the battery isolation switch before leaving the boat at its dock or mooring.

Fuel: Keeping it Clean

Sediment stirred up in fuel tanks by heavy weather will clog the fuel filters, starving the engine or engines of fuel just when it's needed most. This is one of the most common sources of engine failure in both powerboats and auxiliary sailboats. Start the season right by cleaning your fuel tanks.

The first step is to make sure that all tanks are fully drained. Pour the drained fuel into an appropriate container so you can either reuse it or dispose of it properly. When the tanks are empty, unbolt the inspection plates on the top (if there are any) and use a flashlight to inspect the insides thoroughly. Ideally, the inspection plates will be large enough to permit this. If not you may have to remove the fuel gauge and plate and peer in through that opening. When removing inspection plates, check their gaskets and replace any that show signs of deterioration. The tank should have internal baffles to prevent fuel from sloshing around, so you might not be able to inspect the entire tank without removing other covers.

Aluminum tanks can corrode, especially those that are foamed in place. The foam attaches to the tank and prevents the aluminum from oxidizing as it should do to seal any corrosion that may start when the tank is scratched on installation. If the tank doesn't have inspection plates, you may have to get it pressure tested. This can be done on-site, or you can pull the tank from the boat and take it to a testing location. Make sure the tester does not overpressurize the tank, since this can distort it.

On the outside, look for flaking paint, corrosion, and leaks (as indicated by a drip line down the side of the tank). Make sure all pipes exit the top of the tank, since lines coming out of the bottom will allow fuel to drain into the bilge if they ever break. Each line should have a shut-

off valve with which to close it off should it break. Inspect the vent line or breather pipe that should exit the top of the tank, and make sure it goes all the way to the highest point of the deck. Breather pipes that terminate on or below the rail often get submerged as the boat rolls.

Having inspected the tank, clean any sludge out of the bottom by having a hazardous waste truck suck it out. Do not use your shop vac to remove sludge! A spark can ignite the fuel vapor. A person in my town did that and burned his garage and house down. If you don't clean the dirt out, it may eventually find its way into the fuel filters. Put the inspection plates and new gaskets back on the tank. It is a good idea to use a torque wrench to get equal tension on every bolt, but many people don't bother. If you kept your old fuel, run it through a filter to make sure it is clean before putting it back in the tank. Add biocides to diesel tanks if desired. Often, after a winter onshore, a diesel tank will get condensation in its fuel. The water allows algae to grow and needs to be removed before the fuel is burned in the engine. Adding a biocide kills the algae, and a fuel-water separator filter removes the water before it can reach the engine.

On a diesel system, bleed the fuel lines all the way to the engine injectors and make sure they are clean. Then clean the filters and insert new elements according to the manufacturer's instructions. When the boat is back in the water, run the engine to draw clean fuel through the system and to make sure there are no airlocks.

In modern gasoline systems, the fuel lasts about six weeks before it breaks down. If you are going to leave your fuel for a long time, add a stabilizer. If you don't, you'll find water in the fuel tank, which will require a fuel/water separator and filter between the tank and engine.

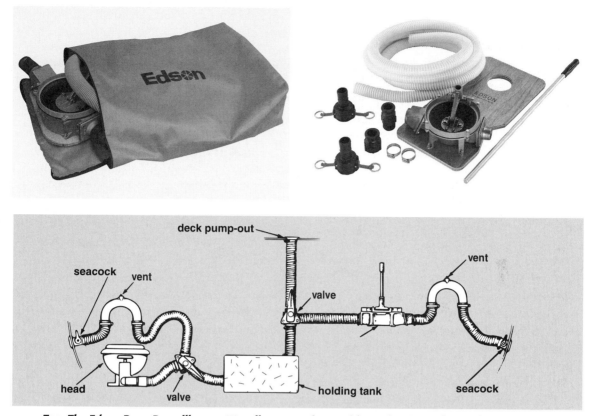

Top: The Edson Bone Dry will pump 30 gallons per minute without clogging. A pump like this should be aboard installed in the cockpit of every boat that intends to go out of sight of land. Above: An Edson manual pump installed in an overboard discharge—not for use in inshore waters.

The main reason pumps stop working is that their pick-up hoses become clogged by junk in the bilge, so when buying a new boat, your first job should be to vacuum up any residual wood shavings or other garbage. Even then, expect the strainer to clog eventually, and have a plan for unclogging it.

Preparing the Electrical System

The electrical system is one of the most important parts of the boat and the one most likely to go wrong, especially in severe weather. Heat, vibration, heeling, and the jolts caused by big seas all cause wear and tear, and drips and splashes of salt water cause corrosion and even shorts. Only by taking particular care of your boat's electrical system can you be reasonably sure it will not fail.

Batteries

Your batteries should be bolted down to the battery tray and the tray tightly fastened to a foundation. Under no circumstances should a battery be able to move. If it moves the terminals could touch metal, short the battery, and cause a fire. If it falls out of its rack, you could find yourself with 60–100 pounds of live battery flying around the engine compartment. If the battery breaks it will spew acid all over the place. Check your battery bank installation carefully.

This breaker panel can handle 12 to 20 volts DC or AC and is available from Blue Sea Systems. (Photo courtesy Blue Sea Systems)

Breakers

Fortunately, breakers do not often go wrong. They can corrode, however, and the wires to which they are attached can also corrode and break behind the breaker panel. The panel should therefore be mounted in a comparatively dry location where there is easy access to its rear. Inspect the back of the panel in the off-season to make sure no corrosion has started, and make sure all the breakers are correctly sized for the loads on their circuits. I have tried many electrical systems, and I find Blue Sea Systems equipment far superior to anything else.

Wiring and Fixtures

Boat wiring should be installed in conduits to protect it from chafe, to enable broken wires to be changed, and to allow new wires to be run when new gear is added. Wiring should also be color coded according to ABYC recommendations, so that an electrician in a distant port can follow the wiring scheme without spending an inordinate amount of time finding out where all the wires are supposed to go. Although still a matter of debate, the growing consensus is that boat wires should never be soldered, since soldering creates a hard spot and typically a wire will break immediately next to the soldered portion. Instead, use U- or O-shaped terminals crimped onto the wire to ensure that cable ends

are held properly. You can cover the joint with heat shrink tubing, though most electricians don't bother. If you happen to remove the cabin overhead or any joinery at any time, check the wiring behind to make sure the cables are not being chafed or that a screw has not been driven through them.

Spare Navigation Lights

Not only should you carry back-up navigation lights, you should also carry spare batteries for them. On one long ocean passage my crew rigged back-up navigation lights after our primaries got wet and failed. Four days later the ship's batteries also failed, which meant resorting to some rather creative methods to keep a red and green bow light working. (Hint: A red or green rag or plastic film over a powerful flashlight works wonders.)

One handy way to supplement navigation lights is with chemical light sticks. My kids love them, and on a long cruise these lights can keep them occupied for a long time. They come in various sizes and several colors, including fluorescent green and a pinkish red for use as emergency navigation lights (although I would explore every other possibility before using them for this purpose). Larger sizes can illuminate the cockpit for an eerie dinner or serve as emergency belowdeck lighting. Smaller sizes are great for attracting fish at night. The kids put them in the freezer to prolong their life, and when warmed the sticks emit just as much light as before they were frozen. Chemical light sticks are available from a variety of sources and come in many shapes. Some have hooks or attached elastic bands, or you can duct tape them to virtually anything.

Extra Lighting

In heavy weather it might be difficult to charge your batteries. The engine may not start or run properly because of an extreme heel angle or filters clogged by dirty fuel. As a result, your onboard lighting may be weak or nonexistent if you rely solely on battery power. Some offshore sailors use bulkhead-mounted oil- or kerosene-fired lanterns in such circumstances, as well as waterproof back-up battery-powered navigation lights with extra batteries, as mentioned above. Smart sailors also keep a supply of flashlights and extra batteries so that every crew on deck has a waterproof light with a lanyard tied to his or her jacket or belt. If anybody falls overboard, the flashlight can be used to guide rescuers, in addition to the strobe light on the crew's life vest.

Preparations Inside the Boat

You may not think there is much you can do to improve your boat's accommodations for heavy weather. But most production boats are built to a certain price point, and as a result you can easily make improvements that make a huge difference to your comfort offshore. For example, if your varnished cabin sole turns slippery as soon as it gets wet, why not use another sole treatment altogether or add some nonskid grit to the varnish to provide your crew with better footing? While you're at it, why not treat your companionway steps to make them safer as well? There is a new product called Ultimate Gloss, manufactured by Ultimate Products, Inc., which gives you the best of both worlds. This varnish gives a high-gloss nonskid sole when it is applied correctly.

Handholds

Walk through your boat when it is upright and when it is heeled, paying attention to where you most commonly grab—or would like to grab—for handholds. You might want to fit additional handholds where there are none. You can also cut handholds in the corners of fiddles provided

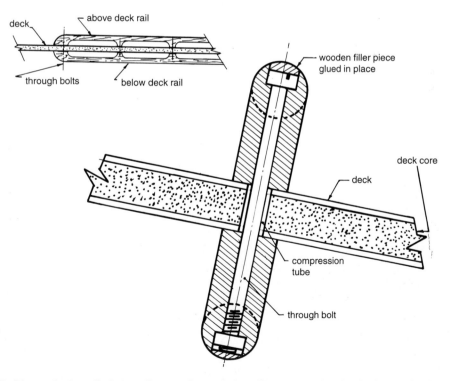

Handholds can be installed virtually anywhere. By installing one under the deck and another above the deck, unsightly nuts and bolts can be hidden in the wood and covered with a bung.

123

they are strong enough to restrain a person's weight. Check that items such as the saloon table are firmly bolted down if you decide to add a handhold to it or if you find that you lean against it as you walk through the boat. Handholds can be installed on the overhead as well, but you will have to bolt them through the deck to make sure they are secure. If you do this, you might want to add a rail on deck as well to hide and anchor the fasteners.

Even below decks, hooking on a harness is not a bad idea and can prevent you from falling in rough seas. In particular, you might want to put a strong point or two in the area above the galley to give the cook somewhere to hook onto.

Bunks

While you can't do much about the size of a bunk once you own a boat, you can fit leecloths to each bunk to make the occupants more secure and ensure that they won't fall out in any weather. I've found that the best leecloth installations are screwed to the plywood bunk flat about half or three-quarters of the way out from the inboard edge. This enables you to tighten or loosen the leecloth to suit the boat's heel angle, and also prevents the edge of the bunk from catching you in the small of the back when you are trying to rest. The outer side of the leecloth is best attached to padeyes through bolted to bulkheads. I prefer to see padeyes located around four feet above the bunk flat. If they are higher, it may be hard to get in and out of the bunk when the leecloth is tied up. Four feet is about the limit that a sleeper can reach to pull on the bitter end of the slip knot holding the leecloth in place.

Whatever you do, don't rely on barrel-bolts and wooden leeboards to hold you in place in severe weather. I have seen barrel-bolt screws tear out of the wood and the entire bunk board collapse when a crewman was thrown against it from *inside* the bunk. The crash was so spectacular that the individual involved would sleep only on the leeward side of the boat from then on.

Another idea for heavy weather is to lay waterproof material over bunks so that your crew can sleep on them without removing their foul weather gear. In storm conditions you never know if you will be needed on deck in a hurry, so many sailors turn in fully dressed. When the storm ends, the last thing you want is to climb into a sodden bunk (although there's a good chance you will be so exhausted by that point that it won't really matter).

You should also put waterproof materials over any bunk under a hatch or dorade vent in heavy weather. Water will penetrate the best hatches and dorades.

Fans Below Deck

It may seem like a minor detail, but if you get caught in a storm in a warm body of water like the Gulf Stream, you may be in 80–85°F (27–29°C) water with the hatches battened down and the vents closed off to keep out the

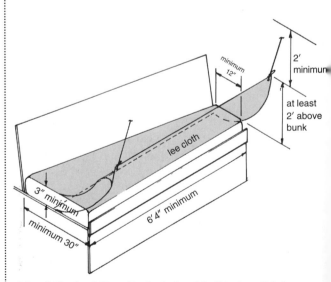

A leecloth should be attached about half to two-thirds of the way under the bunk to allow the mattress to be tilted slightly when the boat is heeled. This also helps to stop furniture from jabbing the bunk occupant in the back when he or she is asleep.

green water that is breaking over the deck. In these conditions the below-deck area will soon become stifling hot if you don't have one or two fans to help alleviate the heat.

I was once caught in this very situation en route to Bermuda and found that fans were essential to keep air moving below. Aboard powerboats, fans or even air conditioning can be kept running continuously as long as the engine is running. Aboard sailboats, fans should be selected to draw as little power as possible, and the engine must be run periodically to keep the batteries charged.

Galley Safety Features

In many ways the galley is the most dangerous place on a boat. Falling knives, scalding food or liquid, and glasses and dishes that can break into shards are among the hazards to be found there. In fact, if you were to list all the misadventures that can happen to you in the galley, you might never set foot there. So what can you do to retrofit a galley and make it safe?

Stoves

I once watched in horror as a cook opened an oven door while the entire gimballed stove tipped forward, sending two pots filled with hot liquids sliding toward her head. Fortunately she leapt aside just in time to avoid one pot and managed to grab the other, which was filled with hot soup, just before it toppled from the stove. It was a virtuoso performance, but she was lucky too.

The motion offshore is almost incessant, so all galley stoves should have clamps on the top to anchor pots and pans, as well as locking *and* damping mechanisms on their gimbals. Use the locking mechanism when the boat is in port to prevent the stove from swinging. Use the damping mechanism at sea when you bend down to open the oven door so that it will not tip forward. Stove swivels should also be constructed so that the stove is totally captive and

cannot jump out of them. Force Ten makes a stove that does not tip forward as the door is opened. In my opinion this is a feature that every stove should have, even though it is a little more expensive. Ideally, a stove should not be able to swivel much more than 35 degrees to either side of vertical.

Another time, I had just come off watch and was removing my foul weather gear when there was a small explosion in the galley. It turned out that while I had been on watch a crewman had made a cup of tea, forgotten to turn off the gas valve at the stove, and then left the burner valve slightly open. The resulting propane leak had accumulated in the stove and ignited when the cook lit the oven. The fire burned the galley bulkhead and was only put out because two fire extinguishers had been stowed next to the galley. (The U.S. Coast Guard requires fire extinguishers aboard boats.)

Liquefied petroleum gas (LPG, or simply propane) is the most popular stove fuel and is found on most boats. Unlike the gas you may use at home, which is compressed natural gas (CNG), propane is heavier than air and will pool in a bilge space or stove cavity where it can be ignited explosively by a spark. The propane

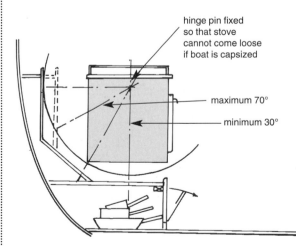

hinge pin fixed
so that stove
cannot come loose
if boat is capsized

maximum 70°

minimum 30°

The galley stove on a sailboat should swing through 70 degrees or so, and should be fastened at the gimbals so it cannot jump out should the boat invert.

tank or tanks should be installed in a self-contained locker that is sealed off from the rest of the boat and vented to an overboard scupper (above the waterline) so that any leaked propane drains harmlessly away. The gas line from the tank(s) to the stove should be installed according to ABYC specifications and should be well clear of stove edges so as not to catch or chafe. There should be a solenoid shut-off valve control next to the stove, and it should be used to shut off the gas line *anytime the stove is not in use*, not just when the crew leaves the boat. If the boat gets into a storm, the movement of the stove could become violent to the point of damaging or even breaking a gas line and allowing propane into the boat. Being blown out of your boat in a storm will not do anything for your peace of mind.

Install a waist-level bar in front of the stove to prevent the cook and crew from falling against the burners in a seaway, if one is not already fitted. The ideal galley provides standing room and a strap to one side of the stove that the cook can use to stay near the stove but also use to pull himself out of the line of spilled hot liquids. In heavy weather, I recommend that the cook wear foul weather gear (for protection from scalding liquids) along with a harness in the galley, although the well-prepared cook should not need to be cooking in a storm.

Stowage in the Galley

I have forgotten how many sailing magazine articles I've seen showing how to build a nice knife rack in a corner of the galley. This seems to me like pure lunacy. If the boat is knocked on her beam ends those knives will fly around the interior like a circus act gone berserk. Unless you can guarantee that a boat will never heel more than 20 degrees, knife racks are dangerous. If you really must have one, adapt your knives so that they cannot come free when the boat is under sail. Otherwise, keep knives in a drawer.

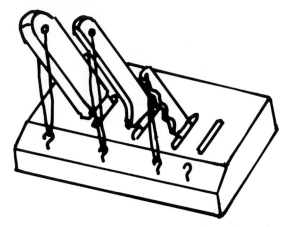

Keep knives constrained with a loop of line through the handle that is hooked when the knife is not in use. If the boat is tossed off a wave, the knives cannot come loose and fly across the cabin.

It's a good idea to stow dishes in racks so they won't become deadly projectiles in a seaway. Cups, for example, should be stowed not on hooks but in a secure rack or holder of their own. The same goes for anything else that isn't nailed down or is easily smashed.

Locker doors should be equipped with a mechanical locking device, since magnetic catches may fly open if a heavy can or dish bangs against them. As the airlines say, be wary when opening lockers after a bumpy passage—some gear may have shifted and could fall on you.

While you are inspecting the galley for loose gear, don't forget the icebox lid. In storm conditions, there should be some way of fastening it, both open and closed.

Heavy items such as canned foods should be stowed as low as possible. A large can falling from a head-high locker can give you a nasty bruise or even a concussion. If you stow canned goods in the bilge, remove the labels and write each can's contents on the top with a waterproof marker pen. This prevents labels peeling off and clogging the bilge pump. It also enables you to see what each can contains without having to

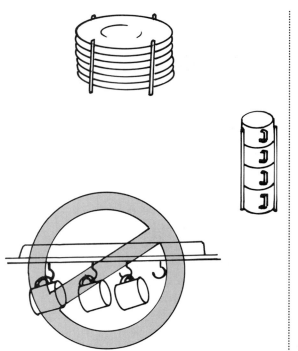

If your boat does not already have them, fit racks for plates and cups to stop them from banging and bouncing around in rough weather.

lift it away from its neighbors. If a can is likely to be stored for a long time, dip it in old varnish to stop rust.

Nonskid

The galley sole should have a nonskid floor—either a removable mat, or a nonskid mat or coating fixed in place. Leftover scraps of sole nonskid mat can be cut to fit countertops. The nonskid materials I recommend are TBS from Wichard, Inc., in Portsmouth, Rhode Island, or Treadmaster M from Simpson-Lawrence in Bradenton, Florida. In a pinch, spread a damp towel on the cabin sole.

The Head Compartment

In a storm, no one should try to relieve themselves over the transom. Instead, fit a kneeler (like a prie-dieu in church) in the head so male crew can kneel down for quick relief. You can also install a safety strap for heavy-weather use by toilet sitters. It should be bolted to the sole, not the toilet seat. Try to imagine yourself bouncing around a cramped head compartment with a broken toilet seat strapped to your rear end, and you'll understand why I say this! Fit handholds in strategic locations around the head compartment.

The head should also face across the boat or fore and aft, not at an angle to the vessel's centerline. It is easier to brace yourself if you have a bulkhead to lean against.

Seacocks

Although there is not much you can do about the number of seacock fittings in your boat without incurring a major expense, you can make sure that they all work properly and are secure. First, check that every hose connection is secured with two hose clamps (jubilee clips) and that both clamps are made of stainless steel with stainless screws. *Never* fit nickel-plated clamps or clamps with nickel-plated screws. They will eventually rust.

Then check that each seacock works properly by opening and closing it, and make sure you can reach it easily. Obtain a selection of tapered wooden bungs and tie one—of an appropriate size—next to each seacock. Should the fitting let go, you can hammer the bung into the hole. At the end of every season, after the boat has been hauled, check every seacock for wear and corrosion, and in a storm, be sure to close any seacock that isn't absolutely needed. The accelerated motions of sailing in heavy seas are sometimes enough to break a marginal fitting or cause the hose to let go.

I prefer bronze seacocks and would use only them if I were fitting out a boat for a transocean trip.

Miscellaneous Equipment

A number of everyday items can come in handy at sea during a heavy blow. These can range from plastic bags to duct tape and from vacuum flasks to a cold pack. Here are some ideas.

Plastic Bags

Stow your clothes in various-sized Ziploc-style bags before a storm hits. Squeeze all the air out and tie the bags off tightly. When the storm is over you will have dry clothes, fully creased and ready to wear.

Duct Tape

One of the most useful items for preparing to weather a storm is several rolls of real duct tape (not the fake stuff that tears every few inches). Use it to seal holes and locker doors, to hold down ropes or lines, and even to hold caps or clothes in place. I have used it for emergency sail repairs, to hold chafing rags in place, to cover sharp corners, and to seal out water from the tops of my seaboots. Duct tape can leave a sticky residue that soon gets dirty, however, so you'll need a solvent to clean the residue after the weather has abated.

Vacuum Flasks

It is difficult to heat water when a storm is raging, so the smart cook will fill a couple of vacuum flasks ahead of time with coffee and hot soup. Nothing is quite so satisfying as coming off watch to a hot drink. Typically, vacuum flasks will keep liquids hot for about eight to ten hours.

Cold Packs

You can use a cold pack to keep food and drinks cold when it is too difficult to run the engine or compressor. You can also apply them to bruises or sprains on crew members.

Plastic Boxes and Cartons

Small plastic boxes, such as those made by Tupperware, are extremely useful on a boat. In the galley a cook can stow sandwiches, sliced vegetables, meats, and other foods in a plastic box for use later, when it might be impossible to work in the galley. A plastic container can also be used to keep flashlight, radio, and GPS batteries dry in the navigation area or to keep spare rolls of toilet paper dry in the head. When putting gear in a plastic box write an inventory on masking tape and stick it on the lid so its contents will be easy to identify.

Pressure-Sensitive Adhesive tape

Single-handed sailor and Caribbean 1500 organizer Steve Black recommends that you carry a roll of pressure-sensitive adhesive tape whenever going offshore. "You can use it for repairing sails, but also for a lot of other things," he says. "It will repair ripped foul weather gear, cover a crack in the deck or in a hatch, hold wiring in place, and has lots of other uses."

Tools

Black also recommends that every boat, whether it goes offshore or not, carry a good set of tools, a few snatch blocks, and an extra sheet or two. "Buy tools suitable for the gear onboard your boat. That might mean buying a single wrench or an adjustable rather than a complete set of wrenches, to keep the weight down."

You want tools that will not corrode into a pile of rust as soon as you set sail. This may mean chrome-vanadium, stainless steel, or nickel-chrome tools instead of the standard forged steel varieties. Cutting tools, however, should be of carbon steel to keep a good edge. Spray tools with Corrosion Block or Bullfrog to prevent corrosion. You might also want to store them in a watertight Ziploc-style bag or in Tupperware containers to help prevent rust.

Nuts, Bolts, and Cotter Pins

So often in my experience the repair of a crucial part has been stymied by the lack of a simple fastener. During one race the tiller extension pulled out of the tiller. A quarter-inch nut and spring washer would have solved the problem, but we didn't have either aboard. We could no longer use the tiller extension, so the helmsman had to sit inboard, affecting our performance. These days I always ship a box of nuts and bolts—not just any old nuts and bolts, but those that are commonly used on the boat on which I'm sailing. For inshore work you need replacement fasteners only for essential parts, but offshore the more the better, although you can often cannibalize additional fasteners from other parts.

You should have a small box with cotter pins and split-rings that suits cotter holes for every part of the rig. Rigs have been known to collapse because a cotter pin dropped out, the turnbuckle (or bottlescrew in UK) unwound and the shroud let go. A check and replacement of any worn pins will give you peace of mind.

Emergency Water

A small supply of emergency potable water is another good idea, in case your boat's tanks get contaminated. Indeed, this is a requirement for boats in the Bermuda Race. You can either buy water bottles from a marine supply company and pay an arm and a leg, or go to the local supermarket and buy several gallon jugs for about a dollar each.

Engine Spares

When traveling inshore you will want to carry a couple of quarts of engine oil, a spare engine belt or two, a spare set of water hoses, a spare engine cooling water pump impeller, and a spare spark plug or injector. Learn how to install all these parts. For offshore passages, a full engine spares kit, hoses, oil, hose clamps, and a full set of belts should be aboard.

Emergency Repair Gear

You should carry enough materials to make repairs at sea, particularly those repairs that might be essential to the survival of your boat. One useful piece of gear is a Syntho-Glass kit. This is basically the same material doctors use to set a broken arm. It hardens quickly and can be used to repair cracks in fiberglass casings, to repair antenna housings, and for many other small jobs. As an alternative to the expensive marine-store Syntho-Glass, buy virtually the identical product at a local pharmacy.

If you regularly wander through waters where deadheads, unmarked rocks, shipping containers, or other hazards lurk, you might want to carry a Navirex Emergency Hull Repair kit from Perimeter Industries, which allows you to seal a 5- by 10-inch hole in the hull in less than 3 minutes while the boat is underway. You do this by pouring a two-part catalyzing mixture onto a sponge, stuffing the sponge into the hole, and holding it in place (while wearing the glove provided with the kit) until the mixture expands and sets up hard to stop the inrush of water. (Don't get your fingers stuck in the hole when the mixture expands or you might become a permanent part of the boat.) That, at least, is the theory. I have been trying to get my editor to loan me his boat so that I can put a hole in it and test this kit, but he seems reluctant.

Epoxies such as Goudgeon's Emergency Epoxy and Sea Fit's equivalent product are great to have in your repair kit but are rarely

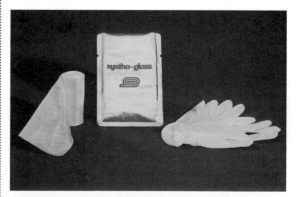

A Syntho-Glass pack showing gloves, hardener, and foam sponge (in liner). This kit is available from Landfall Navigation for about $20.

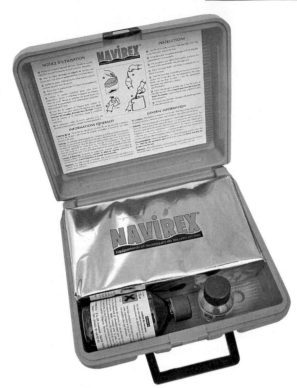

The Navirex Emergency Hull Repair kit. (Photo courtesy Perimeter Industries)

useful inshore, where you can effect your repairs back at the dock. On the other hand, it's not a bad idea to carry some underwater-setting stick epoxy, which works well for repairing a crack in the hull or deck and sets up fairly quickly.

Radar Reflectors

By now most of us have heard about stealth technology of the kind used on the F-117 fighter jet, the B2 bomber, and many newer warships. One major element of stealth technology is sloping the ship's sides and superstructure to reduce radar reflections. Another is the increased use of fiberglass and plastic materials that are nonreflective to radar.

Now think about your boat. It is probably made of fiberglass, has sloped sides, and if it's a sailboat, a thin metal mast that is at an angle to any radar beam whenever the boat is heeled. Sounds like a good stealth vehicle to me. Unfortunately, unless you are James Bond or a U.S. Navy Seal, a stealth vehicle on the water is the last thing you want. What you *do* want is something to tell big ships you are there, by regularly returning a large radar echo.

One byproduct of an ever-increasing reliance on electronic navigational aids is that less and less time is devoted to watchkeeping on the bridges of large ships. Indeed, the annals of cruising are filled with stories of close calls in which not only was no one keeping a lookout on the bridge of a ship, but no one was even paying enough attention to respond to a radio call. The expanding reliance on radar collision avoidance systems or automatic radar plotting aids (ARPA) to prevent ship collisions is not good news for recreational boaters. The best defense is a highly efficient radar reflector.

Before we get into the specifics of radar reflectors, it helps to understand how radar operates and how it detects a target. Most small-boat radars work on X-band with an operational frequency of about 9 GHz—not the best frequency for penetrating rain or differentiating wave clutter from true targets. S-band radar, on the other hand, operates around 3 GHz and can penetrate rain to give a clearer picture of the ocean. The problem with S-band radar is that it has difficulty detecting small or closely spaced targets. Typically, a large ship uses both types of radar—S-band in the open ocean and X-band nearer shorelines.

In order to return a strong "echo," a radar reflector needs to be "painted" or "hit" by the radar beam and to return some of the energy of the beam back to the radar set, where it can be detected by the receiver. Unfortunately, by the time a radar beam has hit a boat's radar reflector and bounced back to its point of origin, it has been degraded to as little as a fourth power of its transmitted magnitude. This tells you that your radar reflector needs to be extraordinarily efficient for its return to be seen by a large ship.

According to the International Maritime Organization (IMO), a ship's radar reflector should give a return comparable to a 10-square-meter (108-square-foot) beam for X-band radar. Small vessels need not adhere to the IMO standard, but it has been found that a small boat needs to reflect a minimum *radar cross section* (RCS) of around 22 to 27 square feet (2–2.5 square meters) to emerge from the background clutter on a ship's radar screen. Most boats won't come anywhere near meeting this standard without a radar reflector.

The leading radar reflectors come in a few styles, of which octahedral or trihedral reflectors (those metallic spheres made of interlocking plates that you see hanging in rigging or mounted on pilothouse staffs) are the most common. More on these below. Alternatively, the reflecting surfaces are bundled inside a smooth, cylindrical, plastic shell that will not chafe sails or snag rigging (see the description of the Firdell Blipper below). Another style of reflector employs lenses to focus an incoming radar signal into a strongly concentrated return.

All too often a radar reflector is installed on brackets mounted on the mast. For many reasons, however—the most obvious being that the mast prevents much of the radar signal from reaching the reflector—this is the worst possible location. Better to suspend it in a sailboat's rigging or install it atop a short mast on a powerboat's pilothouse roof.

A more active way to ensure that you show up on another vessel's radar screen is with a radar transponder, which transmits an amplified return or its own signal when it detects an incoming radar beam. A transponder (see Active Radar Enhancer below) makes you look like a large ship to other vessels, but many big ship captains don't like transponders for precisely that reason: their radar screens can be cluttered with "large vessels" when their eyes tell them they are surrounded by pleasure craft.

Octahedral or Trihedral Radar Reflectors

I was once aboard a yacht that was almost run down by a freighter in thick fog despite the big (18-inch-diameter, 45 cm) intersecting-plane reflector we were flying from a spreader (12 inches, 30 cm, is a more usual diameter). When we contacted the freighter by VHF radio, the watch officer told us that, despite our large reflector, he had been unable to make out our echo against the background clutter.

Octahedral or trihedral radar reflectors (sometimes known as corner reflectors) are designed to bounce an incoming signal off the flat, intersecting plates of which they are constructed. But while this sounds great in theory, in practice it leaves a lot to be desired. Most octahedral radar reflectors only reflect signals back to the sender about 20–30 percent of the time, and whether or

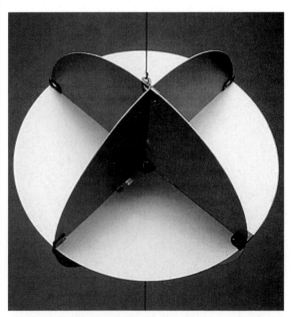

The Echomaster octahedral radar reflector from Davis Instruments. Consider hanging two in the rigging to increase your chances of being seen in fog. (Photo courtesy Davis Instruments)

not a signal is reflected depends on the angle at which the signal strikes the reflector. While an echo might show up on the radarscope during one revolution of the transmitter, it might not show up on the next. Furthermore, the signal may be so weak that a radar operator might not be able to distinguish it from clutter like breaking waves, birds, fishing gear, and so on. In general, it takes a "hit" on three consecutive revolutions to set off the alarm with which most radars are equipped. To be reasonably certain of detection, therefore, you might want to hang a pair of big reflectors in the rigging.

The Blipper

The Firdell Blipper weighs less than 4 pounds (1.8 kg) and is only 20 inches (50 cm) long but is purported to present a radar echo area of 20 square feet (6 square meters). According to the manufacturer it comprises a series of small trihedral cones in a stacked array and can be seen even at 30 degrees of heel, although results from other trihedral cone trials appear to dispute that claim. As with all reflectors, mounting the Blipper on a mast will mask its reflection through at least 90 degrees.

Lensed Radar Reflectors

The Cyclops line of radar reflectors comes with two dielectric lenses made from an advanced polymer in a Luran casing. Two parabolic reflectors focus an incoming signal onto the lenses, which concentrate the signal and reflect it back to its source. According to the manufacturer, the signal from the Cyclops 3, the company's largest reflector, has two peaks that present a 10.5-square-meter (34-square-foot) radar cross section (RCS). The smallest, the Cyclops 1, reflects two peaks equaling a 4-square-meter (13-square-foot) RCS and is suitable for a small, inshore boat. The Cyclops gives its best results from a masthead mount, to avoid a mast shadow.

The Firdell Blipper radar reflector. Do not mount the reflector next to a mast—it will carve a null sector of at least 90 degrees from the reflector's return signal. (Photo courtesy Firdell)

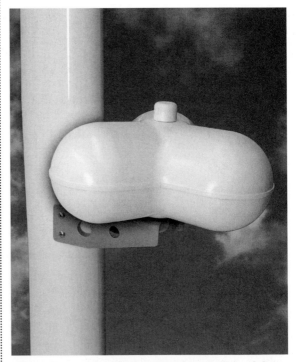

The Tri-lens radar reflector uses the principle of the Luneberg lens to increase radar visibility.

At 18.5 pounds (8.3 kg) the Cyclops 3 is somewhat heavy for suspending from a spreader. The Cyclops 2 weighs 10.5 pounds (4.6 kg), and the Cyclops 1 weighs 6 pounds (3 kg).

The Tri-lens reflector uses three globular layers, rather like the layers of an onion skin, to refract an incoming signal to a point on the opposite side of the globe. (This is the Luneberg lens principle, for those who care.) A reflective material at the opposition point then sends the signal back to the radar transmitter. The three concentric layers of the Tri-lens reflector reduce dead spots and enhance visibility.

The Active Radar Enhancer

This product from Ocean Sentry in England includes a control panel that provides an audible and visual warning that your boat is being painted by radar. Rather than just reflect a radar signal, however, the Active Radar Enhancer (ARE) amplifies an X-band radar pulse and transmits it back on the same frequency at an increased signal strength. The ARE works at a heel angle of up to 12 degrees and provides 360-degree coverage. It weighs 3.5 pounds (1.1 kg) and should be used on or near the masthead for best results. Typically it has a range of 12 miles, although the higher it is mounted, the better it will work. The unit operates on standby mode until it is hit by radar, then it "wakes up," sends its signal, and returns to standby. Its only real problem is one of clutter. If every vessel in a harbor had an ARE fitted to its mast or tuna tower, large ship radar screens would be filled with returns from smaller boats.

Radar Detectors

There are a few products on the market that sense an incoming radar beam and generate an alert to warn the people onboard that a ship is nearby. The C.A.R.D. (Collision Avoidance Radar Detector), for example, sets off an alarm when it is painted with a radar signal and indicates the direction from which the signal is coming. It can detect a signal from up to 8 miles away. This is a good idea for a solo sailor because it warns you of shipping while there is still time to take action.

Choose a radar reflector that will provide a sufficient margin of safety for your boat and circumstances. If you sail in areas where heavy fogs are frequent, such as Georges Bank, you should have the best reflector you can buy and one or two back-ups. In areas that see occasional fog, a Cyclops or Lensref would work well. In areas where large numbers of ships operate, your best bet is not to rely solely on a radar reflector, but to use your own radar, sound your foghorn, keep a constant watch, and monitor and use your VHF radio to let others know you're in the area.

You need a radar reflector that will make you visible to a large ship at a distance of at least six miles, since it can take that long for a large vessel to turn or make other collision avoidance maneuvers. But beware of relying on your reflector when the boat is sailing at high angles of heel; even the most efficient reflector will suffer some degradation of the return signal in these conditions. And no matter what kind of reflector you use, in thick fog it is still wise to use your ears and eyes, stop the engines to listen occasionally, and proceed at a speed that allows you to stop within half the range of your visibility.

Final Thoughts

There is always one more piece of gear you can put aboard your boat to cover some conceivable emergency. Use common sense. If you are unlikely to be aboard the boat at sea overnight, you don't need to include more than one or two nights' worth of extra canned food. If your boating only takes you across the bay and back, you don't need emergency fuel tanks, spare part kits, or spare belts and hoses. You can probably make it back to shore without them.

This spring, go aboard your boat and make a "what if" list that suits your kind of sailing or boating. For example, what if you got a hole in the hull? Could you save the boat with the gear you currently have onboard? What if a through-hull let go? What if your engine or engines quit? What if the rig fell down? What if a front came through, forcing you to power home directly into choppy seas? If you think you could easily motor to land without your rig, why take a lot of spare rigging parts?

Go through the boat and imagine your worst nightmare for the type of sailing that you do. Then think about how you would prevent or survive it, and whether you would need more equipment than you already have onboard. If necessary, add that equipment, but don't weigh your boat down with unnecessary gear.

Almost any boat can be made capable of weathering strong winds and heavy seas. It just takes some effort and expense. The points we've outlined here are only a few of the items you should consider, but they'll get you thinking in the right way. No doubt, after a storm or two, you'll find other ways to make your boat more capable. This is what sailing in heavy weather is about. Preparation for the unexpected is a large part of winning the battle.

Five

Storm Sails

Should you carry storm sails, and modify your boat's rig as necessary to fly them, or should you watch the weather like a hawk and hope to never see a storm? This is a quandary for many sailors. Most hope they will never run into a storm, but those heading offshore or even on long coastal passages usually want their boats set up for bad weather, just in case.

A while ago I gave a talk on heavy weather at a rendezvous for Pacific Seacraft owners. One owner of a 40-footer mentioned that he had carefully picked his weather windows and had only once run into a Force 8 gale (34–40 knots of wind) in more than 40,000 miles of sailing. For him, paying attention to the weather had made it possible to avoid storms. Nevertheless, he carried heavy-weather sails.

Your own answer to this question should take into account the size of your boat, its sail plan, the number of crew, and where you sail. If your boat is less than 35 feet long and you don't sail offshore a lot, you may always be able to reach safety before heavy weather hits. In that case you can probably get by with a single, sturdy roller-furling headsail and a good, strong mainsail with three reefing positions. But if your boat is large enough that heavy-weather sails can be easily stowed, and if your sailing is a little more adventurous, you should probably carry them. One point is universally true: the more confident you are with your heavy-weather sail plan, the sooner you'll adopt it as the wind increases and the more comfortable you and your crew will be.

Headsails

Heavy-air headsails need to be carefully suited to your boat and rig and should be designed as a true complement to your working sail plan. A storm sail of the maximum size recommended by the sailmaker, for example, may be too large for a light hull when the winds really pipe up. A heavy cruising boat, however, may need a little more sail in a moderate gale than a storm jib can provide. No matter what their dimensions, all heavy-air headsails need to be cut extremely flat. (Don't worry, the wind will blow some shape into them!) Also, waves coming across the foredeck can damage a headsail just as quickly as a strong wind. So a good storm sail must be high-clewed, which will also provide better visibility.

Roller-Furling Sails

Most cruising sailors use some form of roller furling, and reefing your sails in this manner is a real laborsaving method of making them smaller as the wind gets stronger. Unfortunately, roller-furled sails can cause problems in a blow since they tend to get baggier at midluff the more you take them in, especially in high winds—precisely what you *don't* want in a storm sail. Although the top and bottom of the sail furl at the same rate, the middle part stretches, so the sail does not roll up evenly with each complete turn of the luff foil. Some sailmakers get around this problem by installing a foam insert at the leading edge of the sail. The insert is bulkiest at midluff, tapering above and below, but will eventually compress to the point where its effectiveness is diminished. For this reason, North Sails (for one) inserts strands of 1-inch (25 mm) rope in the luffs of its sails. Other sailmakers offer a sail cut much flatter in the forward part as another means of making it furl a little tighter.

When you are deciding how best to deal with impending heavy weather you are faced with a difficult choice. Ultimately, roller-furled headsails are best removed during a storm. But on the one hand, if you remove the roller-furling headsail while the wind is still light enough to do so, you will need a reasonably large sail, say a No. 2 or 3 headsail, to take its place. On the other hand, if you keep rolling it in until it is truly time to fit a storm headsail, the roller-furled sail will be impossible to remove, since nobody in his right mind will unroll a full-sized roller-furling sail in winds heavy enough to require a storm jib.

Imagine trying to remove a roller-furled headsail in winds blowing a steady 35 knots and gusting to 50. You put on your harness and go forward. Waves hit the weather side, sending plumes of green water and spray high onto the deck. The rain is lashing down. You pause to unclip your harness when a wave hits. Green water sweeps across the deck, carrying you with it, but fortunately, your secondary tether hook stops you from hitting the mast.

The wind noise is too high to make yourself heard, so you wave to the crew aft. Your wife lets go the sheet, and the sail flogs madly. The bowlines fastening the sheets to the clew whip you once, leaving a stinging welt on your cheek. (Good thing you decided not to use snap shackles there, or you might have lost a few teeth!) You let the halyard go, then try to run forward, but your harness brings you up short. While you unclip and reclip your harness, the sail flogs and works partway down the headstay. You manage to grab it and haul it down farther, but then a wave washes over the deck, taking the foot of the sail to leeward. You grab more of the sail, but now the halyard is stuck. You go to the mast to free it, and the sail sags to the deck. Waves wash over it as you struggle to haul it to windward.

You tie part of the luff to the weather rail, then gather more sail, tying down what little you can gain. Every movement is slow and hard, as the boat rears and bucks like a rodeo bull. Water cascades over you, soaking everything and tearing the sail from its ties. You struggle mightily to retie it, but the effort saps your stamina, so you pause to get your breath, holding onto the weather rail and hoping for a lull in the gale. But the storm's fury only increases, and a wave washes across you. The sail, tethered at the tack and head, flogs and whips across the deck. Then a huge wave fills it with water, and suddenly a long tear opens up at the foot. Now the halyard and sheet are all that hold it on board. You wrestle with it, tying it down anywhere you can. It takes an hour, but finally the sail is strapped along the weather side. The last ties have been put on by your crew and your wife, because you are too exhausted to do any more. When you regain some measure of strength half an hour later, you set the storm jib and then go aft.

It takes an entire day for your body to recover from the ordeal.

As this scenario illustrates, changing sails in storm conditions is one of the most physically demanding and stressful jobs a sailor will ever face—an important factor in heavy-air sailing. As a result, most roller-furled headsails are left on their stays. If this is your plan, make sure you put a few lines around the sail to stop it from unrolling as the wind builds.

Of course, if you carry a roller-furling headsail on a boat that lacks a second forestay, there's no point in carrying a storm headsail because you'll have no way to set it. Be sure to consider how you are going to set heavy-weather sails before you order them or take them aboard your boat, so you won't be left wondering what to do when the wind pipes up.

Twin Headstays and Staysail Stays

To avoid having to remove a roller-furled sail in heavy going, you could fit a second forestay. In fact, many round-the-world solo racers who use roller-furled headsails have a second headstay fitted for just this reason. It can either be a twin headstay a foot or two inside the primary head-

stay or a staysail stay (also called a midstay or inner forestay) about 40–60 percent of the distance from the mast to the bow. When twin headstays are fitted, the second one should have its own chainplate, rather than being connected to a shared triangular link plate as I saw on one boat. If the pin holding the link plate were to break, both headstays would be rendered useless.

The second headstay needs to be at least the distance of the roller-furling drum aft of the primary headstay to be useful, and a bit farther aft than that if you want to be able to tack the boat without having to roll up the primary headsail every time. The best way to attach a storm headsail to a second headstay or inner forestay is to hank it with sturdy clips like those made by the Wichard company.

Many sailmakers now recommend setting a storm jib on a staysail stay (inner forestay) rather than a twin headstay. This places the headsail well inboard where it will be easier to handle and keeps the rig more compact, allowing the boat to ride and steer better in strong winds. A storm jib on a headstay applies pressure well forward of the centers of effort and lateral resistance, which has a disproportionate effect on the boat's balance.

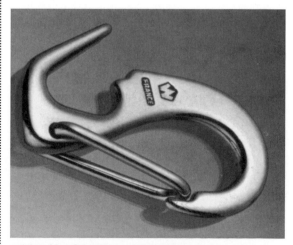

Wichard hanks make a secure method of hooking stormsails to a stay. (Photo courtesy Wichard USA, Inc.)

Twin headstays are set up on the boat in the foreground to enable two different-sized headsails to be used. Note the heavier sail on the staysail or inner stay behind the twin headstays. On this singlehander, almost any combination of sails can be set.

A single headstay with an inner forestay about 3 or 4 feet behind it allows this boat to set a smaller roller-furling sail on the inner stay with a lighter roller-furler on the headstay. In very light winds a gennaker or reaching sail could be set off the end of the sprit. Notice how the transverse struts stiffen the sprit.

A staysail stay must be bolted to a bulkhead or the keel to avoid peeling the deck off the boat, and the load it imposes on the mast (especially when the staysail is flying) must be counterbalanced with running backstays or fixed intermediate backstays to prevent the mast from bowing forward. Running backstays must be set up to windward and released to leeward with each tack to avoid fouling the main boom—not all that much work unless you are short tacking, which you are unlikely to do in a gale. Fixed intermediates load the mast more due to their poor angle of pull, and they prevent the main boom from being eased way out when reaching or running.

If your foredeck space is limited, you may not be able to site an inner forestay far enough aft to avoid fouling the primary headsail when tacking. A common solution is to set up the inner forestay with some sort of quick-release lever, so it can be

A view of BBV with two headstays, staysail stay, and a babystay. Tacking would be a little difficult when using the forwardmost headsail.

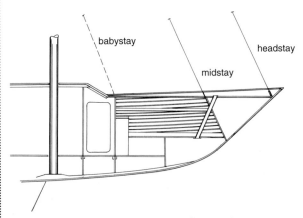

Fitting a midstay (staysail or inner forestay) can save your boat should you encounter rough weather. The midstay should be tied to the keel or a bulkhead to prevent the deck being peeled off the boat.

tied off to the shrouds when not needed. In that case, many sailmakers recommend that the inner stay be made of aramid fiber, which is lighter and easier to handle and store than rod or wire. Installing an inner forestay is not cheap, but it is the *best* solution if you have a roller-furling headsail and are planning to venture out where heavy weather can find you.

As bad weather approaches, you can set the inner forestay and clip on your storm staysail or storm jib. The sail can stay in its bag until needed. For this type of situation, North Sails makes a mesh-bottomed bag that allows water washing over the foredeck to drain from the bag instead of sweeping it away.

Another tip offered by Mike Toppa, of North Sails, is that the storm staysail have its own tack pendant to allow it to be set above the normal staysail. When the storm sail is used, the regular staysail is left on the stay, but stuffed into the mesh bag. That way, should the wind abate, the storm jib can be changed quickly and easily to keep the boat moving through the slop left over from the storm.

In summary, set heavy-weather sails early. The boat will stand up better and generally sail faster, more responsively, and more comfortably. Make sure your heavy-weather sails are shack-

This photo shows a roller furling headstay landing at the masthead and a roller furled staysail stay landing farther down. Running backstays attached to the back of the mast absorb the staysail forces and prevent the mast from bowing.

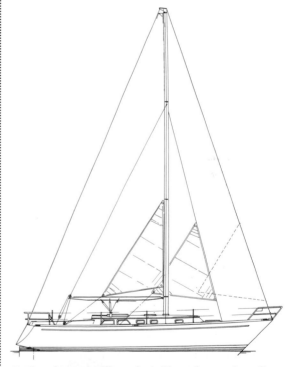

Setting the storm jib on the midstay keeps the sail plan compact as shown here. If the storm jib is set on the headstay (shown dashed) its effect on balance is much more pronounced, making it difficult to heave-to or lie ahull and possibly causing an autopilot to run more than necessary. Note how the head of the storm trysail is taken to the shroud landings and spreader, where the mast is likely to be strongest.

led on properly, and that halyard pendants are not likely to chafe the mast or headstay. (Storm sails are smaller than lighter sails, so they usually have a wire or Spectra pendant from the top of the sail to the halyard shackle. This helps to keep enough halyard on the winch.)

Finally, one minor point bears repeating from the previous chapter: When the going gets rough, back off a little on the hydraulic backstay to allow the rig to flex. If you don't, you risk putting a compression buckle in the mast. This is the reason I prefer to specify 1×19 wire rather than rod rigging for the backstay of a cruising sailboat.

Storm Jib

The storm jib is the smallest and heaviest sail in your inventory. Its size is critical. If too small it will be useless in all but the heaviest winds. Too large and it will be too much for most heavy-weather situations. The Offshore Racing Council (ORC) special regulations specify that a heavy weather jib have an area not greater than 0.135 IG^2, or 13.5 percent of the height of the foretriangle squared, and a storm jib be no larger than 0.05 IG^2, or 5 percent of the height of the foretriangle squared. (IG is the approximate height from the headstay landing on the forward face of the mast to a point just above the deck on centerline.)

These dimensions, based on years of experience, are the ones most sailmakers use, although it's important to bear in mind that they were established in the late 1970s, when boats were heavier and had smaller rigs. If you own a modern lightweight boat with a big rig and a narrow keel, you should seriously consider a smaller storm jib than the rule-recommended minimum. Reports from the 1998 Sydney-Hobart race suggest that storm jibs were too big for many of the lighter boats. When matched to the righting moment of the boat, appropriate sail areas are as small as 3.5–4 percent of the foretriangle height squared.

In Chapter 1 we mentioned that the wind's pressure increases with the square of its velocity, so even when reefed the loads on sails and gear can quickly increase to the point where storm sails are needed. The accompanying figure, adapted from my earlier book *Designed to Win*, shows how the heeling loads on the mainsail increase as the wind gets up. The graph approximates what the loads would be like on today's cruising boat. We can also make up such a graph for the headsail, but this one will illustrate the point. Note how the load drops each time the sail is reefed and it drops considerably when the storm trysail is fitted. Obviously, the wind in the storm trysail can increase quite a lot before it reaches the force achieved before the mainsail was taken down. Note also that the wind forces when the first, second, and third reefs are put in does not decline much, but because the sail area is removed from aloft the heel angle is reduced considerably.

No matter how large or small, a storm jib should always be cut high at the clew in order to keep the foot out of the water, since storm sails

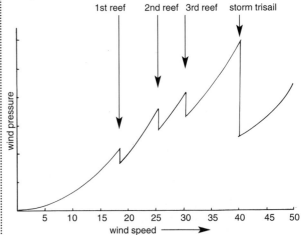

The pressure of the wind is found from the formula $0.00119 \times$ sail area $\times$ velocity$^2 \times$ C, where C is a sailforce coefficient that changes for mainsails and headsails. This graph shows the wind pressure on the mainsail as it is reefed and later, when the storm trysail is fitted. A similar graph can be developed for the headsails, but the sailforce coefficient will change as the sail is rolled up due to its less efficient shape.

are often destroyed by heavy waves thrown up into them. A high clew also improves visibility under the sail, as mentioned previously, and it leads the sheet farther aft, to a turning block that might be on the forward end of the working sail track or on the boat's rail. If the working sail track fails to give you a fair lead, you may have to fit a pad eye for the turning block, which needs to be large enough to accommodate the sheet without chafing it.

Reefable stormsails pose several problems. First, a reef along the foot forms a barrier that prevents water clearing out of the sail as quickly as possible when it's doused by spray or even green water. A second wave washing into the sail before the first one drains off might then overload it. Second, a line of reef points tends to form a weak seam in the sail; reefed stormsails often rip right along the reef line. Be assured, wind and wave pressure put severe loads on stormsails.

Storm jibsheets should never be fastened to the sail with metal fittings such as J-locks, since they can do serious damage to crew or boat when the sail is flogging. Ideally, the sheets should be spliced to the clew, which makes a more compact and less menacing mass of rope than a large bowline. Polyester single-braided line (such as New England Rope's Regatta Braid) jibsheets give slightly more shock-absorbing yield than low-stretch double-braided polyester, yet not as much as nylon line, which is too stretchy for this application.

North Sails recommends Spectra webbing instead of wire for tack and head pendants on storm sails, since it eliminates meathooks, shackles, heavy thimbles, and wear caused by wire against the rig. Webbing is also easier to handle when setting the sails.

Storm jibs should not have battens, as these will break when the sail flogs. Finally, these sails should be strongly reinforced at each corner and along each edge. Remember, this is a sail of last resort. If it is destroyed, you won't have anything else to set.

In an effort to improve visibility in heavy conditions many sailmakers are now covering the top third of storm sails with high-visibility Dayglo orange material.

When you first take delivery of your storm sails, don't just stuff them in the forepeak. Bend them on while your boat is sitting alongside the dock on a calm day. Make sure you can hank both sails on and that the halyard and the head and tack pendants are the correct lengths. Check the sheet leads to ensure that you have a pad eye, track, or rail where the turning block needs to go. This is of critical importance for both the storm jib and storm trysail! There is no point in taking a storm sail out on the ocean only to find that it cannot be sheeted anywhere when you need it.

When storm sails are set, the boat should not be driven close-hauled, but rather steered on a close reach—assuming you can make any progress at all to windward. If a close reach proves excessively uncomfortable or untenable, or if your destination is downwind, you can run off downsea, taking the wind over your port or starboard quarter. (At no time, however, should you attempt to sail beam-to the wind and seas, nor should you sail dead downwind. See Chapter 8 for more on storm tactics.) In either case, the lead should be well outboard. Take the lead to the outboard track or even to the rail in order to open the slot between the storm jib and reefed mainsail (or storm trysail) in heavy winds. If you take the sheet to the rail, make sure the rail or lead block can carry the load of a tightly sheeted storm jib and still give you a clean lead back to the primary winch. Having made all those checks, you can fold the sail and stow it away with a sigh of satisfaction. Murphy's Law pretty much guarantees that if you check your storm sails and have everything ready, you won't need them.

As a final note, some sailmakers offer a working jib that can be reefed (usually by a reef along the foot) down to a storm jib, which is better than no storm jib but, for the reasons stated above, not as good as a purpose-built sail. Well-known writer and sailmaker Jeremy Howard-Williams, in his book *Sails*, recommends that a reefed storm jib only be used in winds up to Force 6 or 7. In heavier winds there is a danger of the foot tearing out and getting shredded.

The Mainsail

When the time comes to reef the mainsail—you've already partially roller furled your headsail or changed down to a smaller one but your boat is still overpowered—you'll want to do so efficiently and properly, which means practicing in light winds. Reef points are relatively easy to tear out, and when one is tied they should all be tied, with equal tension. If you use sail ties passed through reef cringles in your sail make sure they are colored so you won't miss one when it's time to shake out the reef. White Dacron ties often get left in by accident, and as soon as someone sheets in the sail, it rips. Some old-time cruisers use reef lines sewn through the sail. If this is your preference, either ask for the lines to be made of a different color or check carefully to ensure that you have taken them all out before resetting the sail.

The first step in the reefing process is to put in a flattening reef, which takes a lot of the curvature out of the foot of the sail. First be sure you have as much tension as possible on the outhaul to remove excess shape from the sail. Then, to apply the flattening reef, it is only necessary to crank down on a single reefing line that passes through a cringle in the clew—or around the edge of the clew if there is no cringle—about 6 or 8 inches above the main boom. This has the effect of flattening the foot of the mainsail and removing some of the area needed in lighter winds.

When the wind increases further, the time will come for the first full reef, which removes

between 15 and 20 percent of the mainsail's area. To put in a full reef, first tighten the topping lift (or adjust a rigid boom vang to support the boom), then ease the mainsheet until the sail luffs, removing the wind load. Now ease the halyard until you can pull the new tack cringle (that is, the tack cringle at the height of the first line of reef points) down to the level of the boom, where it either slips over a tack hook or is lashed in place. If the former, make sure you slide the cringle over the hook in the right direction. If it goes on backwards, it can rip the mainsail.

With the reefed tack in place, pull the halyard back up until wrinkles form in the mainsail luff. Then take up on the leech-reefing line until you've hauled the leech cringle down to the boom; this is hard work, rendered easier with a well-placed winch. Ease the topping lift, trim the sail, and the reef is done. Well, almost. Now you should tie in each reef point.

Some sailmakers recommend a single "Jiffy" reefing line that is tied off at the outer end of the boom, passes through the reef cringle at the sail's clew, back down to the boom, along the boom, up to and through the tack cringle and down to a winch. My experience with this system is that it often hangs up at the tack end, meanwhile bringing insufficient tension to bear at the clew end. For this reason a cruiser might want separate tack and clew lines.

There is also a school of thought that advocates against tying the reef points, the argument being that with so much strain in the middle of the sail, the reef points will only serve as pressure points to tear the sail. Indeed I have seen that happen, but I have also seen the clew cringle tear out of a reefed mainsail and the boom drop into the cockpit because there were no other sail ties to support it. Find out what your sailmaker suggests.

If the wind continues to pick up, you will have to put in more reefs. Most mainsails provide for two or three, with each removing about

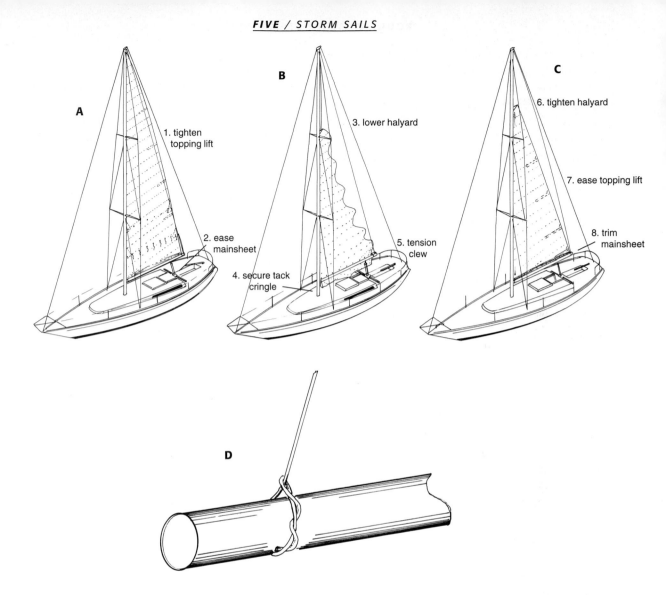

A

1. tighten topping lift

2. ease mainsheet

B

3. lower halyard

4. secure tack cringle

5. tension clew

C

6. tighten halyard

7. ease topping lift

8. trim mainsheet

D

Reefing a mainsail. The first step in reefing a mainsail is to make sure that reefing lines are rigged and are easy to move. You will be surprised how often a reefing line is tied off somewhere. (A) When the order is given to put in a reef, make sure the topping lift or boom vang is set up so that boom will not drop in the cockpit. Ease the mainsheet to take the load off the sail. (B) Lower the main halyard the appropriate amount so that a crew can hook the reefing eye over the gooseneck hook. Only when that task is done should the clew line be tightened. If you use a fisherman's bend to hold the clew line (as shown in panel D) it will be easy to remove when you shake the reef out. (C) When the tack and clew are fastened tightly crank the halyard back up, ease the topping lift, and pull in the mainsheet. If you wish to tie off the reef points, do so at this stage. Most sail problems occur when a reef line is left tied in when the reef is shaken out. North Sails offers colored sail ties so that you will see them when you remove the reef lines before unreefing.

15 to 20 percent of the remaining sail. If you are still overpowered with all three reefs in, it is time for the storm trysail.

I remember a passage in which we set the storm jib on the headstay and reefed the mainsail down to its numbers (about one-third of its full size). While the storm jib took a pounding, it kept the boat going on a close reach for nearly 38 hours. The mainsail, on the other hand, suffered torn reef points, and the only two battens visible above the reef were shattered inside their pockets. The sail was stretched beyond repair, with great scallops along the leech between the batten pockets. In retrospect, we should have set a storm trysail and saved the mainsail. For the cruising sailor this alone is a compelling enough reason to carry and use a storm trysail in heavy weather: it cuts down on wear and damage to your mainsail.

Mainsail reef points should be heavily reinforced, and boats over 60 feet (18 m) long should have reef blocks on the leech, as opposed to the usual cringles (pressed rings), since this part of the sail will be under a tremendous strain.

Again, practice reefing ahead of time in gentle conditions to work out the kinks, instead of waiting for a blow to figure out how it is done. When you know how to reef, you'll do it sooner rather than later—and sooner is better.

Roller-Furling Mainsails

In-mast roller-furling mainsails are smaller than their battened counterparts. They have to be in order to furl around a thin metal bar inside the mast and also because a sail without battens can support no roach. Thus, if you retrofit a roller-furled mainsail on your boat, you'll find that you can carry full sail in winds that once required reefing. When you do have to reef, you'll find that the ends of the reefing device tend to turn more than the middle of the metal bar, and the sail becomes fuller at midluff as it is rolled up, just like a partially furled headsail. The fuller sail

tends to make the boat heel more, so you will need to put more rolls in the sail.

Storm Trysails

The trysail is a sail of last resort, used to balance the storm jib and keep some load on the back of the mast. The storm trysail is traditionally flown loose-footed, not clewed to the boom like a normal mainsail. Instead, it is controlled like a headsail by a pair of sheets, the leeward of which (the one in use) leads to a turning block on deck near the rail. This allows the crew to lower the main boom and lash it on deck, rendering it less dangerous. On some boats with a modern, rod-type vang that supports the boom, however, some sailors tie the clew of the trysail to the boom. The trysail can then be controlled with the mainsheet and traveler, just as the mainsail would be. It is not as efficient, nor safe, but does the job.

Storm trysails are usually of a similar weight to storm jibs and are also battenless. The actual cloth weight depends on the size and stability of the boat and is best determined by the sailmaker. ORC regulations limit the size of a storm trysail to $0.175P \times E$, where P is the height of the mainsail luff and E is the length of its foot, though this may be too large for a light, modern hull with a high-aspect rig. If you own a boat of this style, consider a slightly smaller trysail. You'll be able to carry it in heavier winds.

Ideally, your storm trysail should attach to a designated track on the back of the mast, separate from the track that carries the luff of the mainsail. Otherwise you have to take off the mainsail before you can bend on the trysail—the last thing anyone wants to be doing in the midst of a gale. Sailmaker Mike Toppa remembers that the boat on which he was sailing when a major storm struck the 1998 Sydney-Hobart fleet had 13 mainsail track cars. They formed a stack that topped out 10 feet above deck when the mainsail was lowered. The only way to unhook the mainsail and clear its track for the trysail was to

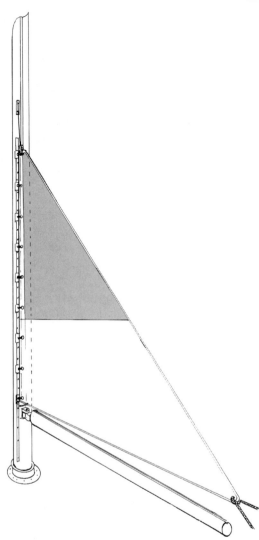

A storm trysail flown from a separate mast track. This one is sheeted to the rail, but on boats with hydraulic boom vangs the trysail is sometimes clewed to the boom and controlled by the mainsheet. Note the location of the storm trisail halyard sheave box. By locating it near the top of the track it prevents halyard slap on the mast. For better visibility in bad weather the top portion of the trysail is coated with Dayglo Orange.

send someone up in a bosun's chair—hardly recommended at the height of a gale.

In heavy conditions at sea, you may need the bosun's chair to get a man high enough to undo the main halyard. If you have a fully battened

mainsail, make a contingency plan to get the mainsail halyard off the sail in heavy winds. The solution may be to install a storm trysail track running from the deck one-third to one-half of the way up the mast with a storm halyard sheave box not far above it. The sheave box helps to eliminate halyard slap on the mast.

In reality, not many cruising boats today are fitted with a separate storm trysail track. Instead you might want to use parrel beads or even lash the trysail to the mast. (Parrel beads are round wood or polymer beads with a line threaded through them. The beads and line loop completely around the mast. The beads act more or less like ball bearings and allow a sail to be raised and lowered without being removed from the mast.) If you do have a storm trysail track, its lower end should terminate near enough to the deck to allow the sail to be fastened to the mast while still in its bag on deck. If you really want to prepare for heavy weather, an additional, shorter halyard running through a special sheave set in the mast just above the top of the trysail track is not a bad idea, since it reduces the length of the halyard, cuts down on wear, and eliminates halyard slap on the mast. The sail should be set with its tack above the gooseneck fitting.

As always, practice setting the sail in normal conditions to make sure it has been built properly and will bend on and hoist easily when you face the real thing. Remember the flip side of Murphy's Law: if you prepare thoroughly, you'll probably never be tested.

Sailing with No Mainsail

If you are caught at sea without a storm trysail, it is not a good idea to try to sail your boat without a mainsail unless you have no other option. A boat under headsail alone makes a lot of leeway, which means that your course made good differs radically from the course you are steering. Don't count on weathering those shoals or headlands under your lee bow!

A headsail unbalanced by any load behind the mast can also invert the mast in a storm, causing it to collapse. In January 1999, the 150-foot *Mirabella* broke her mast sailing under genoa alone, as have many smaller boats.

Adding a trysail or deeply reefed mainsail creates a uniformly distributed load along the back of the mast, which tends to damp a lot of the midlevel vibrations in the spar, steadying it. If you do not have a storm trysail, have your sailmaker add a third or even fourth row of reef points so you can reef your mainsail down well. Obviously, you need to do so long before you get caught in a storm!

Sailing with No Headsail

If you don't carry storm sails aboard your boat and you are surprised by heavy winds, it's better to sail under reefed mainsail alone. But remember that sailing upwind in this manner (just as under headsail alone), you will make a lot of leeway, often about 10–15 degrees instead of the more usual 5–10. You may also end up with a lot of weather helm, depending on the wind angle, as the mainsail tries to turn the boat into the wind. In fact, if you are caught in heavy squalls, such as those that accompany the passage of a strong cold front, it may be best to remove all sails and motor home, rather than risk losing the mast by setting too much unbalanced sail.

Powerboat Steadying Sails

Some slow-speed displacement cruising powerboats derive a little benefit from a steadying sail when powering either directly or at an angle into a wind up to Force 6 or 7. This sail, of necessity, will be small, and made of heavy-duty Dacron. It may or may not have battens (most likely not). Its job is to damp the boat's rolling.

If the sail is set aft of amidships, on no account should it be used downwind in heavy weather, or it might push the stern around and into a broach. In weather more severe than force 7 or so, a riding sail should be removed and stowed. The windage of the mast and upperworks is usually enough to keep a slight heel on the boat and keep it heading into the wind.

Additional Thoughts on Storm Sails

There was one time, aboard a 55-footer, when we had to change from a heavy-weather jib to a storm jib in winds of more than 65 knots. It took two of us more than half an hour, and breaking waves almost washed the heavy-weather jib over the side several times. Always remember that in heavy weather, the foredeck of a sailboat is no place to be, and the faster you can change sails and get aft or below, the safer you will be. Unless you have a full and experienced crew, you will find that changing sails in high winds will take a long time. Allow at least an hour for each sail change. If you are older than 40 or unfit, it will take longer. Judge accordingly, and make your sail changes early. Remember, it's a lot easier to shake out a reef if the wind fails to build than to try to take one in if a squall proves stronger than expected.

Finally, if you do choose to use your existing sails for heavy weather, remember that you will most certainly shorten their life, either by tearing them, ruining battens, breaking fittings, or just stretching out the sailcloth so that the sail no longer has an efficient aerodynamic shape. This is yet another reason why, if you intend to sail offshore, you should carry heavy-weather sails and know how to set them.

Preparing for a Storm in Harbor

Never ignore a storm or hurricane forecast when your boat is in the water. To do so is a sure way to get to know your insurance adjuster. You can make several preparations when you hear a storm forecast, but your actions will be more effective and directed if you've made a flexible plan ahead of time. With your plan in place, track the storm. If your boat is small you might want to haul it out. If it is on a mooring, you might have to double up on the mooring line and/or take measures to prevent the line from chafing. If the storm is particularly severe you might want to take your boat to an especially safe harbor, or *hurricane hole*, keeping in mind that you should get there early to make sure you get a good spot.

The Plan

Know in advance what you intend to do with your boat should a storm or hurricane come your way. Your plan will be shaped by the size of your boat, its distance from your current location, and the policies of your boatyard or marina. The plan must also be flexible enough that it can be adapted to the predicted strength of the storm or hurricane.

For example, if you own a 24-foot trailerable powerboat and live near your mooring, you might simply drive your boat to the local launch ramp and haul it without any fuss. If, on the other hand, you own a 50-foot sailboat and live a hundred miles from the marina where you dock it, the job becomes more difficult. In this case you might have to make an arrangement with the marina operator to have the boat moved to a safe haven, hauled out, or tied off in the marina.

You should plan to take the following actions:

1. For a moderate gale with winds to 35–40 knots (Force 8 on the Beaufort scale), double up on dock lines, install chafing gear and fenders, and make sure the mast is not in line with the mast of the boat in the next slip. Move all halyards to locations around the foredeck so they won't slat against the mast. You should probably do this anyway, whenever you leave your boat, so that you don't annoy your neighbors. If a dinghy or other gear needs relocating, do this too. Topping fuel and water tanks makes the boat more stable, but be forewarned that, should the boat go aground, there will be a bigger mess to clean up.

2. For a strong gale or storm with winds over 40 knots (Force 9, 10, or higher), do all of the above, and remove the roller furling headsail (if you have one), the bimini top, awnings, fly bridge enclosure, dodger, lee cloths, and any other high-windage deck gear. If the storm is expected to have hurricane-strength gusts, you might want to move your boat to a safer mooring. A sheltered, well-constructed marina will keep it safer than a mooring (see the sidebar later in this chapter), but a sheltered mooring with stout ground tackle will be safer than an exposed or poorly constructed marina.

3. For a hurricane, plan to get the boat hauled and chocked up safely on shore. If you can't

get it hauled, have a secure place to put it and determine who is going to move it. Remove anything that might create additional windage, including the mast. Make sure the person who is going to move the boat knows where the keys are, how to operate the engine, and at what time the boat will be moved. Work out who should be notified and provide a backup in case the primary person is unavailable. In a hurricane your best bet is to remove the mast, although that is not often possible. When Hurricane Wilma hit Florida in October 2005, boating writer Tim Banse watched as boats on tightly chained boat stands gradually worked the stands loose and collapsed onto their neighbors. Even on shore, your boat is not totally safe in a hurricane.

Make sure you have the equipment—weather radio, VHF radio, weatherfax, Internet access, and so on—to track the storm as it approaches. Weather-tracking software is constantly being upgraded, and what is good today may not be good in a year or two. Check out the various weather-tracking products at your local chandlery or on the internet and make your decision based on what is most suitable for your conditions and location.

Tracking the Storm

In these days of weather radio and satellite tracking maps, there's no reason not to know about heavy weather long before it reaches you. When you first hear about bad weather approaching, make a plot and mark the weatherman's forecasted positions. As we mentioned in Chapter 1, the traditional sailor's prediction assumes that a storm will swing as much as 20 degrees either side of its forecast track. Plot that cone on your chart. Ideally, your boat should be well clear of this area to ensure that you have the maximum chance of avoiding bad weather. If your boat is in this predicted cone

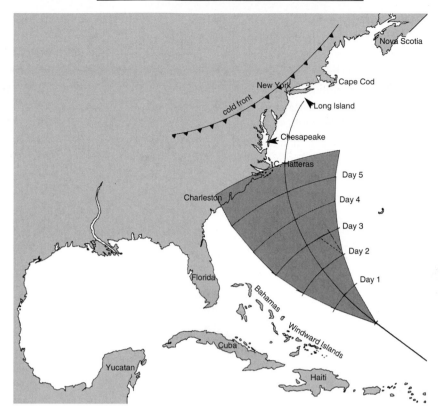

When plotting a hurricane's track, assume that the storm will swing 20 degrees either side of its predicted path. Draw that cone on your chart. If your boat is within that area, start getting your haul-out plans organized. (This plotting method produces a bigger, more conservative cone than the 1-2-3 Rule developed by the Hurricane Prediction Center, also described in Chapter 1.) Although the predicted path of this storm remains offshore until it reaches Long Island, the area from Charleston, South Carolina, to Long Island is threatened. The cold front running southwest to northeast will help keep the storm away from shore, however. Cold fronts help to redirect a storm unless the storm ceiling is extremely high. On the Eastern Seaboard a storm can be pushed into New England by a cold front in the location shown.

and on a mooring or in a marina, be prepared to get it hauled or moved as the storm nears. (And if you are at sea, steer a heading to avoid what I call the *cone of destruction*.)

A cold front located in the track of a storm will often block and help to redirect it. On the east coast of the United States, for example, if you see a cold front approaching from the west or northwest and a storm coming in from the south, the front is likely to redirect the storm to the northeast. Remember that any predictions more than three days ahead are little more than best guesses based on experience.

Putting Your Plan Into Operation

You've planned your course of action. Now a storm is approaching and it's time to put it into action.

Hauling Your Boat Out

In most marinas the sight of yard crews hauling boats out of the water and putting them safely ashore is a reliable indication that a major storm has been forecast. Generally, smaller boats are the first ashore, their owners waiting with trailers to cart them off to a safe haven.

If you want to make sure your boat is hauled when a storm is forecast, check with your marina operator to find out the storm policy. For example, one Rhode Island boatyard maintains a list of clients who have requested that their boats be hauled in the event of a hurricane. "We start hauling boats 48 hours before a hurricane strike is predicted for our area," says the manager, "and we call those owners who have not requested that their boats be hauled. We have other owners who store with us for the winter. We'll get their boats from other moorings or marinas and haul them. Then we go out to every boat in our mooring field regardless of whether they asked for it, install chafing gear, and remove sails and gear that might blow away or get destroyed."

The yard may need you to sign an indemnity form or some other waiver. It may have a policy of notifying you if the staff thinks your boat should be hauled. Check to make sure you are on the priority list to get hauled.

You should also know where your boat is going to be stored. There is little point in hauling a boat if it is only to be stored where the storm surge can reach it. Work out what needs to be done, where the boat should be stored, and who should be notified in advance. Also note that in a severe hurricane, your boat might be blown over, even on shore.

If your boat is under 20 feet—the size of the average car—it might fit in a concrete storage building. You can back boat and trailer into the shed or parking garage, lock the door, and know that it is secure. If it's a large building, being the first boat to arrive will give you the pick of storage spots. Choose one that is not likely to be flooded during a storm surge or heavy rain.

If your boat is large, you might park it in the lee of a strong building. Make sure the boat is tied down both to its trailer and to strong points in the ground. Tie-downs attached to concrete blocks are not strong enough. If the boat is supported on jackstands, make sure the stands are chained tightly together and heavily weighted, and that there are extra stands under the boat. Ideally, you should take the mast out of a sailboat and remove a powerboat's bimini or tower and any other high-windage items. The good news is that even if your boat does blow over on shore, insurance adjusters say it is likely to sustain less damage than a boat that breaks free of its mooring.

Remember that as a hurricane passes, the wind direction will change, usually 180 degrees, so your boat should be protected on as many sides as possible. Also remember that parking your boat between two tall buildings can cause additional problems. Under the right conditions they may act as a wind tunnel, creating gusts two or three times higher than the prevailing wind speed. Even if you're sure you've removed every high-windage item from

The Force of the Wind

Wind pressure increases with the square of the wind's velocity. In other words, doubling the wind speed quadruples its punch. A 20-knot wind exerts a pressure of 1.6 pounds per square foot (psf), whereas a 40-knot gale has a force of 6.4 psf. So let's say your 30-foot boat (minus all removable windage) presents 250 square feet of surface to an incoming blast. In a 20-knot breeze it will only have to withstand 400 pounds of pressure, but at 40 knots there will be a 1,600-pound force pressing against it, and at 80 knots that force would increase to 6,400 pounds—quite possibly close to the weight of the boat.

the deck, check again. Even a dinghy lashed on deck should be removed and stored. Note that the forecast wind speed for a hurricane is only its sustained average, and gusts may be as much as 25 knots higher.

Marina Preparations

When high winds or a major storm are forecast, television weathermen might tell you simply to double up on your docklines and leave it at that—if they tell you anything at all. But in reality, if you are thinking of keeping your boat in the water during a storm, that is only the beginning. Know your marina's storm policy. Do they require that boats be hauled out? Do they want a boat in every other slip? Do they want the marina to be completely evacuated? Your plans hinge on the marina's requirements and your assessment of the marina and the storm. If the marina will let you stay put during a hurricane, ask yourself if the marina itself would survive a direct hit. If it is open to the ocean or large seas are likely to roll in, the docks may be destroyed, along with your boat.

Assess the general condition of the marina. Are the docks strongly fastened to the pilings? Are the pilings partly worn through? If you can rock a piling back and forth, it has probably eroded near the seabed, or mudline. If necessary, ask the marina manager when the pilings were installed. The rate at which pilings get eaten away depends on water temperature, seabed conditions, the material the pilings are made from, and a number other factors—including the presence or absence of woodboring worms and mollusks. Are the pilings high enough above the normal high water level so that floating docks will not float right off them during a storm surge?

Look at the docks and floats. Are they linked properly? Are the links worn? Worn links may break in severe conditions. Are the cleats through-bolted properly? Screwed or rotting cleats may tear out and should be replaced. Are the docks floating evenly or sagging? Check dock boxes, too. A heavy dock box may lower the end of a finger pier, allowing waves to sweep it from end to end, or the box itself may be washed away or fill with water and sink the dock. And a dock system is only as strong as its weakest link; once breakdowns begin, they are likely to escalate. Does the dock have rubber fenders or dock guards around each float? Dock guards will help to protect your boat if its fenders ride onto the dock and the hull grinds against the float.

Also check out the marina breakwater or pilings around the perimeter. A strong storm surge can cover the breakwater and expose the marina to heavy surf, which can break up even the sturdiest docks.

Even if you decide that your marina checks out and your boat can ride out the storm there, your work is not done. You should also prepare your boat for waves and high winds. Among other things you should remove gear that might be destroyed, moor your boat in such a way that it won't be damaged, adjust all fenders so they won't ride up onto the dock, and set lines out to keep your boat in place should storm surge lift the marina floats. Don't forget to remove any excess windage from the boat.

Hurricane Andrew Legislation

In 1994 in Florida, in response to the damage done in 1992 by Hurricane Andrew, the state legislature ruled that a marina cannot force boat owners to remove their boats from the marina when a storm is forecast. (In 1998 Florida had about 750,000 registered boat owners, according to the NMMA.) This law was subsequently upheld in September 1999 when a marina owner lost a lawsuit against boat owners who had not removed their boats from his marina before Hurricane Opal hit in October 1995.

Mooring in a Single Slip

As in all heavy-weather responses, the key to securing your boat in a marina slip is to have tried it when conditions are fairly calm. Get a little practice and make sure you have all the gear you need, rather than running to the marina store or chandlery on the morning of the storm.

One of the most important things you can do if you plan to keep your boat in its slip is to make sure the bow will be facing the strongest wind. For example, New England's fall storms are often nor'easters (which is to say that the wind blows from the northeast, even though the track of the storm is *toward* the northeast). These brutes are well forecast as they track up the coast, so there's no reason to be caught unprepared by one. If your boat is facing south-west when a nor'easter hits, its stern will receive the worst seas.

Tropical storms are different. They are rotary storms and the wind may change direction by more than 180 degrees as the eye of the storm goes by. Don't try to turn your boat during a lull. Instead, position it so that its bow will be facing into the wind for the longest part of the storm or facing the direction in which the worst seas will come.

Next, locate your boat in the middle of the slip and tie it off as shown in the accompanying figure. All lines should be doubled up in such a way that the partners take equal strain. They should also be at least one size larger than your normal docklines and about half as long again. Remember to disconnect shore-power lines. Leave docklines slack enough to allow the boat to move around, but not so slack that the boat can get near the edge of the dock. Protect all lines from chafe. Some people recommend that you take lines across the dock to more distant cleats, thus giving them more length over which to stretch, but these surging lines then become a hazard to anyone who has to walk down the dock.

If possible take docklines to seawalls or solid land-based fixtures rather than relying on the dock. A good rule of thumb is to make your docklines at least as long as the boat. Note that three-strand nylon docklines can generate enough heat from internal friction under severe strain to melt the rope's core. In a storm you may be better off using a braided polyester anchor line such as Brait, a non-hockling, energy-absorbent anchor line made by Yale Cordage line. It won't stretch as much, but it will probably stretch enough. When securing your boat you can also take additional lines to the tops of pilings, provided you allow enough slack in them to account for storm surge. Don't, however, tie a dockline around a piling without fastening it well above the water level. If need be, use your dinghy to take lines to pilings or even

Locate your boat in the middle of a single slip and tie it off with long lines. The mooring lines should be long so they will stretch and enable the boat to move around as gusts hit.

to concreted fixtures or trees (which are strongly rooted and will not blow down) on shore.

Put fenders out on *both* sides of the boat. Fasten the halyards at various points around the foredeck so that even in high winds they will not slap against the mast and cause chafe on the spar. If you have an inflatable dinghy tied on deck, deflate it and take it ashore. If the headsail is roller furled, unfurl it and stow it either belowdecks or ashore in your garage. According to most sailmakers, more headsails are ruined by unrolling in storms than are wrecked by sailing the boat.

If your boat has windows more than 2 square feet (about 0.2 square meters) in area, you might want to install storm boards to prevent flying debris from smashing the glass. At 4 square feet, consider this essential.

Take valuable electronics ashore. Turn off gas lines, and turn off your battery at the isolation switch. Make sure your automatic bilge pump will keep running even when the battery selector switch is turned to "off," by wiring the pump directly to the battery. Most such pumps are activated by a float switch when the bilge water rises above a threshold level. The circuit must be fused to keep the wiring from burning up if a jam in the pump keeps it running continuously. The circuit must also be waterproof. My center-console boat came within two inches of sinking when its nonwaterproof bilge pump switch shorted out. Now I use waterproof Blue Sea switches on all bilge pump circuits.

The U.S. Coast Guard strongly recommends that you do *not* stay aboard your boat in bad weather, since many people have been killed by doing so in the past. It is unlikely that you will be rescued at the height of a hurricane if you elect to stay on your boat. But if you do stay aboard your boat, you can relieve the strain on mooring or docklines by motoring gently into the storm if it is coming from ahead. In this case, fill the boat's fuel tanks before the storm hits.

If you have hatches or vents over bunks and bedding, remove the bedding or cover it with waterproof plastic in case the hatch or vent leaks. You might also duct tape large openings such as engine air intakes and air vents to prevent water ingress. Check that all hatches and vents are tightly closed and that heavy gear is placed on the cabin sole and tied down. I once saw the interior of a boat after an anchor had been left on a bunk during a storm. The anchor had fallen off the bunk and worked its way into the passageway while the boat rocked and rolled to the cadences of the storm. It cost the owner several thousand dollars to repair the resulting damage.

Close all through-hulls, including the engine exhaust through-hull, since this will help to stop water from siphoning back into the boat. Make sure, of course, that the automatic bilge pump through-hull is open. Check that all gear is tightly secured and that locker doors are securely closed before you leave the boat. If necessary, tape doors that might fly open.

Once the boat is set, go ashore and leave it. If you have to row ashore in your dinghy, take the dinghy home and stow it in your garage or basement or a rented storage unit. Take the contents of your dockbox home for storage as well.

Mooring in a Double Slip

If two boats share a double slip, both should be moved away from their respective docks toward the middle of the slip, and the mooring lines doubled up. This will give both boats space to pitch and roll without riding up over the edge of the docks. Make sure that both sets of mooring lines are slack enough to allow the boats to absorb wind gusts and wave strikes—they need room to move around—but not so slack that they collide when the lines stretch. Check that a sailboat's mast or a powerboat's outriggers are not aligned with the masts, outriggers, or antennas of the adjacent boat—you don't want these

STORM SCENARIO

Decision Time Approaches

You are watching the evening news and see that a major storm is developing to the south of you. It is expected to head north and may make landfall near you. You anxiously track its progress over the next few days. Your 30-foot boat is on a private mooring, not tended by a boatyard. Should you incur the expense of hauling out before the storm nears, and how long can you wait before deciding? What should you do?

Your options are:

1. Leave your boat sitting on its mooring and take hurricane precautions.
2. Haul your boat and have it put in your driveway a few miles from the seashore.
3. Move your boat to a sheltered marina and hope that it will be more secure there than on its mooring.

Option 1 may be the most convenient and least costly, but it's also the least secure. If you intend to leave your boat on its mooring, you first need to have confidence in that mooring. Has it been inspected within the past year? Do you know what state the mooring, chain, shackles and mooring line are in? Do you know how large the block or mushroom anchor is? If a storm surge were to lift your boat, could the boat uproot the ground tackle? Unless you have total confidence in your mooring and ground tackle and you are sure your chafing gear will last, you should probably move your boat.

Option 2 is the best choice for keeping your boat safe. According to a Massachusetts Institute of Technology study, after hurricane Gloria in September 1985, more than 96 percent of the boats in Padnarum Harbor that were hauled out and blocked up on land suffered no damage whatsoever. The research did not say what happened to boats afloat, but I remember seeing a huge number of boats lying onshore just after the storm. If you want to be sure your boat will survive a major storm or a hurricane, have it hauled and blocked up onshore. Make sure the mast (if it is a sailboat) and all removable windage and fragile equipment is stripped before the storm hits.

Option 3, moving your boat to a sheltered, well-constructed and well-managed marina, is a better idea than leaving it on a mooring, but not as good as hauling it.

Ideally, when you first put your boat on a mooring, you arranged with a local boatyard to haul it when a hurricane or storm winds above a certain threshold are forecast for your area. When you think it's time for action, confirm that the boatyard thinks so too.

If you don't have an arrangement in place, at least contact a boatyard for hauling while the storm is more than 36 hours away. If you wait longer, the yard may not have time to haul your boat. Most boatyards know how long it takes to haul their confirmed clients' boats, and they will start hauling in plenty of time for those. Last-minute additions to the list may or may not get service.

structures to roll into each other. If possible, lay antennas and outriggers down on powerboats. Put fenders out on both sides of your boat.

Remember that a storm surge can run as much as 8 feet, and a hurricane surge as much as 20 feet above normal wave heights. Ask yourself if your marina docks could lift off the tops of the pilings in such circumstances. If they do, what could you do about it?

Prepare as much as you can early, and hope the rest will take care of itself. One final task you should do before the storm approaches: make sure your insurance is fully paid up and you know exactly what is covered.

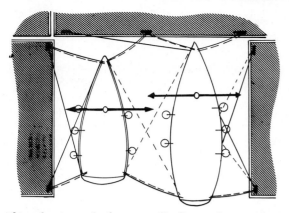

If two boats are in the same slip, first make sure that their masts will not hit if the boats roll, then move the boats toward the middle of the slip as shown. Tie off both boats and place fenders between them. Additional lines are shown dashed. The idea is to form a cat's cradle of lines to keep the boats in the middle of the berth, where they cannot hit each other or their respective docks.

Facing a Storm on a Mooring

If your boat is on a mooring and cannot be moved, check the mooring or confirm that the yard checked it in the spring so that you will know it is secure. If you have any worries, hire a diver to go down the line and make sure there's no corrosion in the chain links, shackles, swivel (if present), and the bale of the mooring itself, before the storm hits. Shackles should be tight and the anchor(s) or mooring block(s) firmly embedded in the sea bottom. If you find corrosion or have any doubts about your chain, replace it or move to another mooring.

Check your mooring pendant for chafe. If it shows any, replace it. Check, too, the cleats on the bow of your boat. They should be strongly fastened to avoid the risk of being torn out of the deck. If you have any doubts about their strength, take a line from the mooring pendant through the yacht's chocks and around the mast or windlass. The latest information I have seen indicates that most mooring lines chafe and break where they pass through chocks. In the future, perhaps builders will mount cleats on the outside of a hull near the bow, so that lines do not have to pass through chocks to reach them. This would reduce chafe on the lines under all conditions.

When a storm approaches, double up your mooring lines or put a bridle around the bow of your boat to take the strain. Any line leaving your boat should have some form of chafe protection. The best protection is a 3- to 4-foot length of fender tubing like that made by Perimeter Industries. It should be placed over your mooring line and secured in place by stitching or with a lashing, so it can't slide down the line. Check too, that there are no sharp edges around the bow of your boat that might abrade or even cut the line. Quite often, the stemhead fitting has a sharp corner, or there is a sharp edge at the corner of the deck or on the bow chock. These edges will chew through a line in a remarkably short time.

In the past I always recommended that boaters put heavy-duty plastic tubing around a pendant to protect it from chafe, but an M.I.T.

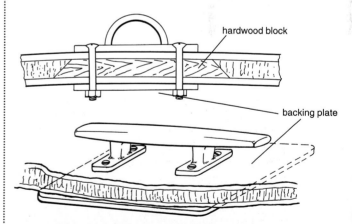

hardwood block

backing plate

Cleats and pad eyes should have backing plates to absorb some of the strain placed on them by mooring lines. If the cleat or pad eye is bolted through a cored deck, the coring should be removed and replaced with a hardwood block, solid laminate, or epoxy fill to prevent crushing. Do not use low-stretch Dacron sheets for mooring or anchor lines. If the line cannot stretch, it may rip the cleat right out of the boat.

study ("Wear and Fatigue of Nylon and Polyester Mooring Lines," by M. Seo, H. C. Wu, J. Chen, C. S. Toomey, and S. Backer, *Textile Research Journal*, July 1997) found that dry nylon lines heat up internally as a result of the friction of stretching and shrinking. Wet nylon is much less affected because water acts as both a coolant and a lubricant. If you keep a nylon pendant dry by putting a plastic cover over it, you might inadvertently destroy the line. Based in part on this study, some experts suggest using a Hazlett rode (a stretchy, polyurethane-composite, bungee-style rode designed to absorb and dissipate shock loads) for the primary mooring pendant, backing this up with a chafe-protected braided polyester (Dacron) pendant. I have never used a Hazlett rode, so I have yet to verify first hand that it is effective.

When a mooring line snaps it is often the buoy swivel that breaks. So, for an extra measure of safety, you can always take an additional line directly from the bow to the mooring chain under the mooring buoy. Also, in the event of a severe storm, you might decide to lay out your own anchor line to relieve the strain on the mooring line. Remember, though, that if the eye of the storm passes over you the wind direction will change. Your boat will swing around and the anchor line will tangle in the mooring line. This might cause your mooring line to lift or part.

Make sure the mooring anchor or anchors are large enough to take the weight of your boat. When Mike Plant moored *Duracell* off Jamestown, Rhode Island, after racing around the world, he put the boat on a mooring that was too light, and during a subsequent storm, the boat lifted the mooring off the bottom. Plant, who was aboard at the time, tried to start the engine, but it failed, which left him with no option other than to sail the boat up the bay, where he hoped he could put into a lee and drop anchor. Unfortunately, it didn't work out that way. Sails and sheets got jammed and Plant sailed the boat onto the beach in Jamestown. Fortunately, the damage was minimal, and the boat was repaired to sail again. If you have any concerns about your boat lifting its mooring anchors off the seabed in an 8- to 10-foot storm surge, move to a heavier mooring before the storm hits.

Finally, rig fenders horizontally along the side of your boat, in case another boat breaks loose and collides with yours. The fenders may not prevent damage altogether, but they will help minimize it. Then go ashore and watch the

Water-permeable chafe protection is available from Davis Instruments and Perimeter Industries. The Davis Instruments removable Chafe Guards fit 3/8- to 7/8-inch (10 mm to 23 mm) line. Each chafe guard is 16 inches (40 cm) long, but I'd prefer a longer chafe guard than this in case the guard wears through and you have to ease it out a little. (Photo Courtesy Davis Instruments)

Duracell coming ashore (top) and on the beach (above) after lifting a cement block mooring. Mike Plant, the boat's skipper, tried to sail up the bay but ended up running aground. (Photo courtesy of Jeff McDonough, The Jamestown Press)

storm from land, not from the deck of your boat. If you do elect to stay on board—and again, most experts say this is not a good idea—make sure that the fuel and water tanks are topped up and your sails are bent on, ready for instant use. Among other things, the additional weight of a full load of fuel and water will help make the boat more stable. And with full fuel tanks you will be able to use the motor to help relieve loads on the mooring lines or even power to safety if necessary. On the other hand, if your boat sinks or runs aground, a full load of fuel will create quite a mess.

What's in a Mooring?

Some boatyards lay out mushroom anchors. Others use concrete blocks. Still others use railroad wheels or heavy pieces of granite, while a few enlightened yards use Helix anchors. Let's consider the pros and cons of each type.

Mushroom Anchors

Mushroom anchors are widely used, but their holding power rests solely on their ability to become silted in. A newly laid mushroom anchor has very little holding power unless it is laid in a pre-scooped hole. The holding power depends on the rate at which the anchor silts in, which in turn depends on the type of bottom.

The mushroom anchor must suit the boat's size, ideally as expressed in displacement or buoyancy. Typically, however, an anchor weight (in pounds) of beam × length × 1.5 has been considered generous. By this formula, a 30-foot boat with 10-foot beam would need a 450-pound mushroom. In heavy weather, however, mushroom anchors often simply pull out of the seabed and drag.

The Dor-Mor Mooring Anchor

The Dor-Mor is a patented anchor that uses weight as well as silting-in to improve its holding power. It comes in sizes from 15 to 2,000 pounds (7 to 900 kg), and according to the manufacturer's information, the anchor has 10 times its dry weight in holding power once it has penetrated the bottom. Its square-edge shape is also said to allow it to dig in much

A Dor-Mor mooring is hard to lift after it has been silted in.

more easily than a round-edged mushroom anchor.

Concrete and Granite Blocks

This style of mooring relies solely on weight to hold it down. Determining the adequate size of such a mooring can be difficult, since the weight of concrete can vary between 100 and 160 pounds (45–74 kg) per cubic foot. Furthermore, when immersed in seawater, that same concrete will weigh only about half to two-thirds its original weight. So a 600-pound concrete mooring might weigh only 300 to 400 pounds (135–180 kg) when immersed. Of course, a concrete block will also silt in, but its holding power is not par-

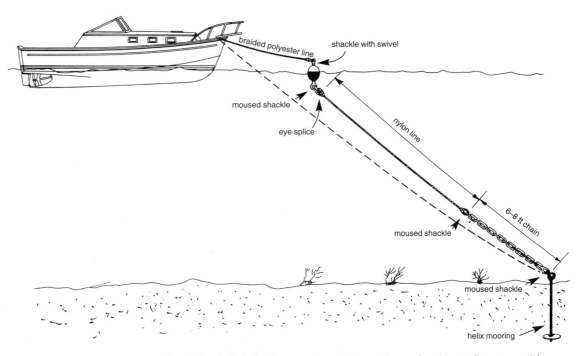

The best mooring system for high winds is laid out as shown here. The anchor is a Helix screw with a shackle at the top. The lower 8 to 12 feet (2.4 to 3.6 m) of the anchor line is chain (exaggerated for clarity), shackled to nylon anchor line suitable for the depth of the water. At the surface is a buoy with a swivel shackle to the line. The boat's line to the mooring buoy is braided Dacron with an optional Hazlett rode and chafe protection at the bow chock. The length of the Helix screw depends on the boat's displacement. For dinghies the screw is about 30 inches (0.75 m) long. For a 3,000-pound (1,360 kg) yacht, it is about seven feet (2 m) long. And for larger yachts the screw anchor is jointed to allow it to be folded.

ticularly high. The rule of thumb is that, to be effective, a concrete block should weigh three or four times as much as a mushroom anchor. Granite, while slightly denser than concrete, also has poor holding powers.

Railroad Wheels

Like concrete and granite, railroad wheels rely on weight to hold them on the seabed. As steel weighs around 400 pounds (180 kg) per cubic foot, it has slightly more holding power than concrete or granite. On the downside, railroad wheels don't have a shape that allows them to grab hold of the bottom, so the only way their holding power is increased is by silting in.

Screw-in Anchors

Recently we installed Helix mooring anchors for dinghy outhauls at our local dock. These anchors screw into the seabed and are probably the most secure form of mooring I have come across. Their holding power comes from the fact that the holding plate is three or more feet down in the mud. Of course, the holding power depends on the type of seabed. The best bottoms are clay and mud, while shale and rocky bottoms are not suitable. When it can be screwed in fully, the Helix provides phenomenal holding power. According to Helix Mooring Systems, one strain-gauge test was terminated when the measuring gauge threatened to break, not when the anchor lifted out. The company claims that several cruisers now carry a Helix anchor. If a storm is forecast or the owners are going to leave their boat for a week or two, they don diving gear and screw the anchor into the seabed. According to one report, nine boats swung off a single Helix anchor during Hurricane Hugo in the Caribbean.

Lying against a Dock or Seawall during a Storm

Suppose you can't get into a marina or you have to moor in a narrow canal or channel. In that

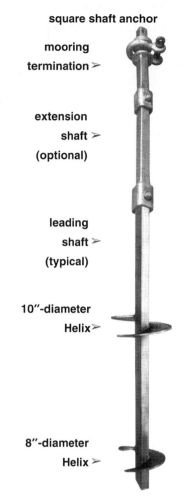

A Helix mooring will carry a lot more load than a conventional mushroom anchor, cement block, or railroad wheel.

case, go as far up the channel as you can to reduce the effect of the storm surge. Also, if the canal is narrow and you can safely put lines across it without having to worry about blocking boat traffic, lay them where you can. Having your boat nestled in a cobweb of lines is a fairly effective method of keeping it from being dashed against canal walls. Put chains or weights on the lines to give them some shock-absorbing catenary. Longer braided polyester lines will stretch more and will also allow the boat to rise with the storm surge.

Table 6–1. Anchor trials.

In a Vineyard Haven test, a 65-foot tug pulled on various anchors until they failed, and the load at failure was recorded. (Courtesy Helix Mooring Systems)

Mooring Type	Bottom Condition	Breakout Force
350 lb mushroom	mud (set 5 ft deep)	2,000 lb
500 lb mushroom	sand bottom	1,700 lb
3,000 lb concrete block	mud bottom	2,100 lb
6,000 lb cement block	sand bottom	3,200 lb
8/10 Helix anchor	soft clay mud	20,800 lb*

*The 1-inch hawser parted. The Helix never failed.

If the canal is wide and you can only lie against one side, you may have to lie alongside a dock wall. This might not be a problem as long as the wind does not blow your boat directly onto the seawall. In fact, if the wind is blowing away from the seawall, you may find yourself in a cozy location indeed, especially if low tide puts your boat below the top of the wall.

To protect your boat when lying against a seawall, you will need lots of fenders. But be warned, this location is only good for winds up to about 35 or 40 knots, even with a breast line. In anything stronger you should move to a safer location. Place the largest fenders you can find between your boat and the seawall. Next, put out a breast anchor with an anchor buoy so that other boats know where your line is. (Try a helix anchor here for increased safety.) If you use a conventional anchor, use 10 or 12 feet of chain next to the anchor to keep the hook parallel to the seabed. With the breast line out from the stern, use a spring to the bow to align your boat parallel to the seawall.

Check that you are far enough from the seawall that your mast won't hit the wall if the boat

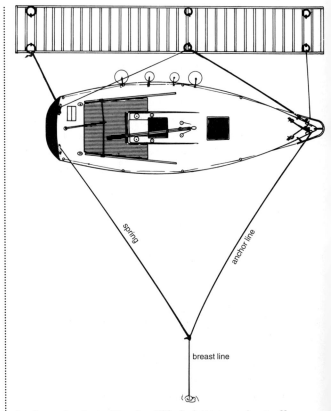

Laying out a breast hook will help keep your boat off a canal wall or seawall during strong winds.

heels toward it. If you have any doubts about the security of your position, lay out additional anchors off the bow or stern—whichever is upwind—to hold the boat even farther off. On no account should you let other boats moor alongside yours in bad weather. The pressure might be enough to crush your boat against the seawall.

Riding Out a Storm at Anchor

The only available mooring is too light, you're too late to get hauled, there is no space available in any of the nearby marinas, and you can't find a hurricane hole. What are your remaining options? Frankly, if you are close to shore, about all you can do is drop your hook and wait it out.

Pick a good spot. The ideal anchoring location is in the lee of a cliff or some buildings, avoiding gaps between closely packed buildings that may act like wind tunnels, accelerating the wind between them at the height of the storm. Remember that as a storm develops the wind is likely to swing, sometimes as much as 180 degrees, so you will need to be protected against waves coming from more than one direction. A sheltered cove might be ideal for anchoring.

Next, you need to know what the sea bottom is like. In the days before electronic depth sounders, mariners used lead lines to determine water depth. In the bottom of the lead weight was a recess filled with tallow or soft wax. By heaving the lead over the side a navigator could obtain a sample of the bottom—silt, mud, sand, or shell—as well as a depth reading. Today, charts show the bottom substrate.

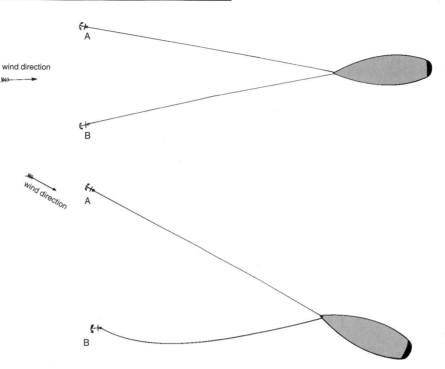

Top: *A layout for two anchors. As long as the wind stays in the indicated quarter, the boat will swing and keep out of danger.* **Bottom:** *If the wind is expected to come from only one direction, you might use this variation instead. Anchor A takes the brunt of the load, and anchor B comes into play only if A drags or the line breaks. B is doing nothing until the boat has dragged A past it. If A fouls B on the way by, you could end up with no anchors at all. If the wind shifts 180 degrees, the anchor lines could end up in a mess.*

Then lay out your anchors. Bruce, Danforth, and CQR plow-style anchors all work best on silt, mud, or sandy bottoms. Anchoring on rock or coral is not recommended in severe weather, and anchoring on coral is prohibited in many areas. Most sailors will lay out two anchors, which is fine as long as the storm blows from one quarter but can cause problems if the wind backs or veers so that the boat is left hanging on just one anchor. If you are planning to leave your boat and go ashore, you might want to lay out three anchors bridled to a common rode,

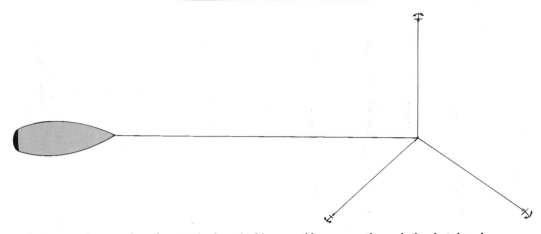

Laying out three anchors from a single swivel is a good heavy-weather solution but does have drawbacks. You need to set the anchors from your dinghy, and if the central swivel and/or the attached shackles break, your boat will be adrift.

hopefully guaranteeing that two are in use at any given time. After the storm you may find that the boat has turned one or two complete circles around the anchor line, and there may be a tangle to unsnarl, but at least you will be securely attached to the bottom, not on the shore.

In heavy weather, the longer the anchor rode, the better it will hold. Anchors hold best when they are pulled parallel with the seabed, but in heavy weather, especially if there is any kind of a surge, a short rode may pull upward more than horizontal. You want a scope of at least 5:1 (five feet of anchor line for every foot of depth) at the height of the storm surge, and 7:1 is better. Some experts suggest even more. Anchor weights and chains that keep the pull as horizontal as possible can all be used in this situation. It is always helpful to buoy your anchor lines in case a tangle gets too tight and you have to attack the mess from the anchor end. Remember to allow plenty of slack in the buoy lines to ensure that you can still find them if there's a large storm surge.

Finding a Hurricane Hole

If you wait until the storm is almost upon you to find a hurricane hole, it will be too late! The time to find a secure hurricane hole is when you are out on your boat before the hurricane season. Check your charts and cruising guides, ask other sailors or boaters, then go and inspect the likely candidates. At that time you can check out the best holes and figure out how you would tie your boat off. Make sure it can be secured properly regardless of which direction the wind comes from. Check to see where you may have to lay out an anchor and where your lines may be taken ashore. Try to imagine the area with other boats in it, then figure out where you would put your boat and how you would lay out your lines and anchors.

The ideal hurricane hole has a single small entrance with a fairly large open area inside for mooring. It is surrounded by high bluffs or tall buildings and has plenty of small to medium trees or tying-off points for lines run ashore. A small boat basin is ideal, as is a cove like Nelson's Dockyard in Antigua. Many hurricane holes were originally used in the days of sailing ships and are still of great value today.

If and when you decide to go to a hurricane hole, try to get there early, and if more than one boat is already anchored, figure out how the other boats will swing and where you should be

A typical hurricane hole is surrounded by high hills or bluffs with a narrow entrance and space for several boats. Here, Nelson's Dockyard in Antigua shows its natural defense against hurricanes.

located to ensure you won't be in their way. If the hole is really crowded and boats are rafted together, check that all masts are free to swing, that all windage is removed, and that the raft has enough ground tackle down. Each boat should have its own anchor, and possibly a second. Yes, the anchor lines will be a mess to sort out afterward, but at least you'll have a boat from which to do the sorting.

What About The Lines?

The lines you use to moor your boat are probably the most important part of the mooring plan. Without lines that stretch and allow the boat to move around, cleats can be ripped off the deck and lines can break, and your boat can be lost. If one line is too short you may have to tie two together, and a knot can weaken a line by 40 percent or more.

Dock Lines

Dock lines should be either nylon or polyester, either of which, if of sufficient diameter, will absorb the loads that winds, waves, and currents can impart while allowing the boat to move around slightly at the slip. Nylon is stretchier, which is a good feature, but as mentioned above, the revelation that nylon can heat up internally under strain has biased me toward single-braid polyester (such as New England Rope's Regatta Braid or Yale Cordage's Braidline). Double-braid polyester, which is used for sheets and halyards, is not sufficiently stretchy, so old jib sheets or halyards are not recommended.

A dock line should have an eye splice (large enough to put over a piling) in one end, and should be at least as long as the boat. Samson Ropes suggests that dock lines be just one and a half to two times the beam of the boat, but longer lines will make it easier to get the boat alongside when the wind or tide is pushing it away from the dock. Have at least one or two lines that are two or three times the length of the boat for these situations. Spring lines, which run from the bow and stern to cleats on the dock amidships, should be about the length of your boat or one and a half times as long. Docklines for storm use should be one or two sizes larger than your fair-weather docklines. For example, if your present docklines are three-quarters-inch diameter, use $\frac{7}{8}$- or 1-inch lines in a storm.

Anchor Lines

Anchor lines should be stretchy to absorb some of the loading on the anchor, so that the hook will stay on the bottom. Three-strand or braided nylon line is the material of choice, since it is stretchy and does not float. Three-strand nylon is stretchier than nylon braid, but either will do. Given that nylon lines heat up and may melt under strain, however, you could substitute a single braid polyester line like New England Rope's Regatta Braid, a 12-stranded single braid. As we mentioned above, this line has more stretch than a polyester double braid but is still not as stretchy as nylon. Some inexpensive nylon lines, especially those not intended for saltwater use, get hardened and thus weakened over time with immersion.

I recommend at least two fathoms (12 feet) of chain spliced between the line and the anchor; the weight of the chain will keep the pull more nearly parallel with the seabed, helping the anchor to dig in properly. The best way to attach the chain to your anchor line is with a shackle through an eye spliced around a thimble at the end of the line. The introduction of smaller remote-controlled windlasses has led to a growing tendency to splice the line directly

An anchor line should be spliced around a thimble that is then shackled to the anchor chain. Splicing the line directly to the chain subjects it to chafe in a storm.

into the chain in order not to bind the windless with the thimble and shackle. This is fine for limited use, but the splice is subject to chafe in a storm.

The Mooring Weight Your Boat Can Lift

Let's assume the displacement of your boat is 30,000 pounds and that it takes about 1,600 pounds to lower the boat an extra 1 inch in the water. So if a mooring weighs 5,000 pounds, and your boat lifts the mooring off the seabed, the boat will be just over 3 inches lower in the water. In other words, it will easily support this much weight. In a storm surge a boat might be lifted 6 or 8 feet, so you must make sure your mooring pendant is long enough to take into account both the storm surge and the wind force driving the boat back.

Seven

Preparing for Rough Weather at Sea

We were only three miles from the harbor entrance and very relaxed. The trip from Ft. Lauderdale to Miami had been easy. Gear was strewn around the boat as we made ready to enter Government Cut and moor at Miami Marina. We talked about having dinner at Joe's Stone Crab in Miami Beach. The trip had been uneventful, and being so close to land we weren't taking normal precautions.

Then the wind lightened. Dark black clouds hovered over Miami, but we paid no attention. We set down our beverage glasses and discussed whether to start the engine and motor in as the wind died. The ominous blue-gray clouds drew swiftly closer, but we scarcely noticed. Flags on beach-front hotels stood out straight just before they were obscured by heavy rain, but our only concern was whether we'd get rained on before we got ashore. We had full sails set, and the wind knocked us flat in seconds. Fortunately, the helmsman had the presence of mind to bring the boat head-to-wind and start the engine.

With no time to don foul-weather gear, we fought to lower the sails. The wind ripped at our clothing, and rain and hail stung our legs and faces as we struggled. A line squall had blown through, and in our haste to enjoy the delights of Miami we had ignored its approach—to our peril. Within 15 minutes we had both sails stowed and were motoring around the entrance buoy into the teeth of a 40-knot wind. (Had we been farther from port we would probably have reefed the sails and sailed through the stronger breeze.)

The wet headsail had been stuffed down the companionway on top of shore clothes, crew bags, and other gear. It took us two extra hours to clean up the mess.

This example illustrates the need to keep a weather eye open and the need for a sea storage plan no matter where you are. If we had kept our gear stowed until we were in the entrance channel, it would probably not have gotten soaked. If we had been paying more attention to the sky, we would have taken the sails down and turned on the engine sooner.

This episode also illustrates the value of good seamanship, whether aboard a sailboat or a powerboat, when the weather pipes up. We were lucky that the crew and especially the helmsman were experienced. A less experienced crew might have found itself in much greater trouble. (On the other hand, perhaps they would have been more vigilant!) This is the reason why you should practice sailing and motoring skills—like making a passage at night, shortening sail, going aloft, or even just heaving a line—so that you will be ready when it really matters. Perfect these skills on a warm, sunny day, and you will feel that much more confident in the face of an impending blow.

The "what if" game is played by all sailors at one time or another, but the ones who benefit from it are those who take the lessons to heart, those who make a checklist and use it often, and those who watch the weather carefully and use binoculars to check the flags and smokestacks of buildings or other vessels under dark clouds.

Preparing to Go Offshore

Storm or no storm, when you head offshore, out of sight of land, it pays to be prepared. And for an offshore passage of several days, it pays to be *extremely* well prepared. Preparation can take many forms, from stowing your gear properly to setting up a watch system that will allow you enough rest to stay alert while on deck.

Stowing Personal Gear

Typically, most sailors just toss their clothes into a sea bag before heading down to the boat, where the clothes are either stowed in the first available locker or dumped, still in the bag, on a convenient bunk. In the latter case, the bag usually stays there until someone decides to climb into that bunk to get some rest, at which time it is dumped on the cabin sole. In the morning the process is reversed.

If you get into bad weather, the watertightness of your sea bag is all that keeps your clothes dry. On one race across the English Channel, we took a pounding from a Force 9

You never know what kind of weather you are going to meet on a long trip. Here, Avance pounds into a gale on a transatlantic crossing.

storm and everything got wet, including the sea bags, which were soaked. Fortunately, before the race, the skipper had offered plastic bags to the crew for our clothes. Sealed tightly in these bags, our clothes stayed dry in spite of the conditions. There is nothing quite like getting soaked in a good storm and then going below, toweling off, and climbing into dry clothes. It raises morale and makes miserable weather seem much less ominous. Even if your sea bag is not watertight, put some clothes in zippered or freezer-style plastic bags. It you want to make absolutely sure they don't leak, seal them with tape or with a kitchen vacuum sealer.

Weems and Plath of Annapolis, Maryland, have taken the plastic bag strategy a step further by introducing the Pack Mate, a triple-reinforced plastic zippered bag with non-return air valves in one end. All you have to do is put your clothes in the bag, seal it, roll it up to force out excess air, and stow it away. Clothes stowed in this way take about one-half to one-third their normal space, and they stay fresh since the bag keeps out the dampness that results in musty odors at sea. With a half-dozen of these bags, your gear will take up less room and stay dry longer.

The Pack Mate bag rolls up, and air is squeezed out of it through a non-return valve. Clothes stay compact and fresh until the bag is opened. (Photo courtesy Weems and Plath.)

Sea Bags

Most sea bags make totally unsatisfactory storage receptacles. Sailmakers, who often manufacture them, make bags with just one large pouch. Some have a so-called watertight compartment, which isn't really watertight. Others just have a large plastic flap to keep your dry and wet clothes separated.

The best sea bags have several compartments of differing sizes. I like to have one compartment for valuables and keys, another (watertight) for passports and money (you will accumulate little piles of foreign money and change if you go from port to port), and yet another watertight compartment for dirty clothes. You also need a compartment for clean clothes, and another for sailing and street shoes. A well-organized sea bag is compact and easy to carry. I prefer to keep it small enough to fit into an overhead bin on an airplane, which means that I have to pack it well and keep personal gear to a minimum.

In the same vein, it's a good idea to use large plastic or garbage bags to protect sleeping bags and bedding. Stow everything carefully so that you don't poke holes in the plastic.

Stowing Ship's Gear

If you go below on your boat and find loose batteries in the chart table drawer, a toolbox full of rusting tools stowed in a locker, spare parts piled on a shelf or locker, and other gear lying around loose all over the boat, it's time to get organized.

First, collect all those loose batteries and stow them in a plastic zippered bag or Tupperware-style container. That way they are stowed in one place and safe from moisture. (And make sure they still have juice before you store them, unless you enjoy fumbling through an assortment of AA batteries during a night watch looking for working replacements for your GPS receiver!) Go through the boat and collect all your spare parts. Stow them in the same kinds of containers and put them all in one place.

If you save the small sacks of silica gel that come with every electronics item you buy, you can place one in each sack to prevent corrosion. Or you can buy Bullfrog corrosion prevention sponges and pads and put one in each bag. I live next to the ocean and find that Bullfrog sponges also inhibit rust in my toolbox at home. If your tools are rusty, you need to take them ashore and get them cleaned and buffed. Lightly oil them and stow them in plastic bags before bringing them back aboard.

Once you have everything sealed away from salt air, stow it and make a storage list, which can be posted in the navigation area so that the entire crew will be able to find any item at a moment's notice. Some computer programs like the CAP'N navigation program also allow you to make gear lists on your computer. *OnBoard*, from Force Ten Software, is a yacht management program that allows you to do the same thing. I find I rarely need to consult my storage list, yet the discipline of creating one helps me get organized and stay that way.

Copy the checklists on these pages and take them aboard your boat. That way you'll have a permanent record of where things are, what you need to do, and when you need to do it.

Before you put to sea, take a walk through your boat and list all the heavy items. Then ask yourself what would happen if the boat were upside-down and these items were to come loose inside the boat. Where would they go? What damage would they do? Could one of them sink the boat? Could it hurt or even kill somebody? If you find loose gear and answer yes to any of these questions, then you need to firmly bolt, lash, screw, or otherwise fix that gear in place.

Starting at the bow, look in the chain locker and ask yourself if the chain would fall out if the boat were to be inverted. If the answer is yes, figure out how to put a catch or lock on top of the locker. Are your anchors secured properly on deck, or if one is kept below deck, is it lashed to a pad eye or rail?

There is not much you can do about bags of sails, but at least they are soft and unlikely to do serious damage to life and limb. Make sure you check each below-deck tank and reassure yourself that it cannot move from its assigned position. Gently try to move it. Bladder tanks are often not well fastened down, so you might want to put a lashing over them. On one boat I inspected, the cabin sole rested on the floor bearers, which rested on the tops of the tanks. When I inspected further I found that the tanks were not even bolted or glassed in place. If this boat had been inverted, everything, including the fuel tanks—which when filled with 200 gallons (760 L) of fuel would weigh more than 1,000 pounds (450 kg)—would have come crashing down upon the occupants.

Moving aft, hopefully you will find that the engine is firmly bolted in place. But can the same be said for the rest of your engine room gear? Check the bilge pumps under the cabin sole. I have seen many installations in which the bilge pump was not secured properly. While you are at it, make sure the bilge pump's pickup hose can reach other bilge compartments, in case a *limberhole* (a drain hole between bilge sections) gets blocked.

Go into (or, in a small boat, at least poke your head into) the engine compartment or battery storage area and check that the batteries, toolboxes, cans of oil and other lubricants, spare filters, and other items are firmly fastened down. The ship's batteries should be fastened to their trays and the trays fastened down. I have seen instances where batteries were fastened to a tray, but the tray itself was not secured.

While you are in the engine compartment, make sure that gratings and metal walkways cannot move, that bilge water is removed regularly (note that engine oil in the bilge is hazardous waste), and that tools are not left lying around.

Make sure there is nothing in the bilges that can clog the bilge pumps. This may require a

Stowage Checklist

Item	Where Stowed	Item	Where Stowed
Anchor line		Nav light bulbs	
Additional anchors		Radar reflector	
Battery meter		Reefing lines	
Blocks		Shackles	
Boat keys		Ship's papers	
Bosun's bag		Stopwatch	
Bosun's chair		Tape	
Bulbs (spares)		Tools	
Burgee		Winch handles	
Dock Lines		Wire cutters	
Engine oil			
Emergency tiller		Spare parts	
Fender board		Batteries	
Fenders		Cabin light bulbs	
Fire extinguishers		Dinghy parts	
First aid kit		Electronics	
Flags		Engine parts	
Flares		Foghorn gas cylinders	
Flashlights		Inflatable pump and parts	
Foghorn		Spare shackles	
Harnesses		Stove parts	
Handline or leadline		Winch parts	
Life jackets		Toilet parts	
Loud hailer			

thorough vacuuming throughout the boat to get rid of boatyard debris. It may require removing paper from any cans stored in the bilge. (Label the cans with magic marker, and when you can no longer read the writing, toss the can out.) It may require that you constantly monitor the strum box to ensure that debris is removed regularly. No matter how clean your bilge is, a good storm bounces the boat around enough that additional garbage will end up there.

While moving through the interior, check small details, such as catches on locker and compartment doors. You want them to stay closed dependably and to open easily when needed. If, for example, the head door has a tendency to jam, you might find yourself

Returning from Fastnet Rock in an Irish Sea gale. Notice that all the crew are wearing harnesses.

trapped there when you need to get on deck in a hurry.

By checking your boat once or twice a season and before every offshore trip, you will make it better prepared to face any unexpected circumstance, not just a storm.

Setting Watches

Always set a watch for overnight passages. If you don't, you'll find that most of the crew will feel drowsy between 3 and 4 A.M. On a multiday passage, if the crew aren't able to establish regular sleeping patterns, they will become increasingly tired, leaving you more vulnerable in a storm. Start the first watch at 8 P.M. That way a new watch will come on deck at either midnight or 2 A.M., depending on the system you use.

There are several ways to set up a watch roster. The one most often used for a reasonable number of crew is four hours on and four hours off, starting at 8 A.M. or noon. With this system the dog watch, from 4 P.M. to 8 P.M., is often split into a pair of two-hour watches. The watch rotation then alternates each night. If you have enough crew you can set up a three-watch system, in which a person is on for four hours and off for eight hours. This will ensure that everyone on board gets plenty of rest.

Another watch system, known as the Swedish system, is ideal for shorthanded cruisers, since daytime watches are four hours long, but the night-time watches run for six hours. This means that every night each crewmember gets six full hours of uninterrupted sleep. Of course, the downside to this system is that the "on" watch need to work a bit harder to stay awake those two extra hours. These watch systems are shown in the sidebar. I have found that a four-on, four-off system is good enough for a three- or four-day trip, although for longer trips I would use a four-on, eight-off, three-watch sys-

Watch Systems

FOUR-HOUR WATCHES

Midnight to 4 A.M.	Middle watch
4 A.M. to 8 A.M.	Morning watch
8 A.M. to noon	Forenoon watch
Noon to 4 P.M.	Afternoon watch
4 P.M. to 6 P.M.	First dog watch
6 P.M. to 8 P.M.	Second dog watch
8 P.M. to midnight	First watch

SWEDISH SYSTEM

Midnight to 6 A.M.
6 A.M. to 10 A.M.
10 A.M. to 2 P.M.
2 P.M. to 6 P.M.
6 P.M. to midnight

Alternatively, this system can start at 2 A.M. instead of midnight. This makes the night watches slightly less strenuous.

tem and rotate the watch by splitting the dog watches every four days. The Swedish watch system puts you on watch at different times every night, and your biorhythms never really have a chance to settle down. This system tends to make you really tired on long trips, so it should be used mainly for relatively short passages.

Remember that when you are on watch, you are responsible for the safety of the vessel and all aboard. Don't fall asleep. If you feel sleepy, get up and walk around the deck or cockpit to stay awake. Drink coffee or Coke. Enough coffee will force you to hit the head at least once during your watch (a nice incentive to stay awake!), and the caffeine will keep you awake.

Sailing at Night

If you are at sea during bad weather, chances are the gale will continue into or through the night. It's natural then to worry about falling over the side and never being found, or mak-

ing a mistake and steering the boat onto the rocks. In the darkness of a stormy night you might get the feeling you are sailing down a dark tunnel as opposed to the wide-open ocean. With little to guide you other than the compass and the boat's direction, this feeling can be unnerving. Indeed, everything seems a little different at night. The sea may seem rougher and the wind stronger. Things seem more concentrated, more intense.

But there is really no need for concern. With a little practice you can put to sea at night without trepidation. And with an autopilot, electronic navigation aids, and safety gear, night sailing is now less stressful than ever. In fact, sailing at night can be a lot of fun. Not many other boats are out there. You have the ocean to yourself. The stars are often much more visible at sea than on shore, and there's nothing like watching the moon rise with wonderful majesty over the eastern horizon as your boat leaves a trail of white-frothed foam.

If you have any doubts about your ability to sail at night, practice first by sailing in the evenings. Sail during the late afternoon and then up to about 10 P.M. Gradually stay out later, until you feel confident about sailing through the night. If you can, pick moonlit nights for your first overnight forays. You'll find that you feel most tired between 2 and 4 A.M. This is when your biorhythms are at their lowest ebb. It's natural to feel sleepy, which is why mariners set up watch systems.

After you have sailed through the night a few times, you may develop a preference for certain watches. I like the early morning watch, because I can come on deck with a cup of coffee or hot chocolate and watch the false dawn. Then it gets lighter and lighter until the first rays of the sun peep over the horizon. As the sun climbs higher I start to shed layers of clothing, and (if I'm lucky) the smell of breakfast wafts into the cockpit. There is nothing quite like a sunrise and cooked breakfast at sea.

*It can be cold and wet in the early morning when the wind is blowing hard. Notice the helmsman in full foul weather gear and harness with tether attached as **Avance** heads toward Falmouth at the tail end of a gale.*

Protecting Your Night Vision

When coming on watch in the dark, your vision will need time to acclimate to the darkness, and normal vision is vital for performing to the best of your ability. It takes between 20 and 30 minutes for your eyes to adapt to the dark with maximum efficiency after being in a brightly lit cabin. Get on deck early and become acquainted with the darkness before you take the helm. Once you can see relatively well in the dark, look only at dim red lights, like those on the compass, and dim your instrument lights so that they will not hamper your ability to see. Use dim red lights in the cabin as well as on deck, to preserve night vision when you go below for a hot drink or a bit of navigation. And rouse the oncoming watch with a shake or call, not by turning on the bunk or overhead light.

Night vision is especially important in heavy weather, when you may be called on for sail handling as soon as you come on deck. The boat's motion is much more violent in heavy winds, and you will need to be fully acclimated to the dark before you can function safely and efficiently.

Helming at Night

Steering is a particular concern for beginning nighttime sailors, yet it's easy to master with some practice. When steering at night, don't stare at the compass and rigidly hold the boat on course. Watching the compass can mesmerize you and even cause you to fall asleep if you are tired. In the words of John Masefield, "All [you] need is a tall ship and a star to steer her by," and this sage advice is as true today as ever.

Look for a star in front of the boat and try to sail toward it. That is much easier than staring at a magnetic heading. Be sure to check your compass course from time to time, however, or you will gradually follow the star eastward across the heavens. When one star rotates away from your bow, look for another. In overcast conditions you can try sighting on a cloud, although you will need to be especially diligent about checking the compass—clouds move faster than stars. You can also feel the wind on your face and maintain the same angle to the wind and sea, but you will have to check the compass frequently.

Of course, in a storm, when clouds are scudding across the sky in front of the boat, helming can be especially difficult. You're unlikely to have stars for reference, and in most cases the clouds are moving much too fast and are too featureless to steer by. You'll need a feel for the boat, what old-time sailors called "sailing by the seat of your pants." Note the movements of the boat beneath you and the wheel in your hands, and feel the wind on your face. Using all your senses, you'll get through. In heavy weather, avoiding knockdowns, broaches, and the worst waves may matter more than a straight course.

You'll do fine.

Night Safety

Make it a rule that everybody wears a harness (and is clipped on) and a life jacket when on deck at night, no matter what conditions are like. If you have to go forward on a powerboat at night, I recommend that you wear a life jacket but not necessarily a harness. If you fall over the side wearing a harness you could be dragged under the boat. One of the afterdeck crew should keep an eye on anyone going forward, to respond immediately if there's an unexpected event.

It also helps to give every watch member a waterproof flashlight or strobe light and a whistle. If anyone falls overboard, these items will

---

Steering By Feel

To practice getting the feel of a boat, try this: while a crewmember maintains a lookout, try to steer your boat with your eyes closed. Sense where the wind and waves are coming from. At first you may find you can only manage it for a few seconds, but later, as you build confidence, you'll be able to steer for prolonged periods with your eyes closed. (I have seen some helmsmen steer for remarkably long periods with their eyes closed, although they wake up eventually when the boat jibes with a loud bang!)

---

help you find them. You can also wear a radio-controlled pendant that immediately alerts the helmsman if you fall off the boat. If you are alone, get a pendant like the Mobi-lert, which stops the boat's engine if you fall overboard. Another option is a Mini-B personal EPIRB, although these expensive items are most often used on offshore trips. Note that a Mini-B alerts the Coast Guard via satellite, and it could take as much as four hours to be rescued. See Chapter 9 for more on crew safety.

On many boats, sailors are issued a flashlight for use on deck. I find that a flashlight ruins night vision, however, and I prefer not to use one unless I have to find something quickly or untie a recalcitrant knot. You can always turn on the deck lights to make a sail change far in advance of a squall or other heavy weather. Just remember that it will take time to get your night vision back.

Be Prepared

Your preparations for sailing or motoring at night should begin long before darkness falls. On a sailboat, make sure your halyards are not tangled and that your sails are well organized below deck so you won't have to fumble around blindly or with a flashlight in one hand if a sail change becomes necessary. If the wind is expected to strengthen, you might place a heavier or smaller sail at the top of your sail inventory. If you are cruising and want to change to a smaller sail, do so before the twilight vanishes. While daylight lingers, check that you have enough battery power to last the night. If not, recharge your batteries immediately, or you will end up disturbing the "off" watch by running the engine in the middle of the night.

Aboard both sail- and powerboats, make sure you know where the spare electronics batteries, harnesses, life jackets, and flashlights are stored. Also make sure you have a good fix on any nearby vessels or landmarks, and that you are proceeding at a prudent speed. Learn what lights other ships will be carrying so you don't find yourself calling down the hatch to the "off" watch to ask what a red and green light on each side of two vertical white lights means. (It means that a ship over 150 feet [50 m] long is heading directly toward you!) If you are unsure, buy a book illustrating the kinds of lights carried by shipping at night (or buy *Rules of the Road and Running Light Patterns*, one of a series of fold-out laminated Captain's Quick Guides from International Marine, available also in a West Marine edition), and keep it aboard if you are going to sail at night. Make sure the VHF is handy to hail any shipping that seems to be getting too close, and have a spotlight handy to warn off large ships visually when the radio doesn't work. (You don't want to experience surfing on the bow of a large tanker, as we once did aboard *Morning Cloud* in the east end of English Channel. In case you think it was our fault, the ship simply followed another vessel that had turned slightly to avoid us. Both vessels were doing about 20 knots against our sailboat's 6.)

As soon as twilight falls, turn your navigation lights on, and before it is completely dark, take a walk around the boat and check that they are all working properly. Bow lights in particu-lar tend to get immersed in spray or solid water, which can result in corrosion that will eventually cause them to fail. Only by checking can you tell if they are working properly.

If you have them, check to see that the radar sensor and/or the radar are turned on. Finally, you might also want to make up a flask of soup or coffee and put out some cookies, candies, or sandwiches so that the on-watch crew don't trash the galley looking for food when they get bored.

Lights Can Be Confusing

When you are out at sea at night, looking toward land can be very confusing. Streetlights, vehicle lights, navigation aid lights, store lights, and all manner of other distractions make it hard to see harbor entrances, and spotting a single navigation light amid landside clutter can be next to impossible without the help of a few simple tricks. First and foremost, you should have a good idea where you are and where the nav aid is expected to be, so you will at least be searching the right sector. Then, if you cannot see it flashing against all the lights behind it, try looking to one side of the anticipated direction. Quite often your peripheral vision will pick up the flash before you can see the light when looking directly at it. Another trick is to isolate the nav aid against the dark ocean by making your way to the highest possible vantage point—the flying bridge or even a mast spreader—and looking down on it.

Once you have located the nav aid, time its flashes carefully using a stopwatch to see if it matches the pattern indicated on your chart. Don't try to time flashes without a watch—you will usually get them wrong. On one trip our navigator directed us toward what he thought was the correct light after timing it by counting "one, one thousand, two, one thousand," and so on. We dutifully turned toward it, even though it seemed well below our course, and the navigator went below. But a few minutes later he yelled at us to come back to our previous course. He had counted the flashes from a lighthouse instead of the buoy we wanted, and the lighthouse was several hundred yards inshore! At night, always double-check your navigation. It is much easier to make a mistake during the hours of darkness than during daylight, and this is never more true than when closing a shoreline.

Night-Vision Devices

Several devices are available to help you see better in the dark, including night-vision glasses of the type originally developed for the military. Early glasses used an infra-red sensor to illuminate an object, but the next generation concentrated available light without relying on infra-red sensors. The newest glasses concentrate and amplify available light to yield a picture that is almost as clear as daylight, and prices have declined substantially. Be aware, however, that in recent years the market has been flooded with cheap Russian-made devices, some of which give a grainy picture. Before buying night-vision glasses, try them at night if possible.

Also be aware that even the best night-vision glasses have their drawbacks. Using them can be rather like looking down a paper-towel tube. You can turn the tube to see anything you want, but you only see what's at the end of the tube. Also, if you turn the latest generation of glasses toward a bright light, the concentrated, amplified picture will flare dramatically, and you may not be able to see properly for a few minutes after.

Everyday Practice Makes It Easier to Weather a Storm

If you make the techniques outlined in this chapter part of your everyday sailing, your adjustment will be much easier if and when you encounter storm conditions. You won't have to throw together last-minute lists of gear—which you may forget in the panic of the moment. And you won't have to re-stow clothes in plastic bags; it will already be done. Your tools will be dry and working properly in an emergency. Heavy gear will be fixed in place. Make a copy of the checklist of what you need to remember in a storm.

Storm Checklist

- Make sure the weather radio is working properly and that you have fresh batteries for all electronics. The ideal weather radio has its own batteries and does not work off the ship's supply.
- Check your barometer periodically. Quite often you'll see the lowest barometric pressure before the weather forecast tells you that the center of the storm has passed. This lowest reading will give you an idea of when the winds will ease up and when they will change direction.

Remove all extra windage (lee cloths, bimini tops, and gear stowed on deck) and stow it inside the hull.
- Get the main companionway washboards out and ready to be dropped into place.
- Check that all halyards are untangled and available. If possible, shackle the halyards away from the mast, so they will not clang on the spar when the storm is at its height.
- Make sure that the cockpit seacocks are open and unblocked.

continued

- Bring the dinghy onboard. If it is an inflatable, collapse and stow it. If it is a hard dinghy, lash it down well and position a sharp knife near the lashings in case you have to launch it in a hurry. In a severe storm you may have to cut the dinghy loose and let it go if waves are pounding it heavily. It could be dangerous to keep it lashed on deck.
- Make sure the crew has seasickness pills ready and that they take them early if required. The pills are a lot more effective if taken before sickness sets in.
- Make sure all harnesses and life jackets are ready. Nobody should be allowed on deck in a severe storm without a harness and/or a life jacket. Wear a life jacket on a powerboat and a harness (preferably with a life jacket) on a sailboat.
- Install jacklines along the deck to clip harnesses to. (On an ocean voyage do this before leaving the dock.)
- Check that the life raft is ready and easily accessible.
- Get the storm sails ready and positioned near the companionway ladder.
- Get plenty of sail ties ready. Gear gets washed around by green water coming aboard, and a sail tie is handy for lashing anything down.
- Make sure all crew members have foul-weather gear and warm clothing available and that they don it before they get wet or cold.
- Identify your most experienced helmsmen and set up a helming roster.
- Make sure heavy items such as battery boxes, stoves, books, tins of food, and even sea bags are fixed securely in place.
- For a severe storm have a diving mask or two ready for the helmsman, and add dry towels to the on-deck crew's gear. (Towels worn like a scarf prevent water going down your neck. Henri Lloyd makes a long, narrow scarf/towel for just this purpose.)
- Close low-height ventilators. In a gale green water will enter the boat through open ventilators and may force its way past closed ventilators. The ideal ventilator during a storm is high enough to stay above most of the green water that cascades down the deck. The vent intake should be about 18–24 inches off the deck. Expect any vents lower than 10 inches high to take in water unless they are tightly closed. Turn all dorade vents to face aft and partially close the intakes. In most cases, you will want to remove all dorade-style ventilators and cap the openings before heavy weather hits.
- Carefully coil and secure any halyard tails and other lines that might be washed away.
- Prepare sandwiches and Thermos flasks full of hot soup for the crew. Turn off propane at the tank when the cook has finished.
- Set up leeboards or leecloths for each bunk. You may want to add extra rolled blankets, rolled sleeping bags, or even a spinnaker to make a berth snug, so that you don't roll around.
- If the anchor is on a bow roller, make sure it is firmly lashed down and the anchor chain is secure.
- Check your navigation lights and make sure emergency lights are ready with fresh batteries.
- If your boat has a hydraulic rig adjustment, you may want to ease off slightly on the backstay tension. Keeping the tension at maximum when the boat is slamming off a wave can lead to compression failure of the rig.

continued

Severe Storm Checklist

To the list above, add the following items:

- Make sure you have stormboards to cover every large window or hatch and that they can be fitted—before the full fury of the storm hits.
- Check your life raft grab bag and make sure everything you need is ready.
- If you have a roller-furling headsail, remove it and get a hanked-on sail ready. Use a heavy-weather headsail until the storm jib is required.
- Hank the storm jib onto the staysail stay and leave it in its bag. Tie the bag and the sail securely.
- If you have a storm trysail, get it ready.
- Prepare a sea anchor for deployment from the bow or a drogue for deployment from the stern. (See Chapter 8 for a discussion of sea anchors versus drogues.)
- Check your position on the chart and make a note of it. Put the note in your grab bag.

(If possible, update your position every few hours.)

- Dog closed any watertight hatches to ensure that water cannot flood the entire boat.
- The engine room intake vents on powerboats need to be sealed, but doing so restricts air into the engine compartment and can shut down the engine. Either seal unnecessary vents and jam the engine room door open to allow air from inside the boat to get to the engine, or allow air and water to enter through the vents but make sure the engine room bilge pump is working properly and is unlikely to clog. In a severe gale, check the bilge pump frequently for clogging.
- Be aware that a powerboat or a large sailboat engine can be back-flooded through the exhaust line. This is unlikely to happen while the engine is running, but guard against it if the engine stops for any reason.

Preparing Food

Storms can often last 36–48 hours if you sail directly through them, even longer if you opt to run off, following their rough seas and high winds. Even during the roughest storms, however, the crew should do their best to eat, and ideally that food should be nourishing enough to replace the energy they burn while battling the storm. In colder climes, most cooks prepare pre-storm soups and stews and keep them hot in vacuum flasks. You can, of course, provide sandwiches, fruit, and cold drinks for the crew, but beware of greasy foods that might make an already queasy stomach revolt completely. Cold foods don't warm a crew directly, but almost any food provides calories to help stay warm. Energy bars or granola-type cereals can help your crew get through the watch.

Using the Stove in Rough Weather

Keeping a stove going in heavy weather is dangerous. You should not attempt it unless the crew is in dire need of hot food. If you do have to use the stove, be sure to wear foul-weather gear and a harness—the former to keep hot soup or boiling water off your skin should a pot fly off the stove, and the latter to keep you from becoming airborne in an especially rough sea. Make sure your harness keeps you in the galley but not directly in front of the stove—that will put you right in the path of any spilled liquids. When heating food in heavy seas, fill pots only halfway, and always cover them with lids (if possible, with a short bungee across the handles to hold the lid in place). Pots should be clamped tightly on the stove and fenced inside deep fiddle rails. Soup bowls or mugs should be arranged so as not to spill hot liquid as you fill them. Few things are more annoying than spending half an hour making a hot drink only to see the mug fly off a countertop and onto the floor. Fill mugs about half full and warn the crew that the liquid may be hot.

Using the Head in Heavy Weather

What goes in must come out, and relieving yourself in heavy weather is a challenge of another sort. Banish any thought of peeing off the transom—in heavy seas this is a sure way to be tossed overboard. The porcelain throne is your only viable option, but you have to approach it with all the care of a student driver sitting for the first time behind the wheel of a car. If you're a guy, don't be too proud to kneel. Standing may strike you as more convenient, but no matter how sure your aim under normal circumstances, in a tossing boat you're going to get as much on the floor and wall as lands in the bowl, and that's unpleasant for everyone. So on your knees, buddy—from this distance it's hard to miss. Whether kneeling or sitting, you need to relax enough to go through the motions—or movements, as the case may be.

If you are successful, pump the head thoroughly. Even a modest amount of liquid will slop out of the bowl in heavy seas, usually straight into your gaping pants. You only have to experience going on watch with water in your pants once to develop a lifetime preference for sitting on the throne with your feet braced high on a bulkhead when possible. And one storm at sea will give you a lasting appreciation for a head compartment snug enough to let you wedge yourself atop the toilet with knees, elbows, skull, anything. Do what you must. This too shall pass.

Preparing Your Mind

When a severe storm is forecast, your first thought may be, "Will we survive?" Of course you will, unless your boat is in poor shape or you plan on doing something dumb. Rather, your thoughts should be, "How can I make sure my boat is in the best shape to survive without damage to itself or the crew?" Don't let your mind play tricks on you, and don't panic. There have been occasions when crews have abandoned perfectly sound boats in the middle of very survivable storms—and some such crews have subsequently been lost, while the boat survived. You can survive a storm—that, after all, is the whole point of this book—especially if your boat has been adequately prepared and you keep your wits about you. Yes, it will be trying, it may be terrifying, and some of the crew may get banged up a bit. But with appropriate precautions, surviving a storm is relatively easy. Plus, you'll have something to talk about when you get to shore.

Going Aloft

It was a quarter to six in the evening and just about to get dark. A southwesterly wind was blowing at 25–30 knots apparent, and we were sailing *Avance*, a 100-foot Jongert. We were a thousand miles at sea, heading east, running hard under spinnaker. The spinnaker guy was stretching six feet or so in the gusts, then shrinking back to the pole end as we debated whether it would snap. One of the crew flicked the instrument display to true wind. It was 35 knots, gusting to 40. Time to get the spinnaker down, someone said, although still we waited, telling ourselves that as soon as the other watch came on deck we'd all work together to get it down, then set the big genoa instead, snug for the night.

Moments later a tremendous bang shook the entire rig. We checked the guy. It was still attached. The boat slowed. The spinnaker floated out in front of the boat.

"The halyard's gone," somebody yelled.

Safer than breaking the guy and possibly the spinnaker pole and the headstay, I thought as I ran forward.

"The kite's under the boat," another voice yelled, and I realized that we had our work cut out for us.

On the foredeck the crew sweated and swore as they pulled 14,000 square feet of sail back aboard. Even with the boat head to wind, it took nearly an hour. Miraculously the spinnaker came aboard with no holes, so we could hoist it again. But there was one problem—we didn't have a halyard. Someone would have to go to the masthead and reeve another one.

To cut a long story short, after the wind abated I went up about a hundred feet above the deck to the masthead and reeved a new halyard. But first I took several precautions to make sure I descended the right way—slowly.

First I attached the hoisting halyard to the bosun's chair with a bowline—*not* the snap shackle—and then snapped the shackle to the chair as a backup connection and taped it shut. (I've seen too many sails collapse on deck when a shackle inadvertently opened to trust my life to one.) After that I put on a harness, which I clipped to the shrouds as I was being hoisted. This solved several potential problems. First and foremost it would keep me close to the rig all the way to the top: the farther up a mast you go, the greater the back-and-forth motion as the boat pitches. I knew that at the masthead I would be gyrating back and forth some 50 or 60 feet as the boat sailed across leftover seas. Another advantage of the safety harness was that it left my hands free to hold on and to steady myself. And of course, it provided me with a backup in case the halyard or bosun's chair failed. In harbor I don't usually bother with a belt-and-suspenders approach, but this far at sea I wanted an extra measure of safety. (I could have tied the safety harness to a second halyard, but halyards were in short supply at

A shot from the masthead of a 55-footer after installing a new spinnaker halyard. My knee is to the lower left of the picture.

that time—reeving another was the reason for going aloft!)

We also attached a line to the underside of the chair, since the weight of the halyard could exceed my weight and pull me to the masthead unexpectedly. As it was, the weight of both halyards after I had reeved them through the block required that the line on the chair seat be used to pull me down.

With the spare halyard tied to my chair (but not to me—if it had snagged it might have pulled me out of the chair) I was winched aloft, pausing at each spreader to reclip the safety harness. Eventually I arrived at the masthead, where I clipped my harness to the spinnaker U-bolt and reeved the new halyard through the block. Scanning the horizon, I saw no other vessels in sight. While I was up there I checked the wear on the sheaves and inspected the other halyards for signs of chafing. Then the boat pitched heavily, and I banged back and forth uncomfortably as I tied the new halyard to the chair so that the end would follow me down. Dispensing with the safety harness—I now had two halyards—I yelled for the deck crew to let me down, and the experienced hand on the winch lowered me fast while I walked backwards down the mast. He stopped me a few feet short of the deck, then lowered me slowly the rest of the way. No jerks, just one long, smooth ride from the top.

Going aloft is easy if you know what you are doing. To do so safely, however, you need to know what you intend to accomplish, take the right tools, and plan the ascent and descent with appropriate safety factors in mind. Here's how to do it right:

1. Plan exactly what you are going to do at the top of the mast so you will take aloft the correct tools for the job and will be properly positioned when you get there. If you are going to reeve a new halyard, for example, make sure you will be able to reach the halyard block. Once it's reeved, tie the halyard to your chair for the trip down. Remember that the weight of a halyard is often enough to prevent the chair from coming down on its own. If you have to fit a new sheave, replace a block, or adjust an antenna, make sure you have all the parts you are going to need. If you are not sure what needs to be done, study the problem with binoculars while you are still on deck.

2. Make sure you have the right gear to hoist you aloft. In harbor a bosun's chair is fine, but at sea I prefer to wear a harness clipped to the halyard, either with or without a chair. In other words, if you are going to play around at the top of a mast at sea, use a belt-and-suspenders approach to ensure that you will come down only when you want to, at the speed you want.

3. Don't rely on a halyard snap shackle while you are going aloft. Tie the halyard to the chair with a bowline and then snap the shackle to the chair. Finally, tape over the shackle so that it cannot come undone. Before you go aloft, check everything yourself; don't rely on others. If you are in doubt about your safety aloft, don't go; wait until you return to harbor.

4. Make sure the person handling the winch knows what he or she is doing. A winch override when you're halfway up the mast might force you to sit on a spreader or support your own weight to take the load off the halyard while the override is undone. This is not a pleasant experience, especially in a seaway.

5. Make sure the person tending the winch cleats off the line when you reach the masthead. I know of one instance when the winch handler held onto the halyard tail, then reached for a tool, inadvertently dropping the man at the masthead several feet. When you are at the masthead, you will not welcome such surprises.

6. Make sure that the tools you are taking with you to the masthead are in a closed bag and are attached to the chair with lanyards. Buckets are great for work on deck, but they tend to get hung up on spreaders and rain tools on the unsuspecting deck crew. That gets *them* a little testy—and knocking your winch handler unconscious is not in your best interests. And tools usually bounce on deck, then dive off the boat, never to be seen again. Tie a lanyard on your wrench and hammer, and

you can retrieve them if they slip out of your hand.

7. As you go up the mast, take the opportunity to check out all the mast fittings. You never know if there might be some kind of damage or wear aloft that was invisible from the deck.

8. If you are going aloft to repair a tear in a sail, always hang a rope from the underside of the chair leading down to the deck. That way, instead of swinging like a trapeze artist from the masthead out to the repair site, a crewman on deck can control your position. I once went aloft to repair a tear in the mainsail and found that it was easy enough to slide along the sail to the repair site, but once out there I couldn't stop myself from slipping around the leech to the other side of the sail. This did nothing for the sail shape, of course, and getting back to the weather side of the sail proved difficult. The on-deck crew get annoyed when they have to lower you, sort out the mess, and haul you back up again.

9. If you have to work on the mainsail track or the mainsail, you'll find it easier to lead the halyard around the spreaders and go up on the weather side, just abaft the spar, rather than on the forward side.

10. If you have to go up the headstay and no sail is flying, put a large shackle block around it and clip it to your chair. This will keep you close to the stay. Remember to tape the shackle closed and the block's pulley on the outside of the stay. Don't believe you can merely hold onto the headstay by hand as you are being hoisted. If you slip, the clang when you hit the mast will make your eyes water.

11. As you go aloft at sea, try to hold onto the leeward shrouds and use the spreaders to help you make midcourse adjustments. That way, if you slip, you end up hitting the headsail or swinging away from the

mast. If you can wrap your legs around the spar on the way up, it will also help you keep from losing your grip.

12. If you are asked to tend the winch, make sure you pay attention to where the mast climber is. Typically, the climber needs extra time to negotiate spreaders and diagonal shrouds, especially if he is inexperienced. Also make sure you have at least three wraps on the winch, and don't inadvertently pull them off when you are watching the mast climber. Don't use the self-tailing gear on the winch when hoisting a crew member. It can slip. Tail the halyard by hand, and don't let it slip.

13. Once the mast climber has reached the objective, cleat the halyard off securely. Make sure you can undo the line when the time comes.

14. When it is time for the mast climber to come down, try to pay out the line easily and evenly. Nothing is more disconcerting when coming down a mast than to drop a few feet, stop, drop a few more feet, stop, and so on. Quite often the person descending the mast can walk backward down the spar and descend quite fast. Remember to stop the descendee as he or she nears the deck.

15. Finally, stand out from under the person coming down the mast.

As a final note, if you are prone to seasickness, you probably shouldn't volunteer to go up the mast at sea. The movement at the masthead can be violent, and tossing your cookies from aloft is guaranteed to disgust the crew on deck as well as the owner, who will need to launder the sails.

Gear to Help You Go Aloft

Of all the gear that's been designed to help you go aloft, some is specialized and some is ridiculous. Here we'll look at some of the more popular options.

Mast Steps

Frankly, I don't like mast steps. They snag sails and halyards, they add weight, and I believe they also add a false sense of security. I have seen people go aloft using mast steps without a harness or safety halyard, which is running a big risk if you go any higher than six feet or so. Having said that, if you are sailing single-handed, going aloft is almost impossible without steps. (In my youth I could shinny up the shrouds, but now I'm old and cranky and weigh too much to haul myself aloft.) If you have superior arm strength, you can go aloft using a halyard and belay it to itself as you climb, but I don't recommend it.

The Bosun's Chair

Many sailmakers make a bosun's chair. If you buy one, it needs a strong seat that is completely sewn in. Avoid any wooden seat that can slide out of its canvas sling. I prefer an all-canvas chair in any event. A wooden seat can be a real pain in the butt (or the groin), and catching your leg between a wooden chair and the mast can give you a nasty bruise.

I like a chair with Velcro-closure pockets. Loops or shackles sewn into each pocket, to which you can tie tool lanyards while working aloft, are also good. I prefer at least four pockets, all located above the seat. If the pockets are too low on the chair, you'll find it hard to get at tools and materials while you are sitting in the chair. Try the chair before you have to use it aloft, and make sure everything works for you.

The chair should have a strong point underneath to which a downhaul line can be attached should you have to walk onto the sail. Also check the shackle rings to see that they are securely sewn and unlikely to rip out.

Harnesses

Make sure your harness and tether meet all Offshore Racing Council specifications, and when you are using them, hook the halyard to the harness rings, not the tether. I once went aloft to untangle some snarled halyards and had to hook my harness onto the spinnaker shackle, climb out of the chair, untangle the halyard I had just come up on, then climb back into the chair, all while racing along at 8 knots.

Spares to Make Your Job Easier

Carrying a spare halyard or two makes it easy to set a new sail if a spinnaker halyard breaks. On one Fastnet race we carried three spare rope halyards, and I replaced the same halyard three times when it broke at the masthead, the last time in Force 7 conditions. After that we carried twin headsails downwind from Fastnet Rock to Bishop Lighthouse rather than risk yet another break. Since that time I have always carried a spare halyard on long cruises.

Identify the tools that fit the gear on your mast. You can easily do this while the mast is sitting in the boatyard over the winter. Then you will know exactly what tools to take with you, which will shorten the time you have to spend at the masthead. Put lanyards on tools that you will often use aloft.

Preparing for a Cold Front

Not all storms last long. You may find yourself out on the water when a severe cold front blows through. While a cold front is not a low-pressure storm, it is often accompanied by strong winds and heavy seas. Be conservative. Remember, you don't have to get home by water. If you feel conditions are unsafe—or could soon become so—put into the nearest harbor and take a bus or a cab home. Your boat won't object to being left in a strange place for a day or two.

But what should you do if you are not within easy reach of a harbor when a cold front roars through? You could easily find yourself having to sail home in 15–25 knots of wind, with gusts to 35. Not Southern Ocean caliber to

STORM SCENARIO

Going Aloft in a Good Breeze

Low, gray clouds scud overhead, and intermittent rainsqualls obscure the horizon. Your 38-footer is driving through the waves with a full-hoist 100 percent blade jib. The forecast is for increasing winds, peaking at about 35 knots. A single reef in the mainsail balances the jib perfectly. Suddenly, there's a bang from the rig. Balance and control are lost as the mainsail collapses onto the deck. The halyard has parted. What do you do?

1. Sail under headsail only.
2. Drop the headsail and turn on the engine to maintain speed through the waves.
3. Keep the headsail up and use the engine.
4. Figure an alternative method of using the mainsail.
5. Go aloft and fix the halyard.

Your answer should depend on your sailing skills and where you are. If you are in reasonably flat water and will get home in an hour or two, sail under headsail only. You can turn on the engine as you wish to help control the boat. I would not take the headsail down—doing so will make the boat's motion unstable and uncomfortable. The headsail damps the rolling substantially. On the other hand, sailing upwind through rough seas for any length of time under headsail alone might jeopardize your rig. (See "Sailing Home Upwind" on the following page.)

If you are farther offshore and will spend more than 24 hours with no mainsail, especially if the wind is increasing, you should do something about fixing the halyard. But most mainsail halyards run inside the mast, so this will not be easy. Having a spare messenger rigged to the masthead crane is ideal if you remembered to set one up before the mast was stepped in the boat. Alternatively, you may want to rig some form of block at the masthead to take a jury-rigged, temporary external main halyard. Or you could hoist a reefed mainsail on a spinnaker halyard that has been led around the back of the mast. You'll have to keep a careful eye on the halyard for chafe, and you won't be able to set a full mainsail, but it will get you home without wrecking the rig.

If you're in the middle of the ocean, however, you should make a serious attempt to rig a new halyard, and that means someone has to go aloft and run a messenger down the inside of the mast. Another crew should be positioned at the halyard exit box to pull the messenger out as it appears. Use a small piece of wire or a wire coat hanger to pull the messenger out of the mast.

You should not go aloft in heavy weather. The masthead whips forward incredibly fast as the boat pitches. If you really, really have to go aloft, wear a harness and wrap the tether around the mast to keep yourself close. Wrap your legs around the mast and hold onto the shrouds. Let the crew winch you up. If you try to climb, there's a good chance you'll lose your grip and be bounced away from the mast. Once at the masthead, hook the harness tether into the spinnaker halyard block U-bolt or some other strong point. That way, if you lose your grip, you'll stay attached to the mast. Do what you have to do and get down on the deck again. Don't spend longer than you have to aloft in strong winds and heavy seas.

be sure, but enough to qualify as a handful. Let's assume fairly typical conditions: the wind has been blowing out of the south or southwest, and has generated 3- to 5-foot seas. But when it swings around to the north and strengthens with the passage of the front, strong crosswinds will make for very confused seas.

The time to be most concerned is just before a front arrives and just after it passes. Its arrival may be heralded by what weather experts call a *gust front*, which can pack gusts up to 40–50 knots. The north winds that trail the front may also be boisterous, producing confused seas.

If you have not been listening to your weather radio, the first sign of an approaching front will usually be steely black or dark gray-blue clouds approaching from the north or northwest. If you see clouds like this, you should turn on the weather radio to find out just how fast the front is approaching and what wind strengths it contains. If thunder and lightning are forecast in the front, head for port ahead of it if you can. Once in harbor, tie up next to a boat with a taller rig than yours, on the theory that lightning will hit the taller mast first. Try not to be the last boat at sea when a severe cold front with thunder, lightning, hail, and rain is approaching.

Often the wind will die just before the squall hits, which offers you an excellent opportunity to get your sails down and turn on the engine while you wait for the frontal winds to strike. Unless you have an experienced crew and heavy-air sails, I strongly recommend that you do just that. If you elect to wait for the new wind to hit, turn the boat so it is facing into the wind. Then, if the wind is strong, you can more easily reef or drop the sails or just let them flog. If you turn away from the wind, you will be pushed downwind by the new breeze. You may find that your sails are jammed against the mast or spreaders by 40-knot winds and are impossible to get down. If that happens, you can round up into the wind, though the maneuver will be hairy in a small boat in building wind and seas, or you can cross your fingers and hope that you have enough sea room to sail downwind for a while.

If you decide to proceed under power, instruct a crew member to roll up the headsail and take three or four turns with the sheet around the headstay to keep it from unrolling and getting shredded. Drop the mainsail, put sail ties around it (or stow it below) and then lay the sail cover over it if you have time. Try to get your sails down far in advance of the blow. You don't want severe winds to hit when you have sails all over the deck.

Sailing Home Upwind

Sailing to windward in a small boat in gale conditions is wet, tiring, anxious work. Your boat may be sailing along nicely one minute, then stopped dead by a large sea the next. Try cracking off the sheets a little. Sailing with eased sheets will give you better boat speed and may allow you to sail around large waves. When helming, watch the seas carefully. You can often bear away as a large sea comes at you and turn the boat slightly into the wind after the sea passes, working your way carefully through big waves. Your crew can often help by calling out when large waves or strong gusts are about to hit.

If the lee rail is continually under water, you have too much sail hoisted. Try reefing the mainsail or rolling up some of the jib. If necessary, change to a smaller jib. You might not have enough power to pound into a big sea, but the boat will stand up and sail better, and your crew will thank you.

If you don't have any smaller sails, take the headsail down and sail under mainsail alone. You will make more leeway (be sure to allow for this in your navigation), but you will reduce the chances of losing your mast. If you take the mainsail down and sail under jib only, the compressive load on the mast with no mainsail to counteract it along the trailing edge could bring the rig crashing down around your ears.

When pounding upwind into a sea, make sure that all hatches are closed and securely dogged down. Slide the hatch cover over the main hatch, and if there's any danger that water can go below, put the washboards in.

Wear warm, dry clothes. After sailing all day in shorts and tee-shirt, you don't want to risk hypothermia by beating into a strong, cold northerly wearing minimal clothing. If necessary, put on your life jacket. Not only will it keep you warmer, it will keep you afloat in the unlikely event that you go overboard.

Downwind Tactics

If you have to sail downwind to the harbor, don't over-canvas the boat. Take it easy, and try to avoid any large, confused seas that threaten to board your boat. Remember that sailing downwind you will spend more time in the stronger winds.

The favored sailing angle in heavy winds is a close reach or a broad reach. A reach leaves you the option of bearing up or down to dodge a particularly brutish sea, and even though you're sailing faster, you'll have a little more time to evaluate what's coming than when close-hauled. The motion is likely to be more comfortable as well, and you'll be better able to power through a sea—less likely to be stopped dead. You will need to pay attention at reaching speeds, and you may have to reef to prevent being overpowered. You may find that waves are thrown up into the headsail on a reach, so fit a headsail with a high-cut foot if you can.

If a front is coming and you are not racing, don't be caught with a spinnaker up. Exciting as it is to learn that your boat can plane as fast as a waterskier, it's disconcerting, too. The risk of gear damage is all too real, unless of course the spinnaker is blown out when the first gust hits.

I experienced exactly that situation in the middle of the night off the south coast of the Isle of Wight in an Admiral's Cup series years ago. Three boats were racing side by side, and we were in the middle. As our anemometer registered a 45-knot gust, our $3/4$-ounce spinnaker vanished. When I went forward to take it down, only the luff tapes remained. All our sailmaker would have to do was fill in the middle again!

We slowed dramatically as the spinnaker ceased to pull us, but this was just as well. The boat to our port, which was flying a heavier spinnaker, broached right across our bow, forcing the boat to our starboard into a broach to avoid hitting her. Shortly afterward the wind stabilized, and we put up a heavier spinnaker. But the other boats took some time to recover. Hairy? Yes. But it also was a great learning experience and one that allowed us to get ahead of our rivals, which is what racing is all about.

If you have a kite up and are beam-to the wind when a gust hits, expect to go over on your ear or to find out very quickly where the edge of control for your boat is. You should rehearse your broaching drills for just this occasion. (I suggest you have a rescue boat standing by when doing so, and try to do it when the water is warm.)

On a white-sail reach with main and jib only, you *will* go fast and you *will* need to have a crew operating the mainsheet traveler and mainsheet. As a puff hits, the boat will heel over, often until the rail buries. At that point the helmsman may start to lose control. By easing the mainsheet traveler you let the mainsail flog, yet the sail maintains its airfoil shape for when you haul it in again. Only after the traveler has been eased all the way to leeward should you let out the mainsheet. If you let go the mainsheet every time a puff hits, you will have a differently shaped mainsail when you pull it in again.

The helmsman should sit to windward along with all the crew, looking for gusts and big seas. All the weight to windward and aft will help keep the boat more upright and the rudder deeper in the water. Just before a gust hits, feather the sails into the wind slightly. The main will probably flap slightly, but you'll be able to bear off again after the gust passes. If you fail to feather the puffs in this way, the boat will heel farther and you will have to ease the mainsheet to get it back under control.

When running, don't go dead downwind, as that's asking for an inadvertent jibe. If you do have to sail downwind, you'll do better to "tack downwind"—jibing from one broad reach to the other. If the sea is really confused, put a *preventer* on the boom, a line leading forward to prevent the boom from slamming across the boat in an accidental jibe.

If you have any doubts about your ability to jibe in a strong wind and heavy sea, *wear ship* instead. That is, turn the boat into the wind, tack, and bear off onto your new course. Balance deliberation with smartness in this maneuver; if you turn upwind too slowly, you might get caught in irons—not a situation you want in these conditions.

When jibing in heavy weather, make sure the maneuver is tightly controlled. First, jibe the mainsail by easing the preventer and pulling the mainsheet in. As the mainsail approaches the centerline, everybody should duck, and the helmsman should *gently* turn the boat, holding it dead downwind for a few minutes while the crew brings the boom across the centerline. As soon as the boom is across, let the mainsheet out. Make sure you are not standing in the bight, and don't let the sheet run through your fingers—it will remove skin. Now the boat is running wing-and-wing. Put the preventer on the main boom to prevent it from jibing back. At your leisure, bring the headsail across to the new jibe and bring the boat up onto course. When bringing the headsail across ease it from one sheet winch to another keeping it under control all the time. If you allow the headsail to blow forward, you may end up wrapping it around the headstay.

A cold front passing through on a summer's day is nothing to be afraid of. Keep an eye on the weather and be prepared before it hits. Typically, when a front comes out of the north or northwest, the winds are strong and gusty as the front passes through. But afterward the sky clears and the sailing is often delightful, though much cooler. Keep your head and enjoy the ride.

Preparing for heavy winds and highs seas means having your boat and crew in the best shape possible to weather the conditions. You will have made most preparations long before you actually encounter bad weather, and these preparations set you up to get through it with little or no damage to your boat or ego. If you have prepared carefully, you should survive even the worst weather, unless you are just plain unlucky enough to hit a semi-submerged object or meet a giant wave with your number on it. Even long-distance voyagers encounter bad weather less than 2 percent of their time afloat, and the percentage of bad weather that's *really* bad is just as small. A coastwise boater is extremely unlikely ever to have to cope with survival conditions.

Eight

Heavy-Weather Techniques

Have you ever seen your boat's anemometer register 45 or 50 knots or more? If you have, you've been at sea in a Force 10 gale.

Looking to windward in these conditions is virtually impossible. When the seas mature in such a gale, you find yourself gazing from the bottom of a wave trough up at a wall of green water topped by a frothing white breaker. Waves tower over the boat, and you wonder if your little vessel will make it up the heaving green slope. With a thundering crash the crest plunges, hurling tons of green sea water toward you. As you struggle to point the bow of the boat at the oncoming deluge, it passes with a rumbling and hissing worthy of the bowels of Hades. Finally, the bow surfaces from beneath several feet of solid water, water that continues to boil its way back to the cockpit. The storm jib slats briefly as you spin the wheel to lay the boat off on the back of the breaker. A fraction of a second too late, and your heart leaps. It's a moment when time itself seems to stand still.

Below deck, the storm lanterns flicker and gutter as gravity takes over. On deck your stomach surges as the boat becomes airborne. For less than a second there's nothing below; the boat is falling off the breaker. Then, with an almighty crash that shakes the vessel to its keelbolts, it hits the water again. A minute or two later, you are again on top of the wave crest, the wind screaming, tearing at your clothes, blowing spray into your eyes, laying the boat over almost flat. You turn away to shelter your face from the stinging spume. How much longer can this go on?

Steering your boat in such conditions is hard work, requiring stamina, good helming technique, and luck. The lucky boats are the ones that are not in the wrong spot when a giant wave climbs toward the heavens, then succumbs to gravity and descends like a horseman from hell into the yacht's cockpit or rolls the boat over completely.

If you get caught at sea during a gale or storm, you have two groups of tactics to choose from: active and passive. As the wind and seas build you may at first try to continue toward your destination or evade the worst of the storm—an active response. If conditions get so rough that carrying on endangers your boat or crew, the next logical choice is to *heave-to*, and then perhaps to *lie ahull*, assuming your boat will ride safely in these attitudes, and not all will. These are passive tactics. When breaking seas render these simple responses untenable, you might try lying to a sea anchor, but more likely it will be time to revert to an active tactic—meaning one that requires active steering—running off before the storm, possibly trailing warps or a drogue.

In this chapter we will look at these three phases of storm response in turn—carrying on, adopting passive tactics, and running off. Once you find the right tactic for your boat and the conditions, you'll find the motion easier, and you may even get some sleep while the storm blows itself out. Oh, and yes—you do have one other option. You can call the Coast Guard. Remember, though, that when the Coast Guard responds to a Mayday call, they will take you off your boat, leaving it to sail or drift on alone, possibly never to be seen again. And if the Coast Guard finds that there was no real need for a rescue (your boat wasn't sinking, nobody was hurt, or there was no imminent danger), you may be asked to pay the cost of the rescue, which could amount to $100,000 or more.

Before you get caught in bad weather, learn what tactics best suit your sail- or powerboat.

For example, many modern sailboats with deep, short-chord keels lack the underwater lateral plane to heave-to successfully. Such boats will keep falling off to lie beam-to the seas—the last thing you want—and this tendency is only heightened when the boat is using a reefed main and a storm jib set way forward on the headstay. Nor is such a boat likely to lie successfully to a sea anchor. Rather, it will tend to skitter from side to side, and your tactics will have to take that into account. (Hint: If your boat oscillates back and forth on a mooring or anchor, it will probably do so on a sea anchor as well.) By comparison, long-keeled sailboats will often lie docile for quite some time when hove-to, and may also lie to a sea anchor successfully.

It's always a good idea to practice heaving-to with a reefed mainsail (or storm trysail) and headsail (or storm jib) in moderate conditions before you have to try it in heavy seas. You might try it for the first time on an afternoon when the wind is blowing 15–20 knots, and later in somewhat stronger winds. Build confidence in your abilities before you set out to cross an ocean.

Carrying On

If getting to your destination fast is critical, if your boat simply will not heave-to or lie ahull safely, if you lack the sea room to heave-to or run off, if sailing or powering through a storm might carry you away from the worst of it, or if the conditions simply aren't bad enough to force a halt, you'll have reason to carry on as long as possible. This takes a different sort of boat handling from what you may be used to, as well as a fair amount of skill. It also requires flexibility. If your sailboat won't tack in heavy weather, *wear ship* (see below). If you cannot jibe without stressing the rig to its failure point, roll up or take down the sails and use your engine to power over to the other tack. Be willing to try whatever it takes.

Broaching

The wind is strong, but you're still able to carry on. What are the risks? One of them, certainly, is broaching.

Let's say you're at the helm of an offshore racing boat, careening downwind in a 30-knot breeze with spinnaker set. You are sailing on adrenaline, hyper-alert to the slightest nuance of the boat's performance. The wheel seems almost alive as it kicks in your hands. The boat surges down a wave and the vibration starts, in the rudder blade first, then in the keel area. Soon the entire boat is humming. You know you are on the edge of control. When one deep trough spans your boat from bow to stern, the roiling stern wave breaks right at the corner of the transom, the roar filling your ears. It feels like the boat is on the thinnest of tightropes. The spinnaker starts oscillating, first to port, then to starboard. You try to anticipate it and stop the oscillations, but you get a second or two out of phase. Now you are reacting to the rolling instead of anticipating it.

Everyone onboard knows it is only a matter of time before you lose it. The boom plows a groove in the sea surface, making spray fly. Somebody hauls on the sheet, but you tell them to leave it, and they let out the vang instead. The boat rolls the other way, and the spinnaker pole digs a spray-edged furrow. You steer away from the roll, trying desperately to stop the oscillations. The boom hits the water again, and spray flies. Once again the vang is eased and the boom bounces across the water like a skipped stone. The boat straightens and rolls again, but this time you're too late. The pole digs in, the foreguy stretches to an impossible length, and the boat spins around the pole, which is now pointing at the seabed. The spinnaker collapses and blows inside the headstay. Sheets are eased and the boat slowly sheds water and comes upright. Sails flog as the crew attempts to bring everything under control and get back on course.

Congratulations. You have just broached to windward.

I remember once teaching advanced racing techniques to a crew of sailors. We had spent several days learning how to start, round a mark, and slam-dunk another boat. When Friday arrived, about the only thing we hadn't been able to practice was broaching. Leaving the dock, we encountered a typical New England northerly—first gusting and hauling ahead, then lulling and moving aft as we sailed to windward. By now the crew were confident in their own abilities and had started to sit on the rail and talk among themselves without heeding the trim of the boat. They were relaxed—a bit too much so. From my usual instructor's post, sitting on the stern rail with one hand on the backstay, I watched a puff of air stir up little whitecaps as it moved toward us and called out, "Puff coming. Stand by on the main." But the crew were too busy telling jokes to hear my call. I tried again, but to no avail. The helmsman heard me but didn't bother to relay the warning. Complacency had set in. I gripped the backstay and made sure I was on the high side.

The puff hit. As the boat heeled, it quickly became apparent that nobody was tending the mainsail, and the helmsman turned the wheel to counter the increased wind forces. "I can't hold it," he yelled. The bow spun into the wind. The crew on the rail, their legs over the side, were tipped backward, feet pointing to the heavens. They were in no state to help. As we lay over in the water, I popped the mainsheet and we came upright again. A deliberate broach? Sure. But it got the crew's attention. Since that time I have sailed with that crew often, and they pay a lot of attention when somebody calls out, "Puff coming."

A sailboat can be overpowered under virtually any conditions, either upwind, reaching, or downwind. You don't need to be flying a spinnaker to broach downwind. All you need is for the wind in the sails to create more rotational force on the hull than the rudder can control. Design features can also make a boat hard to steer and give it a tendency to broach. For example, IOR boats from the 1970s often had a distorted stern to give them a rating rule advantage. Under certain conditions this stern shape could induce turbulence over the rudder and cause the boat to broach.

Of course, not all sailors carry spinnakers in heavy wind—only cruising fools and racing sailors who relish the rush and exhilaration do that. The important part of sailing in strong winds is knowing how to keep your boat under control at all times. Remember to change down or reef your sails early.

Keeping the Forces in Balance

A broach can happen at almost any time. In heavy weather, an improperly balanced boat can spin out of control to windward or to leeward. And a cruising boat losing control in heavy waves can easily be knocked down and capsized. The key to prevention is setting your boat up with a balanced helm under almost all conditions, keeping the boat under control, and recognizing the conditions that threaten that control. It starts with understanding why sail forces must be in balance with hull forces. We'll

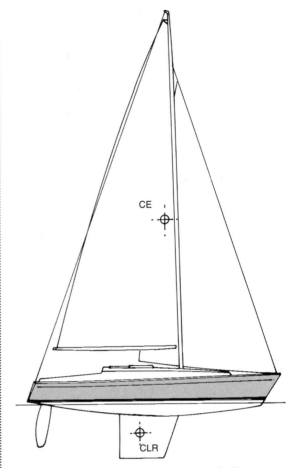

In a properly balanced boat, the center of effort is slightly forward of the center of lateral resistance.

Centers of Effort and Lateral Resistance

For lack of a better definition, sail forces are said to act through the *center of effort,* or CE. This point is taken as the geometric center of the sails. Hull forces are said to act through the *center of lateral resistance,* or CLR, the geometric center of the hull. These centers are illustrated in the accompanying figure. In practical terms, both forces act farther forward than their geometric centers, but their relative positions remain as pictured, with the CE slightly forward of the CLR. The CE is said to have a slight *lead* over the CLR.

find out what happens when those forces get out of whack, then we'll see what happens when a boat broaches and how we can control the tendency.

Keeping Control Upwind

As the illustrations show, when a boat is sailing to windward, forces are created on the sails and on the hull. The sail forces are countered by the hull forces, and in a balanced boat all the forces are in equilibrium. An increase in wind speed increases the sail forces, and further increases in wind speed heel the boat more, moving the center of lateral resistance (CLR) as well as the

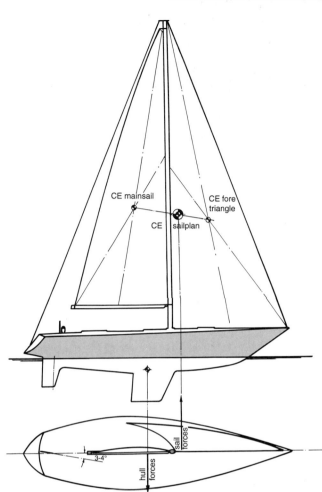

The overall center of effort is derived as shown from the geometric centers of the individual sails. In a properly balanced boat, the slight lead of the center of effort leaves a small residual weather helm that is counteracted by three or four degrees of rudder angle.

center of effort (CE). We'll talk more about these movements in a moment.

When the dynamic equilibrium is upset in this way, the boat starts turning to windward. Under normal conditions, the helmsman counters this turn with the wheel to increase the rudder force and bring the boat back into equilibrium. But if the sail forces increase so much that they can no longer be countered by the rudder, they need to be reduced by reducing sail

area. In other words, the main traveler should be eased out, or if the steering is consistently overmatched, the mainsail should be reefed. Easing the headsail would not give the desired effect. Sail forces tend to move aft when the wind increases, and easing the traveler down on the track and if the loads are still too high, easing the mainsheet moves them forward again and back into equilibrium.

Keeping Control on a Reach

It's a perfect day, and you are sailing a close reach. There is nothing strenuous on the day's itinerary, just an easy jog to an offshore island, dinner in a restaurant, sleep aboard, and return home the following morning. As you sail along, the cirrus clouds thicken and lower to become altostratus, blocking the sun. The crew grumbles good-naturedly about losing the sunshine. It's just a front coming through, you tell yourself, nothing to worry about.

Then the apparent wind increases to 22 knots, with gusts to 28. Now the leeward rail is submerged almost constantly. The crew rolls in some genoa and the boat heels less, but the helm is heavy. It takes two turns or more of wheel to bring the boat back on course after a puff. This should tell you that you're about to lose control. When the wheel is turned hard against the stops to stop the boat from rounding up, you have reached the limit of control. At that point, if the wind keeps building, the boat will spin into a broach, and that's what you want to avoid.

How do you avoid it? As we saw in the example above, a broach is caused by putting too much wind force on the sails aft of the normal CE. To move the wind force forward again, all you need do on a sloop or cutter is to let out

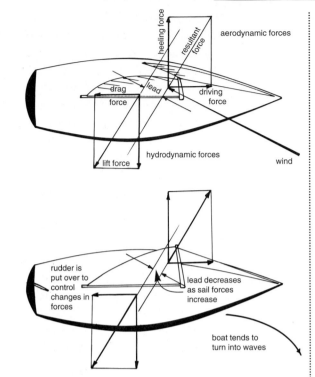

Wind hitting the sails generates an aerodynamic force, which is resolved into heeling and driving forces. To simplify, these aerodynamic forces are assumed to act through the CE. A boat moving through the water (A) generates hydrodynamic forces that can be resolved into a lifting force and drag. These forces are assumed to act through the CLR. When the wind increases and the boat heels (B), the sail forces move both aft and to leeward, and the lead becomes smaller. This unbalancing of forces serves to increase weather helm and is corrected with the rudder. But if a gust of wind overpowers the rudder's ability to keep the boat on track, the boat will spin into a broach.

the main traveler, then the mainsheet. The problem becomes a little more complex if you are sailing a ketch or a yawl on a beam reach.

I was once sailing on an 84-foot ketch, flying a mizzen, mizzen staysail, mainsail, staysail, and spinnaker. When a gust overpowered the boat, I knew we needed to ease the aftmost sail first. "Throw off the mizzen," I shouted. It was let go. "Throw off the mizzen staysail," was

the next order, and it too was let go. "Let go the mainsail." It went out. With these three sails flogging—and bear in mind that the mainmast was about 90 feet tall—the boat continued to slide majestically into a broach. At some point the helmsman yelled that he still had no control. I called for the staysail to be let go, and it joined the other sails flapping. The lee rail went under, and all 90,000 pounds of this magnificent ketch spun into a broach.

After we had sorted ourselves out, I figured out what had happened. Throwing off our sails had indeed lowered the pressure on the rudder, but the helmsman had held the rudder to the stops for so long that there was no longer a clean, attached flow of water passing over it. It had stalled, which reduced our chances of recovering from the broach as sails were thrown off practically to nil. If we had thrown them off earlier and allowed the helmsman time to bring the rudder back in line, the water flow would have been reattached, and we would not have continued into the broach.

On a reach, the first step toward controlling the boat is to reef the mainsail. That will reduce weather helm and bring the boat more upright. If your boat still shows a tendency to broach, consider putting another reef in the mainsail before rolling up the headsail. Then, if the wind keeps increasing and the lee rail once again submerges constantly, it may be time to partially furl the headsail or change down to a smaller one. Your aim is to keep the rig in balance. As you shorten sail, alternately rolling in the headsail and reefing the main, you will ultimately be left with a very small piece of headsail and a double- or triple-reefed main.

A large headsail tends to move the CE farther forward as you reef the main or let it flog temporarily to relieve pressure on the helm, but as your heel angle increases, you nevertheless have to reduce the size of the headsail in order to control the helm. Of course, if the boat heels until the lee rail is underwater but you still have helm control, the headsail should be reduced in size first.

As we saw above, on a two-masted boat you should reduce the sail area aft first. In fact, on many yawls and some ketches, it is standard practice to remove or reef the mizzen when the boat turns onto a reach so that it cannot push the boat into a broach. One last caveat is that large, flat-bottomed, dinghy-style keelboats should be sailed more upright than vee-hulled boats to get the best performance.

Keeping Control Downwind

A downwind broach can develop in a number of ways. If the mainsail is sheeted in too far, a gust of wind can force the boat's stern around. A headsail may start oscillating and spin the boat out of control. And a jibe, deliberate or accidental, offers another great opportunity for a broach. To make the jibe easy, the mainsheet should be pulled in almost to the centerline before the boat is turned. As soon as the boat is on the other jibe, the sheet should be allowed to

STORM SCENARIO

Heavy Weather Control

A roller-furled headsail becomes fuller when partially furled, which increases heel angle. (We discussed this earlier, in Chapter 5.) Unless the mainsail is hauled in really tight, it too is likely to be a little too full for the conditions. In heavier winds, a flatter sail is better. When the wind increases further, you need to get rid of more sail. What are your options?

Option 1. Furl the headsail completely and sail under mainsail alone.

Option 2. Drop the mainsail and sail under headsail alone.

Option 3. Get rid of both sails and turn on the engine.

Option 4. Set a staysail and keep the reefed mainsail.

Option 5. Set heavy-weather sails if you have them onboard.

Option 1. If you furl the headsail completely and sail under mainsail alone, the boat will make a lot of leeway. Allow for this in your navigation. Typically, the average boat under full canvas makes between 5 and 7 degrees of leeway. Under mainsail alone, you will see 7–15 degrees.

Option 2. Under headsail alone you'll also make a lot of leeway, and more important, you will have removed the sail load along the aft side of the mast. This allows the middle of the mast to flex forward as the boat pitches in a seaway, and if this motion becomes severe, the mast could collapse. If you must sail under headsail alone, make sure that the mast is tightly stayed with a midstay and runners.

Option 3. If you are near a port, engine power is an option, but in midocean you may need to conserve your fuel for a more desperate situation. And if you remove all the sails, the boat will roll considerably more than with some sail set.

Option 4. If your boat has a staysail stay (midstay) and a heavy staysail, setting it will keep the sail plan compact, help you make less leeway, help prevent a lot of rolling, and in conjunction with a reefed mainsail should balance the boat properly. This is the option of choice unless you have storm sails.

Option 5. If you have storm sails onboard, setting them will help your boat sail properly with the sail plan in balance and at a minimum heel angle.

As the wind increases still further, your options become more limited. At some point you will have to sail out of the storm, adopt passive tactics, or run before it.

run out. Any delay in letting out the sheet can force the boat into a broach.

As heavy seas roll under the hull from astern, the CLR may move forward and aft, affecting the boat's balance regardless of the sail configuration. If the helmsman is not paying close attention, this action alone might force the boat into a broach.

In other situations, downwind broaching occurs when the boat is flying a spinnaker and the sail starts to oscillate. As the boat rolls, the sail forces (acting at the center of the sail plan high overhead) move first to one side of the hull forces, then to the other. This creates a transitory horizontal lever arm, or couple, which causes the boat to turn. If this turning moment becomes large enough to overcome the rudder, the boat will broach, rounding up until it is beam-to the wind, sometimes with the rudder so far out of the water that it is completely useless.

How do you stop this kind of broach? As one veteran offshore sailor put it, "Keep the boat under the sail, man!" But that's often more difficult than it seems. It requires that the helmsman anticipate where the bow of the boat is likely to be before it gets there. If he waits until the sail forces have acted and then tries to stop the broach, it's unlikely that the rudder will exert a large enough force to do so. In fact, if he acts too late, he may only exacerbate the turning forces and encourage the broach. By acting early and decisively, the helmsman can stop the broach by increasing the rudder force while the turning moment is still low.

The crew can also do their part by pulling the spinnaker pole and clew farther aft to make the chute flatter, and by moving the sheet and guy turning blocks forward to the point of maximum beam to stop the sheet and guy forces from acting at the stern, where they have the largest lever arm. This helps cut down on oscillations. The crew should also ease the sails before a broach starts.

In short, you can reduce or eliminate broaches by being attentive to your sails and helm, not being overcanvased, and sailing within your experience. If in doubt, play it safe. It takes nerve and skill to sail a boat right on the edge without broaching.

Keeping Control of a Powerboat

A few years ago I was returning to Newport, Rhode Island, aboard a large powerboat. We headed north with a typical Narragansett Bay southerly blowing about 20 knots over our stern. I was standing next to the helmsman when suddenly the boat surged down the front of a wave, buried its bow in the back of the wave ahead, and slewed to port. We heeled over so far that the starboard rail almost buried. Two guests in the cabin slid to starboard; a third was left hanging onto a handrail. Drinks and plates of hors d'oeuvres crashed to the starboard side. At the helm, the skipper struggled to get the boat back on course.

What we had experienced was a broach. When we recovered and cleaned up the mess, I learned that that the boat was prone to broaching when going downwind in heavy seas. Later, when I saw the boat out of the water, I could see that it had the classic features that made it so: a deep forefoot, a wide transom with no skeg or lateral surface, small rudders, and a single prop.

What causes a powerboat to broach? In his 1946 book *The Naval Architecture of Planing Hulls*, Lindsay Lord attributed frequent broaching to a lack of lateral plane aft and too narrow a stern. In *High Speed Small Craft*, Peter Du Cane defined the causes and cures of broaching more succinctly. According to Du Cane, a boat traveling downwind in a strong sea is liable to broach if the following conditions are met:

- First, the boat must be traveling as fast as, or slightly faster than, the wave train. In this condition it will spend a relatively large

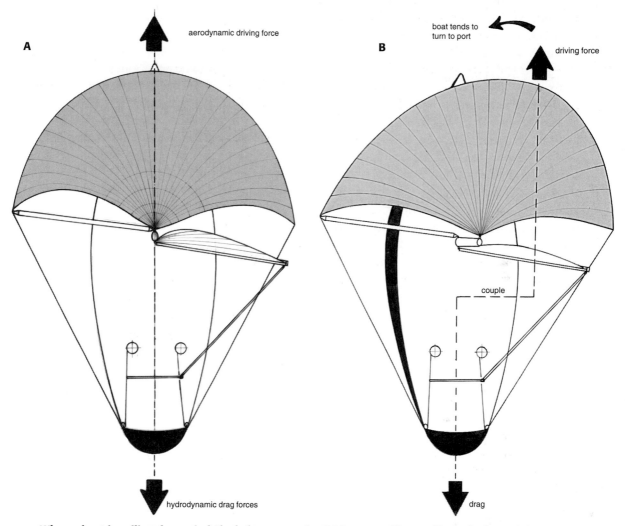

A

aerodynamic driving force

boat tends to turn to port

B

driving force

couple

hydrodynamic drag forces

drag

When a boat is sailing downwind, the helmsman and sail trimmers will try to "keep the boat under the sail"—that is, to keep the aerodynamic forces generated by the sail plan directly above the hydrodynamic forces acting on the hull, as in (A). But if the boat starts to oscillate, these forces get out of alignment and form a couple, as in (B). At first the rudder can exert enough force to counteract the couple, but if the rolling increases, eventually the sail forces overpower the rudder and the boat spins into a broach. Note that a downwind broach can occur to either side.

amount of time traveling along the crest and then down the front of the wave. As it surfs down the wave front its speed increases. By the time it hits the bottom of the trough it is usually going fast enough to bury its bow in the wave ahead, slowing the boat. The following wave then slams into the boat's

transom, which creates a turning moment that starts the broach.
- Second, the boat must lack lateral resistance aft. In effect, it must have no skeg and possess a rounded hull form and shallow stern sections that provide no "grip" on the water. This will allow the broach to continue.

- Third, the boat must have small or otherwise ineffective rudders to limit the helmsman's control. Note that most powerboats have small rudders when compared to a sailboat because the boat moves faster through the water. The higher the speed, the smaller the rudders can be.

So how do you minimize broaching in a powerboat? The most effective method is to slow down when traveling in a following sea. Make sure the boat is moving slower than the wave crests. It might take you longer to get home, but you will not have that knot in the pit of your stomach every time a wave passes the boat. If you're trying to hustle into harbor ahead of a squall, try steering diagonally across the waves rather than taking them square on the transom.

If you are looking at a new boat, check the hull shape. The forefoot should not be deep enough to trip over, and a widely flared bow and/or wide shoulders (full bow sections) will provide reserve buoyancy forward and prevent the bow from *rooting* (digging too far into the wave ahead). Look also for a large rudder or rudders and a transom that is neither excessively narrow nor very wide. If you favor a round-bilged hull over a chine hull with deeper sections aft, make sure the boat has an effective skeg to provide longitudinal stability and help prevent broaching. Twin props and twin rud-

How to Avoid a Sailboat Broach

If your sailboat has a tendency to broach, here's what you can do to stop it:

1. Fit a larger and slightly thicker rudder to give you more control. A very thin rudder will stall early and stay stalled. A rudder with a thickness ratio (ratio of blade thickness to fore-and-aft chord length) of about 12 or more percent will not stall as early and will regain flow sooner than a thinner rudder.
2. Cut down the length of the mainsail foot along the boom if the boat broaches when sailing to windward. A long foot increases sail area aft of the CE and helps to turn the boat into a broach. When you shorten the boom, the CE moves forward.
3. If the boat was designed back in the 1970s and has a bustle, filling it and fairing the after part of the hull will significantly reduce the tendency to broach.
4. Move the mast forward to move the center of effort (CE) forward.
5. When sailing downwind, don't let the spinnaker oscillate. Strap it down tightly with the sheet and guy run through turning blocks at the widest part of the boat.
6. Don't overpower the boat by flying too much sail as the wind increases.

How to Avoid a Powerboat Broach

If your powerboat has a tendency to broach, here's what you can do to stop it:

1. Slow down. Go slower than the waves passing you, and the boat won't have a tendency to race down the face of a wave and dive into the back of the one ahead.
2. Fit larger rudder(s) to exert more control over the boat's direction.
3. Slow down. It's the easiest and best way to stop a broach.
4. Fit a skeg to give the boat greater directional stability.
5. Slow down. (Get the message?)
6. In really hairy conditions (big following seas), trail a drogue on a bridle and long line to help you slow down and keep the boat's stern to the wind.

ders also give more control in a seaway. With the right design, a little care and good seamanship, you can make broaching a terror of the past.

When Carrying On Gets Dicey

Broaching is a potential hazard even in a stiff breeze of 20 knots or so. In stronger winds and bigger seas, however, the hazards multiply. How strong? It depends on the size of your boat, the competence of your crew, and the handiness of your gear, among other factors. But when your boat feels overpowered even under reduced canvas, you'll know you're there.

You will want to sail a close or broad reach under reefed main or trysail and a storm or other small jib, while carefully monitoring the weather. (You can also motor a sailboat or a powerboat either directly into or a few degrees off the wind, or run before it under power.) Sailing close-hauled—smashing through waves to weather—puts too much strain on the rig and hull, and sailing directly before the wind leaves you vulnerable to a broach or uncontrolled jibe. Nor should you sail on a beam reach, as that leaves you vulnerable to a knockdown or even a capsize if the seas are large enough.

In the northern hemisphere, if you are in the dangerous semicircle of an approaching storm (and a veering wind—one that is shifting clockwise—is a fairly reliable confirmation of this), with no time to get to the safer side of the storm, sailing a close reach on starboard tack is probably your best option for evading the worst of what's coming. If you're in the so-called "safe" or "navigable semicircle" (as revealed by a backing breeze), or if you're close enough to reach harbor before the storm arrives, a broad reach on starboard tack is probably the better option. In the southern hemisphere, port tack will be favored.

Make sure your storm sails are small enough for your boat. (We discussed this in Chapter 5.) Storm sails that are too large can either

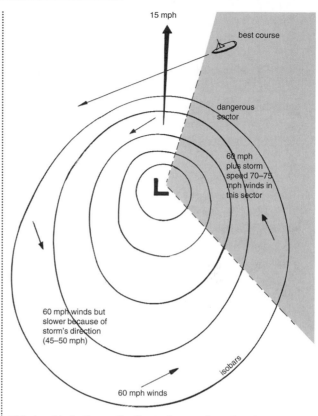

This boat is in the path of a major northern hemisphere storm but still has time, if barely, to sail a broad reach to the safer side of the storm's forecast track, where the system's speed of advance (15 knots) will partially counter its wind speed. In this case the sustained wind speeds in the safe sector might be 40 knots, versus 65 knots in the dangerous sector—a huge difference. If unable to make it to the safe side before the storm arrives, however, the boat would be better off sailing a starboard-tack close reach away from the approaching center.

overpower your boat or drive it too fast into heavy seas. Matching the speed of the boat to the conditions is one of the arts of sailing in heavy weather.

A powerboat can also employ an active approach, heading off and keeping the waves either directly astern or on the quarter. The angle at which you take the waves will depend on the windage near the stern of your boat. For example, a boat with a big, flat transom, such as one with an aft cabin, might fare best by taking the waves at a slight angle to avoid following seas slamming into the transom and slewing the boat around. A boat with windage forward and a lower transom might do better by taking the seas directly on the stern.

Boat speed in these conditions will vary, but should neither be so fast that the boat blasts through the seas, nor so slow that the small rudder (or rudders)—typical of a powerboat—becomes ineffective or that overtaking waves break over a low transom. In most cases a speed about half that of the wave train will most likely avoid broaching while maintaining steerageway. Active throttle control may be needed to prevent waves from breaking aboard. Even then, you'll find that a powerboat surges down the front of a wave at speeds approaching the speed of the wave train. To slow the boat and keep it under more control, especially in breaking seas, you can use a drogue on a bridle as discussed below. If you want to keep the seas on a stern quarter, the bridle can be adjusted to move the drogue out to one side and make it easier to control the boat.

Keeping a Lookout in Heavy Weather

There are two schools of thought on maintaining a lookout on deck in heavy weather. One school says that it makes no sense to expose more than one person to the elements when other crew can sit below in relative comfort and then go on deck feeling refreshed when needed. The other school claims there should be a second person on deck at all times in case something happens to the helmsman. For example, if a wave comes aboard and fills the cockpit, the only way a person below deck can come to the aid of the helmsman is to open the companionway hatch. Under these circumstances, opening the hatch could allow a lot of water into the cabin.

The lookout's job in a storm is not so much to watch out for other boats as to help the helmsman cope with both the routine and the unexpected. The lookout should wear a harness at all times on deck and be dressed in foul-weather gear over plenty of warm clothes. It is easy to get cold while sitting on deck in bad weather. Both the helmsman and the lookout should wear goggles or transparent face masks to help them look into the spray and rain. For most sailboat crews, keeping a lookout will mean little more than staring astern or to leeward, simply because it is too difficult to look to windward in heavy weather. If the boat is sailing downwind, the lookout can check for large following waves, but most of the time there is little to do in a storm other than hang on.

On a powerboat, keeping a lookout is easier. Usually the skipper and crew can sit inside the cabin and steer from this warm, dry haven. It is at night that powerboats have problems, as the glare from instrument lights reflected off the inside of the windshield can make it hard to see out. Red lights and a dimmer will help tremendously in this situation. For the powerboat crew keeping a lookout, seatbelts can be a boon. A seatbelt will enable the lookout to keep his or her seat as the boat bounces off waves, rather than having to stand for several hours.

Steering a Sailboat in Heavy Weather

The helmsman's job in daylight is to watch the seas and steer the best course to avoid launching the boat off the back of a wave. Under these conditions the boat's actual heading takes a back seat to weaving through the seas. In the dark, the job becomes much more difficult. The helmsman cannot see the waves, must sense the movement of the boat, and be able to feel the right time to bear off down the back of a wave. Inevitably there will be a few hard landings during momentary lapses of concentration, but far less than if the helmsman adhered strictly to the course.

When entering heavy weather, the first thing the skipper should do is put the most experienced helmsman on the helm and set up a roster of other experienced helmsmen. Storm conditions are not the time for a novice to start learning how to steer the boat. Steering in severe conditions is largely a matter of anticipation and instantaneous reaction to the waves and seas. You have no time to watch the instruments. When a sea comes at you, you must react with the correct helm movement. Unfortunately, there are few rules to guide what is really a set of instinctive reactions to wind and sea. We mentioned earlier that you should avoid sailing dead downwind if possible in moderate to heavy weather, but if circumstances force you to break this dictum, reef or take the main down and run with headsail only. In extremely heavy weather, go with no sail at all and trail a drogue, as discussed below.

I remember a heavy-weather Bermuda race in which the off-watch crew could tell exactly who was driving the boat. As we close-reached toward Bermuda at about 45 degrees off the wind, one helmsman would steer up the crest of a wave, then bear off at the right moment as the wave passed, maintaining contact with the back of the wave and making the "off" watch significantly more comfortable. The other helmsman, however, kept the boat right on course as if we were sailing in moderate conditions. Over and over we would feel the boat rising as a wave passed under it, the growing crescendo of water noise along the hull adding to our unease. Then the noise would cease completely as we reached the crest, and the oil storm lanterns would gutter and flicker as the boat went into free-fall. At this point the crew held tightly to anything they could find, and then a second or so later there would be an almighty crash as the boat hit the sea again.

This of course can be as bad for the boat as for the sailors on board, since each slam causes deflection in the hull structure. Repeated slamming can eventually lead to a fractured bulk-head or even to hull or rig failure, and should be avoided if possible. On another trip to Bermuda years ago, when boats were more heavily built than they are now, we opened a crack about 2 feet long in a $^3/_4$-inch plywood bulkhead and separated a 5-foot section of the bulkhead from the hull, all by sailing off the crests of a few storm seas. And yet we were lucky. Several competitors lost their masts, and the storm caused severe damage ashore when it hit the coast.

In addition to steering carefully, if you are sailing on a close reach, make sure your boat has the appropriate amount of sail set. The right amount will depend on the size of the boat, the strength of the wind, the air temperature, the sea state, and even crew fatigue. You need enough speed to drive the boat through the wave crests, but not so much that the vessel blows through the crest and flies into the approaching trough. That means reefing early and deeply. Off the wind, minimal sail is usually sufficient. In severe weather, some boats have been known to go downwind at 8 or 10 knots under bare poles. When a wall of green water is roiling regularly down the deck, you have too much canvas up and are driving into the backs of the seas ahead.

On the other hand, undercanvasing in heavy winds can be as bad as overcanvasing, since a boat with too little canvas may not be able to maneuver fast enough to avoid a breaking sea or turn fast enough to run off before a gust.

Unfortunately, in heavy seas, it can be difficult to determine just how much sail is needed. One moment you may find yourself in a trough between waves and virtually at a standstill, even with a reasonable amount of canvas set. Then, as the boat rises to the crest of the next wave, where the wind is howling, it may feel way overcanvased. In this situation it is better to set less sail and keep the engine running to help you steer in the trough than to endanger the boat when it is exposed to the full force of the

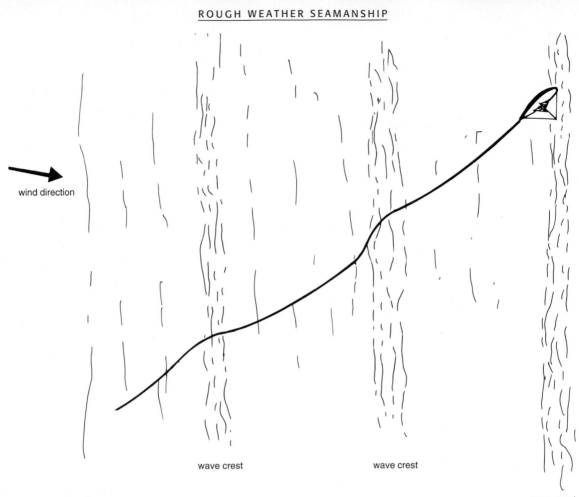

Steer up slightly into an oncoming wave, then lay the boat off on the back of the wave to minimize the number of crashes that you subject the boat and the "off" watch to. Don't bear off too far, however, or you might put the boat beam-on to the seas.

wind. Again, there are no hard and fast rules when sailing in heavy seas.

Steering a Powerboat in Heavy Weather

On a powerboat, steering in heavy weather is less critical than the proper operation of the throttles, which should be close at hand where they can be adjusted instantly as events dictate. For example, suppose you see a large wave bearing down on the boat when powering to windward. A quick increase in speed might put the boat over the top of the wave before it breaks on the foredeck. Then again, a quick deceleration may slow the boat enough to achieve the same effect. If the boat is going too fast and becomes airborne as it breaks through a wave, the throttles should be cut back to prevent the engines from over-revving.

Powerboat rudders are typically small, and a powerboat operating at slow speeds in heavy weather might not be easy to control. Intelligent use of the throttles can help keep it on course, heading into or slightly to one side of the wind. Steering in heavy conditions requires concentration to keep the boat just jogging into the wind and seas. Going too slowly into the waves risks the boat being pushed backward by a large sea. This is extremely dangerous, since the rudders will then act in the opposite direction and could cause the boat to broach backwards.

Note that in severe conditions the helmsman should keep the boat under control using wheel and throttles while other crew keep a lookout, navigate, and do any other necessary chores. The helmsman will be plenty busy keeping the boat going in a straight line, and will need to concentrate on the job.

Sailing Upwind in a Storm

There may come a time when you'll have no choice but to sail upwind during a storm, most likely to escape a lee shore. Quite frankly, you'll probably find it a virtually impossible task. Waves will slam into the bow and push it to leeward. The boat will make so much leeway that you will seem to go sideways faster than you can sail forward. Heel angle will vary dramatically, depending upon where you are in the wave train. In heavy weather you can barely see forward, as spray and rain drive into the helmsman's eyes. When you are trying to sail on the edge of a luff, even a slight misjudgment will put the boat aback and possibly take the rig out. All these factors conspire to make sailing to windward extremely difficult in a storm.

If possible, sail toward the storm's weaker side. If this means you have to tack during the height of the gale, pick your moment carefully. Don't simply slam the boat over as soon as you have decided to make the maneuver. Wait for a lull in the wind and seas. The best point at which to tack is just before the boat crests a wave. That way the boat will have its bow into the wind on the backside of the wave and be through the tack as the crest passes under the hull. On the other tack the boat will slide down the back of the wave and build speed as you get the new sheet in. If you tack on top of the wave, there is the danger that the boat will have its bow in the air as the crest passes and you will simply fly off the top of the wave with no forward speed. If you tack in the trough, you may not have enough power to get the bow fully through the wind.

If you cannot bring the boat head to wind in a heavy sea, the alternative is to wear ship—that is, to lay the boat off onto a broad reach, jibe, and bring it back onto a course as if you have tacked. Old-time square-rigged sailing ships that were hard to tack would often wear ship to achieve this result. Needless to say, jibing in heavy weather is a risky proposition. You must bear off through a beam reach—the most vulnerable attitude in a big blow—then head up through a beam reach on the other tack, quite possibly with a lack of control after the jibe. This is not something you want to attempt unless you have no other option. We give some hints on heavy-air jibing below.

Running Away from a Storm

Sailing on a broad reach is sometimes the easiest way to ride out a storm and is also a good evasive tactic if you judge yourself to be in the navigable semicircle of an approaching storm, as mentioned above. Bear in mind, however, that if you are in the dangerous semicircle of the approaching storm, a broad reach will keep you in the storm a lot longer than a close reach. Also, on a broad reach, the boat will probably move quite quickly even with few or no sails up. You may have to set a drogue to slow your progress, as discussed below. You may also underestimate the true wind strength, because sailing downwind makes the apparent wind weaker. Any sail that is set should be set at the bow so that it will keep the center of effort in the forward part of the boat and keep it tracking in a straight line. But remember that, as we saw in a previous chapter, setting a headsail alone can lead to compression failure of the mast. When you sail a broad reach with a small headsail set, make sure you have running backstays set up properly to stabilize the rear of the mast and a babystay or midstay to help prevent the mast from inverting as the sail halyard load is exerted on the top of the spar. For the same reason, you might also want to crank the mainsheet down hard against the topping lift to help keep a slight curve in the mast.

If you have to jibe when sailing downwind, you run the risk of taking the entire rig out of the boat—especially if you have to jibe the main. A jibe in heavy weather is best performed by a top-notch crew who know what they are doing. If you really must jibe, the best plan of action is to reduce sail area to a minimum and then jibe the sails one at a time. Jibe the mainsail by winding the sheet in on a winch. After the jibe, let the sheet out smartly to avoid overpowering the helm and letting the boat be caught beam-on to the waves, or even broach. Jibe the headsail by trimming it slowly from one winch to another. In other words, ease the old sheet out slowly as another crew member winds the new sheet in. Do not cast off the old sheet and try to trim in the new sheet. The sail will blow forward of the headstay, where, at best, it will merely wrap itself around the stay and be very difficult to trim in again. At worst, it will shred itself to pieces as it whips out in front of the boat, or will get itself so tightly wrapped that it can't be trimmed without sending a crew member onto the perilous foredeck.

An alternative to jibing is to gradually harden up onto a close reach and then tack. If you decide on this approach, pick your moment carefully. You do not want to be caught beam-on to the seas as a wave breaks. Ideally, you will be abeam of the sea just after the wave crest has passed the boat and before the next crest approaches. As soon as you get on the other tack,

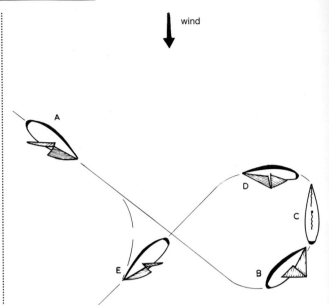

Tacking ship in high winds is an alternative to jibing and possibly taking the rig out of the boat. (A) The boat is brought around slowly on the backside of a wave. (B) At the bottom of the trough the boat is through the turn and (C) heads into the wind. As a new wave approaches, the boat continues its turn through the beam-to position (D), reaching (E) its new broad-reach course before the crest arrives. The dashed line shows the turn if the boat jibed.

ease the sheets until you are on the course you would have made had you jibed.

The Passive Approach

If wind and seas preclude carrying on under reduced sail or power, if the crew is exhausted and needs to rest, if you have sea room to leeward but not enough to run off before the gale, or if running off would take you away from your destination, you can try a passive approach.

Passive responses to a gale include heaving-to, lying ahull, or lying to a sea anchor. In passive mode, the boat is made as secure as possible and left more or less to its own devices. The crew goes below and turns in or reads while the storm rages around them, with one crew member ready to go on deck in case of some sudden need.

A sailboat's hull shape has a lot to do with the success of a passive approach to riding out a gale. Long-keeled hulls can usually be made to heave to or lie ahull successfully, but more modern hull shapes—those with minimum wetted surface, deep, narrow bulbed keels, and balanced rudders—may simply be unable to ride out bad weather passively. If you want to know whether your boat is capable of a passive approach, try heaving-to, lying ahull, or lying to a sea anchor in 20–30 knots of wind before you get into a gale.

A passive approach for a powerboat might consist of setting a sea anchor and dropping back on it. In this case, the vessel's forward windows may take a beating and may need storm shutters. If the boat has too much top-hamper forward and veers around excessively under a sea anchor, exposing its vulnerable sides to breaking seas, you might have to let go the sea anchor and try something more active. You might try "jogging" slowly into the wind, using just enough power to drive the boat through the wave crests and avoid being driven backward on the upslope of a wave, yet not so much power that the boat buries its bow in the oncoming wave fronts.

Or you might try running before the gale at an angle calculated to take you away from the storm's path, constantly looking over your shoulder while playing your throttle or throttles, speeding up when an overtaking sea threatens to swamp your transom, slowing down when your boat threatens to bury its bow in the back of the wave ahead. This is exhausting, nerve-wracking work, and you'll have plenty of time to wonder why you let yourself get caught out in such weather rather than listening closely to the forecasts and beating the storm to port. One thing you cannot do with a powerboat is to take the seas beam-to, whether under power or lying ahull. A powerboat is simply too vulnerable to capsize when beam-on to steep seas.

Lying Ahull and Heaving-To

In days gone by, lying ahull during a storm was a common practice. The crew would take down the sails and leave a long-keeled boat to drift under bare poles. The problem with lying-to like this is that the boat will likely drift more or less beam-on to the seas, which is not a good situation to be in when there are large breaking waves. Lying ahull is a good tactic for an exhausted crew in a reasonably stable boat in the early part of a storm, when the winds have neither yet had time nor achieved sufficient velocity to generate large breaking waves. If breaking seas are present, or if your boat does not have a large lateral underwater profile (a long keel), do not lie ahull. It is unlikely to work on a lightweight, high-performance, bulb-keeled yacht.

Heaving-to differs from lying ahull in that some sail is left set. When you decide to heave-to, you are really saying that you have confidence in your boat. A boat that is hove-to will make some leeway—as much as 4 knots—but the crew will be safe below, and may even get a little sleep. To heave-to properly, sheet the storm jib on the windward side and push or lash the helm to leeward. Some boats set a storm trysail, while others heave-to more successfully under a deeply reefed main. Most yawls and ketches should have their mizzen sails removed and heave to under staysail and reefed main, although I have heard of some long-keeled yawls heaving-to successfully under staysail and mizzen. Again, this tactic is best employed by boats with large lateral underwater profiles. It does not seem to work for a modern hull with minimum wetted surface, a bulbed fin keel, and a spade rudder.

You should experiment in moderate conditions to find out what works best for your boat. The force of the mainsail or storm trysail should be just enough to push the bow up into

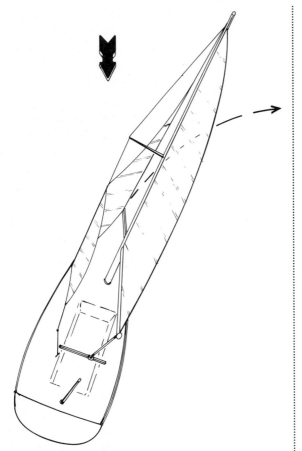

Heaving-to. Sheet the headsail to windward and let the mainsail drop slightly to leeward. Lash the helm down or put the wheel brake on to hold the rudder down slightly. Make minor adjustments until the boat balances properly and then enjoy the ride. This boat is hove-to under full canvas, which is unusual. Perhaps a singlehander is taking a nap in a gentle breeze at sea! Practice heaving-to under storm canvas so you'll know how it works on your boat.

the wind against the force of the headsail trying to push the bow to leeward. Note that when you are hove-to there is no guarantee that the boat will not get thrown over on its beam ends or even further by a large sea. However, a boat with plenty of stability will come back upright again—at least in theory!

If you own a fin-keeled boat, try to keep the sail plan as compact as possible when heaving

to. Widely spaced sails can exert a temporary movement on the hull that may cause the hull to pivot around the keel, especially if the bow of the boat is in a lull while the stern is exposed to a strong wind. If your boat is an older full-keeled vessel, the long keel makes it easier to heave-to.

A boat has a better chance of lying ahull or heaving-to safely when steep breaking seas are either absent or widely separated. A moderate gale is one such time; a decaying storm marked by long wavelengths and seas that are not particularly steep may be another. But when steep breaking seas are erupting all around—either because the storm is that strong, or because two wave trains are colliding, or both—the boat's crew should take a more active approach to survival, by running off before the storm. The possibility of taking a breaking sea on the beam is too great if hove-to or lying ahull in such conditions, and could result in severe damage and/or capsize.

It's especially important to take a more active approach in areas of strong currents or tidal influences, since wind and current in opposition build particularly steep, vicious seas. Off the east coast of North America, for example, the Gulf Stream exerts a strong influence, and many boats have been rolled by a combination of heavy seas and high northerly winds as they made a stream transit.

When lying hove-to, every item on deck that contributes to windage should be removed. Take down and stow a roller furling headsail if possible, remove the dodger and any lee cloths, take the life raft off the deck, and get the dinghy below if it is an inflatable. You might even cut a hard dinghy loose in extreme conditions, provided you have a life raft available—as you certainly should if you're out there to begin with. High freeboard forward will make heaving-to more difficult; again, experiment in moderate conditions to find out what works for your boat. If you find that heaving-to or lying ahull is untenable, you will either have to set a sea anchor or run off. If the latter, don't let the boat get beam-on to the seas when bearing off. Turn the boat the moment the crest of a wave passes. Do not try to turn as the boat is rising up a wave front.

Lying-To on a Sea Anchor

If your boat does not balance easily when hove-to or lying ahull, or does not like jogging to windward, you may have to lie-to on a sea anchor. This technique can be used both by sail- and powerboats. Several companies make parachute-style sea anchors that have functioned well in storms. They are available in a range of sizes to accommodate various kinds and sizes of boats. Lying to a sea anchor appears to be especially effective for multihulls, which, being light and beamy, could find themselves in great danger if they ever get caught beam-to a heavy sea.

You must have plenty of sea room when lying-to a sea anchor. Expect 1–3 knots of leeway. Boats have been lost when they drifted onto a lee shore under sea anchor.

From which end of the boat should you set a sea anchor? There are two schools of thought on this question. Some sailors advocate setting a sea anchor from the bow and letting the boat drift backward, while others say that it should be set from the stern, since the rudder is at risk of damage if the boat is allowed to drift stern first. I, for one, firmly believe that a sea anchor should be set from the bow. This keeps the bow—the strongest point in the boat—pointing into the storm, and hatches are less likely to be forced open by boarding seas (so long as they have been installed properly, with their openings facing aft). Setting a sea anchor over the stern, on the other hand, leaves the fat end of the boat facing the seas, rather like the side of a barn facing an oncoming torrent. The forces involved are impressive in any event, but even larger when the stern faces the seas. The wave train will be moving much faster than the boat, and the chances of being pooped are high. This makes the cockpit highly vulnerable to flooding and exposes the companionway to potentially damaging seas.

Some sailors recommend canting the boat a few degrees to the wind by taking a breast line from the transom to make a bridle with the anchor line. But while this apparently works for long-keeled, traditionally styled sailboats, you should experiment in moderate weather before trying it on your own boat in heavy seas. If it works for you, use it.

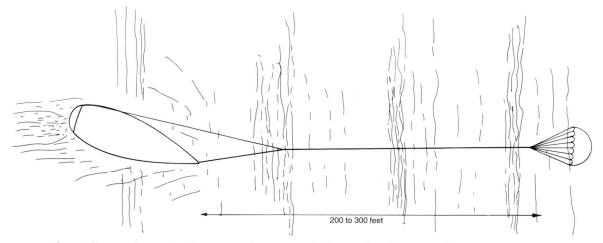

200 to 300 feet

A breast line can be used with a sea anchor to cant the boat a few degrees to the wind. Some sailors say this gives an easier ride than lying back on an anchor line.

The sea anchor line should be extremely strong, since the forces exerted on it in a storm are very high. Remember that both wind and sea are at work on a boat lying to a sea anchor. Some authorities say the anchor should be set on the third or fourth wave crest away from the boat, while others say it should be set at least 200–300 feet (60–90 m) behind the boat. As with a drogue, a long line serves two functions: First, it absorbs shocks as the boat snubs against the sea anchor—an important consideration, since in extreme conditions a sea anchor can impose strains large enough to rip deck hardware out of the boat. (For this reason the anchor line should be three-strand nylon or single-braided—not double-braided—Dacron.) Second, it allows the anchor to operate at sufficient depth to keep it open. Too short a line may jerk the anchor out of the water and collapse it, rendering it useless.

Setting a sea anchor requires careful maneuvering to bring the boat head to wind in a storm-tossed sea. The engine may be a major help aboard a sailboat, and on a powerboat you may need to use a little more throttle to bring the bow around. Once the boat is head to wind, set the anchor off the bow, making sure that the inboard end of the line is cleated or wrapped around the windlass *before* you pay out any line. Ideally, the sea anchor will fill and settle near the boat. When you are sure that it is full you can pay out more line and allow the boat to drop back from it. Always keep a turn of the anchor line around a cleat or around the windlass as the boat drops back. (Victor Shane's book, *Drag Device Data Base*, shows several methods of setting a sea anchor.)

The sea anchor should be strongly fastened through the bow chocks. Ideally, you should run the line back around the mast in case the cleat or windlass tears out of the hull. Powerboats should use the windlass as the main anchor point for the line. Fit chafing gear wherever the anchor line touches the hull, or use chain where

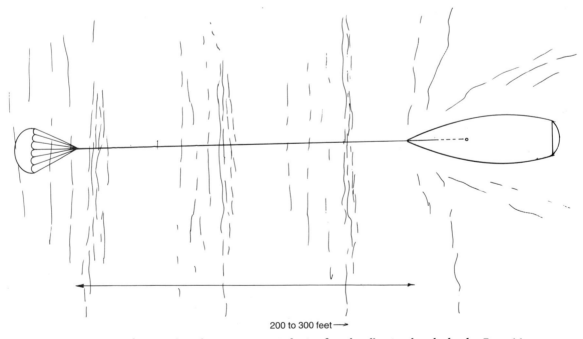

200 to 300 feet →

Lying to a sea anchor requires that you pay out plenty of anchor line to absorb shocks. Expect to make about 1–3 knots of leeway.

it runs over the bow chock. Chain should also be fitted with chafing gear to prevent it sawing into the hull. Chafing gear can consist of rags wrapped around the line, an old piece of garden hose wired in place, or leather strips wrapped and sewn around the line. Unfortunately for the on-deck watch, the line needs to be checked every few hours for chafe. If you do not have chafe protection on the line, wear can be reduced by pulling in 5–10 feet (1.5–3 m) of line every few hours, so that it does not occur in the same spot. By taking in the line you put the chafed spot around the windlass or cleat. Recovering line in this fashion will be extremely difficult or impossible while the storm rages, however.

Victor Shane notes in his book that as the anchor line stretches and shrinks after being deployed, it creates a sawing motion where it passes through the bow chock, and that many sea anchors have been carried away from the resultant chafe. With this in mind, he recommends that cleats be set well up near the bow or at the side of the hull, so that the anchor line does not pass through a chock or over the rail but goes directly to the anchor, reducing or eliminating chafe. This is a great idea that should be filed among the features to look for when buying a stormworthy boat.

Shane claims that in some cases boats don't lie well to a sea anchor due to *lack* of wind strength. In many reported cases the wind simply wasn't strong enough to drive the boat back on the sea anchor and keep the bow into the wind. The boat tended to veer to either side of the anchor line.

If you set a sea anchor, take particular care to minimize windage forward, or the boat may surge to port and starboard. This can be a real problem on a powerboat with a high foredeck and a lot of flare. Remember also that when lying-to a sea anchor your boat is moving backward, albeit slowly. This puts strain on the rudder, which should be rendered immobile with the rudderstock brake or by lashing it in place. Full-keeled sailboats that provide a full-length rudder attachment are less vulnerable to rudder damage when lying to a sea anchor—yet another reason why passive tactics seem to work best for traditional hulls.

Not all sailors think that sea anchors are a good idea. In his book *Heavy Weather Sailing*, K. Adlard Coles wrote that they put too much strain on a boat in extremely heavy weather or survival storms and may cause more damage than running away from the storm. On the other hand, a number of multihull sailors have ridden out severe storms using sea anchors. This discussion has raged for years, with people such as Victor Shane promoting the use of sea anchors (he also owned a company that made them), and other skippers who would not use them. Before deciding whether you want one on your boat, find out how it lies to a regular anchor. If it veers around it may well veer around on a sea anchor also. There are no hard and fast rules. You need to get out there and figure out what is best for your boat.

Running Off

There may come a point in a storm—particularly if your boat has a high-aspect fin keel and spade rudder and does not heave-to, lie ahull, or lie happily to a sea anchor—when you can neither carry on under reduced sail nor continue passive tactics. Perhaps the prevalence of breaking seas around your boat convinces you that lying ahull or heaving-to is simply unsafe. Perhaps you've already been knocked down once by a big sea that caught you beam-to. It is time to run off. This is an active tactic, requiring an alert helmsman and perhaps one other crew member on deck. It also requires ample sea room if continued for any length of time.

We've covered the basics of running off earlier in this chapter under "Carrying On." You might be under storm canvas, keeping the wind on your quarter so as to avoid an accidental jibe. You might be under storm jib alone, with mid-stay and runners set tightly to protect the mast from buckling. You might be under bare poles.

Sailing with a Drogue or Trailing Warps

As stated earlier, the biggest problem when sailing downwind is that the boat is likely to sail too fast, to the point where it might drive into the back of the next wave and bury its bow under tons of water, possibly even pitchpoling, or somersaulting, as a result. To slow down, and also to help prevent a broach, you should stream warps or a drogue over the transom. A warp is basically a long rope—maybe an anchor rode—paid out over the transom until it creates enough drag to slow the boat. A drogue is any object designed to provide resistance that will slow the boat when tied to the end of a long rode. It might be improvised: a sail, an anchor, an oar, a bottomless canvas bucket, a tire, or a hatchboard. Or it might be a purpose-designed device as discussed below.

When streaming a warp or warps, do not pay out a lot of line all at once. Slowing the boat too much can lead to *pooping*, in which overtaking waves come aboard over the transom, flooding the cockpit and attacking the vulnerable companionway.

Some sailors tie the ends of the warp to the corners of the transom and feed the bight over the stern, since this will create more drag than two single lines, while conserving the amount of line paid out. If you follow this plan, lead the ends of the warp around the primary winches so that it will be easier to adjust and haul back aboard when the gale abates. You may need to vary the amount of line you put out in order to regulate the vessel's speed. As long as you watch your speed carefully, you should be able to maintain a reasonable comfort level.

If you decide to trail a drogue to slow the boat, the best choice of equipment, in my opinion, is the Galerider drogue made by Hathaway, Reiser, and Raymond. It looks like a large canvas bucket and is heavily reinforced at the ends and where the ropes are attached. Its wire leading-edge ring allows it to be folded to take up less space when stored, and it has a narrower hole at the trailing end. It is set on 200–300 feet of nylon or braided line. Be extremely careful when setting a drogue—it can drag line over the stern at an incredible rate. I find the easiest way to set it is to pass the line out through the chocks, bring it back over the rail, then attach it to the drogue on the afterdeck. Put a bridle line on the drogue line so that you can stream the drogue directly astern. If you stream it from a corner of the transom, the boat will sail at an angle downwind. Wrap the drogue line at least three times around a primary winch, then lower the drogue into the water. Pay the line out slowly from the winch to control how far it streams behind the boat. If you simply toss the drogue and line into the water, it will run out aft at a great rate, and when it "bites" the line could snap or tear fittings out of the boat.

A drogue should stream a minimum of 200 feet astern of your boat so that, if the boat surges, it will not pull the drogue to the surface. The extra line will also help absorb some of the shock as both boat and drogue work in the seas. Current wisdom says that a drogue should be set just behind the third wave crest so that it stays in the water constantly and doesn't get pulled across the wave trough. Other experts, however, use distance as the parameter and adjust the length of the drogue line according to the way their boat behaves.

Some reports suggest using a longer line to keep the drogue submerged, while other users have shortened the line quite successfully. Boat speed seems to be the critical factor. A faster-moving boat tends to pull the drogue nearer to the water's surface, while a slower-moving boat makes the drogue more effective. By adjusting the length of the drogue line, the boat's cap-

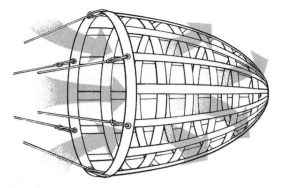

A Galerider Drogue. The drogue is 30 to 48 inches in diameter and 30–56 inches long, depending on the displacement of the boat.

tain can control the vessel's speed to best suit the conditions.

For example, when Michael and Doreen Ferguson were using a Galerider drogue aboard their 41-foot cutter *St. Leger* during a major storm to the north of New Zealand, with winds in excess of 60 knots, they noticed that a bight would appear in the floating polypropylene line as the boat slowed in wave troughs, which threatened to tear the steering blade off their wind vane. They shortened the distance to the drogue so that it stayed behind the first wave crest astern the boat and then sailed this way for the next 60 hours. Ultimately the boat survived, even though three sailors on other boats lost their lives and seven other boats sank in the same storm. According to Doreen Ferguson, she and her husband would occasionally see a small half-moon section of their Galerider drogue, but it still worked just fine. The short tether even allowed the wind vane to steer the boat.

Then there are those who maintain that the length of the drogue line is of minor importance as long as it is trailed from the boat's stern. "Think about a surfboard," says Donald Jordan, inventor of the Jordan Series drogue. "A

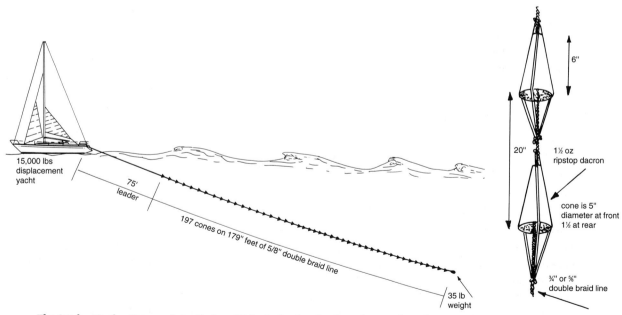

The Jordan Series Drogue is trailed on 75 feet of nylon leader. The number of cones varies according to the displacement of the boat. The drawing shows a 15,000-pound, 35- to 40-foot boat. Larger boats need more cones. For example, a 30,000 lb. displacement cruiser should have 130 cones on 220 feet of line.

wave imparts no energy to it unless it has motion. If a boat is not moving, it gets no energy from a wave. If a boat is moving, wave energy will accelerate it until it reaches the speed of the wave." The Jordan Series drogue is intended to gradually absorb energy from the wave and allow it to pass the boat without allowing the vessel to accelerate into a possible broach. Jordan studied drogues and boat motions after retiring as chief engineer for Pratt & Whitney and as a professor of engineering at MIT, so he brings a solid engineering and analytical background to the problem. Jordan Series drogues consist of a series of small cones attached to a nylon line as much as 325 feet (100 m) long.

Who should carry a drogue? As a rule of thumb, if you are going to sail more than 50 miles offshore, you should have one aboard. Sailing at 5 or 7 knots puts you at least 7–10 hours away from port, and strong winds can develop within 4 hours.

Running Off Under Power

As in a sailboat, it is easy to go too fast in a powerboat when running before a gale. This can be dangerous. The boat might surf down the front of a wave so fast that it buries its bow in the back of the wave in front and broaches. Slowing the boat using the throttles alone may not be enough at such times, and might in fact reduce rudder control precisely when control should be at its maximum. In this case, a drogue or warp towed astern might be helpful to slow

the boat and keep the stern facing the seas. According to Skip Raymond, President of Hathaway, Reiser, and Raymond, setting a drogue on a bridle and adjusting the lengths of the bridle arms allows a skipper to keep his boat at a slight angle to the seas.

More Thoughts on Using a Drogue

Some sailors don't use drogues at all. In his book, *The Long Way*, French solo sailor Bernard Moitessier tells of running with warps while transiting the Southern Ocean during the 1966–67 Golden Globe around-the-world race. When he removed them he found that his boat sailed better. (This was the first single-handed around-the-world race, and although Moitessier looked like a sure bet to win, he gave it up to sail back to Tahiti and Indochina, where he'd spent his childhood. The race was eventually won by Sir Robin Knox-Johnston aboard *Suhaili*, the slow but stout little ketch that I helped him fit out in Portsmouth, England, before he left.)

Moitessier then sailed with the wind off his quarter through Force 9 gales without using warps or a drogue. He also noticed that his steel-hulled boat, *Joshua*, performed better—surfing in heavy waves—if he lightened it, so he tossed a number of weighty items over the side. Weight may be a factor (along with experienced full crews and expert helmsmen) in the success of the relatively lightweight boats now racing in such modern solo events as the Vendee Globe

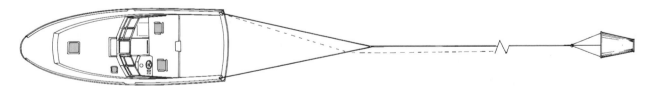

Use a bridle to adjust the angle at which the drogue follows the boat. This will help you to control the boat when heading at a slight angle to the wind. The dashed line shows how the port-side bridle could be shortened to help steer the boat to port.

and such crewed events as the Volvo Ocean Race (formerly the Whitbread Round the World Race).

It's important to note that a drogue fitted on the end of a long line may cause problems in a severe wave strike as a result of line stretch, which can be considerable. When it is loaded to 50 percent of its breaking strength, a nylon line may stretch to more than 20 percent above its original length. Under a sudden wave strike, a boat with 300 feet (90 m) of nylon line out could move some 66 feet (20 m) or more before the effect of the drogue comes into play.

Let's look at the ramifications for, say, a boat sailing downwind at an average speed of 8 knots under bare poles with a drogue deployed. That speed might surge to 12 knots when surfing down a wave face and drop to 4 knots on the back of a wave. As the boat accelerates off the wave crest and proceeds down the face, the line stretches and the drogue limits boat speed. When the boat reaches the bottom of the wave, it slows and the stretch is reduced. Let's say it

is now at 10 percent of the breaking load, and the remaining stretch is around 12 percent or 24 feet (7 m). Boat speed is low, and steering is not very efficient. Suddenly the boat is hit with a large breaking crest, and its speed starts to build. But the line stretches rather than resisting this surge, so the stern is forced around by the breaking sea until the boat is beam-to the wave. At that point the boat may broach and roll.

The Jordan Series drogue, with its large number of small cones positioned along the length of the line, is designed to eliminate just this kind of wave-induced capsize. The drogue exerts a constant drag on the line instead of the variable drag exerted by a single large piece of gear at the end of a long, elastic tether. On the downside, however, the Jordan Series drogue may actually do its job a little too well, as it tends to slow boat speed considerably—to 1 or 1.5 knots. Some sailors, including me, believe that this is extremely slow when waves may be approaching at 20 knots from astern. Virtually

Drogues

Old-time sailing ships used drogues extensively to prevent the ship from being pooped by a following sea. According to the *Oxford Companion to Ships and the Sea*, Sir Francis Drake used a drogue as long ago as 1585. A drogue can be simply a bucket, a cone-shaped canvas device, or even an old sail or several lengths of heavy line towed behind the vessel to slow it down. A drogue operates differently from a sea anchor—it is intended not to stop the boat, merely to slow its progress.

Here, are three drogues that are currently available:

Para-Tech. Para-Tech's drogues are available for boats between 20 and 150 feet long, and prices range from a few hundred dollars

upward. The Para-Tech looks like a cone-shaped bucket with no bottom.

Galerider. Galeriders come in four sizes for boats from 10,000 to 90,000 lbs. Prices vary from around $300 to $600.

Jordan Series Drogue. The Jordan Series drogue is available in several forms. Sizes are available for boats from 10,000 to 50,000 lbs. The cones can be purchased for between $400 and $600, depending on the size of your mono- or multihull. You can buy kits for a few hundred dollars, while fully assembled drogues cost around a thousand dollars depending on boat size. The Jordan Series drogue comprises a series of small cones sewn onto a long length of rope.

(Data provided by manufacturers.)

all the experienced sailors I have polled on this point preferred a little more speed and more control over the boat's course.

The solution might be to use a drogue line with less stretch than a three-strand nylon rope—maybe a nylon double-braid. In my opinion, this would reduce the possibility of a wave-induced capsize while running under a drogue, but without the slower speeds associated with the Jordan Series drogue. Then again, if the possibility of a wave-induced capsize existed, I might use a modified Galerider setup: the Galerider or other drogue 300 or more feet (90 m) behind the boat, and a second, much smaller, Galerider-style drogue closer to the boat—maybe 60 to 100 feet astern or just behind the first wavecrest. Both drogues would be set on braided line, and the drogue on the shorter line would ensure a faster response in the event of an especially large breaking sea.

Ultimately, the question of whether or not to set a drogue can only be determined during the course of the storm. If you try one method and it doesn't work, you should try another. Experiment in lighter winds, rather than finding out in the middle of a gale or severe storm what does or doesn't work. Again, different boats will require different techniques, and it is up to you to find the one that best suits your boat.

Too Much Drogue?

Veteran sailor Sheila McCurdy, who has sailed across the Atlantic five times in boats under 50 feet long and has done a number of boat deliveries, confirms that too much drogue can be as bad as not enough, and that you don't want to go too slowly in a seaway. "We were sailing a 47-foot McCurdy and Rhodes design to Bermuda and got into some bad weather on the northern edge of the Gulf Stream," she says. "We set a Galerider drogue and ran off before the wind. The Galerider slowed us so much that we were only doing about 1 to 2 knots in the troughs, and the boat swung sideways. As soon as the trough

passed and we were on the front face of the next wave, the boat straightened out and moved properly. We finally hauled the drogue in and ran off, keeping the wind on the quarter."

In discussing it later, Sheila thought that the storm had not been building long and that the wind was not strong enough to warrant setting the drogue. "The seas weren't really huge, and the boat wasn't over-accelerating down the front face of the wave," she says.

This is an example of setting out too much drogue too early, and slowing the boat to the point where it becomes almost uncontrollable. According to Sheila, the ideal solution would have been to change the length of the drogue line so that it wasn't stopping the boat in the trough, or to exchange the drogue for warps, which have less drag. "That would have given us more speed, kept the boat straight, and enabled us to sail it properly."

Survival Mode

In addition to carrying on, using passive tactics, or running off, there is one more response to heavy weather—an adjunct to any of the others, but especially to running off—which we'll call survival mode. In survival mode, you do anything you can to keep your boat afloat and your crew alive. It demands that you know your boat intimately and are able to handle it under all conditions. Hopefully, you will have plenty of sea room to leeward and will be able run off, keeping the wind and waves at an angle to the stern of the boat.

In survival mode, everything that causes windage on deck has been removed. You have long since battened down all the hatches, and where possible fitted storm boards over large areas of glass. Every piece of loose gear both on deck and below has been secured. Sail bags or clothing bags are packed into bunks to keep resting crew members in place. (A comfortable bunk quickly becomes much too large when a boat is sailing off big waves.)

STORM SCENARIO

Sequence of Action

1. When you hear a storm forecast on the weather radio, plot the storm's direction and set a course for the nearest safe haven, if there's one you can reach before the storm hits. If not, head out to sea and aim for the storm's navigable semicircle, if possible. Even under sea anchor you can drift as much as 100 miles in a severe storm, so you need plenty of sea room to survive a major storm.
2. Get harnesses, storm boards, lee cloths, storm sails, life jackets, life raft, grab bag, and water jugs ready. Make up flasks of coffee and soup and plenty of sandwiches. Pack bunks with spinnaker sail bags to keep crew secure when sleeping. Pack clothes into plastic bags and use twist ties to keep them closed. Remove all items of extra windage on deck and fasten down loose gear.
3. Reef sails as the wind builds. When your crew needs rest, or when your boat is laboring excessively even under reduced canvas, it may be time to heave-to and get some rest, depending on the configuration of your boat. Continue to plot the storm's course and speed, and record barometer readings and wind speeds. Note that you may experience deeper barometer readings and higher wind speeds than forecast over the radio. Radio weather broadcasts are usually at least two to three hours old. Your onboard instruments will tell you what is happening around you. Use weather forecasts to get the big picture.
4. If the storm builds to the point where heaving-to or lying ahull no longer seem safe, it's time either to set a sea anchor or run off. If you are running off and the boat speed increases to more than half the wave speed, set a drogue from the stern. If you choose to set a sea anchor, batten down everything and set it from the bow.
5. If the storm continues to increase, check for chafe regularly and swear to God that you'll go to church every Sunday when you get back ashore.
6. Most important, do not abandon your boat unless it is really sinking. You stand a much better chance of survival in a boat than you do in a life raft.

An important precaution for a survival-mode storm is to make sure that you have at least two functioning bilge pumps onboard, only one of which should be engine-driven. Engine-driven and electric pumps are of no use if the battery gets flooded. A large bucket and a hand-operated bilge pump are much more reliable. Regulations issued for blue-water racing events by the former Offshore Racing Council (ORC), now the International Sailing Federation (ISAF), call for at least one pump operated from on deck. In my opinion, this should be the largest pump you can find. If you have a choice, a pump such as Edson's Bone Dry (30 gallons or 114 liters per minute) or the Whale Gusher is ideal, as discussed in Chapter 4.

Surviving a killer storm at sea requires good seamanship, a well-found boat, and a lot of luck. Luck means not being in the spot where a freak wave dumps a million tons of sea water. It means not being on top of that wave as it descends. But if you read the barometer and the weather forecast accurately, track the storm, and respond by dodging it, making port, or at least finding its navigable semicircle, you'll make your own luck.

Nine

Keeping Your Crew Safe

Keeping your crew aboard the boat and keeping them safe is a critical responsibility for the captain. In rough weather each member of the on-deck crew should wear a personal flotation device (a PFD—in other words, a life jacket), as well as a harness to keep him or her aboard. A strobe light and perhaps even a personal locator device on the PFD will help guide you back to any crew member who does go over the side.

Still, there's more to keeping your crew safe than supplying them with safety equipment. You also need to be prepared for worst-case scenarios. For example, should the boat be holed by floating debris or damaged in a storm to the point of flooding at a rate faster than your pumps can handle, you'll need to know what to do and have the gear to do it, starting with an adequately sized life raft, an EPIRB, flares, a strobe light, a VHF radio, and—if you're more than a hundred miles or so offshore—a single sideband radio (SSB).

Personal Gear

If you're crewing someone else's boat, you may trust the boat's owner to carry the right personal gear aboard and make it available for your use. It's better, however, to carry your own gear and know how to use it. I have tested a lot of equipment and have chosen what works best for me. You should make similar choices.

Life Jackets

Before you buy your next PFD, I suggest that you jump into a pool wearing the life jacket you use now. Better yet, jump off your boat into shallow water wearing your life jacket and try climbing back aboard. If it's the inflatable sort, try this experiment when it's time to replace the water activator. What you find out may surprise you. It may lead you to change the way you store and use life jackets. It might even save your life.

The ideal personal flotation device is one that keeps you afloat under all conditions. You might prefer a conventional life jacket, but the trend is toward the inflatable variety, which is less restrictive and more comfortable when not in use. Inflatable life jackets are available in both manual configurations, which require you to pull a cord to inflate them, and in configurations that inflate automatically when the life jacket gets wet. There have been reports of automatic life jackets inflating after being hit by spray or rain, but you can prevent this by replacing the water-activator on a regular basis. The worst problem with inflatable life jackets is that all too often they are not maintained as they should be. Just like a life raft, an inflatable life jacket needs to be inspected regularly, and the CO_2 cylinders and water activators should be replaced every spring.

Follow the U.S. Coast Guard's advice and wear a PFD at all times, especially in bad weather. In fact, make wearing a life jacket mandatory on your boat as soon as the wind pipes up, or on a powerboat as soon as you leave the dock. Inexperienced crews in particular should wear life jackets at all times when they are on deck, since they may not be accustomed to the roll and heave of a sail- or powerboat offshore. I prefer an inflatable life jacket with a harness when I'm offshore, and a Stormy Seas vest (see below) when near shore.

The results of a national study released in 2003 dramatically underscore the benefits of

The author in drowned-rat mode, trying out inflatable life jackets.

wearing a PFD. Observers looked at more than 85,000 boats and almost 230,000 boaters between 1997 and 2002. The study tells us that more than 90 percent of children aged 1 to 5 wear life jackets, but the percentage drops with age. Only 10 percent of boaters over 65 wear one consistently.

Almost 80 percent of the boats observed in the study were powerboats, 40 percent of them under 16 feet long and another 40 percent ranging from 16 to 25 feet. The users were 65 percent male, and 80 percent were between 18 and 60 years old. Some 80 percent of the study was in water temperatures higher than 70°F, 60 percent in little or no current, 70 percent in waves less than 6 inches high, 95 percent in clear weather, and 80 percent in air temperatures between 70 and 90°F (21 and 32°C). The study also concluded almost 100 percent of PWC (personal watercraft) operators wear PFDs, and most kayak paddlers wear them as well. PFD use decreases as boat length increases.

Coast Guard statistics show that in 2004 there were around 12 million registered boats in the United States and 676 fatalities, of which 484 were drownings. The executive summary of the U.S. Coast Guard Boating Statistics for 2004 suggests that 90 percent of those who drowned could have been saved had they been wearing life jackets. The report also concludes that more than 70 percent of the fatal accidents happened to boaters who had not received boating safety instruction, and that one-third of the accidents involved alcohol. Boats under 25 feet long were involved in more than 80 percent of the accidents.

The messages are pretty clear, and one of them is that *life jackets save lives*. Finally, these and other reports note that hypothermia is a major killer, especially if the water temperature is below 60°F, which is not unusual in spring and fall), and that people going out on small boats should not only wear life jackets but dress for possible immersion. If you buy an inflatable life jacket, consider one with a built-in harness so that you will have a double safety factor. (Some reports recommend against harness-type life jackets for women due to the waist belt position relative to a woman's breasts.)

Small children should wear both a harness and a life jacket. The life jacket will keep them warm as well as protect them from falls. There are numerous manufacturers of children's life jackets. Older children can wear either a small adult jacket or a children's jacket.

Life jacket stowage is another problem that every boater should address. On many boats the jackets are stowed in an out-of-the-way locker where they are not only difficult to reach but liable to become mildewed and smelly. Next time you are aboard your boat, try to get your life jacket out and on in less than a minute. If you find that it takes longer than that, you need to find a better storage place. Keep in mind that if you had a fuel explosion aboard your boat, you probably would not even have a full minute

to get it on. Often, if you think creatively, you can find a spot that is both convenient and out of the way without much trouble. *Sportfishing* magazine editor Dean Clarke, for example, helped pioneer a canvas hood under a T-top on a center console to keep life jackets close at hand. Why not follow his lead and look at a second layer of canvas under a bimini on your boat to keep life jackets nearby? Then again, if your sailboat has canvas dodgers around the cockpit, why not sew in pouches for life jackets? Remember that a good life jacket may be all there is between you and your obituary.

Life Jackets Put to the Test
Most inflatable life jackets are reasonably comfortable to wear, but clear differences emerge between brands in emergency use.

When testing both the Mustang and SOSpenders vests, for example, I found that their freshwater-activated igniters inflated even as I was sinking, dragging me back to the surface quickly, but that it was then extremely difficult to climb into a life raft or swim. I did

A lifejacket being put to the test by the author. The life raft was loaned by Zodiac, and I boarded it from the water while wearing a lifejacket.

eventually manage to get aboard, but almost overturned the life raft in the process.

By comparison, the Stearns fanny or belly pack life jacket I tested forced me to tread water for a few minutes while I inflated the life jacket and then pulled it over my head. If you are not a good swimmer, you should probably avoid this style of life jacket. According to Stearns, many people simply hold onto the life jacket without putting it over their heads. Others get the life jacket over their head while floating in the water.

Stormy Seas Vest

This is a great product, and probably the best-kept secret this side of the California coast. It looks and feels like a normal vest, but contains a buoyancy chamber that is inflated by a compressed-air cylinder hidden in a Velcro-fronted pocket. In fact, you would be hard-pressed to know that it is a life jacket as well as a vest. This vest is *not* Coast Guard approved, but company president Michael Jackson (no, not him of the white glove) says that he does not want Coast Guard approval for his jackets. He believes that Coast Guard–approved jackets have more buoyancy than they need, which makes it hard for a person in the water to swim. Having tried swimming in a number of Coast Guard–approved life jackets, I know exactly what he's talking about. Jackson says that his life jackets will support you even when they are only about two-thirds inflated (if you want to inflate them more, simply use the mouth tube), and that you *can* swim wearing a Stormy Seas vest or jacket. Jackson knows what he is talking about, having twice fallen off a deep-sea fishing boat in the Bering Sea. This, he says, is why he is now making lifesaving gear.

I tested the Stormy Seas life vest in 50°F (10°C) water off the coast of Rhode Island in October. When I jumped in, the vest inflated

---

PFD Standards in America and Europe

In America, the highest category of life jacket is the Type 1 PFD (personal flotation device). A Type I life jacket is designed to turn an unconscious person face up and has a minimum of 22 lbs. of buoyancy to support an adult in open, rough water. In Europe, where SOLAS (International Convention for the Safety of Life at Sea) life jackets are required, the amount of buoyancy is much higher—35 lbs. This makes SOLAS jackets bulkier, harder to wear, and harder to store. European inflatable life jackets must also have 35 lbs. of buoyancy, but they are still more comfortable than standard life jackets.

A Type II PFD serves the same functions as a Type I but has only 15.5 lbs. of buoyancy. This type is best suited for calm inland waters or where rescue patrols are nearby. A Type III PFD also has 15.5 lbs. of buoyancy, and is designed to keep a conscious person vertical or slightly on his back in calm waters. Type III PFDs have three specialized subgroups: flotation aids, waterski vests (for waterskiing enthusiasts), and floatcoats (a coat that has built-in buoyancy). Each meets the Coast Guard definition of a Type III, but each serves a slightly different purpose. Type IV PFDs are throwable devices such as cushions, horseshoes, or life rings. All have at least 16.5 lbs. (7.5 kg) of buoyancy. Type V PFDs are special-use units such as white-water rafting vests.

The Coast Guard requires one PFD onboard for every crewmember, plus one Type IV throwable device. ORC (Offshore Racing Council) regulations for offshore boats require two throwable devices, such as horseshoes with poles and drogues.

automatically, and I bobbed to the surface. The vest easily supported my 200-pound weight, and more importantly, I could easily swim around, just as advertised. It was a simple job to inflate the vest further using the mouth tube, if I needed to do so. And climbing into a liferaft or onto a boat was easier than when I was wearing a Coast Guard–approved PFD. While you should have Coast Guard–approved life jackets aboard your boat at all times, the Stormy Seas vest is warm and comfortable and can save your life.

Note that you may have trouble traveling with compressed-air cylinders. The Transportation Safety Administration allows these cylinders to pass through airport security checkpoints, but airlines themselves may prohibit them. If you are traveling to join a boat, you might want to mail or send air cylinders ahead of your trip or pack them in checked baggage.

Life Jacket Lights

ACR Electronics makes several models of life jacket lights, as does McMurdo, CFX of Israel,

The Stormy Seas vest modeled by the author. The author added the reflective patches on the shoulders for better night visibility.

and other companies. The idea is that any person going on deck—especially at night—should wear a life jacket with an emergency light attached. If that person goes overboard, the water-activated light flashes a clear signal to mark the wearer's location. When buying such a light, make sure it is SOLAS-approved, as SOLAS requirements in this area are more stringent than those of the U.S. Coast Guard. Check too, that the light will activate in both salt and fresh water, and that it attaches easily to the life jacket or to clothing where it will be clearly visible if the crew falls overboard. The ideal location is high on the shoulder. We'll discuss these lights in use later in the chapter.

Clothing

I am often asked by beginning sailors, "What should I wear when I go out on a boat?" My recommendations are based on the trials and errors of 40 years of sailing. For an afternoon sail in temperate waters, the same casual clothes that you wear for recreation at home will probably suffice. If the afternoon is cold, you'll want additional layers—for example a sweater, fleece pullover, and/or a windbreaker that you can put on for that long beat to windward and remove again when you turn downwind. Two thin sweaters give more warmth than a single heavy one. A warm parka—or a fleece and windbreaker—make a lot of sense on the water, especially in the spring and fall.

In tropical conditions, most sailors wear shorts and a tee shirt, with leather sailing shoes and no socks. As the weather gets colder, they'll add long pants, heavier shirts, and sweaters. I use a zippered Polartec or Patagonia fleece in spring to keep body warmth in.

Your shoes should be rubber soled with non-skid soles. Ordinary sneakers or walking shoes are good enough for casual use as long as their soles don't leave scuff marks on the deck, but if you plan to go out regularly, buy a pair of canvas or leather sailing shoes.

Foul-Weather Gear

Henri Lloyd developed the style now known as the "ocean racer" in 1972, using a proprietary fabric. At that time the gear was considered to be leading edge, and I am now on my fourth set of Henri Lloyd foul-weather gear since then. At first I wore Henri Lloyd because it was part of the crew uniform on the boats I raced. But my present set is one I purchased for myself, because I consider it to be the best gear around. Having said that, however, I hear from other sailors that Musto, Helly Hansen, and Gill now have equally good gear, a lot of which has been developed for and tested in various around-the-world races. Do not buy cheap foul-weather gear if you intend to spend a lot of time at sea. When it is cold and rainy, gear that leaks makes life miserable and could put you off sailing forever.

Much of today's foul weather gear is made using Gore-Tex breathable fabric, which lets your body moisture out and stays dry and comfortable. This is a big advantage when you have to work hard enough to break a sweat—while grinding a winch, say—then sit on the rail in cold weather afterward.

When buying foul-weather gear, make sure it has reflective shoulder patches, a high pants-front with adjustable suspenders, Velcro closures at wrist and ankle, and legs that will slip on over your sailing boots. I prefer zippered to buttoned jackets, with a Velcro flap to prevent wind from penetrating the zipper.

For offshore and cold-water sailing, my Henri Lloyd jacket has a built-in harness and jacket liner, but for sailing in warmer waters I prefer an offshore jacket that's a little lighter. Bear in mind that even a light offshore jacket

The author wearing his Henri Lloyd foul-weather gear in the deep ocean. I am at the midstay, trying to feed the sail into the roller furler after it ripped and stuck in the feeder. At this point we were about five days from land on an Atlantic crossing. (Photo by Dan Nerney)

may be too heavy for sailing on a sunny afternoon, when all you need to cut the wind is a lighter windbreaker such as the Henri Lloyd Breeze or the Gill Antigua. Another alternative is Helly Hansen PVC gear, although I don't recommend this kind of gear for colder sailing areas.

When the weather gets very warm, a vest may be all you need.

Powerboaters usually have the luxury of steering from below deck when the weather gets bad, but on a small boat that may not be possible. Gear such as the Carhartt PVC rain gear outfit (available for under $100 for a top and bottom set) may be all a fisherman needs in rainy weather. If the weather is cold, a fleece or warm jacket may be needed under the rain gear. For heavier use, Cabela's Gore-Tex Guidewear with a Thinsulate liner will do the job admirably. A parka and pants cost around $200.

When shopping for foul-weather gear, check that the seams are watertight and the pockets do not let water in. Helly Hansen gear has the tightest zipper pockets I have seen, but some manufacturers simply put a grommet in the corner of the pocket to allow water to escape.

Look too at the collar height. A low collar allows the back of your neck to get cold, and you will need to wear a towel in scarf fashion to stay warm. Heavy-duty offshore sailing gear features a high collar for full protection. Gill makes foul-weather gear with three heights of collar for just that purpose.

Should You Have a Float Coat?

Clothing that keeps you afloat if you fall overboard sounds like a good idea, but does it really work? To find out, I tried several types of clothing with built-in flotation. I tried gear from specific manufacturers, but all the major manufacturers make clothing similar to the garments discussed here.

The Mustang Bomber Jacket

I had heard that this Coast Guard–approved flotation jacket rides up on your torso when you fall into the water, so I decided to give it a try. After putting it on I jumped about 10 feet off a dock, figuring that would put the jacket to the test. It did not ride up. In fact, it supported me nicely when I was in the water.

The jacket is bulky but comfortable, ideal for fall or spring sailing. Its rubber padding cuts the wind over your arms and chest, although your rear end tends to hang out (at least mine did) and get cold. It supports you in the water, so it offers a safety factor not found in conventional jackets.

The Mustang Suit

This Coast Guard–approved suit is bulky, but I loved it anyway. It is warm and very buoyant, and its bright yellow color makes it highly visible. The suit has Velcro fasteners on the sleeves and ankles, lots of pockets, and is really comfortable. Pull the hood up and only your hands, face, and feet are visible. What great protection from bad weather! If I were out on the water year-round, I would include this outfit as part of my daily gear.

Like so many good things in life, however, the Mustang suit has a drawback: it is so warm that you would want to wear it only when the air temperature is below about 45°F. If I were sailing offshore in a cold climate, I would definitely have one of these suits aboard. Stick a GPS in one pocket, food and water in another, a chart and a VHF in still another, and you could sail (or ski!) anywhere.

Like the Stormy Seas life vest, the Mustang suit supported me beautifully in the water, and I was able to swim without any difficulty. The only real problem came when I had to get out of the water. The waterlogged suit is heavy. I figure the water added an extra 50–75 pounds to my weight. If you wear one of these suits routinely, make sure you have a good, strong ladder that extends well down into the water, so that if you fall overboard you can climb out easily. Also—and this is true of all survival suits—be sure to read the instructions before you get into an emergency situation, so that you will understand what your suit can and cannot do.

Hats and Hoods

Even though most foul weather gear comes with a hood, I find that the rubberized old-fashioned style sou'wester hat that you can often pick up at a surplus store is far superior to anything that the foul-weather gear manufacturers supply. If you cannot find such a hat, make sure your foul-weather gear hood has a peak and a drawstring to pull it tight around your face.

Gloves

I never use gloves because I feel more capable and dexterous without them, but I have second-guessed myself many times during cold watches on deck. In extremely cold conditions they should be considered a necessity. Many manufacturers make sailing gloves with and without fingertips. The best gloves have non-slip or leather palm and finger surfaces that give a good grip and keep your hands warm.

Boots

I have tried many kinds of boots and have put them to severe tests, including swimming, standing waist deep in water, and surviving several storms in them. Boots are constricting, and when the weather is warm I prefer to wear sailing shoes, even if they are sopping wet. For cold weather, on the other hand, sailing boots are essential. Without them your feet will get insufferably cold, and you will be an unhappy and ineffective sailor. I much prefer a knee-high, nonskid-soled, lightweight boot such as those made by Musto. Although many sailors wear them, I have found that dinghy racing

boots with drawstrings and holes at the top fill with water easily. Neoprene boots, either with or without zippers, keep your feet warm and come with nonslip soles, but neoprene can become incredibly smelly. Low-cut sailing boots are neither fish nor fowl, in my opinion. If you are going to wear shorty boots, why wear boots at all? They fill with water far more easily than the taller boots, and then you must slosh around with a boot full of water for the entire watch. Wear the higher boot, and at watch's end simply drop your foul-weather pants around the boots and then climb out of boots and pants at the same time. It will be that much easier to get your gear back on when you go back on watch. In fact, using this method, I find that I can dress in full foul-weather gear in a minute or two.

Knife

It has been said that all seamen need a knife, but I have never carried one except for a small Swiss army knife. Generally, a knife is only used for cutting lines after careful consideration of where and when to cut. For that reason, I prefer to have a knife taped or lashed to a handy fitting, either near the mast or in the cockpit.

A knife complicates your trips through airport security, and the stainless steel blade you need for rust resistance won't hold a good edge for long. Moreover, you will need to keep your knife on a lanyard so that it doesn't get lost, but lanyards tend to tangle with other gear on the boat. If you decide that you need a knife, I suggest one with a fixed blade or one that can be opened with one hand. If you are flying, pack it in your checked baggage.

A Wichard one-handed knife.

Sunglasses

Sunglasses aren't the first item you think of for heavy conditions, but you'll need a pair during a stiff blow on a sunny day. Get the darkest polarized glasses you can find. Glare off the water can give you a severe headache at the end of a long day of boating and can even cause long-term eye damage. Having smashed or lost many pairs of sunglasses on boats, I recommend that you either tie them on with string or use a Croakie (a floating strap) to hold them in place. Many magazines hand out free Croakies at boat shows, so if you have the chance, grab one or two.

If you routinely go out on a powerboat you'll need glasses that will not blow off. The best type is held in place with a tight headband.

Diving or Face Masks

If you go snorkeling off your boat, you are already equipped with a diving mask. When steering the boat in severe weather you may need it so you can open your eyes when facing stinging rain. Of course, you will spend a lot of time wiping the mask, but that's considerably easier than having to look through squinted, swollen, caked, and stinging eyes. I'm told that the best diving masks are the ones with a light-colored rubber rim; they are less tunnel-like to look through.

Man Overboard

I've fallen off a boat three times, and every time it hurt, although in different ways. One time I fell off my own boat while I was working on it in my yard. I missed the stone wall and landed in a privet hedge. The freshly cut branches gave me a bloody back, but at least I was not going to die from hypothermia or drowning.

Another time, 20 miles at sea and running hard under spinnaker in growing darkness and 12–18 knots of wind with a full racing crew, it came time to jibe. We took the lazy guy off the spinnaker pole, and just as I clipped it back in on the new jibe, a gust filled the sail. It lifted me off the deck, over the lifeline, and dropped me neatly alongside the boat.

I surfaced spluttering and gasping for air. My first reaction was panic. What should I do? I was not wearing a life jacket and had to swim. But where should I swim? The seas made it impossible to see more than a few feet, and I knew that I was miles from the nearest land. Fortunately, the crew tossed a man-overboard (MOB) pole over the side, and I saw it. I figured that they would see the pole when they could get the rig squared away and return upwind, and if I were near it I would be seen too. The pole had a drogue (a cone-shaped sea anchor) and a life ring attached, but it still blew downwind faster than I could swim.

For 25 minutes I swam, until the boat came back under power with the spinnaker plastered all over the mast. (The crew said it took so long because they had to vote whether to come back for me! I figured they needed me to take the spinnaker down, which is why they decided to turn around and get me.) They saw the MOB pole first, and circled it. Then they saw me. They approached under power, two men leaned over the side and simply hauled me aboard. Safe on deck again, I had learned some lessons I'll never forget.

The first lesson is not to panic. I was able to concentrate on swimming toward the MOB pole, and that simple act kept panic from overwhelming me. The second lesson is to stay warm. I was fortunate. It was late summer and the water temperature was near 70°F. I was wearing foul-weather pants, a shirt, and a sweater. I was also wearing a brand-new pair of boots, which I probably should have kicked off to make swimming easier, although being a frugal Englishman I didn't want to lose them. The third lesson I learned is to wear a life jacket or harness. Had I been wearing a harness on the foredeck I might have been hurt by a stanchion, but I would have stayed aboard. And had I been wearing a life jacket, I would not have had to work so hard at staying afloat.

My third unplanned swim came when I fell off a J/22. That time I held onto the spinnaker sheet and got a tow until the spinnaker collapsed. As soon as the boat stopped, the crew hauled me back aboard. Not a big deal, just a wet moment.

A man-overboard rescue breaks down into three distinct parts. The first is locating the MOB, the second is getting a line or rescue device to the person in the water, and the third is getting him or her back aboard the boat. Before turning to those specific topics, however, we should discuss how to avoid going overboard in the first place.

Don't Go Overboard

The surest defense against loss or injury of a person overboard is to prevent anyone from going over the side in the first place, and there are several ways you can minimize your chances of

MOB SCENARIO

Falling Overboard while Entering a Slip

You are backing your trawler yacht into a slip. The boat has high freeboard, so your crew decides to stand on the stern platform to put the stern line onto the dock. Your view from the helm is obstructed by a dinghy stowed on deck aft of the bridge. As you back into the slip, the crewman on the stern platform falls into the water. What is the probable scenario?

1. The crew gets sucked under the boat, into the props, and is killed or maimed for life.
2. The crew grabs onto the stern platform and manages to hold on. Fortunately, the platform is large enough that his or her legs stay clear of the props.
3. The crew manages to swim clear of the boat, gets to a nearby dock ladder, and climbs out of the water.
4. The crew grabs the swim platform, but there are no handgrips on it and he is about to slide off when a bystander yells at you to stop the boat.
5. You've thought about this situation, and because your view aft is obstructed, you have fitted additional controls on the wing of the bridge to make sure you can see any crew on the stern platform. When docking, you watch all crew carefully. You also make sure that all crew members wear a PFD when outside the safety lines or bulwarks.

Obviously, Option 5 is preferred. If your view astern is obstructed, either figure out how to remove the obstructions or fit additional controls that allow you to get outboard and see all your crew at all times.

Options 2 to 4 require quick wits on the part of the crew, but you can make it easier by taking a look at your boat next time it is at anchor. Go for a swim and try to climb out of the water. If you cannot, consider fitting a stern ladder that can be lowered by the person in the water, and add handholds on the edges of the stern platform. (If you put them on the top, crew could trip over them.) Make sure that a person in the water holding onto the stern platform will not get his or her legs anywhere near the props. Finally, you might consider ways of getting docklines to the dock without having anyone on the stern platform. This might entail leaving them on the dock on holders, or using a boathook to get them onto the dock cleats. It might mean cutting a boarding gate through the bulwark to make it easier to get ashore.

falling overboard. One of the most important on a sailboat is to wear a harness and tether when the wind and seas are up or when it is dark and you are working on deck—even if you are at the helm. A harness with a Coast Guard–approved inflatable life jacket is even better. I recommend a tether with a quick-release hook on either end and a third hook in the middle to which a second part can be attached—the Wichard tether, for example. In bad weather this allows you to hook one of the tether parts to one strong point while transferring the first part to another as you move forward or aft. This way you will never be completely unhooked. In heavy weather especially, always attach your tether to a jackline or pad eye *before* you leave the safety of the main cabin or cockpit.

If you are cruising, shorten your sails slightly at night so that you will not have to go forward and work on the foredeck in darkness. If you have radar, it can spot rain squalls well in advance so that you and your crew can reduce sail and get off the foredeck before they hit. If you have to go forward at night, make sure somebody is watching you from the cockpit so that if you slip and fall off, you'll be seen im-

mediately. Use handholds whenever you go forward, and make sure the person helming the boat warns you before turning or tacking. I have seen a crew member go right off the bow because the helmsman turned the boat quickly without warning the foredeck crew.

Harnesses

In the 1971 Fastnet Race a strong gale blew for three days straight. Back then, harnesses were neither required nor even thought necessary. Aboard *Quailo III*, owner Don Parr insisted that the crew wear harnesses whenever they were on deck, but many other boats didn't bother. Since that time, they have become essential equipment on all boats. Even on a 100-foot sailboat crossing the Atlantic recently, our skipper insisted that the crew wear a harness or life jacket when on deck in all conditions. Interestingly, harnesses were preferred by almost every crewman over life jackets. Out in the deep ocean, the natural preference is to stay with the ship rather than stay afloat awaiting rescue.

Today's harnesses are much improved over those worn years ago, although it took the loss of a number of crew overboard to get harness

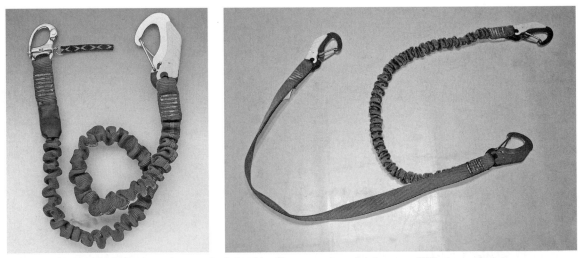

Wichard quick-release tether on the left. This allows you to unhook yourself if you are being dragged underwater. At right is a three-hook tether; one hook is attached to your harness and the other two hooks are attached to the boat. (Photo courtesy Wichard USA)

Harness Standards

The webbing on all harnesses should be strongly sewn (in many cases it is double- or triple-sewn). All harnesses should have a breaking strength of more than 1,500 kg (3,306 lb.), and the harness tether must have a breaking strength of more than 2,080 kg (about 4,600 lb.). The webbing must be at least 38 mm (1.5 inches) wide and be made of nylon or polyester. The loss of crew in the past, plus ORC testing, showed that many rope tethers broke before the harness or harness hook let go. To prevent injury to crew (by falling across the cockpit or deck), tethers should not be more than 2 meters (6.5 ft.) long and should also have a midlength hook to accept a second tether part, so that one tether part can be attached at all times. Tether hooks must be of a type that cannot come undone accidentally.

Check tethers regularly to ensure that the webbing has not been weakened from UV degradation, and replace them if in doubt. (This is the reason I don't like webbing jacklines along the side decks. They tend to suffer rapid UV degradation, often in as little as one season.)

standards raised. The ORC has established requirements for harnesses and tethers that are universally accepted in the sailboat racing world, including a tether made of nylon or polyester webbing rather than rope. Rope has been known to snap.

Helping Yourself If You Do Go Overboard

There are a number of things you can—and should—do to help yourself if you fall over the side. If you sail with an inexperienced crew, show them how to handle the boat if you fall overboard. For example, discuss how to start the engine, turn off the autopilot, retrace a course, and get you back aboard. Then stand aside and let them practice. It may be your life that is saved.

If you and your crew routinely wear inflatable life jackets, I strongly suggest that you go to a local pool or beach and get into the water to see how they work. If the jacket does not inflate automatically, make sure you know how it does inflate. You won't be in a position to read the instructions when you're bobbing around in the ocean. Also be sure to replace your inflator cylinder and charging element at the beginning of every season.

The Firefly Plus strobe light from ACR Electronics (Photo courtesy ACR Electronics)

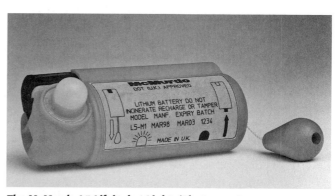

The McMurdo L5 Lifejacket Light. (Photo courtesy McMurdo)

Make sure each crew member has a flashlight handy for nighttime sailing. Ideally, a water-activated, SOLAS-approved strobe light such as those made by ACR Electronics, McMurdo, and Pains Wessex should be attached to your harness or inflatable life jacket.

Man Overboard Drills

Yes, they're tedious. Yes, they seem like a waste of time. And who can see the damn soccer ball bobbing out there on the water anyway? But if your crew ever has to do it for real, you'll be glad that you practiced, especially if you're the one in the water.

When practicing man overboard drills with your crew, toss an old soccer ball over the side and see how long it takes to disappear from sight. A soccer ball is about the size of a human head and is equally difficult to spot in a seaway. Work out a strategy for getting back to the swimmer quickly (see "Rescuing a Man Overboard," below), then give it a try. It may be that you simply yell "Man overboard!" and jibe all standing. You may want to turn and retrace your course carefully, or stop the boat by throwing the sails aback and then dropping them before turning back toward the swimmer. Your preferred solution will depend in part on your boat's turning radius, on how long it takes to get the sails down, and on your point of sail at the time of the accident. Test your theories before you have to put them into practice. You might also want to practice your MOB drills at dusk, at night (tape a strobe to the soccer ball for a realistic scenario), and when there is a sea running to show your crew how difficult it is to find a head in the water.

Getting Back Aboard

Try getting aboard your boat from the water while wearing a life jacket. Unless it has an open transom, a low swim step, or a well-placed ladder, you may find that you cannot get aboard unaided. You might even find it surprisingly difficult to get back on board with the help of your crew, especially if your boat has a high freeboard or there's a sea running. You need to work out a boarding strategy. An Armstrong or Garelick transom ladder that goes deep into the water is one solution. Another commercial solution is the man-overboard ladder from Wichard that simply sits on your boat's rail until needed and is opened if anyone falls overboard.

Lowering the mainsail over the side with the boom and topping lift holding it up is another strategy. Crawl into the mainsail, then tell your crew to winch the sail high enough, using the main halyard, for you to get onto the deck. Using the main halyard itself as a lifting device is yet another method.

A device called the Tri-Buckle is available from England. This is a triangular, sail-like sling that clips onto the toerail of your boat while the top portion is hooked onto a halyard. The MOB swims to the device or is dragged to it and pulled inside. The halyard is then cranked up, and the person is deposited on the deck of the boat between the stanchions. This device is simple and works remarkably well. The Tri-Buckle makes it possible for just one person to get an MOB out of the water fast. Remember, the person in the water may be tired from swimming and burdened with sodden, extra-heavy clothing.

Don't imagine that you're fit enough to pull yourself over the side of your boat without fail. While testing this notion, I once found that I could kick myself far enough out of the water to reach the toerail of a sailboat, and from there manage to reach the lower lifeline. After that it took a lot longer to pull myself up out of the water and hook a foot around a stanchion. When I tried again after swimming around for a while, I could not hoist myself and my soaking clothing high enough to hook a foot over the rail. The harder I tried, the more tired I became. I swam around to the transom and tried to board there, but that was even more difficult.

Using a rope to get aboard was almost as hard. When I was young I used to be able to shinny up a rope in the gym or climb the mast using the halyards and shrouds, but that was then. Now I find climbing a rope up the side of a boat extremely difficult, and if the boat is moving it is virtually impossible. By contrast, getting aboard via a transom ladder or over a transom step on a sail- or powerboat is fairly easy, and I believe that the current trend toward an open transom or a transom with steps is a good lifesaving feature that should be encouraged. Every powerboat should have some form of ladder or transom step to help people get aboard easily. I tried all of these tests in a calm sea and daylight. I would hate to have to repeat them in a raging gale at night.

Try various strategies in warm, protected water. Anchor your boat near a shallow beach and put on your life jacket. Then get into the water and try to climb back aboard without help, having first lowered a ladder or stationed crew to help out if needed. Here are several methods you might try:

1. Try getting aboard your dinghy and from there onto the boat. Imagine yourself doing this in a gale.
2. Try climbing into the folds of your mainsail and being winched aboard.
3. Try climbing a stern ladder or steps.
4. Try being winched aboard wearing a harness attached to a halyard.
5. Try climbing the anchor chain or climbing aboard over the outboard motor using the prop as a step.

Don't quit until you know that you can get aboard easily and quickly. Remember, speed is of critical importance. If you spend a long time in the water, hypothermia can set in, or you will tire and never be able to haul yourself aboard.

Designing a Cockpit for Safety

A few years ago my design office worked up a cockpit design with several additional safety features. We decided that the cockpit needed comfortable seats, and each should be at least 6 feet 4 inches long to enable a person to lie down when the boat was heeled. Among other things, this would keep sleeping off-watch crew inboard, where their harnesses could easily be hooked on.

To allow sitting crew to brace their legs comfortably against the leeward side underway, we decided initially to limit the cockpit width at seat level to 2 feet. This made fitting a cockpit table very difficult, however, and we were forced to increase the cockpit width at the sole to more than 3 feet (90 cm), and make the dropleaf table strong enough that it could be used as a foot rest.

This made for a huge cockpit—far larger than the CCA rules permitted—and one that might sink the boat if it were filled to the coamings. To prevent water flowing into the boat's interior we placed a bridge deck at the forward end of the cockpit. For an offshore boat I consider a bridge deck essential, even though it makes the companionway ladder one or two steps longer. For a harbor cruiser it is not so necessary, and on most production boats bridge decks have been eliminated. In order to allow water to flow out of the cockpit quickly, we ran the sole all the way back to the transom. Many people don't like open transoms, but we used this feature to add several more potential life-saving features.

By making the cockpit sole wider, we not only gained a cockpit table, we also made

continued

room for a person to get past the steering wheel without leaving the cockpit. Behind the cockpit we put a removable helmsman's seat. At sea, this seat is locked in place and immovable, but in harbor it can be removed along with the steering wheel to give an easy walk-through area. (We specify a special Edson steering wheel nut to make the wheel easily removable.) This also allowed us to change the helmsman's seat to suit different people should the boat be sold and the new owner want something different.

On one side of the cockpit, we placed a hatch that opened into the sail locker. Not only did the hatch have a lift-up lid, but the side hinged down to allow a large sail to be stuffed inside quickly. The owner and I felt that getting a sail aft and into the cockpit was safer than leaving it tied down on the foredeck. The sail bin was arranged so that sails, lines, and sail-handling gear could be easily located, removed, or replaced.

Crew Shelter
Rather than expose the crew to the elements, we enclosed the forward end of the cockpit with a hard dodger. This had the advantage of allowing instruments to be fitted on the cabintop, and it provided a good landing for the forward end of the bimini top when the boat was anchored in the Caribbean. Several of the windows in the hard dodger could be opened to provide cross ventilation. In bad weather, or when only one crew member is on deck, the favored seat is immediately behind the hard dodger. Consequently, we made sure that no instruments or dials were fitted into this bulkhead.

We took care to design 6 feet of headroom under the hard dodger without making the boat look ungainly. This enabled winches and the radar screen to be installed there, and wind gauges were fixed to the overhead of the dodger forward of the hatch, where they could be seen easily and were well away from people ascending or descending the companionway.

No cruising crew wants to be at the helm when the wind is honking at 40 knots. It's miserable, wet, and hard work. Consequently, this boat is fitted with an autopilot located under the hard dodger, where it can be adjusted while the crew remains sheltered and maintains a good lookout.

Safety Concerns
Going on deck at night can be risky when the breeze gets strong. Consequently, we fitted jacklines immediately outside the cockpit on strong, through-bolted pad eyes. If heavy weather is forecast, the jacklines can be shackled in place quickly and easily. Each jackline ends 5 feet (1.5 m) from the transom. Most harness tethers are 6 or 7 feet (1.8 or 2.1 m) long, so if the jackline ends right at the transom you could be dragged behind the boat and unable to reach a rail to get back aboard. Ending the jackline a few feet ahead of the transom prevents this possibility.

Inside the cockpit, we made it possible to clip on a harness without leaving the safety of the cabin by putting pad eyes on the aft face of the bridge deck and running jacklines along the cockpit sides just below seat level. This allowed the crew to move around the cockpit or steer without unclipping, yet kept the jacklines in an unobtrusive location.

Having run the cockpit sole aft to the transom, we installed transom steps. I firmly believe that transom steps and a deep ladder are lifesaving features that all cruising boats should have. I recommend a fold-down ladder that allows anyone to get a foothold and climb back aboard unaided. We made the transom steps into a fold-down locker that houses the life raft. This puts the life raft in a relatively safe location (it won't get washed off the deck or stolen), where it can be hauled out in an emergency and rapidly kicked into the water. Inside this locker there's a strongpoint for the life raft tether. To the side of the transom steps we installed lockable twin lockers for propane tanks.

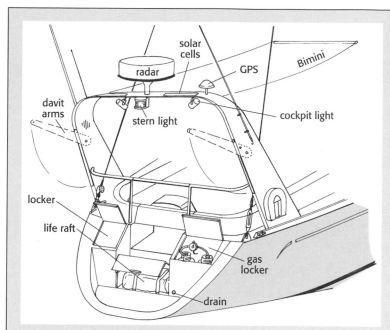

This allows the tanks to be vented over the stern and makes it unlikely that anyone will store gear in the tank locker. Finally, we expanded the lowest step of the transom to make it easy to board from a dinghy, and we added small grab rails to help people get out of the water and out of a dinghy.

The Radar Arch

The integrated cockpit includes a radar arch on which the radar and radio antennae are mounted, as well as a bank of small solar cells to keep the batteries fully charged. On the outside of the arch hang two horseshoe life rings, each with its own strobe, rescue streamer, and automatic MOB pole, and at the aft end of the arch there are fold-down dinghy davits. We also

Lucayo, a 48-footer designed by the author, shows some of the features highlighted in this sidebar, though not the hard dodger. Left: The boat about to be launched at Brooklin Boatyard in Maine. The yard worker standing on the transom step shows how easy it is to board the boat. To the starboard side of the transom is the sailboard stowage (two round handles in the transom). On the port side is the MOB pole stowage. Right: The cockpit area, moments after launching. Lifering holders have yet to be mounted on the radar arch.

continued

installed a spotlight on top of the arch, plus stereo speakers, dimmable cockpit lights, and a shower unit for use when you climb out of the ocean.

Gated stainless steel pushpit rails behind the arch help to give the helmsman a sense of security despite the open cockpit. A removable fiberglass or wood gate under the cockpit seat would stop children from crawling out over the transom.

In harbor, a bimini can be fitted from the front face of the radar arch to the aft side of the hard dodger to give maximum protection from the sun. While harbor-bound in bad weather, drop sides could be fitted to the bimini and fastened to the back of the cockpit cushions.

Rescuing a Man Overboard

If you are at the helm when you hear the dreaded call "man overboard," your first reaction should be to check the compass course and then punch the MOB button on your GPS receiver. Meanwhile, other crew should start tossing the MOB pole, horseshoe, cushions, life rings, and other floating gear over the side to lay a trail back to the person in the water. These items will also give the swimmer something to focus on and swim toward.

One person should be told to watch the person in the water as long as possible, pointing continuously at the victim. Nothing should distract the designated spotter from his or her job. It is extremely difficult to keep visual contact with a head floating in the water, so the watcher should not be called on for any other chore. If you are the watcher, do not take your eyes off the swimmer for an instant. Once visual contact is lost, you'll find it incredibly hard to reestablish in any kind of a sea.

There are numerous methods for getting back to a man overboard as quickly as possible, most of which have been developed by sailors, since sailboats are notoriously slow to turn around under sail. We'll look at the two leading methods for returning under sail.

Sailing a Figure Eight

In a figure eight pickup, a sailboat immediately comes onto a beam reach, then tacks around and crosses its original path on a broad reach before rounding up head to wind alongside the man overboard. At least, that's how it works in theory. The idea is that by turning onto a beam reach, you increase boat speed in preparation for the tack. After the tack, you ease sheets and turn almost 270 degrees from your previous beam reach to cross your outgoing path. You hold that course long enough to dive to leeward of the MOB, then come into the wind alongside the victim so that he or she can be hauled back aboard quickly.

The problem with this scenario is that it presupposes the crew can tack the boat fast and bring it back alongside the MOB quickly. Unfortunately, most boats are sailed with only one or two crew. A fast tack requires at least two crew onboard the boat, maybe three for a larger boat. On a boat with a midstay, often the headsail must be rolled up before the boat can tack. Easing sheets and bringing the boat head to wind requires more than one person in many cases. Add to that a person to watch the MOB, and you need at least two people onboard to attempt such a maneuver, even though it may be the only option.

When U.S. Naval Academy cadets practiced sailing a figure eight and making a crash stop (see below), they found that the figure eight kept the boat within a hundred yards (thirty meters) of the victim and within easy spotting distance. The cadets were able to return to the

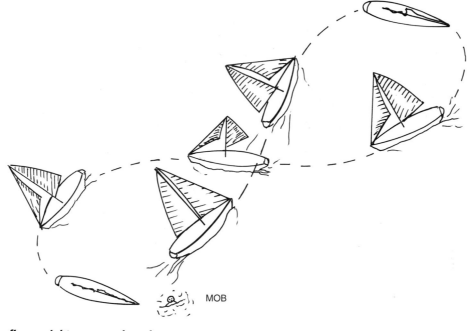

The figure-eight man-overboard maneuver.

MOB within a few minutes of the person going over the side.

Making a Crash Stop

A crash stop entails rounding up into the wind instantly and stopping near the MOB with the jib backed. In effect, the jibsheet is not let go when the boat tacks, so that the boat heaves-to near the MOB. In the Naval Academy tests, this recovery method proved faster than the figure eight by about half a minute, but only if the crew reacts quickly. Many people onboard a boat freeze when someone goes over the side, and only figure out what to do after a minute or two. In the case of a husband-and-wife crew, the task of returning to the victim single-handed may well fall to the more inexperienced team member. The Naval Academy boats were fully crewed, and the victim could be retrieved from the water after a crash stop within two minutes.

A crash stop is the best maneuver when a person goes overboard and is still attached to the boat by their tether. In several instances people have been dragged along beside a boat and drowned after falling overboard. In our own experiments, we have found it impossible to pull a victim back aboard a boat that is moving at more than 4 knots, nor can the victim help himself. At faster speeds, the MOB creates such a large bow wave that he cannot breathe. (We almost drowned our volunteer finding this out!)

Using the Engine

The figure eight and crash-stop maneuvers are certainly good to know and to practice, but if you are running downwind when a person goes

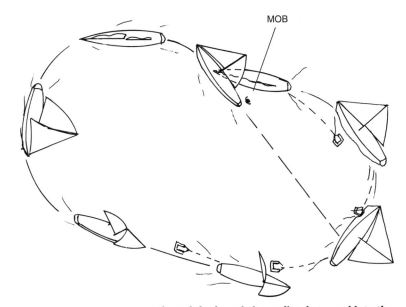

MOB

The "crash stop" maneuver. When a person goes overboard the boat is immediately turned into the wind. The jib is not released to aid in quick tacking. (You may want to reconsider this tactic if you are flying an overlapping genoa.) The boat runs downwind deploying the Lifesling if it is fitted. My recommendation is not to deploy the Lifesling too early as it will create drag and slow the boat. Opposite the MOB the boat is jibed and brought around to the MOB. If you have a Lifesling you may want to get the MOB into the sling and bring them aboard. If you do not have a Lifesling bring the boat to a halt near the MOB and toss a looped line. No crew should go into the water until given permission by the captain.

overboard, getting the spinnaker down, turning around, and sailing back to the MOB could take 20 minutes. For that reason, I now recommend that as soon as somebody goes over, the boat be put about and the engine turned on immediately; check that all lines are clear of the propeller before putting the engine in gear. With quick reactions you can spin the boat around very quickly, even with the spinnaker plastered against the mast. You can also simply cast off the headsail sheet and start motoring back to the MOB. In some tests that I have witnessed, the boat continued to sail away from the MOB while the crew made decisions. This is the absolute worst thing you can do, given how difficult it is to keep track of a person in the water in even the calmest seas.

Turn the boat around! Even if you are stopped, at least you are not moving farther away from the MOB. A boat sailing at 8 knots will move away at about 13 feet per second or 800 feet—almost three football fields—per minute. At that rate the victim would be a quarter-mile away within two to three minutes. If

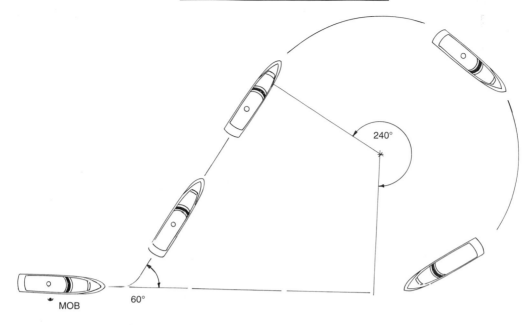

The Williamson turn as executed on larger craft. Turn 60 degrees to port or starboard, then turn 240 degrees in the opposite direction until you come back on a reciprocal course toward the MOB.

the crew took 20 minutes to get the spinnaker down, the boat would be nearly two miles from the swimmer before turning, and sailing back upwind would take at least another 20–30 minutes. The faster you can turn around, the nearer you will be to the MOB and the greater your chances of a successful recovery. Ideally, returning to the MOB will be merely a matter of motoring up the line of cushions and other floating objects that were tossed over the side.

Sailing books rarely discuss maneuvering under power, but if you turn on your engine to dock the boat, to leave the harbor, and to maneuver in tight corners, why not use it to rescue a MOB? Of course, when you get near the swimmer, you will have to stop the prop rotation to avoid injuring him. But the minutes you save by motoring could make all the difference.

Tell your crew to hang on tightly before you make a sharp turn to get back to the MOB. The last thing you want is *another* MOB. If possible,

let the MOB swim to the boat rather than bring the boat alongside the victim—that way you can stop the engines. (The propellers will often continue to turn slowly if the engine is left in idle.) Lower the boarding ladder as the victim comes alongside.

Practice MOB routines with your crew. There's no need to put a person in the water; simply toss a cushion over the side unexpectedly. If just two of you sail the boat, let one person sit back while the other retrieves the cushion. That way, both people onboard will know what to do should the other go overboard.

The Lifesling

The Lifesling is designed to be thrown to a person in the water. It is reputed to have a range of up to 60 yards, but it is difficult to throw and the effective range is more like 10 yards. A newly improved version shown here has a

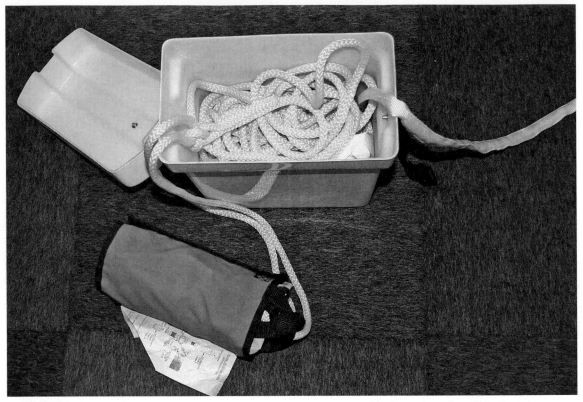

The Lifesling. This is the latest version of the Lifesling. It is easier to throw than the original version. I easily tossed this one about 100 feet.

longer range and is easier to throw. Once the Lifesling reaches the MOB, the swimmer climbs into it and is pulled aboard.

Personal Locator Devices

According to Lt. Commander Paul Steward, COSPAS/SARSAT liaison officer for the U.S. Coast Guard, the current trend in lifesaving is for devices that greatly enhance a boat's chances of locating and therefore rescuing an MOB. These devices range from a personal flare pack to a pocket EPIRB, and you should seriously consider equipping your crew with them if you plan to go offshore.

Miniflare Kit

The Miniflare 3 by Pains Wessex Schermuly is a personal kit of eight flares that you can carry around in your pocket. Each flare can be fired to an altitude of 240 feet (about 70 m) and burns at an intensity of 10,000 candelas for 6 seconds. This gives each flare a visible range of 1 mile during the day and 5 miles at night.

Emerald Marine Products Alert System

This system is a radio device designed to operate at 418 MHz and has a 2,000-foot (600-m) range. (Note that because the system operates on 418 MHz, it cannot be tracked by a Coast Guard vessel, nor is it part of the COSPAR/SARSAT rescue system.) It can shut down engines, initiate an automatic turn, broadcast an automatic radio mayday, sound an onboard alarm, and induce other programmable reactions. When the Alert System transmitter is worn on a life vest and the wearer falls over-

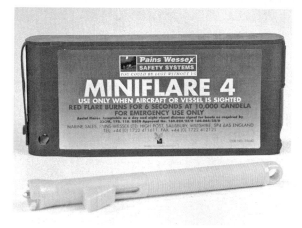

The Miniflare from Pains Wessex Schermuly.

The Mini B300 ILS Personal EPIRB. (Photo courtesy ACR Electronics)

board, it automatically starts transmitting. It also has a strobe light that flashes 10 times per second to help locate the user. The unit runs on two AAA batteries.

Alden SatFind 406 Pocket PLB

The Alden Personal Locator Beacon is a satellite-based system that operates like a normal EPIRB. If the wearer falls over the side, the PLB emits a homing signal, allowing the wearer to be rescued.

Emerald Marine Products Alert System. The system includes a UHF transmitter with a strobe light, pouch, lanyard, and batteries. (Photo courtesy Emerald Marine Products)

ACR Mini B 406 EPIRB

ACR Electronics sells a small personal 406 EPIRB that is worn by a crew member. Should the crew fall off the boat, the EPIRB automatically starts transmitting.

The Sea Marshall

The Sea Marshall is a man-overboard locator beacon, or in the world of acronyms, a PLB (Personal Locator Beacon). It works on a frequency of 121.5 MHz (the worldwide emergency homing frequency) and, according to its brochure, can transmit signals from the man in the water up to 3 nautical miles, depending on the height of the receiver antenna aboard the yacht. The range is up to 15 nautical miles to a helicopter at 10,000 feet and 35 miles or more to an aircraft flying

The Sea Marshall can be worn by an on-deck crew or by a diver and is activated either automatically (when the MOB goes over the side) or manually (as for a diver). It is powered by a lithium battery with a shelf life of more than 10 years and will transmit for up to 30 hours.

The MOBi-lert

Of all the devices I've looked at, the MOBi-lert is probably the most intriguing. It consists of a set of pendants that normally sit in a charger unit. When a crew member goes on deck, he simply takes one of the pendants out of the rack and puts it around his neck on the lanyard provided or simply places it in a pocket.

The pendant is a rechargeable electronic transmitter that keeps in touch with the master unit in the cabin of the yacht. Once it is removed from the charger rack, it is armed. The moment communication between the pendant and the master unit is broken (due to water immersion), an alarm sounds. Depending on the model and the number of pendants, up to six crew can use separate color-coded pendants at any one time. A central console can be set up to allow the helmsman or the watch captain to monitor the crew while they are wearing one of the pendants. Each pendant has a battery life of around eight hours, and when the first pendant is exhausted it can easily be exchanged for a fully charged one.

If a person falls overboard the circuit is broken, at which point the unit can do several things depending on how it is programmed. It can:

1. Record the exact time and location of the fall overboard.
2. Trigger a second alarm in another part of the yacht to alert other crew.
3. Release a man overboard pole or life ring.
4. Cut out the autopilot.
5. Stop the engine.
6. Cause a sailboat to head up into the wind and stop.
7. If you cannot recover the MOB, it will release an EPIRB to alert the Coast Guard and other authorities.
8. Provide a complete audit of the event to allow the crew to analyze the incident after the person has been rescued.

The MOBi-lert was developed in Australia and is now available worldwide. Other, similar devices include the Virtual Lifeline and the Marline MOB.01 and MOB.02.

ACR AquaFix Personal Locator Beacons

Both the AquaFix 406 and 406 GPS Personal Locator Beacons (PLBs) transmit on the international emergency frequency 406 MHz directly to COSPAS/SARSAT satellite systems and on the search-and-rescue (SAR) homing frequency of 121.5 MHz. As its name implies, the GPS unit also transmits a constant GPS position to enable a searcher to home in directly on the MOB. Both units contain a flat stainless steel antenna wrapped around the housing, which comes in a holster and is considerably larger than the MOBi-lert. Unlike the MOBi-lert, however, these units can summon rescue services worldwide.

Other, similar devices include the Fastfind and Fastfind-Plus from McMurdo. All these devices seem to have been designed for hikers and airplanes, then introduced to the marine industry later. They all contain built-in safeguards to prevent accidental triggering, but these require the MOB to use both hands to operate them—the last thing he wants to do. These PLBs are also expensive, which raises the question: if you have five crew on deck and only one PLB, who gets it?

In summary, I admit to being impressed by the thought and ingenuity that went into the MOBi-lert. Using the boat as the rescue platform, without alerting the rest of the world's rescue services, makes sense to me. That, too, is why the Sea Marshall is appealing. It can be used by a yacht to home in on the MOB without alerting rescue services, but should the yacht fail to find the MOB, emergency rescue services can be alerted to aid in the search, homing on the 121.5 MHz signal. If only it also had a GPS transmitter unit . . .

If Your Boat Is in Trouble

On a recent trip to Bermuda, the boat I was crewing had to veer sharply away from several whales cavorting in the middle of the ocean. We didn't see them until almost too late. If they had hit the boat, they might have put a hole in it. Without some method of containing the leak, we might have sunk. In this section I'll look at equipment you should have aboard to save the entire crew, rather than just one person. I'll also mention a few products that I have not tested, but that might prove useful.

EPIRBs

According to the Coast Guard, the easiest way to locate a boat is to home on its Emergency Position Indicating Radio Beacon (EPIRB) signal. So an EPIRB is probably the most important item to have aboard your boat.

There are two types, the 121.5 MHz and the 406.5 MHz EPIRBs, but the 121.5 EPIRB has been phased out in favor of the 406.5. When activated, both types send a signal to a satellite that relays the signal to a ground station. Its receipt at the ground station initiates an SAR (search-and-rescue) response, and subsequently guides rescuers to the boat in distress. Consequently you should not turn your EPIRB on and off. Once it's activated, leave it on.

A 121.5 MHz EPIRB costs 20–30 percent less than a 406 model, but sets off a lot of false alarms, is not as effective in general, and will be discontinued by 2008. According to some experts, 121.5 MHz EPIRBs average about 1,000 false alarms per real rescue, while the 406 EPIRB has about 8–10 per real rescue. In Britain, the coastguard estimates that 98 percent of all 121.5 EPIRB calls are false alarms. The 121.5 EPIRBs suffer from another problem, too. They may not be "heard" by aircraft in areas of radio clutter.

The 406 MHz EPIRB is specifically designed to work with COSPAS/SARSAT

The Pains-Wessex 406 EPIRB in its hydrostatic release.

(search-and-rescue satellites), but they must be registered before they will be effective. A registration form provides the rescue services with the owner's name, telephone number, address, and type of vessel. See Chapter 11 for a description of how the COSPAS/SARSAT EPIRBs work.

GPS-Linked EPIRBs

Since the advent of the original EPIRB, a number of safety companies have taken the technology a step further by integrating it with GPS technology to make finding distressed mariners that much simpler. The GPIRB, for example, is a 406 MHz EPIRB with a GPS chip from Northern Airborne Technologies

ACR's Rapidfix GPS-linked EPIRB. (Photo courtesy ACR Electronics)

installed. Other manufacturers have similar devices. For example, ACR Electronics makes an EPIRB that can be interfaced with your onboard GPS. A light shows you if the EPIRB is getting a signal from the GPS, so you are as-

sured that the signal is current. From Pains Wessex/McMurdo comes the Fastfind, mentioned above, which also has a GPS linked to an EPIRB.

A device like this cuts rescue times dramatically, since rescuers no longer have to home in on the transmitting beacon but can go directly to the EPIRB's location.

SARTs

Search-and-rescue transponders (SARTs) are the latest development in rescue equipment. They are intended to be deployed in life rafts, where they sense a rescuing vessel's radar emissions and emit a response signal that gives the life raft's position to the searching vessel's radar. While this technology is not yet widespread, its use is growing.

SART range is limited to the range of the searching vessel's radar, but that can be up to 72 miles. (Although some navy ships have over the horizon capability, most commercial ships have a 48- to 72-mile range.) When using a SART, do not locate it near a radar reflector, because the reflector can confuse the emission signal.

The Simrad SA50 SART is the smallest SART currently available. It has a simple, tubular shape and an overall height of around 11

Making Sure Your EPIRB Is Working Properly

1. As soon as you buy your EPIRB, register it with the correct vessel information. Forms are provided with the EPIRB.
2. Make sure that your EPIRB is installed properly in an area where it is unlikely to be stolen and where it would float free if the boat were to sink.
3. The ideal mount will be near the life raft. The EPIRB can be tied to the life raft so that it will emit signals if the raft is used. Don't tie the EPIRB to your boat, however. If the boat

were to sink, the EPIRB would go with it. Make sure that the EPIRB will not be immersed in sea water should the cockpit flood. (Some EPIRBs turn on automatically when submerged to a certain depth.)
4. Regularly check that the batteries work and that all self-tests are performed. Check too, that the hydrostatic release is operable.
5. Send your EPIRB for maintenance checks regularly. Remove the battery first so that the unit cannot accidentally emit signals.

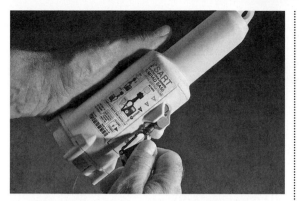

The Simrad SA50 SART is much smaller than its predecessors. The unit remains in standby mode until interrogated by a radar signal, then sends a pulse that displays itself on a radar screen. (Photo courtesy Simrad/Saltwater Communications)

inches, which makes it ideal for pre-packing in liferafts. Additionally, it is simple to program for automatic activation when the liferaft is deployed.

All conventional SARTs use lithium batteries, whose distribution is controlled by complex air, land, and sea transportation rules. But the Simrad SA50 battery pack incorporates an innovative circuit design to achieve a non-hazardous classification, so the SART and its replacement batteries can be shipped without additional cost or paperwork.

Calling for Help

When all else fails and your boat is disabled, sinking, or in immediate danger, radiotelephone remains the most powerful means of summoning search-and-rescue help. In coastal waters a VHF radiotelephone, which has a range of 15–50 miles, is the first recourse for emergency calls. The U.S. Coast Guard and other coast guards around the world monitor VHF Channel 16 continuously.

If you're operating more than 25 miles offshore, your VHF emergency call might go unheard unless another boat relays it to a Coast Guard station for you. That's why offshore

boats carry single sideband (SSB) radiotelephones, which transmit on medium and high frequencies. The MF distress frequency, 2182 kHz, gives you a range of 25–100 miles or more, and is monitored continuously by the Coast Guard. The HF distress frequencies are 4125, 6215, 8219, 12290, and 16420 kHz, and these are your choices for a high-seas distress call. These frequencies are not continuously monitored, but your chances of being heard are good.

If your VHF or SSB radio is capable of digital selective calling (DSC) and is properly registered and interfaced with a GPS receiver, your distress call will automatically broadcast your vessel's identity and your location. See Chapter 11 for more on emergency calls.

The Grab Bag

If everything goes well, you'll find your boat in good shape after the storm. But if things go wrong, and you have to take to your life raft, you'll need a substantial list of items to make your time adrift more bearable. These items should be assembled in advance and stored in a grab bag or "ditch kit"—that is, a single bag you can grab as you leave the boat in an emergency. Locate the grab bag close to the companionway and keep it ready at all times, so that you will be fully prepared should your boat be lost. Ideally, a grab bag should have enough volume that it will float if you miss when you are throwing stuff into the life raft.

If you are going on a long offshore voyage you can do no better than read George Sigler's book *Experiment in Survival* (Vero Technical Support, 2001), in which the author recounts how he and a fellow named Charlie Gore sailed a Zodiac inflatable from California to Hawaii while surviving on fish and on water they made in a solar still. They did this voluntarily to test the limits of survival on the ocean. Some of the thoughts and gear listed here were generated by reading this book.

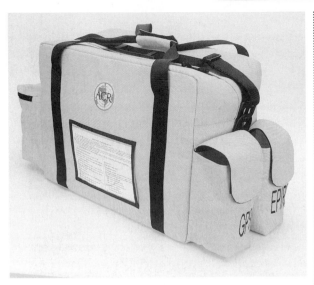

The RapidDitch bag from ACR Electronics is SOLAS compliant and makes it easy to store everything you need in an emergency. (Photo courtesy ACR Electronics)

What to Put in a Grab Bag

In addition to the items that should already be in your life raft, you'll want the following gear. Contrary to many authorities, I believe that you should prepare to survive on the ocean first, then prepare for rescue. So I have organized the following lists into three groups: survival essentials, rescue essentials, and additional gear.

Survival Essentials

- Clothing for warmth and protection. Ideally this should include long-sleeved cotton or woolen shirts and long pants.
- Spare containers of water and a PUR reverse osmosis hand-operated watermaker. You might also include a solar still or two if they are available from a surplus store, or a large plastic sheet. Use the plastic sheet to let water condense on the underside and drip into a container. It doesn't give you much water, but it helps. (Note that the hand-held watermaker requires a lot of physical effort, which

could make you sweat. Use it after dark to cut down on water loss.)
- A first aid kit with sunburn and sunscreen lotion, antibiotic creams, and zinc oxide.
- Fishing tackle. Include at least 100 yards of 100-pound (45 kg) test line, plus 100 yards of 50-pound (22 kg) test line, wire leaders, good-sized stainless steel hooks (that won't rust), and a few artificial lures. You don't need a fishing pole—a spool will do—but you do need something to prevent fishing line from cutting your hands. If you have a spear gun, it would help to have it in the fishing kit.
- A sharp knife and a board to cut on. Cutting on a moving rubber life raft can lead to slashing the raft. Most authorities recommend a blunt-ended knife to avoid cutting the raft, but I find it difficult to fillet fish with such a knife.
- A mirror. ACR's Hot Shot signal mirror with float and whistle is ideal. You can aim it at passing ships, although there are a lot of reflections on the water and you may not be seen.
- Multivitamins and glucose tablets.
- Life raft repair clamps such as Clamseal.
- A Day-Glo orange tarp or space blanket (a very thin blanket with foil on one side. When wrapped around you it directs heat back toward your body. The idea was developed by NASA, hence the name), to be used as a cover, for catching rain, and even as a makeshift solar still.
- A small bailer and a sponge or two.
- Prescription medications.
- Eyeglasses and/or the darkest sunglasses that you can find.
- A spare chart of your cruising area (waterproof if available), pilot charts, a pencil, eraser, and dividers. If you can find room, two small triangles will also help with navigation.
- A watch or timepiece.

- Toilet paper.
- Seasickness pills or tablets.

Essentials to Get You Rescued

- A 406 EPIRB. (If the battery is accessible, you should carry spares.) The EPIRB would normally be kept on its own mounting but should be placed in the bag in the event of a catastrophe.
- At least two white flares, two red flares, and two orange smoke signals. You can also use the DistresS.O.S light from ACR Electronics. This light flashes a constant SOS signal. It is battery-powered and is Coast Guard-approved to replace flares.
- The RescueStreamer distress signal (more on this below).
- Two dye markers.
- A VHF radio. If possible, one with DSC. Both Steve Callahan and Dougal Robertson, in their respective books (*Adrift* and *Survive the Savage Sea*), mention that a number of

An inexpensive GPS can be highly useful in an emergency. (Photo courtesy Magellan)

ships sailed past them without stopping. This also is a good reason to carry a search-and-rescue transponder (SART).

- A small strobe light with spare batteries.
- A can/bottle opener if you put cans or bottles in the grab bag.
- A waterproof flashlight. (Two would be better, with spare batteries.)
- Emergency food rations and vitamin tablets. Note that dried foods use water to rehydrate and are not good survival foods.
- An inexpensive GPS (waterproof if possible) such as Garmin or Magellan with spare batteries. Store the batteries separate from the GPS.

Additional Non-Essential, but Nice-To-Have Gear

- Personal gear such as passport, ship's papers, spare eyeglasses, and valuables.
- Spare Ziploc plastic bags for keeping clothing dry.

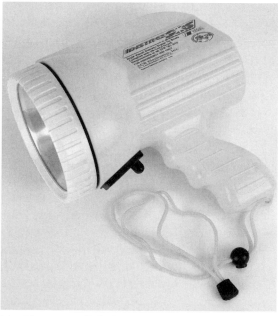

The DistresS.O.S light is Coast Guard approved and can replace flares. (Courtesy ACR Electronics)

- Chocolate bars.
- Multivitamin, iron, and glucose tablets along with beef and yeast extracts that can provide a lot of nutrients from a small container.
- Some form of grater or strainer to wring fluids out of fish.
- A camera to document your experience for the book you will write when you come ashore.

All gear should be of the lightest make possible and retained with string, so that if your life raft capsizes it will not be lost. It's a good idea to store small gear in Tupperware-style boxes. These boxes will come in handy for many other things, such as catching rainwater or storing fish strips. The bag itself should be of a waterproof material, with many pockets, and you should try not to load it up with items that duplicate the equipment in the life raft. Your goal is to supplement this equipment. Still, in an emergency, almost everything can be put to some use, and if your boat is sinking slowly you might want to load other gear into the life raft.

A grab bag may seem like something you think you will never need, but if you are going to embark on a long offshore cruise, it should be part of your planning.

Distress Flares

Ready to abandon ship? Then carry all the flares you can, not just the ones packed in the life raft valise, since flares make it much more likely that you will be seen. According to Coast Guard rescue swimmers I have spoken with, bright white flares work better in heavy seas than smoke flares because in heavy weather, smoke tends to lie down between the waves.

If and when you do need to shoot off a flare, be careful where you point it. The direction can make a big difference in its effectiveness. And whatever you do, don't point it directly toward the rescue helicopter or plane, even if you think that's the best way of being seen.

"This is the worst thing you can do," says Coast Guard rescue swimmer Alan Fijn, who jumps from helicopters in severe weather to help mariners in distress. "We can see the flare, but it is coming directly toward us and we have little or no idea where it is coming from. The ideal flare is fired at 90 degrees to the aircraft. That way we can follow the smoke trail back to the life raft. In the helicopter, for example, the pilot can see out the front, and if the flare comes up in front of him, he will see it, but often he will be beyond the point at which he can track the trail back to the life raft. The crew sitting in the back of the aircraft cannot see forward, but can see a flare out to the right side of the aircraft. If it comes up on that side we can find the life raft in seconds."

Given these comments, it would appear that a flare fired in front of but not directly at the aircraft, followed by a flare to one side, might be the best way to get the pilot's attention and also enable the crew to see where you are.

So what flares should you pack in addition to the life raft pack? Flares that meet the SOLAS regulations are designed for use aboard all commercial shipping around the world and are usually packed in life rafts that may be shipped worldwide. You also need flares aboard the mother boat itself, but only ocean-racing sailboats subject to ORC regulations are required to carry more than the Coast Guard minimum on board.

The ORC standards are good for all boats, sail or power. They recommend a minimum of four red hand flares and four white hand flares for boats that sail close to shore (category 4 racers in ORC terminology). Boats that sail offshore (category 1 yachts) are required to carry a minimum of 12 white parachute flares, four red hand flares, four white hand flares, and two orange smoke signals. Boats that sail in the waters in between (categories 2 and 3) must carry four red hand flares, four white hand flares, four parachute flares, and two smoke signals. All flares must be checked yearly and discarded if they are past their expiration date. In my opinion, cruisers and powerboaters would do well to adopt these numbers as a minimum standard.

Flare Tests

Aided by the Jamestown, Rhode Island, fire department, I once had the opportunity to test fire some Coast Guard–approved and SOLAS-approved flares from a boat (after the local Coast Guard station broadcast a Pan-Pan message to alert local shipping to our testing). First we tried some parachute flares, and found that the Coast Guard–approved flares reached an altitude of about 500 feet (150 m) and lasted 4–7 seconds. I fired one flare when the boat's pilot, harbormaster Sam Patterson, was facing the other way, and he did not see it at all. The SOLAS-approved flares reached a height of about 1,000 feet and lasted 40–60 seconds. (In spite of the Pan-Pan message, telephone and radio calls to the coast guard increased every time we launched a SOLAS flare.)

We next tried a number of handheld flares to see how they would work, and found that the Coast Guard–approved flares lasted 4 or 5 minutes, while the SOLAS-approved flares lasted nearly three times as long. We also found that Coast Guard–approved flares dripped hot slag on the deck and needed to be held over the side to avoid catching the boat on fire. Finally, I dunked the flares in the water to see what would happen if they got wet. The Coast Guard–approved flares went out underwater, while the SOLAS-approved flares bubbled and stayed lit.

Turning next to the orange smoke flares, we found it hard to distinguish between Coast Guard– and SOLAS-approved models, although the SOLAS flares lasted almost three times as long. Again, Coast Guard rescue personnel have told me that smoke tends to lie down between the troughs of the waves and is difficult to spot from the air, so in an emergency situation you would be well served by not depending on smoke flares exclusively.

Based on this testing, I recommend that you buy *only* SOLAS-approved flares for your boat to ensure that you will be seen in an emergency. The difference in price is only a few dollars.

ACR's DistresS.O.S Signal light

The DistresS.O.S Signal Light sends out a Morse code SOS signal automatically when turned on, and the beam is reputed to be visible for up to 18 miles at night, though line-of-sight limitations will normally be more restrictive than that. The battery lasts a long time and can be directed at a potential rescue vessel, so it is certainly a useful adjunct to a flare pack. In my opinion, it is more effective than the Coast Guard–approved flare packs offered by some manufacturers.

Distress Flags and Mirrors

Unfortunately, a boater flying a distress flag (black square over black ball against orange rectangular background) is just as likely to be asked what country he is from as he is to get rescued. A reflecting mirror is useful if you are in a life raft or maybe in the desert, but reflections abound on the ocean. If you are on a boat with a broken engine or a boat that is sinking slowly, flares will bring help faster than reflections from a mirror. Of course, if you've run out of other options, distress flags and mirrors work better than nothing, and they have been used by shipwrecked mariners to attract attention since time immemorial.

I recently tried a new Hot Shot mirror from ACR Electronics. This mirror, about the size of a 3 × 5 card, has a peephole in the middle. To use it you look through the peephole to see a red dot. When the red dot is lined up on your target, the mirror is aimed properly. This is an inexpensive device that I recommend for anyone going afloat.

The RescueStreamer Distress Signal

Another interesting rescue device is the RescueStreamer Distress Signal from the Rescue Technologies Corporation of Aiea, Hawaii. It makes a swimmer or life raft much more visible to a rescue helicopter. The original signal was tested by the U.S. Navy and found to be visible from 1,500 feet (460 m) of altitude. The device is a 12- to 40-foot-long ribbon that floats on the surface of the water. It is lightweight, Coast Guard–approved, and costs $40 to $120 depending on its size. It is now available with lights to aid in night rescues, although I think the light unit looks flimsy compared

The RescueStreamer distress signal makes it easier to be seen from an aircraft. (Photo courtesy Rescue Technologies Corporation)

with the robust streamer. The manufacturer is continually testing the streamer with other lighting options, so a better light may come soon.

Life Rafts

In France and many other European countries, life rafts are mandatory aboard boats over 39 feet (12 m). The U.S. Coast Guard does not require every recreational boat to have one, but for sailboats racing offshore, the ORC mandates a life raft with enough space to hold every person in the crew. The best life rafts are self-inflating, have two or more buoyancy compartments, include a canopy to protect the occupants against the elements and a package of safety equipment, and conform to SOLAS requirements. When buying a life raft, buy the best quality that you can afford. Sailors from several boats who had to take to rafts in the 1998 Sydney-Hobart race found that the less expensive rafts broke apart in extremely heavy winds and seas, and although one man was rescued after spending many hours floating on just the rings of a raft in the hurricane-force winds, two of his companions drowned. Check, too, the number of rings or tubes in the life raft. With at least two separate tubes, if one is holed, the other will keep you afloat while you make emergency repairs.

By keeping the occupants out of the water, a life raft goes a long way toward preventing hypothermia, but you can nevertheless get very cold from heat loss through the uninsulated floor. If you have to take to a life raft, try to remember to toss in a couple of cushions that you can sit on. A life raft gathers the crew together so that the group's heat can help to keep everyone warm—as long as the closures work. Ideally, the closures should be zippered and backed with a Velcro flap.

In addition to keeping its occupants afloat and reasonably warm, a life raft also makes a much larger and easier-to-spot object than the individual heads of people floating in the water, and through the use of a canopy it helps prevent severe sunburn or exposure. Another consideration when purchasing a life raft is that most models only guarantee *sitting* room for the rated number of occupants. This can leave a group of sailors feeling pretty cramped if they have to spend much time there. The ideal raft should have a rated capacity at least 50 percent higher than the number of people it will be expected to hold. If you have a five-person crew, you should get an eight-person raft to allow everyone room to stretch out.

The first thing to do when you get into a life raft is take a seasickness pill, since the motion of a raft in a rough sea induces almost universal seasickness. Then find some line and tie everything to the raft. That way, if it capsizes, nothing will be lost. Despite manufacturers' claims to the contrary, even the most heavily ballasted rafts will capsize given a large enough sea. You can help prevent a rollover by gathering crew weight on the windward side to prevent the wind from getting under the raft.

Another way to prevent or at least reduce capsizing is to trail a Jordan Series drogue to slow the drift rate of the raft and keep it from being rolled in a seaway. The effectiveness of this technique was confirmed in tests carried out by the British National Maritime Institute (now known as British Maritime Technology). One drawback, however, is that a drogue needs to be attached somewhere, and without a strong attachment point it could rip a hole in the raft or, in a worst case scenario, rip it to shreds.

In a demonstration at a Zodiac life raft factory, I saw a life raft inflate in less than 45 seconds, plenty of time to allow the crew to get off a sinking vessel. According to the experts at Zodiac, packing a life raft in a plastic canister is the most secure method of carrying it. The canister protects the raft against UV degradation, keeps it waterproof, and can be stepped on without damaging the raft. Canisters can be

A life raft like this one from Zodiac can save your life if you have to abandon ship.

difficult to handle and store, however, and some people prefer a soft valise.

Life Raft Survival

If you want lessons in surviving in a life raft, you can do no better than read Dougal Robertson's book *Survive the Savage Sea,* Steve Callahan's *Adrift,* Maurice and Maralyn Bailey's *Staying Alive,* Bill Butler's *66 Days Adrift* (International Marine/McGraw-Hill, 2005), and George Sigler's previously mentioned book *Experiment in Survival: Across the Pacific with George Sigler.* The Baileys spent 117 days in a life raft. The Robertson family of two adults and three children, along with another crew member, survived 37 days in a 9-foot dinghy after their boat was holed and sunk in less than a minute by whales. (It is of interest to note that their life raft sank after 10 days because it was old and the rubber chafed through.) Callahan survived 76 days in a life raft after his small boat hit a submerged object and sank. And Bill Butler survived 66 days with his wife in a small life raft after their boat, too, was sunk by whales (not far from where the Robertsons' boat suffered the same fate).

Sigler's experience, in particular, is instructive. He contends that people should not wait for rescue, but should actively make their own way toward the shore, and that life rafts should be boat-shaped to enable people to sail toward land. No place in the ocean, he notes, is more than 2,000 miles from land, or a maximum of 60 days' sail at an average speed of 1.4 knots.

With hard candy and a solar still, he and Charlie Gore sailed across the Pacific Ocean to prove that it could be done. Unlike Callahan and the Baileys, they were only able to find fish a few hundred miles off Hawaii, but they made distilled water from the solar still. Sigler's weight dropped from 185 to 128 pounds during the trip, but both men survived their self-imposed ordeal.

There are striking similarities in all these accounts. No one drank seawater, although Sigler added 3 ounces of seawater to their 10- to 12-ounce daily ration without ill effects. Sigler mentions that Thor Heyerdahl, in his book *Kon Tiki,* also reported adding a little sea water to fresh water. And apparently a small amount of sea water adds minerals and enzymes not present in distilled water. All agree, however, that you should not drink pure sea water, since those same minerals that help in small amounts can be deadly in larger quantities. All survivors collected water, the Robertsons from rain, Callahan and Gore/Sigler from their solar stills, and Bill Butler from a reverse-osmosis hand-operated desalinator that he unreservedly calls a lifesaver. Sigler points out that people can survive for up to 60 days on as little as 10 ounces of water per day. All agreed that the runoff water from their life rafts tasted of rubber residues and was undrinkable except in the worst cases.

The Robertsons and the Butlers (in the Pacific) got most of their food from inquisitive turtles, while Callahan (in the Atlantic) speared dorados (mahi-mahi) that swam around his raft. Gore and Sigler carried stainless steel hooks and almost caught a 16-foot shark by accident. Both Robertson and Callahan lost numerous fish hooks and lures because they had no wire leaders, which allowed the fish to bite through their monofilament lines. Sigler took wire leaders but had little more success because fish are few and far between in the middle of the Pacific Ocean. Apparently it is one of the areas of the world ocean where there is little plankton and thus little marine life. All suffered saltwater boils, dehydration, weight loss, sunburn, cuts, and cramped conditions. All suffered nausea upon entering the life raft, a condition that can be especially deadly (because of dehydration) to smaller children.

The Robertsons and Callahan fired off a large number of flares at the first vessel that passed near them, only to have that ship sail right on by. They fought hard to survive, using the lessons they had learned from other survival accounts and aggressively pursuing a survival strategy. At no time did they sit back and wait to be rescued. All attempted to sail toward the nearest land. Sigler and Gore saw several ships, but only one stopped to talk to them. They were able, however, to talk to airline pilots flying to Hawaii using VHF radio, and reported their position several times.

Life Raft Navigation

Today we have GPS, but Robertson had to keep track of his position with a watch at noon, while Steve Callahan used a simple pencil sextant to estimate his latitude. By aiming a pencil at Polaris, the north star (near Ursa Major in the sky and above the north pole), and a second pencil at the horizon, Callahan obtained an angle of latitude which he then measured against the compass rose on his salvaged chart. Basically, if Polaris is directly on the horizon, you are on the equator. If Polaris is directly overhead you are at the North Pole. Any angle in between gives you an approximate latitude, which can be accurate to within 30 miles. Like Robertson, he timed the sunrise in order to estimate how far west he was.

Both Robertson and Callahan's navigation techniques were based on sound experience, and in both cases proved remarkably accurate. (Robertson's estimated position was off by 5 nautical miles in latitude and a little under 100 nautical miles in longitude.) This is a good reason to learn celestial navigation, in addition to relying on a GPS. Remember, no matter how reliable your handheld GPS, it will be useless if you don't provide it with batteries. You should also learn where the major ocean currents run and where the major shipping lanes are, since by sailing along well-known or well-used routes, you increase your chances of rescue. Remember, however, that your chances of being seen on the vast expanse of the ocean remain small, even in the best of circumstances.

When NOT to Abandon Ship

Do not abandon ship unless the boat is actually sinking. In fact, there is a well-known axiom that you should only step *up* into a life raft—that is, don't abandon ship until your boat is about to slip beneath the waves. In the Fastnet storm of 1979, for example, 24 yachts were abandoned, all but one of them after suffering 90-degree knockdowns. Of these 24, six were abandoned before help was at hand, and of these six, only two were not recovered after the storm. Only two yachts were abandoned because they were in immediate danger of sinking. Of the abandoned boats' crews, seven people were lost after taking to their life rafts. Virtually all of the abandoned yachts were knocked down beyond horizontal, and 19 abandoned yachts were recovered later. According to the Fastnet Report issued by the RORC, only five yachts sank out of the 303 that started the race.

As recounted in the book *The Perfect Storm,* the Westsail 32 *Satori,* owned by Ray Leonard, set sail just before the nor'easter hit the western North Atlantic in October 1991. When caught offshore in the storm, Leonard, with two women as crew, felt sure that his boat would survive and decided to lie ahull. He and his crew took down all sail, lashed the helm, and took to their bunks to wait out the storm. During the severe weather the boat came within 70 miles of the storm's center, and after about 12 hours of rough seas the boat was rolled, spending 30 seconds on its side before righting.

About three hours after the knockdown, Leonard set a storm jib on the staysail stay and let the boat sail on its own. Then there was a second incident, when the boat was knocked over to about 90 degrees before righting itself again. During this knockdown the life raft tore from its mounting and inflated, and Leonard had to cut it loose. At this time one of Leonard's crew called the Coast Guard, and a Falcon jet was dispatched. The Falcon pilot discussed the situation with the crew of the *Satori*, and ultimately, against Leonard's wishes, the boat was abandoned and the crew was airlifted by helicopter after a rescue swimmer went into the 30-foot seas to help them into a basket. Ordered off his vessel by the Coast Guard, Leonard jumped into the sea, but the grab bag he was carrying tangled in the lifelines and had to be left behind. The day after the storm, Ray Leonard set out to find his boat. Six days later it washed ashore on the beach at Maryland's Assateague State Park with the grab bag still on deck. The boat was refloated and is still sailing.

Even in the 1998 Sydney-Hobart storm, two boats that were abandoned by their crews were found afloat a few days later and were towed back to port.

As a rule, stay with your boat unless it is in imminent danger of sinking, and don't ever try to swim to shore, even if it seems only a short distance away. Staying with a floating hulk is more likely to get you rescued, since even a barely floating boat is easier to spot than a head in the water. And according to experts, most people seriously underestimate how close they are to shore.

A good example of the value of staying with the boat occurred in the Bristol Channel in England in early 1998. Three men went sailing on their catamaran, and the seas increased to the point where the boat's main crossbeam broke. The men lowered the mast and lashed it to the hulls to make a triangular raft. Then they activated a 121.5 MHz EPIRB and began firing off flares at intervals. Six hours later, a helicopter from RAF Chivenor in North Devon arrived and lifted the men to safety. They were saved because they were wearing protective clothing and life jackets, had carried an EPIRB and flares, *and did not attempt to swim to shore.*

(They would have been rescued sooner had they used a more reliable 406 EPIRB.)

If you still aren't convinced that you should never abandon ship when there is even a slight a possibility that your vessel can be saved, consider this: if your boat, weighing several tons, is in danger of being rolled over or sunk by large seas, imagine how unpleasant it will be aboard a life raft, which only weighs a few pounds and has much less resistance to being buffeted by the waves. In fact, experience has shown that the motion of a life raft is likely to incapacitate the crew far more than if they were aboard a rolling boat, since a life raft follows the contours of the waves and is completely at their mercy.

Hypothermia: Why It Can Be Deadly

If you saw the movie *Titanic*, you saw many passengers in the water when the ship went down. Headlines of the time assumed that the victims drowned, but today we know that they died of either cold shock or hypothermia. Cold shock occurs when the body is first immersed in cold water. Victims feel almost paralyzed, gasp for breath, and often struggle to stay afloat, which actually dissipates the body's heat more quickly. The only way of surviving cold shock is to curl into a ball, slow your breathing in order to slow the adrenalin rush, and hope you can get out of the water in a few minutes. If you have a face mask on your foul-weather gear, pull it down over your face. Research has found that people float best at about a 45-degree angle, but this usually puts your head downwind, with the wind and waves in your face. Pulling a mask over your face will prevent cold water from hitting you, allow you to breathe more easily, and delay the onset of hypothermia.

In cold water, simple tasks first become difficult, then impossible. When enough time passes, you fall into unconsciousness and either drown or die from hypothermia, your body's core temperature dropping to the point where your vital organs cease to function. In freezing water, *Titanic*'s passengers would have become unconscious in 10–15 minutes and would have died in less than 45 minutes. Reports from survivors indicate that a lifeboat that went back to rescue people in the water found nobody alive after half an hour.

The causes of hypothermia were first investigated when the Luftwaffe became worried about the number of German pilots who were being lost when they bailed out of their planes over the English Channel in winter. Rather than experiment with pilots, however, the Nazis exposed Dachau concentration camp victims to immersion in freezing cold water. Many prisoners died before the Nazi doctors found that immersion in a hot bath immediately after retrieval from the water was the best way of staving off the onset of hypothermia. Normal body temperature is 98.6°F (37°C), and if it drops just 2 or 3 degrees, you will experience mild hypothermia. You will begin to shiver, your hands and feet become cold and painful, and while you will still be alert and fairly able, your reactions might slow to the point where you find it difficult to perform a simple task such as tying your life jacket. At this point you are not yet in great danger, but you should do everything you can to get warm. Treatment aboard a boat might consist of getting into a sleeping bag with something warm (a bottle of heated water, for example), drinking warm, sweet, nonalcoholic drinks, and resting for several hours.

If your core temperature continues to drop to between 92°F and 90°F (about 34° and 32°C) you will have developed moderate hypothermia and should be warmed as above. In this case you should take warm drinks only after you have started to get warm again.

If your body's core temperature drops further still, below 90°F (about 32°C), you will be suffering from severe hypothermia. At this point all shivering stops, since your body no longer has the energy to warm itself up. You may appear confused or even drunk, your speech may be slurred, and you may actually refuse help. Ultimately, you will lapse into semiconsciousness and your muscles will go rigid. At this point you can still be warmed, but should be taken quickly and gently to the nearest hospital, since you are now in great danger. Be aware that at this point the victim needs to be treated gently. Rough handling of a severely hypothermic victim may cause cardiac arrest. The victim should have no food or drink and should be put in a sleeping bag in a bunk and warmed as soon as possible. One well-proven way of achieving this is to have another person climb into the bunk with the victim.

When a body's core temperature drops below 82°F (about 28°C) the victim may lose consciousness or appear dead. The skin is cold and waxy, and the pulse weak or undetectable. The victim's body is rigid. The only hope of recovery is to get to hospital as soon as possible.

There have been cases in which people have fallen into extremely cold water and been revived without major problems, so if one of your crew goes overboard in such conditions and appears dead when you get him out, don't give up. Try CPR, and keep trying until emergency services declare the victim alive or dead.

Remember, you can get mild hypothermia on bright sunny days or cloudy, windy days. Water causes the most rapid onset of hypothermia, but cold air can induce it too. Cold water leads to a cold wind blowing across the boat and possible hypothermic effects. Make sure that you have warm clothing available when you go out on a boat.

Seasickness

It is said that there are four stages of seasickness. In the first, you are afraid you will have to ask the captain to head for shore. In the second, you are afraid that when you ask the captain to head for shore, he will refuse. In the third, you are afraid you are going to die. And in the fourth, you are afraid you won't die. Then there's the joke about the only cure for seasickness is to go and sit under a tree. Seasickness affects a large number of sailors, but most get over it after a few days at sea. To help minimize symptoms, the right diet, a careful approach to going to sea, and the right medications are effective.

Afraid That You're Going to Get Seasick?

There are several ways to delay or prevent seasickness, but almost all of them start onshore or before the onset of rough weather. First, eat properly. A pre-departure party followed by breakfast at the local diner is one of the worst things you can do before going to sea. The alcohol imbibed at the party and a few high-fat sausage links will set your stomach up for a "technicolor yawn," as seasickness has been called. Ideally, the evening before the trip should be spent sleeping on board the boat to allow your body to get used to its motion. When onboard, drink plenty of water to get your body well hydrated—seasick sailors can get severely dehydrated. Alcohol also dehydrates your body, and ideally, should not be consumed for at least 48 hours prior to departure. Some sailors swear by Coca-Cola to stave off seasickness. Others advocate ginger ale or chewing ginger capsules to settle the stomach. Still others claim that wristbands help. These act by putting pressure on wrist points that acupuncture experts say affect balance and the inner ear.

Finally, you can resort to drugs. The most popular is Dramamine, an over-the-counter medication taken for motion sickness of all kinds. This is effective in most cases. TransdermScop, a scopolamine patch, is also a useful drug, but only available by prescription. Trans-

dermScop can have side effects, including dizziness, dry mouth, and "spacey-ness," and should be tried ashore before it is tried on board a boat. In general, a patch lasts two to two-and-a-half days. Sailors who have traveled extensively outside the United States say that a drug called Stugeron—available over the counter in Britain, Bermuda, Mexico, and other places—is highly effective.

If You Do Get Seasick

Yawning and a headache are early signs of the onset of seasickness. Scopolamine won't cure seasickness if you did not apply the patch beforehand. More benign methods might help alleviate symptoms. Ginger capsules, wristbands, and antacids may make you feel more able to cope. Sitting on deck, watching the horizon, and getting plenty of fresh air can also help to delay the onset. If all else fails and you get seasick, ride the rail—the leeward rail—with your harness on and your tether clipped on. If possible, sip water between bouts to keep yourself hydrated.

Children in Rough Weather

In some ways children are more resilient in bad weather than adults, in part because they trust that an adult will get them out of the situation they are in, so they maintain lower stress levels. If you get into heavy weather with children aboard, make them wear life jackets and survival clothing—not so much because they can get washed overboard, but because a life jacket will keep them warmer and help pad their small bodies should they fall or be thrown against furniture.

In heavy weather, most people, especially children, are better off in their bunks than trying to stand in a bouncing boat. Quite often, a child will simply go to sleep in heavy weather and emerge at the end of the storm well-rested and happy. If your child gets seasick, administer a child's seasickness pill to help him or her get through the heavy conditions.

Surviving a Panic Attack

It's easy to panic during a storm. Everyone aboard wonders if he or she will survive the bad weather. But tell yourself that you *can* survive heavy weather—that many sailors have done so before you, and that comparatively few have died. Ask yourself, what is the worst thing that can happen? The boat can capsize and sink? You can fall off? You can fall and hurt yourself? In the pages of this book we have looked at the many ways to keep you and your boat out of trouble. Remember, too, that there is an entire SAR (search-and-rescue) network just beyond the horizon that can help you, provided you let them know early enough. An early Pan-Pan broadcast lets the Coast Guard know you are experiencing difficulties. It is an alert that gets you priority, but not rescue. If you preface your call with Pan-Pan-Pan on VHF Channel 16, all other users should clear the channel to allow the Coast Guard to get back to you. As with a Mayday call, the Coast Guard will ask what the problem is. For example, you might put out a Pan-Pan call if the mast on your sailboat has fallen down and injured a crew member, but your boat is in no danger of sinking.

A Mayday call or an EPIRB transmission sets a huge organization into search-and-rescue mode. As U.S. Coast Guard HH60 helicopter pilot Lt. Brian Washburn says, "If it's humanly possible, we will rescue them." If you are more than 300 miles offshore, other search-and-rescue elements can be alerted to help. But if you panic and scream into the radio, it is unlikely that the Coast Guard operator will understand you. You must be able to calm yourself and tell the Coast Guard exactly what the problem is

and what type of service you require. According to many Coast Guard radio operators, the hardest part of their job is calming people down enough to elicit the required information.

For your part, you need to keep the boat upright and the crew aboard. This means paying attention to life jackets, harnesses, flares, and the EPIRB. Make it a general rule that at night, or when the wind surpasses a certain speed, everybody on deck wears an inflatable life jacket/harness combination. Make sure that every crew is clipped on. Learn to watch the weather before you go sailing, and avoid having to sail home in worsening weather. Practice retrieving a man overboard, setting a sea anchor, setting a drogue, and setting storm sails in light winds (15 knots or less), then try these maneuvers again in 20 or 25 knots of wind. Get experience handling your boat in lighter winds before you head offshore where a storm might find you. And attend safety-at-sea seminars led by speakers who have been on the ocean in heavy weather.

With experience you will gain the confidence to handle your boat in heavy weather and get other crew members through a storm safely.

Psychological Needs of the Crew

When you are out in heavy weather, you will probably have to reassure your crew several times. Yes, the storm will end. Yes, you will survive. Yes, it is windy, but the wind will calm down eventually. You will probably hear yourself saying these things several times during the course of a storm (but think of the stories you'll have to tell later).

As long as you have taken every precaution before heavy weather hits, you should survive. Of course, lady luck can always turn against you. You could be in the wrong piece of ocean at exactly the wrong moment, but you can't do anything about that. You can, however, reassure your crew and get them through the worst.

Practical Storm Tips for the Crew

1. In a storm, the best thing you can do if you are below deck is to get into your bunk. This will keep you from being thrown around as the boat is knocked around by waves and sea. If you have to move around the cabin, wear a harness and always know where your next step is going to be.
2. Take your seasickness pills early. Don't wait until bad weather is upon you.
3. If you have to go on deck, make sure you are wearing adequate clothing to keep warm. You don't want to get hypothermia. It is easier to stay warm than to warm up again after hypothermia has set in. A towel around your neck will help keep water out. A foul-weather hood drawn tight will help keep water off the towel. Dress in layers, so you go can below and peel off one layer if you get too hot. Wear gloves in cold, rainy weather. Wear boots to keep your feet dry.
4. WEAR A LIFE JACKET AND A HARNESS on deck at all times.
5. If possible, hook on before leaving the cabin. Make sure that at least one tether is hooked on at all times when you are on deck. If you are sitting in the cockpit, there is no harm in hooking up both tether lines, although you will have to unhook them in an emergency.
6. When working on deck at night, make sure you have a working strobe light at-tached to your harness, and keep a flashlight in your pocket. If sail changes have to be made, turn on the spreader lights so you can keep track of crew working forward. If possible, appoint one person in the cockpit to watch crew forward exclusively.
7. Try not to open foredeck hatches in heavy weather. Drag sails aft or tie them down. (In very heavy conditions, sails tied down forward may be lost.)
8. If you are steering, watch the waves. You don't need a lot of helm movement to keep the boat on track, but you don't want to let the boat sail off the top of a hollow wave either.
9. Try to make hot drinks and sandwiches early so you don't have to make them during a storm. Make sure the crew get hot drinks at least once per watch.
10. If you have to relieve yourself, go below. Do not under any circumstances try to use the taffrail. Try to void your bladder before serious weather sets in. You can also pee in the cockpit while tethered. It'll wash away soon enough.
11. Think positively. Tell yourself that you will get out of this. You will go ashore and have fun again. In a few hours the bad weather will be over and you will continue with your trip.

Even if you have to take to a life raft, with proper preparation you can survive. Sigler and Gore survived four gales in their life raft. Callahan survived several gales in his, and so did Bill Butler and his wife. With good seamanship you can survive.

Remaining Calm

Preparation is always an antidote to panic. If you and your boat are prepared, there are few situations that can unnerve you. It is the un-prepared (and often inexperienced) sailor who panics in a bad situation.

If you get into a serious situation, first assess the damage. If you call the Coast Guard, the operator will ask you many questions about the situation. You will need to answer clearly and concisely if rescue is going to come quickly. Before you call the Coast Guard, try to figure out if the situation is redeemable or if the boat is damaged beyond repair. The loss of a sail hardly requires the attention of the Coast Guard, unless it ripped half the deck away with it and you are in danger of sinking. If a person is injured, screaming for help will not bring it to you as quickly as telling the rescue services calmly what the problem is.

In a serious situation, take a few deep breaths. Concentrate on doing everything you can to help an injured person or to figure out what the damage is and whether the boat is likely to sink. If you can project an aura of calm, the people around you will probably calm down and you can all work toward resolving the situation.

Ten

Damage Control

Y ou and your wife have done everything you can to prepare your boat for going offshore, but you hit a submerged log when you are 20 miles out, putting a hole in the hull. The pumps seem to be gradually losing the battle against the inrushing water. It's only a matter of time, you think. You tell your wife to put out a Mayday, then you desperately pull up the cabin sole boards. The hole is right there, just aft of the main bulkhead, a half-moon jagged tear about 3 by 4 inches.

You grab a pillow and try to stuff it into the hole, but the water pressure is too much, and the pillow washes out. Again you stuff the pillow into the hole, this time using your other hand to wedge a small section of floorboard over the pillow. That seems to slow the incoming water, and the pumps gain on it. You press down on the floorboard and slow the water even more, but your arms are beginning to ache and you don't know how long you can hold the makeshift bung in place. When your wife finishes the Mayday call and comes to help, you ask her to help hold the bung down. She braces herself between table and the hull, and the bilge pump starts to suck the water down.

What to do next? What can you wedge in place to hold your temporary bung down? Maybe a length of ³/₄-inch cabin sole board can be wedged between the tabletop and the wood on top of the pillow. You reach for it and wedge it into place. It fits, so you hammer it home. Now the pump can cope with the water level for brief periods while you're away from the bung, so you go on deck and retrieve the whisker pole (or the outrigger). By cutting it to length with the hacksaw that you carry onboard and wedging it between the deckhead and the wood over the pillow, you make the seal even tighter.

You call the Coast Guard and let them know what you have done. Telling them that you have slowed the influx of water, you request that a cutter with a dewatering pump meet you in case your temporary plug carries away on your return trip to port. This time your quick thinking has saved the boat, but can you be sure that you have all the equipment that you need to make other repairs at sea?

In addition to practicing crew-overboard drills and carrying engine spares, a life raft, and heavy-weather sails, every boater should know the basic techniques necessary for onboard emergency repairs, and every cruising boat should carry the tools and materials to make them. Over the years many boats have been lost unnecessarily when the captain and crew failed to take the simple measures necessary to keep them afloat and operative. Be prepared to fix things when they go wrong, and with a little luck you'll never need your other emergency gear.

In this chapter we'll discuss the tools and materials that you should have on board, then we'll look at a few of the sorts of breakages that could occur in rough weather—a representative sampling to illustrate the kind of creative thinking that will get you out of almost any jam.

Tools

The tools you use on a boat are slightly different from those you use on land. You need regular woodworking tools for interior work; rigger's tools for mast and rig work; bosun's tools for sail work; mechanic's tools for the engine, pump,

and generator; and special tools to deal with emergencies such as a mast failure.

Every boat should carry a good tool kit that includes a selection of wrenches, with a minimum of two adjustables. I also recommend one or two Vise-grips that can be used as pliers, wrenches, or clamps should the need arise. You should carry one or two hammers—a 1- or 2-pound claw hammer or ball-peen hammer are probably best. Drill a hole in the handle and put a length of string through it. When you are working up in the rig or on deck you can tie the string to your wrist—the seabed around boat berths is littered with tools that have slipped over the side. A hacksaw with many extra blades will be useful should your rig collapse and you have to cut through rod rigging. If you have wire rigging, bolt cutters might work just as well, but cutting rigging on a heaving boat might prove impossible no matter what your gear—in which case you'll need pliers and vise grips to yank cotter pins and clevis pins. You might also need a regular cross-cut saw for woodwork, although saws are hard to keep rust-free on a boat.

Armed with a few tools and an ample supply of spares, even if you are fairly unhandy, you can repair most breakages and keep things going until you get to port. In the following sections we'll look at techniques you can use to get your boat home. We won't cover every eventuality, just a few of the more common problems. To solve problems with specific items of gear, you should carry maintenance manuals or have access to manufacturers' websites, so you can track down the drawings and information you'll need to repair broken gear.

If possible, buy stainless steel or bronze tools that will not rust in the marine environment. While a high-carbon steel knife will keep its edge longer, it will also rust badly, so use a stainless-steel knife and sharpen it often. If you can't find nonrusting tools, spray the ones you

A Minimal Tool Kit

A few tools allow you to do a lot of repairs and maintenance. I prefer to keep several frequently used tools in a small pouch or holster near the companionway ladder, for quick access.

Frequently Used Tools

- Pliers (and/or Vise-grips)
- A knife
- An adjustable wrench
- A fid or spike
- A shackle key
- PSA tape (Ripstop or similar)
- A few needles and a roll of sailmaker's twine
- Duct tape

Woodworking Tools

- A cross-cut or rip saw
- One or two sharp chisels (blade sizes of ¼", ¾", and maybe a ½" are most useful). Make sure your chisels have guards over the sharp tips.
- A claw hammer
- A tape measure
- A small square

Rigger's Tools

- A sharp knife
- A selection of fids for splicing cored ropes, plus a Swedish fid for three-strand rope
- A good lighter or burner to seal the ends of freshly cut polyester lines
- Tape to bind around lines before cutting
- A sharp knife or scissors

Bosun's Tools

- A whipping or roping palm
- A selection of needles
- A selection of twine of various thicknesses
- Beeswax
- Pliers (both needle nose and square nose)

Mechanic's Tools

- A selection of wrenches to suit the engine and engine-room gear
- One or two Vise-grips
- A selection of screwdrivers (slotted and Phillips head)
- A ball-peen hammer
- A hacksaw with at least 12 extra blades
- One or two adjustable wrenches

Special Tools

- Bolt or wire cutters
- A hacksaw with blades that will cut stainless steel wire or rod rigging
- At least 12 spare hacksaw blades
- A mini-vise is helpful but not essential

Spares and Other Gear

- Spares kits for engine, pumps, and generator
- Spares kit(s) for winch(es)
- Extra hose clamps (Jubilee clips)
- A selection of Ripstop and sailcloth of various weights
- Pieces of leather of various thicknesses for chafe patches
- Spare sail ties
- Spare watermaker parts (if you have a watermaker)
- Extra bolts, washers, and nuts to fit the mechanical gear onboard
- Extra cotter (split) pins
- Extra shackle pins and cotters
- Bungs
- Wire
- Electrician's tape, duct tape, Mariner's Choice self-bonding tape. You might also include some of the popular anti-rust products in your toolbox to keep tools from rusting.
- A lubricating spray or two
- A lubricating grease or two

have with oil, or use Bulldog sponges and sprays that prevent rust.

Repair Materials

This year, before you go afloat, go through your boat and tie a wooden bung of the appropriate size to every through-hull on your boat. Should the hose, hose clamp (jubilee clip in Britain), or seacock fail, you will then have a bung handy to hammer into the hole. Bungs cost only a few cents each and can be invaluable in an emergency. You should also carry a roll or two of duct tape, electrical tape, a few nuts and bolts (sized to suit the engine, genset, winches, or other onboard gear), a few wood screws (I carry a small box of different sizes of sheetrock screws), and a reel of stainless wire. On one trip we ripped a fitting off the mast, and the only way to hold it in place was to wire it around the mast. Small items like this can cut out a lot of hassle and get you home safely should something break.

In addition, there are specific repair products that can save you a lot of time and trouble if you have them on board. True, when sailing in sheltered waters, you can probably get to shore with the broken part and have it fixed there. But if you are going to sail in deeper waters or wander across oceans, you might want to carry some of the following gear.

The Navirex Emergency Hull Repair Kit

In Chapter 4, I mentioned keeping a Navirex emergency hull repair kit from Perimeter Industries aboard your boat. This is a good idea if you plan on going more than 2 or 3 miles offshore.

Epoxy

In addition to the stick epoxy I recommended in Chapter 4, you might want to carry a can of regular epoxy with a fast-setting hardener. (The fastest one I have tried is MAS Fast-epoxy hardener, which takes less than seven minutes to set up.) On one trip to Bermuda, after some 40 hours of being pounded by the weather, we emerged relatively unscathed and headed toward the island, only to find that the main bulkhead had separated from the hull over a distance of about 40 inches. The fiberglass had simply cracked along the plane of the plywood. Rather than sail 600 miles back to our departure port with the damage, we opted to repair it on arrival by drilling through the bulkhead and fiberglass and inserting a few bolts. After the bolts were in place, we glassed over the entire area using a quick-setting resin, which made the repair solid.

In addition to a small package of two-part epoxy, you should also carry some fiberglass cloth. A typical kit can be made from a square yard of 6-ounce fiberglass cloth and a packet of West System epoxy or Interlux's Epiglass resin and some glue powder (thickening agent). The entire kit takes up less space than a large box of cereal, and if you add a roll of 3- or 6-inch-wide (75- or 150-mm) cloth tape, you will be able to make temporary repairs to most bulkhead bonding problems or more serious breakages.

Syntho-Glass

Syntho-Glass was also mentioned in Chapter 4 and should be among the spares on your boat.

Caulking

A tube of silicone caulking is another item that can be very handy, especially if you have to remove a piece of deck gear and rebed it. Silicone caulking can be used for just about any above-the-waterline sealing or bedding chore except one that will be painted afterward, since it will not take paint. If you want to paint the finish, use a polyurethane caulking wherever you want a permanent sealant (hull-to-deck joints, for example) and a polysulfide caulking to bed deck

A selection of caulking compounds. You will need a caulking gun to dispense these compounds. If you keep caulking aboard, add a pair of latex gloves and a small can of acetone to make cleanup easier.

hardware, caulk a teak deck, or for any other job that you might conceivably want to disassemble at some point in the future. (Note: Both polyurethane and polysulfide attack some plastics and are not recommended as portlight sealants. Use silicone there.)

On-Deck Problems

The most common on-deck problem for both sail- and powerboats is line chafe (and sail chafe on sailboats). To prevent chafe, carefully cover (tape over) or round off cotter pins, anchor rollers, and all other exposed sharp metal edges. Look at the edges of cleats, pulpits, anchor platforms, and chocks. On powerboats there are fewer deck areas where chafe can arise, but it can still be a problem.

Check over all blocks and tracks to make sure they operate freely. If they don't, give them a shot of lubricant, and if they still don't turn or slide as designed, check for bent pins and shafts. If you are going to sail across an ocean, carry spare track cars and pins. The failure of a pin on one boat I sailed on caused the car to slide aft with such force that it wiped two other cars and the end stop right off the track. Fortunately, we were able to remove a spare car from the other track and continue on our way.

Winches are reliable provided you maintain them properly. Of the failures I have experienced with winches, most have been due either to overloading the unit, bending or breaking pawls, or improper maintenance allowing the pawls to clog. Often seawater reacts with winch grease to form a solid mess. Clean and regrease or oil your winches regularly. A set of winch spares and a manual showing all the winch parts will usually solve any problem. If you don't have one, get a manual from your winch manufacturer.

Another common problem on deck is bent stanchions. If a stanchion is bent a few degrees, it can usually be straightened. But if it is bent more severely, you may have to heat it to straighten it. Often this will leave a blue mark where the metal has been heated, and the only solution is to replace the stanchion. You can do this while the boat is at the dock, but if you are going to cross an ocean, carrying a spare is often a good plan. While you are checking your stanchions, look at the lifeline wire. If it is plastic-covered, there may be nicks in the cover that will let water inside to corrode the wire. Later, when you lean against it, the corroded section lets go and splash, you are swimming. You may be better off with a non-coated stainless steel lifeline wire that will not rust or corrode.

Check your navigation lights and carry spares for the existing lights as well as backup lights that can be bolted or taped into place. The absence of functional navigation lights in a busy channel can be hazardous. If you plan on sailing overnight, make sure your lighting batteries are large enough to let you run the navigation and compass lights all night. Nothing is quite so annoying to the "off" watch as having to run the engine to recharge the batteries halfway through the night.

When working on deck, your first rule should be this: when something won't operate properly, find out what the problem is before cranking or hammering on it. If you can't get a sheet or halyard in because it feels tight, you may find that the halyard has jumped off a sheave, in which case cranking it in on a winch will only make the problem worse. If the sail won't sheet in to the winch after a tack, it may be caught on something like a stanchion or a piece of line. In either case, winching in the sheet may result in a ripped sail. Check first.

Sail Repairs

As soon as you decide to buy a sailboat, you must make decisions about your sails. But first, you must decide where you are going to sail. If you are going to stay close to home, any sailcloth will do, the size of your wallet being the only restriction. If you are going to cruise the world, however, select a Dacron sail. According to many sailmakers, Dacron can be repaired in Botswana just as easily as it can in Rhode Island. If you have an exotic material, it will be repaired with Dacron in many parts of the

Sail-Repair Tools

Selecting the right sail-repair (bosun's) tools is essential. Here's how to choose the best:

THE SAILMAKER'S PALM
For hand-sewing, a sailmaker's palm is essential. A palm is used instead of the seamstress's thimble. There are two types: a *seaming palm* and a *roping palm*. The seaming palm is used for ordinary sewing—for example, sewing two pieces of material together. A roping palm is slightly heavier and is used for sewing ropes to canvas or awning material. The only difference between a seaming palm and a roping palm is that the roping palm has a thumb guard to allow a user to take a quick turn around his thumb and pull the stitch tight. Both palms are made of leather and should fit snugly on the user's hand. In the middle of the strap, where it fits into the palm of your hand, there's a metal cup called the *pellet*. This cup has indentations to help you push the needle through the material.

Don't buy the cheap, soft leather strap that passes for a palm if you can afford a better one. If a needle slips it will go right through one of these straps and directly into the palm of your hand. Instead, buy a heavy-duty palm that will protect your hand. You can get left-hand or right-hand palms from some good chandleries, but both are becoming harder to find. If a palm is too tight or doesn't fit right, soak it in water and then wear it for a short time to make it fit more comfortably.

NEEDLES
Needles should be sized to suit the job and the twine being used, so it's important to carry an assortment. The best needles for canvas repair are triangular in cross section, to make an opening wide enough to pull the twine through. If you use too large a needle with a fine twine, you will make large holes that can eventually lead to ripping of the fabric. Ask your local sailmaker to supply you with a variety of needles.

BEESWAX
In the old days, a sailmaker would grease his twine with beeswax to make it easier to pull through the material and to preserve the twine from abrasion by the sailcloth. Today, beeswax is not easily found, but most sailmaker's twines come prewaxed.

continued

KNIFE

A good, sharp knife is essential for sailmaking. It can be used to trim twine, to cut canvas and rope, and even to shave with.

SCISSORS

Scissors are handy for cutting sailcloth and tape, and on a long trip for cutting the crew's hair.

RUBBER

A rubber is a squarish metal tool with a wooden handle used for pressing down on a crease and flattening the stitching, rather as a seamstress does with a pressing iron before sewing. In a pinch, you can use the back edge of a heavy knife to rub down a seam.

---

world anyway, so why go with a leading-edge, high-tech cruising sail that might not be repairable?

Once you've decided on your sail material, next decide what tools and repair materials your boat will carry. Most sailmakers recommend that you carry at least one roll of pressure-sensitive adhesive, or PSA tape, which comes under various trade names such as Ripstop, Stickyback, and others. With PSA you can repair virtually any sail. Most sails rip for one of two reasons—either they catch on something in the rig, or the sails are old and the material has degraded. In either case you will be left with a ragged edge. Drying the sail and then applying PSA is the easiest and best solution. After you

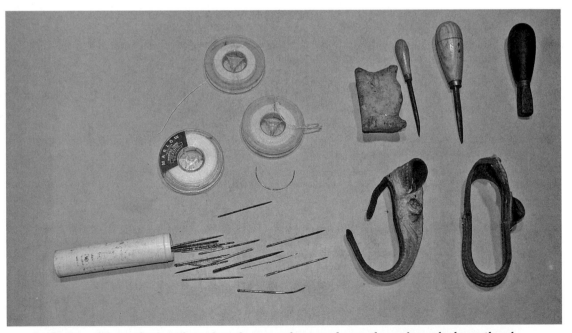

A selection of the author's sail repair tools. Two palms are shown: the roping palm has a thumb guard for wrapping a line around the sailmaker's thumb and pulling it tight; the sailmaker's palm is simply for sewing sails. The collection of needles is stored in a cigar container, but even that is not sufficient to prevent them rusting. A lump of beeswax is essential for greasing sewing line. The three handled tools are a pricker for pinning the sailcloth to the table to hold it tightly, a rubber for creasing sail cloth and a very thin fid for making tight eye splices in the ropes attached to sails.

have applied the tape, you should sew over the rip using a zigzag stitch. PSA tape comes in several styles, woven Kevlar being one of the most popular. Remember, particularly if your sails are old, that in heavy weather high waves pose as much of a threat to your canvas as the wind. If you take care to change down to heavy-air sails in time, you can save yourself a lot of trouble down the road.

Spare Sail Materials

In addition to basic repair materials, a prudent skipper about to leave on a long trip will carry a square yard or two of Dacron for sail repairs and maybe a yard or two of spinnaker nylon to suit the spinnakers or light-air sails. A skipper about to leave on a transoceanic trip might carry a sewing machine and a few yards of Dacron or nylon of a weight to suit the sail inventory.

When repairing sails, select your tools with care. You should use the smallest needle and thread consistent with the strength of the material. A large needle and humongous thread not only create an ugly appearance, but make big holes in the material. Quite often an old sail or awning will rip again along the sewing line if a large needle and thick thread are used.

What to Repair

If you are out for the weekend and your sail snags on something—say, a stanchion while coming about in a squall—cover the resultant hole as soon as possible with PSA. It is relatively easy to repair a small rip in a sail, and if you don't repair it there's a good chance that it will gradually increase in size. Interestingly, a sail usually doesn't rip when you are under sail, unless it is overstressed or the boat is pitching hard and throwing lots of water or spray into it. Instead, most sails rip during a maneuver or when they are allowed to flog. In fact, flogging degrades sail fabric faster than any other factor in sail handling, and today's heavier sail fabrics

tend to break down even faster with flogging. (Twenty years ago, one way that sailmakers would test the endurance of a sail fabric was to tie a strip of sailcloth to their car antenna and drive for a few miles. The flogging from flapping in the breeze would very quickly break down all but the strongest fabrics.)

Should you miss a small rip, and the sail tears from luff to leech, haul it down as soon as possible. If you are close to your sail loft and don't need the sail immediately, take it in for repair. If you are in the deep ocean and need to get the sail repaired, first wipe the edges of the tear with a damp sponge to remove salt. Once the fabric has dried, apply PSA to both sides of the rip. Have somebody hold the edges of the sail together as you apply the tape. If you create a hard spot (where the sail bunches up) there's a good chance the sail will rip again, starting at the bunched area.

If your sail is more than five years old and has seen a lot of use, you might think twice about repairing it. The fabric of older sails tends to break down fairly quickly, especially if it is not UV resistant. You might put in a lot of work just to have the sail rip again. Dimension Polyant reports that some sailcloths lose as much as 50 percent of their strength within two or three months of continual use. (Note that you do not use your sails for two to three months at a time unless you are sailing around the world.) Some fibers, such as high-tenacity polyester (Dacron), Spectra, and Vectran, last a lot longer—up to six months—but UV gets them all (except carbon fiber) in the end. Unless you do it yourself, a repair may be a false economy.

If the sail is ripped into several pieces, a repair may simply not be feasible. In that case, you might decide to make fender bags, a tote or two, or maybe a tail bag out of the remains.

If the sail has a large hole, use a piece of fabric large enough to cover the hole. Tape the edges of the fabric to the sail with PSA tape and then sew the patch to the sail fabric. This will give you a stronger patch than if you cut the patch larger than the hole and simply sew it to the sail. Remember, too, that when you get to port, a sailmaker will probably have to redo your repair, so don't make too large a mess.

Types of Stitching to Use

When sewing two edges together by hand, use a zigzag stitch or herringbone darn so that the edges are held together firmly. If you are sewing two pieces of material together, use a flat seam stitch. Stitches should be pulled hand taut, with uniform tension. Rub down each seam after it is sewn to get the stitches to lie flat. Sewing ropes to canvas requires a roping stitch, which in its simplest form involves little more than pushing the needle through the rope and then the canvas, then spiraling back over the edge of the canvas to make the next stitch.

A sewing machine will make the best stitching. If you are going to sew sails on an ocean race you should carry a heavy-duty or sail-

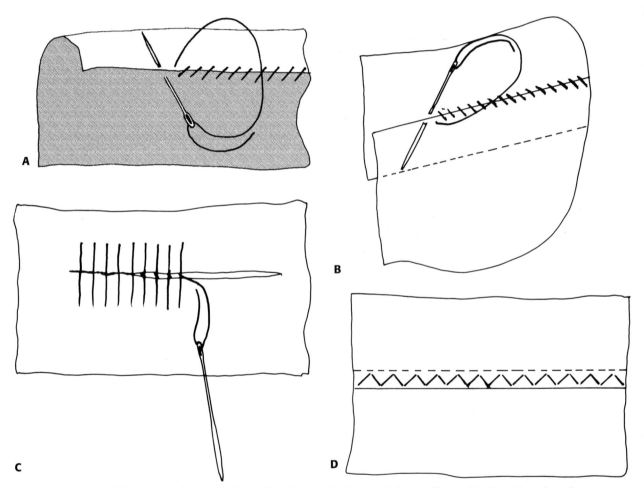

The stitching to use when repairing sails. (A) A herringbone stitch, usually used to hem the edge of a sail. (B) A flat seam stitch used to sew two pieces of fabric together. (C) A sailmaker's darn for repairing small tears. In this one the thread is passed through the tear and then back over itself on the back side. (D) A machine-sewn zigzag stitch, the most common type of stitching seen today.

maker's sewing machine. A heavy-duty home machine will do many of the repairs that your sail covers, bimini, or sail bags might require, but it will probably not cope with heavy sail fabrics.

Mast Failure

If your boat's mast comes down, it is not a catastrophic failure as long as nobody is hurt and the boat isn't holed. The first step when the rig comes down is to secure the spar so that it cannot poke a hole in the hull or deck. If it can't be secured, you may have no choice but to cut it free. The decision may depend on where it has broken. If a mast breaks high up, you can usually save the top, since typically there are a lot of lines, halyards, and cables attached to the broken part to enable you to secure it alongside. Put a fender between the hull and the broken spar and tie it down tightly using winches and tackles so it won't work against the hull or deck and cause further damage. If the mast breaks at or near deck level, you may not be able to save it. If you have to cut it free, try to save anything you can. Spare parts may come in handy for a jury rig.

Close to shore, check to make sure that there are no lines in the water, and motor in to your boatyard or marina. Then you can make arrangements to get the mast replaced or repaired. Far at sea, you will probably have to make a jury rig.

Jury Rigs

There are several methods of making a jury rig. Among the most popular is to make a pair of sheerlegs from whatever spars remain on the boat. You can do this, for example, by lashing one end of a spinnaker or bearing-out pole to the remains of the mainmast or boom, securing the unlashed ends to either rail abreast the mainmast step. Then hoist the assembly with temporary rigging set up both fore and aft and transversely to keep the sheerlegs in place. The accompanying illustration shows how the sheerlegs might look just before being hoisted to the vertical. When you set sails on the jury-rigged spar, avoid cutting them if possible. You may need them for the new mast you're going to have to buy! Instead, reef them by tying off the corners.

After hoisting your jury rig, try to set a course down or across the wind. The boat

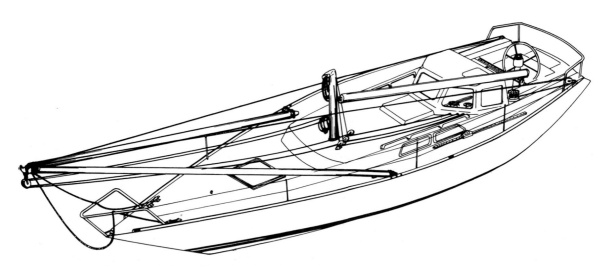

Setting up for a jury rig by making sheerlegs from spinnaker poles.

probably won't sail to windward well. In most cases it will simply be a matter of time before you can get to land and have the spar replaced.

One problem with a jury rig is that the radio antennae you had at the top of your mainmast will probably have been wiped out when it came down. For that reason, if you intend to sail in the deep ocean, you might want to set up your radio antennas so that you will still have a method of contacting shore should you lose the mast. You could try, for example, setting the SSB antenna on the stern or on a radar arch.

If you are going offshore in a two-masted boat, try to ensure that the masts are independently stayed. That way, should the mainmast come down, the mizzen will stay standing. The remaining mast then serves as a hoisting point for the jury mast, making it much easier to set up a jury rig.

Engine Problems

According to Murphy's Law, engine problems always occur in heavy weather. Engine failure can be particularly dicey aboard a powerboat, which is at the mercy of wind and sea without its engine. One typical problem is a fuel blockage caused by the sediment that is stirred up as the boat bounces around in heavy seas. Luckily, with a little preparation you can prevent this problem. A drain fitted at the bottom of your fuel tank, for example, will allow you to periodically draw off both sediment and water before they can become a problem. Efficient filters (including intake filters) will also keep the fuel lines clean in calm weather and virtually eliminate residues settling to the bottom of your tank.

Another problem in heavy weather is gear flying around the engine room. Loose tools can end up in the sump, or worse, they can land across battery terminals and cause a short. Fastening heavy items down and storing other gear where it will not move usually eliminates such problems.

It's also a good idea to pump the engine bilge often to prevent oily residues from slopping out in bad weather. Otherwise the waste might spread around the entire engine area or into other parts of the boat. You might also use one of the bilge cleaners such as Bio-Sok or Clean Water Solutions' enzyme mix to get rid of oil in the bilge and then pump the harmless residues over the side.

Here are some of the more common engine-room problems. Many can be minimized with careful preparation.

Starter Motor Problems

You'll know your starter motor has failed when you push the starter button and the motor simply whines and refuses to engage. Usually this is caused by the failure of the Bendix gear or the spring that thrusts the Bendix gear against the flywheel. If this happens, you'll have to change the starter motor.

If the starter motor doesn't make even a whirring or whining sound, it isn't getting power, and you have a dead battery or loose connection. In this case, checking the battery voltage and tightening connections will often fix the problem.

Alternator Problems

When the engine runs an hour or more without charging the battery, usually the battery has died, the alternator has broken, the alternator belt is loose or broken, or there is a loose connection somewhere between the charger and the battery. You will need a little skill and a multimeter to sort this one out. First, visually check all the connections and belts. Using the multimeter, verify that the battery is flat or not being charged. Then start the alternator and determine whether AC voltage is coming from the alternator. Check the diodes or rectifier that change AC current to DC. (For specific instructions, consult your engine manual or a diesel engine book such as *Troubleshooting Ma-*

rine Diesels, by Peter Compton, International Marine, 1998; or *Boatowner's Mechanical and Electrical Manual*, Third Edition, by Nigel Calder, International Marine, 2005.) Quite often the diodes blow and AC is not being converted to DC current.

Next check all the electrical connections using the multimeter. If a wire is chafed, the electrical current may be shorting out between the alternator and the battery. If you still can't find out what's wrong, head for your nearest boatyard. If your engine is diesel, it will usually keep running without electrical power, but a gas engine will stop and you will need a tow home.

Battery Problems

A flat battery is the most common problem of all. This is why your battery isolation switch should allow you to switch from one bank of batteries to another. Often the battery is run down by a bilge pump being left on while the owner is away. In this case, a solar battery charger is a worthwhile investment.

If the battery will not hold its charge, have it checked by a competent mechanic. It may be dead, with no possibility of being salvaged, and a new battery may be the only answer.

Propeller Problems

You backed up your powerboat and felt a grinding thud from astern. The prop hit a log. When you run the engines ahead, the vibrations threaten to tear the stern off your boat. What have you done? A quick swim shows that you've torn a blade off one prop and bent the blades on the other. How do you get home? With both props mangled, you'll probably have to call for a towing service. Once in harbor, you'll have to either hire a diver or get the boat hauled and have new props installed. The good news is that if only the blades are bent, the old props are repairable. Several companies can do the job fairly quickly and easily at a cost of about 40–60 percent of a new

prop, depending on the damage. (Hale Propeller in Old Saybrook, CT, is one of the leading companies doing this type of work.)

If you are a diver and carry a spare prop and a prop-puller, you may be able to change one prop and use it to get you home. Before you deem yourself ready to make such a repair, however, make sure you know exactly how the job is done and whether you can generate the leverage required while underwater. Powerboats powering long distances should always carry an extra prop as an insurance policy. If your props are not badly damaged, you may be able to limp home at slow speed and then get them repaired. On no account should you run a damaged prop at high speed. A fractured blade may fly off and put a hole in the hull.

Getting a rope wrapped around your prop or props is always a possibility, especially in waters where fixed fishing gear—such as lobster pots—abounds. In this case you'll have to go swimming unless you have a set of rope cutters on your prop shaft. If you have to dive in, equip yourself with a pair of goggles and a sharp knife. Be careful not to slash your hand, and be absolutely certain no one starts the engine while you're working on the prop. (Hide the keys!)

Propeller Shaft and Related Problems

Several years ago a client of mine drove his boat across a sandbar, snapping both shaft connectors. Both shafts then slid out of their shaft logs and sank with the props, whereupon the boat filled rapidly and sank on the bar. Fortunately, the boat was awash at low tide and could be salvaged. The shafts and props were recovered by divers without major damage.

The first sign that should have alerted the owner was the shuddering as the props hit the bar. The second was the automatic bilge alarm, which he had chosen to turn off earlier because it gave false alarms each time a few drops of water found their way into the bilge. The third was the fact that the boat had stopped moving through the water.

If you have even the slightest suspicion that you've hit anything, check immediately for flooding. If you find none, check again after another few minutes—it's better to be safe. Don't turn your bilge alarm off, and when the alarm sounds, check the bilge immediately. If the boat stops when the engines are running in gear, go and check. Carry softwood bungs the same diameter as your prop shaft, located near the shafts, so that if a shaft does drop out, you will have a fighting chance of hammering a bung into the hole. The larger the diameter of the prop shafts, the harder this will be, but you still have a chance of saving the boat.

Steering Failure

One of the most serious problems that either a sailboat or powerboat can experience is the failure of the steering gear. The cause might be clogging or a ruptured seal with hydraulic steering; broken wires, blocks, quadrant, or pedestal with cable steering; or broken cables or clips with a push-pull (or push-push) system. Alternatively, the quadrant arm or internal fittings in the rudder might fail, or the rudder blade could break off while the rudderstock remains in the boat. In the worst case scenario, the entire rudder blade and rudderstock could simply drop out of the boat.

Powerboat Steering Gear

In general, smaller powerboats have push-pull or push-push cable steering, while larger powerboats have hydraulic steering. For powerboats with cable steering, the comments below in the sailboat section apply. For boats with hydraulic steering, a failure can mean a difficult or impossible repair at sea. It can be done if you carry spares and extra hoses and a maintenance

manual. Usually, the hardest part is bleeding the system after the repair is made.

If you cannot repair the steering system and your boat has twin engines, you may be able to steer well enough by varying the throttle settings. If your boat has an emergency tiller, you should be able to fit it to get you home. Check that your emergency steering system works properly each spring before you launch the boat.

If your boat has a single engine, you may be able to get some semblance of control by using a board over the transom as a steering oar or by trailing a drogue on a bridle. Adjust the bridle to turn the boat's bow, as discussed in Chapter 8.

Sailboat Steering Gear

The simplest steering system of all is a tiller fitted directly to the rudderhead. But if a sailboat is equipped with a steering wheel, the system most often utilizes cable, in one of several ways. In perhaps the most common configuration, the wheel turns a sprocket in the pedestal. A length of chain, which looks like bicycle chain, runs over this sprocket. Wire cables are attached to each end of the chain, and these cables travel through a series of sheaves, or turning blocks, back to a radial drive or quadrant fitted to the rudderpost. Turning the wheel turns the rudder. When complex cable-

Getting a Powerboat Home after a Steering Failure

If the steering system on a twin-engine powerboat fails, you can still get home. By varying the engine speeds, you can turn your boat until it is lined up in the direction you want to go and then head for home. When you get close to your slip, you can either dock using your throttles or call for a tow from your yard launch. If you have difficulty getting your boat to go in the direction you want, you may have to resort to a drogue, as described in Chapter 8.

routing problems are encountered, enclosed-cable conduits are sometimes substituted for open cables. The result is known as *pull-pull* steering. On smaller boats a single *push-pull* cable might be substituted for the two cables of a pull-pull system.

With cable steering, if a turning block, cable, pedestal, or quadrant fails, you can usually fit an emergency tiller directly to the top of the rudderstock and steer the boat. Before going offshore, make sure you know how to do this on your boat. It can be surprisingly difficult.

On large sailing yachts, as on powerboats, the steering gear is hydraulic, and the com-ments made above for hydraulic powerboat steering apply.

As for the rudder itself, even if the internal fittings that support the rudder fail, it may still work partially (more on this later). If the rudderstock simply drops out of its bearing, the first step is to stem the influx of water. You can do this by stuffing rags or hammering a large bung into the bearing. Once the water flow is contained, you can set about making an emergency rudder. You will have to steer with the sails and take it easy on the temporary rudder, but you have a good chance of getting home under your own power.

Make sure you can fit an emergency tiller to the top of the rudderstock before you head offshore.

Jury Rigging a Sailboat's Steering System

You are 12 hours from land and your steering fails. What do you do? You first need to determine what type of breakage it has suffered, and for ease of repair, steering system failures sort themselves into three distinct categories: cable or linkage failure, quadrant breakage, and rudder breakage. We'll look at each of these in turn.

Cable or Linkage Repair

The easiest failure to repair is a cable breakage, the failure of a turning block, or the linkage between cable and quadrant or radial drive. All the work can be done inside the boat, and the problem can often be solved at sea. If not, you can just fit the emergency tiller and sail the boat home.

Let's say, for example, that your steering fails and you find a broken cable. If you have a spare length of cable on hand, you can either replace the broken length or sister a new piece to the old so that it spans the break, applying bulldog clamps (also known as cable clamps) to either side of the break. Or perhaps you find that the bolts holding a sheave have pulled through a bulkhead, or a steering wire has jumped off a sheave. On a push-pull steering system the clips holding the conduit rigid may have popped loose, or an end fitting may have let go. All these repairs can be done by a mariner with some basic knowledge of the system and a few spare parts.

For instance, one time when our steering let go, we found that a sheave had pulled a fiberglass pad away from the hull. There wasn't much we could do to glass the pad back to the hull while the steering system had a strain on it, so we drilled a few holes in a temporary frame and rerouted the steering wires slightly. This entailed several hours of hanging in the sail locker with our feet in the cockpit, but the repair got us home.

Quadrant Breakage

Fortunately this sort of failure is rare, but when the quadrant breaks away from the rudderstock, or the hydraulics let go, you cannot usually make the necessary repairs from inside the boat. In this case, the emergency tiller is the only way to get the boat home without calling for a towing service. One way to get around the problem, however, is to fit the autopilot on its own quadrant and use that to take you home. Another is to predrill a small hole in the top of the rudder blade to which you can attach rudder control lines. In normal use this hole can be filled but should the rudder break, the filler can be punched out by a swimmer or a person in a dinghy, and a line run through the hole with an overhand stopper knot on either side. Turning a rudder this way will not be easy, but it might get you home.

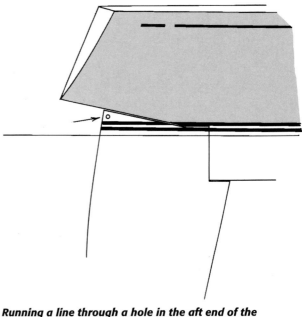

Running a line through a hole in the aft end of the rudder blade might help you get home should the steering fail.

Rudder Breakage

The third and most serious kind of steering system failure is a breakage in the rudder blade itself. In this situation, you must either go over the side to make a repair or forget your rudder altogether and get the boat home by steering some other way. Most rudder breakages occur at the forward ends of the flanges where they are welded to the rudderstock, and the welding process has heat-treated and weakened the metal. This weak area fatigues in use until it breaks. Repairing this situation requires pulling the rudder out of the boat, cutting into the core, and rewelding the flanges. It can only be done ashore, unless you carry welding facilities on the boat.

Flange breakage is more likely on rudders built with a single centerline flange. The figure on the following page shows a better, stronger rudder construction.

I once experienced this type of rudder failure. The occasion was another of the many Bermuda Races in which I've participated, and after the failure we could still partially steer the boat because the remaining stub of the broken flange was still long enough to bind on the rudder's fiberglass skin. It took several turns of the wheel to move the rudder, but we reached Hamilton, Bermuda. There we dropped the rudder out of the boat and cut into the skin to find the problem, and then we took it to a boatyard to get the flanges rewelded. When that job was completed, the rudder was refilled with foam and reglassed before being refitted into the hull. The entire job took about two days.

If you ever need to drop a rudder, be aware that on some boats the rudder bearing sits right on the hull skin, not atop a tube that surrounds the rudderstock and extends above the waterline, as it did on our boat in Bermuda. If that's the case, you will have to haul the boat before dropping the rudder. And another caution: if

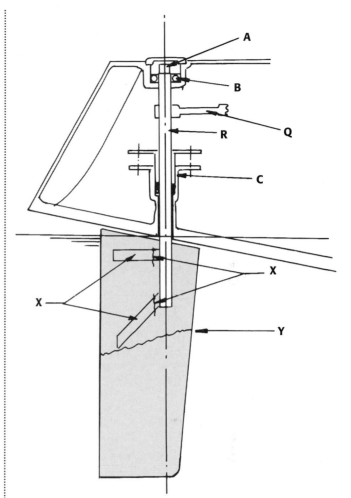

Typical rudder construction on production sailboats. Points X is the most likely point of flange breakage, directly behind the area where the flange was heated when it was welded to the stock. Point Y is the most likely point of breakage for the rudder blade itself, just below the rudderstock termination. R is the rudderstock, A is the emergency rudder fitting, B is the top bearing, C is the rudder stuffing box, and Q is the quadrant.

you do decide to drop a rudder while the boat is afloat, remember that some rudders do not float. You make the situation a lot worse if you allow your rudder to sink!

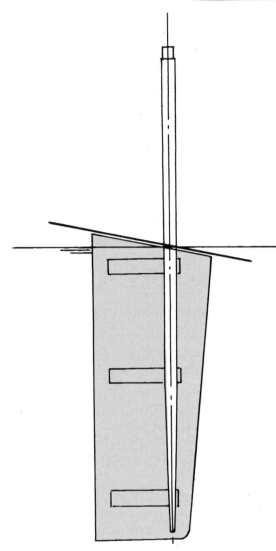

A better method of constructing a rudder blade. Here the flanges are wrapped around the stock and welded at top and bottom. The rudderstock goes to the bottom of the rudder for additional strength. This method of construction is more expensive, but more secure.

The most serious rudder problem of all is when the rudderstock itself breaks in two, leav-ing the rudder blade floating in the boat's wake or drifting to the bottom of the ocean. In this situation, of course, you need a new rudder, which can only be supplied on land. But if you are out at sea, you will need to get home some-how. Several boats have successfully used cabin sole boards, bunk boards, and/or spinnaker poles to jury rig a rudder. Preparation is the key. Work out how you would fashion a jury rig be-forehand so you can make your repair that much more effective if it is ever needed. Re-member that, when using a makeshift rudder, sail trim becomes critically important. Trim the sails so they impose minimal strain on the rud-der, and you will usually go faster and farther than if the crew has to work at steering the boat.

Of course, anything is possible at sea, and even the best contingency plans can go awry. One of our designs got caught in a gale and bent its rudder blade after the pin on the skeg dropped out. Not only could this damage not be repaired at sea, but the bent blade jammed, and the boat could sail in only one direction, and with great difficulty. The vessel barely made it back to port.

Hull Damage

Hull damage can occur at any time, and is the most serious of all types of damage. A through-hull can pop out, a hose clamp can fail, or you might hit a submerged object such as a log or a steel shipping container. The latter can be es-pecially dangerous, and these containers are the suspected cause of a number of sinkings in recent years. Containers have been known to stay afloat for months after falling off ships, and once covered with sea growth they are even less visible. In general, if the hole is less than 36 square inches (225 sq cm), you stand a reasonable chance of saving your boat. If it is larger, only very swift action and a dollop of luck will save it—no matter how powerful your pump, it will not be able to keep up with the inrush of water.

So what do you do when your boat's hull springs a leak? The first job is to find the leak, and fast! Then stuff anything you can find into it to slow the inrush of water, while you consider your next steps. Every moment is vital. Make a careful plan now so that you will know what to do should the time ever come. If you're ready for it, it won't happen.

Damage Control

There's a bang from somewhere forward, and you hear water trickling into the boat. What do you do? Pray? Inspect the damage? Run forward? Launch the life raft?

Here's a step-by-step review of the procedures you need to establish:

1. Go forward to find the source of the problem, turning on the electric bilge pumps as you go.
2. Make sure a crewman calls the Coast Guard, giving the boat's position, a description of the boat, number of crew, and nature of emergency. Until you're know how serious the damage is, the call should be a Pan-Pan call. If it's immediately apparent that you're sinking, make it a Mayday call.
3. Find the source of the leak and categorize it. Type 1 damage is relatively minor. For example, a hose clamp on a through hull might have let go, or the stuffing box seal might have blown out. Type 1 damage can usually be contained easily if you're prepared, but left

unattended it can sink the boat. Closing a through hull may sound like an easy way to stem a torrent, but it's only easy if you check all the through-hull fittings at every decommissioning and make sure they are lubricated and turn easily.

4. Type 2 damage is more serious, and can sink the boat if immediate attention is not given to it. Type 2 damage might be a through-hull fitting or seacock that has let go, or a 3-inch-diameter (7.5 cm) hole in the hull. In the case of a seacock letting go, you should have a wooden bung at hand to simply hammer into the hole. You may get wet, but a few taps from a hammer will put it firmly in place. Of course, since it is hammered in from the inside, the bung could be forced out again by water pressure. Have a backup plan in case this should happen.
5. Type 3 damage—a hole in the hull between 3 and 10 inches (7.5 and 25 cm) in diameter—is more serious still, as in the scenario with which we opened this chapter. Your first priority is to slow or stop the flow of water so that your pumps can handle it. In this case you need to do several things (preferably all at the same time!). You need to get something into the hole to stem the inrush of water—a cushion, pillow, folded blanket, anything, even your rear end—and then, once the flow of water has slowed, you need to figure out a more permanent solution. One option is to tie lines to each corner of your smallest sail. Heel the boat (by moving stores, setting sails, or getting crew to one side), and work the sail over the hole. The sailcloth will help reduce the water pressure so that you will be able to get at the hole and work up a more permanent solution.
6. In your spares locker you should have a premade device that you hope you will never have to use, consisting of two pieces of 1/2- or 3/4-inch plywood, each about 4 by 6 inches in area, that sandwich two layers of thick

felt. Through the center of the sandwich runs a single ³/₈-inch (10 mm) bolt, with large washers epoxied in place on the outside surfaces of the plywood. Note that the wood is not square, since you must be able to feed it through the hole. Carry a 10- by 14-inch sandwich, too, just in case. In an emergency, the outside piece of plywood and outside layer of felt are worked through the hole and placed against the hull on the outside. You will be working against sail pressure and water seeping into the boat, but you should have plenty of adrenalin rushing through your veins at this point to help see you through. If you filled the hole with pillows, cushions, or sails from the inside, you may have to go overboard and put the plywood in place from the outside to avoid a tremendous inrush of water. If so, be sure to use a tether to keep you with the boat. Put the second piece of felt and wood over the bolt on the inside of the hull, then bolt them tightly together. Add other wood screws from the inside until the two pieces of plywood are tightly clamped against the hull. You may also want to add caulking to the felt, although this might just make more mess without really helping to stem the water flow. Now you can remove the sail and see how well your hole repair holds up. Even if it leaks slightly, the boat's pumps should be able to keep up.

7. A different approach is to stuff a pillow or cushion into a plastic garbage bag, put that plastic bag into another one, and stuff it into the hole from the outside—if you can reach the hole. Water pressure will suck the bags and pillows into the hole, hopefully bunging it up fairly tight. If you can't reach the hole, use a boathook to push the bags into place. Once they are over the hole, they'll get sucked into place quite quickly. This is a variation on the old-time sailor's technique of putting a *fothered* sail over the hole in the hull. (A fothered sail was one that had rope yarns sewn through it close together.) Today, larger ships carry collision mats for a similar purpose. When you are out sailing, think about what else you could use on your boat to bung up a leak.

8. A Type 4 leak is catastrophic. It is a huge hole, more than 12 inches (30 cm) in diameter. In this case it is unlikely you will be able to contain the inrush of water, and your thoughts should turn to surviving the loss of your boat. Hopefully your insurance is paid up.

Make an Emergency Plan

Whenever you travel by cruise ship, the crew will hold a lifeboat drill to acquaint everyone aboard with what to do in an emergency. When you set off on a long passage on your own boat, you should go through a similar drill so that, in an emergency, you don't have to waste time telling people what to do.

The drill should include:

1. Location of the life raft, life jackets, harnesses, emergency tools, bolt cutters, grab bag, through hulls, and dinghy.
2. Emergency radio procedures. Show the crew how to contact rescue services and the information they may need to relay.
3. The role each crew member will play in a particular type of emergency. For example, in a Type 4 emergency you may set one crew to getting the life raft over the side (1 minute to get it over the side, 45 seconds to inflate it, 20 seconds to set off the EPIRB); and another crew to get stores into it (3–5 minutes, provided the crew knows where all the emergency stores are). This crew member should load half-filled jugs of water (half- or three-quarters-filled jugs float),

flares, grab bag, emergency rations, EPIRB, handheld VHF, and GPS. A third crew should try to contact rescue services (3–5 minutes) and give them all the relevant information. Your job might be to ascertain the extent of the damage and see if the boat can be saved. If you are sure it can't, you can help get supplies into the life raft or move navigation gear and other essentials from below deck to the cockpit for others to load into the life raft.

One factor that becomes very clear from all the book accounts of survival is this: when a boat is about to sink, you need to get everything you will need into the raft to maximize your chances of surviving.

Keel Failure

Bad news! Your keel just fell off! The good news is that even though your boat has capsized, it will probably stay afloat if you can keep it from filling with water. Fortunately, this is a rare occurrence. Usually it happens because the keel bolts have corroded through or they were not installed properly to begin with. It is also more of a problem with high-aspect racing keels, like those on modern America's Cup boats.

Keel-bolt corrosion occurs mostly on older wooden boats on which the bolts are rarely checked. In a good survey, the surveyor may ask to withdraw a keel bolt and check it for corrosion. If you are buying an older wooden boat, this is a wise precaution. Corrosion usually occurs right at the hull-keel joint.

Another reason a keel might drop off is that the builder neither put nuts on the bottom of the keel bolts nor bent the bottom of the bolts over to get a better grip on the lead ballast. In a proper installation, the keel bolts may be welded to a flange, the bottom of each bolt might be bent over, or each bolt might be fit-

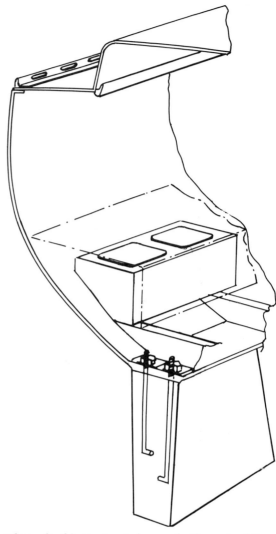

When a keel is constructed properly, the ends of the keel bolts are either bent over or welded to a keel plate and molten lead poured around it. This ensures that the lead cannot slide off the keel bolts. This view also shows how tanks are fitted under bunk flats (dashed line) in a typical cabin layout.

ted with a large washer and nut. Hot lead may also be poured around the bolts and the entire package allowed to cool down. With any of the above methods, the keel will not come off the bolts.

Another problem can result when the weight of the lead ballast compresses the material used in the fiberglass hull and water starts to leak into the boat. This can be fixed temporarily by tightening the keel bolts, but at the first opportunity the boat should be hauled and the keel installed on a new incompressible bed. Usually the first sign of keelson compression is a gap between the hull and the keel. A hairline crack is okay, but a crack that expands to $\frac{1}{4}$ inch or more is a problem that should be attended to immediately.

What can you do if your keel falls off? First, set off your EPIRB. Then make sure you are ready to abandon ship. Don't, however, leave your vessel until you are sure it is going to sink, since a boat in any condition is preferable to a life raft. Englishman Tony Bullimore survived for three days inside his overturned hull in the Southern Ocean before rescue services found him. You can live inside an upturned boat, or you can sit on the upturned hull and wait for rescue. Your decision will depend on the proximity of rescue services, your boat, and your will to survive.

Eleven

For Those in Peril on the Sea

Numerous agencies around the world have been established to rescue people when they get into trouble at sea. The United States Coast Guard (USCG) has several roles—not all of them looked upon favorably by boaters—but nobody is more relieved than a crew in trouble when that red-and-white-striped helicopter or ship shows up.

In Britain, the Royal National Lifeboat Institution (RNLI) has a search-and-rescue (SAR) mission similar to that of the USCG and has developed many rescue techniques that are now used worldwide. The RNLI is an all-volunteer organization supported entirely by charitable contributions. If you are a sailor or boater in British waters, this is one organization you should support. (We'll have more to say about the RNLI later in this chapter.) Britain and Ireland also have a coast guard, but in contrast with the USCG, the UK Coastguard serves only to listen for mariners in distress and then coordinate the organizations that perform the rescues. The RNLI has only its lifeboats, so it is effective as far as 50 miles offshore. Beyond that point the responsibility falls to the Royal Air Force, the Royal Navy, and other services.

Holland, Germany, Portugal, and Sweden have lifeboat services similar to the RNLI, while Norway's rescue service receives partial funding from private industry, as some of its lifeboats accompany the Norwegian fishing fleet for extended periods at sea.

France, Finland, and Iceland also rely on volunteers to man their boats, but the government provides the boats and support. In these countries the lifeboat service is part of a larger coast guard organization, just as the USCG rescue units are part of the overall Coast Guard tasking.

Down under, the New Zealand Rescue Coordination Centre and the Australian Maritime Safety Authority (AMSA) perform search-and-rescue functions similar to those of the USCG and the RNLI. AMSA investigates marine accidents, enforces marine safety, protects the environment, and provides the facilities for six coastal radio stations (at Sydney, Brisbane, Melbourne, Perth, Darwin, and Townsville) that operate under the SOLAS Convention and offer marine safety information, monitor distress frequencies and GMDSS (Global Maritime Distress and Safety System) communications, coordinate rescue operations, and communicate with coastal shipping. Distress calls are monitored in the 2, 4, 6, 8, 12, and 16 MHz marine radio bands from each station.

The Australian national search and rescue plan (AusSAR) falls under the auspices of AMSA. AusSAR's approach, of necessity, has to be flexible, because SAR units are not dedicated and kept on alert, but rather are assembled as the need arises. In a rescue situation, local assets are used first, then long-range assets such as the Australian navy or air force. If other assets are required, they are chartered on an as-needed basis. The bulk of the funding comes from the national government.

The Global Maritime Distress and Safety System (GMDSS)

The foundations of the Global Maritime Distress and Safety System were laid by an international 1978 Safety of Life at Sea (SOLAS) convention as a means of integrating existing means of communication at sea and augment-ing them with new digital communications modes then in development. In 1979, the United Nation's International Maritime Organization (IMO) developed the GMDSS outline and plan, an amalgam of land-, ship-, and satellite-based radio systems that can send and receive distress signals over both short and long distances. SOLAS-regulated ships (essentially, all commercial ships worldwide of more than 300 gross tons) have been required since 1999 to carry the digital radios needed for digital selective calling (DSC), which will be central to the future effectiveness of the GMDSS. All VHF radios manufactured since 1999 have been DSC-equipped, and although digital radios are not required on recreational boats, they do confer significant advantages, as we'll see.

The strength of GMDSS lies in its use of multiple radio frequencies and communications technologies to provide coverage everywhere on the world's oceans. The system divides the oceans into four so-called Sea Areas:

Sea area A1 comprises near-coastal waters up to 25 miles offshore, the limit of reliable ship-to-shore VHF radio transmissions.

A2 lies from 25 to 100 miles offshore (sometimes as far as 200 miles offshore), the limit of reliable medium frequency (MF) transmissions on single sideband (SSB) radio.

A3 covers the high seas between latitudes 70 degrees north and south, an area covered by SSB high frequency (HF) transmissions and by the Inmarsat satellite system.

A4 covers the polar regions, where COSPAS-SARSAT satellite communications are the only option.

The result is a layering of communications networks that work together to provide comprehensive worldwide coverage. Furthermore, GMDSS shifts the emphasis from ship-to-ship distress signals to ship-to-shore communications, allowing search-and-rescue responses to be precisely coordinated by shore-based person-

Table 11–1. GMDSS Coverage

Sea Area	Coverage Area	Distress Services (Digital)	Distress Services (Voice)
A1	From coast to 25 nm	VHF 70 (156.525 MHz)	VHF 16 (156.800 MHz)
A2	From 25–100 nm (sometimes as far as 200 nm)	MF 2187.5 kHz	MF 2182 kHz
A3	High Seas below 70° N and above 70° S	HF and Inmarsat	HF
A4	Polar Regions	COSPAS-SARSAT	No assured coverage

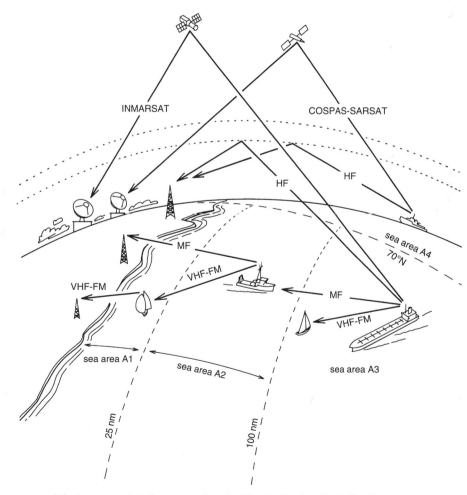

Sea areas and their appropriate frequency bands. (Illustration by Jim Sollers)

nel. The result is better use of all available assets and faster, more efficient rescues.

Note that small vessels—those of less than 300 gross registered tons and pleasure craft—are not regulated under SOLAS conventions, but their distress calls will nevertheless be monitored, relayed, and responded to under GMDSS protocol provided they carry the necessary radio equipment. Currently, as we'll see below, this primarily means VHF and SSB radiotelephones and EPIRBs. There is talk of using newer technologies (satellite phones, mobile phones, automatic distress signals) for SAR operations, but these technologies are not in use as of early 2006.

VHF Radio Distress Calls

Regardless of GMDSS, the most powerful method of calling for assistance in coastal waters remains your VHF radio, and the procedure for making a Mayday call on an analog VHF radio remains unchanged, as follows:

1. Select Channel 16 and press the transmit button.
2. Slowly and clearly say "Mayday, Mayday, Mayday"; say your boat's name three times; give your radio call sign; say "Mayday" and your boat's name again.
3. Give your position, either as latitude and longitude (preferred) or as a bearing and distance from a charted object.
4. Briefly describe the nature of your distress and the assistance you require.
5. Describe your boat by type, color, and size.
6. Say how many people are aboard, and whether they need medical attention.
7. Sign off by saying "out."

Repeat this procedure until someone acknowledges.

If your VHF radio is equipped with digital selective calling (DSC), if it is properly in-stalled and registered, and if it is interfaced with a GPS receiver, a distress call is largely automated, as follows:

1. Lift the cover over the "Distress Button," press the button, then immediately release.
2a. If the display reads "Undesignated," press and hold the Distress Button for five seconds. The radio transmits a "Mayday" alert in digital format containing your identity and location over Channel 70 to the Coast Guard and to other vessels.
2b. Alternatively, if the display provides a choice between "Undesignated" and "Designated," selecting the latter calls up a menu that allows you to specify the type of trouble you are in. Then press and hold the Distress Button for five seconds to send the signal.
3. When the call is acknowledged digitally by another DSC-equipped radio, you will hear a tone.
4. If the radio does not switch automatically to Channel 16 for voice transmission, press the Cancel/Clear button.
5. On Channel 16, send a voice message concerning your situation as described for a Mayday on Channel 16 above.

See the advantages of a digital radio in an emergency? If it is properly interfaced with GPS, it automatically transmits your position to SAR personnel, and if it is properly registered, it automatically identifies you by means of your Maritime Mobile Service Identity number, or MMSI.

Nevertheless, analog VHF radio remains a powerful safety tool. The IMO had planned to discontinue compulsory VHF radio watch on Channel 16 on February 1, 2005, but that change has been suspended indefinitely. For the time being, at least, you can count on the Coast Guard and commercial shipping monitoring Channel 16.

Calling the U.S. Coast Guard for Help

Unfortunately, the United States Coast Guard is stretched thin by its many missions, and there is a vast disparity between its actual communications capability and the capability the public thinks it has. If you pick up your VHF radio and simply shout "Mayday," you might well drown or die of hypothermia before you can be located. Typically, Coast Guard rescue coordinators triangulate a position by taking a bearing on your radio signal from two or more stations before sending a rescue craft.

If you have a 406 MHz EPIRB with GPS capability (see below), it will automatically broadcast your position, but ultimately most SAR operations depend to a large extent on the ability of the people whose lives are in immediate peril to calmly explain their identity, their location, and the nature of their distress. The catch is that the more urgent the distress, the less likely are boaters to be able to communicate the necessary information calmly, and the less likely is their equipment to be functioning properly.

Still, if your goal is to get help fast, you need to know exactly where you are, what your boat looks like, how many people are aboard, and the nature of your distress. And all this information has to be transmitted clearly to allow the Coast Guard operator to record it and get rescue personnel heading toward you.

In an article in *Motor Boating and Sailing*, Executive Editor Dan Fales listed a VHF radio as one of the top three pieces of equipment onboard. Lt. Jaramillo of the U.S. Coast Guard agrees. "It is one of the best pieces of gear to get in touch with us," he says. Jaramillo especially likes the ICOM portable units that are small and reasonably compact. "Every vessel that goes to sea should have, at the very minimum, charts, a GPS, and a VHF radio," he adds. "That way they'll know where they are and what hazards are around them, and they can get in touch with other boats or the Coast Guard."

Beyond VHF

Ship-to-shore VHF communications become unreliable beyond a range of about 25 miles. VHF is essentially a line-of-sight transmission, so its range is limited to the sum of the distances to the horizon from the sending and receiving antennas. When you're more than 25 miles at sea—in GMDSS Sea Area A2—you can still make a Mayday call on VHF radio, but you will probably need an intermediate boat to relay your message to shore-based Coast Guard personnel. If there is no intermediate boat within VHF range, you could be out of luck unless you have a single sideband (SSB) radiotelephone aboard. If you have SSB, you can broadcast a Mayday on 2182 kHz (medium frequency) just as you would on VHF Channel 16. Alternatively, if your SSB is DSC-equipped, you can broadcast a digital Mayday on 2187.5 kHz just as you would on VHF Channel 70.

Medium frequency transmissions on SSB radio will reach shore from 100 miles out, and sometimes from as much as 200 miles out, depending on atmospheric conditions. If you're farther out than that—on the high seas—your primary choices are to transmit a high-frequency (HF) Mayday on SSB radio or to broadcast a distress message via Inmarsat.

Five HF bands—4127 kHz, 6215 kHz, 8219 kHz, 12290 kHz, and 16420 kHz—are reserved for analog distress calls, and the corresponding bands for digital calls are 4207.5 kHz,

6312 kHz, 8414.5 kHz, 12577 kHz, and 16804.5 kHz. The distress call format is as described above, with the added complication that a high seas user must decide which frequency band is appropriate to the time of day and his boat's position. It may be wise to make calls on two or three different bands that bracket the one you think is best.

If your boat is equipped with an Inmarsat terminal and antenna, you can broadcast a distress signal to one of the system's nine satellites—in geostationary orbit above the earth's equator—from anywhere except the polar regions. The satellites will relay the message to earth stations, which then feed it into the GMDSS system.

Inmarsat C terminal equipment is smaller, lighter, and less expensive than its Inmarsat forerunners and is finding increasing use on yachts. An Inmarsat-equipped boat will have the characteristic domed antenna visible on deck. This equipment enables you to send digital text and numeric messages from a keyboard, and to receive such messages—including weather bulletins, search-and-rescue information, and any other safety information that might be of interest to mariners—on your Inmarsat monitor. GMDSS regulations require all large commercial shipping to have Inmarsat capability.

Last, but hardly least, every boat on the high seas should carry at least one emergency position-indicating radiobeacon, or EPIRB. The older 121.5 MHz EPIRBs have been superseded by the superior 406 MHz models, which are digital and broadcast the boat's identity number along with the distress signal. Many 406 EPIRBs can be interfaced with a GPS receiver, in which case they broadcast the boat's position as well. Obviously, this feature greatly increases your chances of rescue. Category I EPIRBs can be activated manually but will also activate automatically when submerged to a depth of 3–10 feet, and will float free of their holders when submerged. Category II EPIRBs must be manually activated. EPIRB signals can be received by satellites anywhere in the world—even the polar seas.

Of course, getting your distress call heard from the high seas is only the first part of the problem. The second, for SAR personnel, is reaching you. When rescue services can't reach you in time due to distance, weather, or both, your best bet might be AMVER.

Automated Mutual-Assistance Vessel Rescue System (AMVER)

When the 106-foot sailboat *Lene Marie* sank in heavy seas 200 miles north of Bermuda on November 9, 1996, the crew were rescued from their life raft by the refrigerated cargo ship *Arctic*, flying the flag of the Netherlands Antilles. The *Lene Marie* had begun flooding in 20-foot seas and 40-knot winds and called for help, which arrived initially in the form of a U.S. Coast Guard C-130, a four-engine turboprop aircraft that located the life raft. The C-130 then vectored the *Arctic* into the area, where it picked up the seven crew and took them to Flushing, Netherlands, the *Arctic*'s destination. The *Arctic* and more than 12,000 other ships are part of AMVER, the U.S. Coast Guard's Automated Mutual-assistance Vessel Rescue system. AMVER is an entirely voluntary program that is open to vessels of any nation. Even during the Cold War, Soviet ships participated. Recently Chinese ships have committed their services to the program. In fact, a Chinese ship, *Gao He*, recently rescued a retired U.S. Navy captain, William Radican, whose 37-foot boat *Seaweed* was sinking in 18-foot seas and 25- to 30-knot winds. *Gao He* delivered Captain Radican to its next port of call in Long Beach, California, two days later.

According to AMVER maritime relations officer Rick Kenney, "No one is turned away. We like to enroll ships over 1,000 gross tons, but we won't say no to a smaller vessel with a professional crew. We are currently enrolling some of the larger megayachts." Today, roughly 40 percent of the world's merchant shipping fleet participate in AMVER. According to Kenney, the service is seeking still more participants. "Every ship increases the number of boats on a plot and makes the chances of a successful rescue that much greater," he says. Every four hours around the clock, participating ships automatically relay their position to a coordination center in West Virginia. A chart showing each ship's location is made available via the U.S. Coast Guard to any rescue organization worldwide. "All we do is pull up the part of the sea where a vessel is in distress, and AMVER ships in the vicinity are shown. We can then ask a vessel to participate in the rescue," says Kenney.

A boat in distress cannot call participating AMVER ships directly. Requests for help must go through the U.S. Coast Guard, because it is the only agency that can access confidential information from Lloyds of London about each ship. Only the rescue coordinator, such as the U.S. Coast Guard center in Boston, can call on a ship to help. The rescue coordinator can access the AMVER system and determine what ship is in the area and what assistance is needed. For example, if a vessel's crew has a heart attack, the rescue coordinator might look for a ship with medical personnel onboard, which might not be the nearest ship. In heavy seas, he might send a supertanker to provide a lee for the distressed ship. If a life raft has to be rescued, he might send a ship with low freeboard. The response depends on what is available. "The rescue coordinator will also look for ships steaming into the area, rather than having a ship turn around," adds Kenney. "These are, after all, merchant ships in business to make money for their owners." The AMVER system has saved more than 1,500 lives to date in the deep oceans of the world beyond the range of shore-based rescue personnel.

When You Need Help in U.S. Waters

The U.S. Coast Guard's HH60 Jayhawk helicopter is a squat, ugly machine with a black bulbous nose, thick-bladed rotors, a thick, flat platform to port, and a hoisting gantry to starboard that gives it a lopsided look. Aft of the black nose it is painted Day-Glo orange and white, with a large red Coast Guard stripe slashed diagonally along the side. But for sailors caught out in heavy weather in North American waters, nothing is quite so beautiful as this machine. When it hovers nearby, your prayers have been answered. Somebody has come to remove you from the maelstrom, the life raft, or the slowly sinking wreck that you have been enduring for the last several hours. At the same time, however, you are suddenly faced with some very important questions. Chief among them, what exactly do you do now? How do you get from the relative safety of your boat to the greater safety of the helicopter?

Before answering that question, it makes sense to think a bit more about how the Coast Guard operates, how it responds to the various calls it receives, and the risks its members run on a regular basis when called to do their duty.

Jayhawk helicopter pilot Lt. Brian Washburn at Otis Coast Guard Air Station on Cape Cod, for example, noted that one of the most important requirements of a successful rescue is that everybody work together. That includes both rescuers and those being rescued, since no one can do the job on his own.

"We are part of a team," he says, "a team that encompasses every person in the Coast Guard." Unspoken is the fact that this team puts its collective lives on the line every time it takes a Jayhawk helicopter, a Falcon HU 25 aircraft, a 41-foot motor lifeboat, a 110-foot cutter or any other "asset," as they are called, to sea in bad weather to save a life.

"Up to a certain wind speed and wave height it is our duty to rescue people," notes Petty

An HH60 Jayhawk helicopter hovers near a Coast Guard patrol boat in a rescue exercise. The rescue basket has been lowered and is being pulled in toward the boat by its tether. Rotor downwash roils the sea surface.

Officer Tom Kish, "but when it gets rougher than that, it's a hands-up situation." In other words, the risky rescues are all-volunteer. Think about this the next time you rush to call the Coast Guard in a non-life-threatening situation.

"There is weather that we won't send some of our craft out in," adds Lt. Jg. Craig Jaramillo, Assistant Operations Officer, U.S. Coast Guard Group Woods Hole, "but no matter what, if you are in trouble, we'll get an asset out to you somehow. If we have to call in a 110-foot boat, we will. If the waves are bigger than 15 feet, we'll bring a 210- or 378-foot boat or a C-130 aircraft, whatever we can get out there. If someone is broken down or is in trouble and we don't have an asset available, we send out a UMIB (Urgent Marine Information Broadcast) to ask for anybody in the vicinity to go and assist the vessel. If there is nobody nearby that can help,

we can access the AMVER network and find out if a ship is in the area."

Jaramillo points out that you might have a long wait if there are no assets available. For example, if the Coast Guard has to send a 110- or 210-footer out in heavy weather, the boat may make only about 6 knots in 15- to 20-foot seas. If you are 40 miles out, it'll take time to get to you. For this reason, he says, it's a good idea to call the Coast Guard early, before a situation reaches a critical stage. "If a bad situation develops, let us know about it," he said. "We can then develop a communications schedule and talk to you every 10 or 15 minutes. If the situation clears up, that's okay. But if it worsens we need to know early, because we can't get 40 or 50 miles out in a few minutes."

With this in mind, if you have a non-emergency situation, but one that could develop into an emergency—let's say your boat's mast has fallen down or the boat has sprung a leak—the correct course of action is either to call the Coast Guard directly on Channel 16 or to make a general Pan-Pan call, which alerts the Coast Guard to the fact you have a problem that is one step below a Mayday.

Each rescue call goes to a regional Rescue Coordination Center (RCC), where officials determine how the call is processed and what assets will be allocated to it. If the boat in trouble is inshore, a 41-footer, 47-footer, or larger vessel may be dispatched. If the boat is holed and sinking 150 miles at sea, an HU25 Falcon jet aircraft may be scrambled, since it flies at 380 knots and can quickly locate survivors and drop a life raft, a dewatering pump (Coast Guard language for a large, self-powered bilge pump), or a locating buoy as a first step toward eventual rescue. If the distressed vessel is 300 miles or more out, an AMVER ship may be asked to assist. Again, all these decisions are made by the rescue coordinator.

When a plane such as a Falcon does arrive, it may stay in the area (depending on its fuel load) until a Jayhawk helicopter or a boat arrives to take over the handling of the situation. According to Washburn, his helicopter can be off the ground quickly but may still take up to an hour to get to a location far at sea. According to Kish, a 44-foot motor lifeboat can operate in 50-knot winds, 30-foot seas, and 20-foot breakers, but only powers at 12 knots. A Coast Guard 41-footer is a faster design at 26 knots, but it can only operate in 30-knot winds and low-breaking seas. Both boats could take several hours to get to a vessel in distress.

Once a helicopter arrives, the pilot will usually stay astern of your boat, and your crew should wear harnesses (as well as life jackets, of course) to stop them from being blown over the side by the downwash from the rotor blades, which can generate winds of more than 100 mph that have been known to overturn small boats. Typically, the pilot will try to hover so that the boat is 5–20 feet outside the area of

A Coast Guard 41-footer is a common sight around major harbors.

downwash, but especially in heavy weather conditions it may be difficult to hold that position. The helicopter will hover for a few minutes while its crew makes a risk assessment of the situation, after which the on-scene commander will decide on the best course of action. While this is going on, be sure not to let your guard down. Many mariners in distress will relax as soon as they see their rescuers, which could invite disaster if the boat is allowed to turn broadside to a breaking sea, pumping efforts lag, or other essential activities are discontinued. There will be time to relax after you have been successfully evacuated.

During this time, you should establish voice contact with a handheld VHF on Channel 16, then follow the instructions you receive precisely. Once the risks have been determined and a course of action decided upon, the action starts. There are no standard procedures, but generalizations are possible. For example, if somebody is injured and the boat has a reasonably flat area, the helicopter may lower a litter or a basket along with an emergency medical technician, who will give first aid to the injured person and then go back up with the litter. After that, real treatment will start in the helicopter. If the injured person is ambulatory, a basket may be lowered for the patient to climb into, in which case you should let the basket drop into the sea or touch the boat before you touch it; otherwise, you could get a nasty jolt of static electricity. Anyone climbing into the basket should keep torso, arms, and fingers inside while being lifted off the boat. It takes a minimum of 6–8 minutes to get lifted into the helicopter.

If your boat lacks a flat, uncluttered area on which a basket can safely be lowered, you may be instructed to get your crew one by one into your tethered life raft for evacuation. Either way, if the situation requires that people be taken off the boat, the Coast Guard may use a rescue swimmer, someone who is trained to jump out of the helicopter, swim to your boat, and help you get aboard the helicopter. Next time you're caught out in a storm, ask yourself if you would want to jump into the water and swim to a boat to help a bunch of strangers. And rescue swimmers do it voluntarily! Do bear in mind that even though rescue swimmers are trained to swim to your boat, they need help to get aboard.

Rescue swimmers I have spoken to say that when they arrive on the scene, all mariners in distress should be wearing a PFD, preferably a type 1. The crew in distress should slow the boat if possible, since boarding the vessel in distress from the water is often the most difficult part of the entire procedure. If you have a swim ladder or a boarding ladder, put it down. When the swimmer is near the boat, stop the props. Let the swimmer come to you. Whatever you do, don't back down on a rescue swimmer!

If the conditions are really bad and you have trouble stopping the boat, set a sea anchor and lie to it. The boat will move backward at about 1–1.5 knots, but the swimmer will still be able to get close. This also has the advantage of putting the boat's bow into the wind, which makes it easier for the helicopter to hover nearby. If you do not have a sea anchor, set a drogue or sail from the bow to slow or stop the boat.

If the swimmer can't get aboard, the rescue crew may tell you to jump in the water and swim to him. Typically, if the boat is moving forward, the helicopter will drop the swimmer just ahead of the boat, and as the boat passes the swimmer, *one* person should jump toward him (children and women first). The swimmer will then maneuver that person into the basket and may even ride up with him or her. Remember that the basket can only hold one person, so if more than one person jumps into the water, those extra people will be forced to swim until the basket comes back down, which might mean a good 10 to 15 minutes in the water, depending on the situation. According to Fijn, a rescue swimmer at Otis CG base in Cape Cod, a swimmer's "worst nightmare is having several people in the water at once in heavy conditions. Then we have to get one into the basket, help the others stay afloat, and keep ourselves afloat."

You should also remember that the swimmer is there to help you, so do what you are told. Don't panic and don't fight him. If you do, you put not only your own life in danger but his as well. In fact, all the rescue swimmers that I talked with were quite frank about this. "I'll hold his head underwater until he does what I tell him or passes out," one told me. "I am trained to save lives, and I must be in control when we are in the water."

A rescue by a Coast Guard boat is often quite similar, the one big difference being that you shouldn't have to jump into the water. As with a helicopter rescue, you should always be wearing your PFD and monitoring a handheld VHF radio so that you can follow all instructions. Typically, the rescue-boat operator will tell you to steer a straight line downwind, although in some situations upwind is better. Put all your fenders out and let the Coast Guard boat come alongside you instead of trying to close with the rescue vessel. The 44-foot motor lifeboat is made of Corten steel, and the 41-footer is made of heavy-duty fiberglass, specifically so that it can come alongside a boat in distress in rough conditions. Again, the Coast Guard trains for this type of situation and is available to do it every day, year round. They should be in control of the situation when lives are at stake.

Using Your Cell Phone

U.S. Coast Guard SAR crews say that more and more people are calling them on cell phones to report problems. Though communications are good, cell phones give the Coast Guard problems when it comes to locating a boat. "We can't home in on a cell phone signal, which can make it difficult to locate the boat," says Petty Officer Tom Allen. "With a marine band radio we can get an LOP (line of position) and locate the vessel, but not with a cell phone." Lieutenant Jaramillo says that he likes the cell phone. "It's a great *backup* system, and we have one on most of our cutters, but we are finding that a lot of boaters are not using marine band radios (VHF). They use their cell phone as a primary communications system." Cell phone coverage extends only 10–30 miles offshore.

Precision Aerial Distribution System (PADS)

One of the assets that might be deployed in a rescue situation is a commercially developed SAR dropping system known as PADS. This system uses a static line to drop rescue equipment from an aircraft. The static line is attached to a long streamer or trail line that can be dropped with some precision directly over or very near the distressed vessel. The manufacturer's "Storpedo" canisters can hold radios, supplies, food, water, or fuel and can be parachuted to a vessel in distress.

Wavetalk

Wavetalk is a digital marine satellite phone system that uses an antenna about the size of a bicycle helmet. It can be used almost anywhere in the world where Westinghouse satellites are visible. Satellite service is provided by the American Mobile Satellite Corporation in the U.S. and by TMI Communications in Canada. Modem communication is at 4800 baud. This means that you can call direct, fax, or e-mail a shore station easily. Currently the cost for the marine unit is under $5,000. Airtime costs vary, depending on the service provider.

STORM SCENARIO

Newport to Bermuda

The Newport-Bermuda race is held every other year, and yachts sail a distance of 625 miles from Newport, Rhode Island, to Bermuda. In recent years, 150 or more boats have taken part in the race. The following is an entirely fictional account of how a disaster could unfold.

Friday, 2:30 P.M. Twenty-four yachts, between 38 and 42 feet, cross the starting line on their way to Bermuda in Class E. Each yacht carries between five and seven crew. Some of the boats are lightweight production race boats with accommodations stripped down to the rule minimum. They can reasonably expect to be in Bermuda by the following Wednesday. The weather forecast is for moderate winds over most of the course, but heavy clouds to the south of Bermuda bear watching.

Saturday, noon. Winds have been light since the start, and the class E yachts are strung out between 80 and 110 miles from the start. The heavy clouds have coalesced into a tropical disturbance that could develop into a storm, but the disturbance is still 150 miles south of Bermuda.

Sunday, noon. Winds are still fairly light, and the Class E yachts are well into the Gulf Stream. A few have made it through the stream and are in an eddy on its south side. The leaders are 250 miles down the course, but tail-end Charlie is only 187 miles from the start line. The tropical disturbance has developed into a tropical storm with winds to 50 knots and is moving north at 13 knots. It is expected to pass west of Bermuda shortly after daybreak on Monday.

Monday, noon. The lead Class E yachts are now 370 miles down the course and are facing a southwesterly wind and heavy swells from the storm. The storm has swung to the east and will pass around the north side of Bermuda, about 100 miles from the island.

Tuesday, noon. The storm is making its turn to cross the fleet. The leading Maxi boats have made it to Bermuda and are already docked in Hamilton. But none of the Class E boats is closer than 180 miles from the island, and tail-end Charlie still has 308 miles to go. All the Class E boats are feeling winds up to 50 knots and 30-foot seas. The storm is now forecast to become a hurricane within 12 hours.

Tuesday, 10:43 P.M. A 42-footer, one of the largest Class E boats, reports that her mast is down. The call is made by hand-held VHF to another yacht, which relays the message to race HQ. Winds are reported to be 60–70 knots, with gusts to 80.

Tuesday, 11:54 P.M. A mast is down on another Class E boat, a 39-footer. The boat reports that the spar has holed the hull and the crew is bailing frantically. A 40-footer is standing by the casualty. Both boats are about 230 miles from Bermuda. The U.S. Coast Guard has been alerted and is sending a Falcon jet with a dewatering pump. The boats are out of range of the HH60 Jayhawk helicopter, however. Winds are reported to be 75 knots or more, and seas are reported to be cresting at 30–40 feet. The air is filled with spray and rain.

Wednesday, 1:08 A.M. A 38-footer, one of the smallest boats in the fleet, reports that it has been rolled over, its mast is gone, and two crew members are injured, although the boat is still afloat. A 40-footer has turned back to give aid. Both boats are about 200 miles from Bermuda. The Coast Guard is sending a 210-foot cutter from Norfolk, Virginia, and a freighter in the area has been asked to stand by.

Wednesday, 2:43 A.M. The wooden cutter *Validote*, a 48-footer out of Padanarum, Massachusetts, reports that it is taking on water. The crew thinks that a plank has sprung. Winds are reported to be a sustained 80 knots, with gusts to 100.

Wednesday, 2:47 A.M. Man-overboard! *Mation*, a 50-footer only 8 miles off Bermuda, reports that one of the crew has been swept overboard. His harness tether was an older style, and it parted. He was wearing an inflatable life jacket and has a strobe. The crew can see the strobe light and are attempting rescue.

Wednesday, 3:04 A.M. *Validote* reports that the water is coming in too fast for the pumps. The crew are getting the life rafts ready. The eight crew will distribute themselves between the two, four-man life rafts.

Wednesday, 3:06 A.M. Two 40-footers unable to see each other in the conditions collide in the dark. One boat is sinking, the other is badly damaged. The crew of the sinking boat have launched their life raft. Five men are in the life raft, two have made it onto the other boat. The life raft is tethered to the surviving boat.

Wednesday, 3:14 A.M. *Mation* reports that a second person who went overboard to get the first man was lost when his safety line snapped. Both men were last seen drifting downwind faster than the boat could travel. The boat is chasing both men.

A 50-footer has *Validote* in sight and is standing by. *Validote* has one life raft inflated. The 50-footer reports that *Validote* is down by the head and recommends that the crew take to the life raft. The first life raft leaves *Validote* with four men and two women aboard. The 50-footer passes within 40 feet of *Validote* and a line is passed to the life raft. Two women and a man get onto the 50 before the life raft capsizes. One man goes into the sea from the raft. He catches a line from the 50 and is hauled aboard. Two more men scramble aboard the 50. The last man slips between the life raft and the hull. He is seen to hit his head and drifts away from the raft. One of the 50-footer's crew leaps into the sea with a lifeline and grabs the man. They are hauled aboard.

Validote sinks, and the last life raft is cut free with three men aboard. The 50-footer is joined by a 47-footer, whose crew passes a line to the raft. All the men are transferred, but not before one breaks a leg. The rescuers head for Bermuda.

Wednesday, 3:17 A.M. A 40-footer is rolled over and dismasted. The crew are still aboard but are thinking about abandoning ship. A nearby vessel tells them via VHF to stay aboard unless the boat is sinking.

Wednesday 3:21 A.M. *Mation* reports that the two crew overboard have been recovered. One is OK, but the other is being worked on by the boat's owner, who happens to be a doctor.

A storm scenario of this magnitude has not yet befallen the Bermuda race, but similar disasters have marred two other major ocean races: the Fastnet Race (from England, across the Irish Sea to the Fastnet Rock and back) and the Sydney-Hobart Race. Given that the range of an HH60 helicopter is about 300 miles and the Bermuda race is 625 miles long, there is a gap of about 200 to 300 miles in the latter half of the race that rescue helicopters cannot cover. As of this writing there are no rescue helicopters, facilities, or formal deep-sea rescue services based in Bermuda.

What is the lesson? Simply that, if you go to sea, you should certainly know how to call for help, but you should also know how to help yourself. That's what this book is for. If you're prepared, you'll probably never be tested. That's Murphy's Law.

More on the RNLI

For British or Irish mariners, nothing gives as much relief as the sight of the blue and orange RNLI lifeboat butting into a head sea to perform a rescue. The organization has been saving lives at sea since 1828 and became the Royal National Lifeboat Institution in 1854. An all-volunteer organization funded by charitable donations, the RNLI operates more than 300 boats at 222 lifeboat stations around the coast of the

United Kingdom and the republic of Ireland and makes rescues as far as 50 miles offshore.

According to the RNLI, it sends out its lifeboats more than 18 times on the average day around the coast. (Many lifeboats actually launch down ramps when needed and are then retrieved after a rescue. Others sit on moorings.) More than half of all launches in a typi-cal year are to pleasure craft in trouble. To give you an idea of the work done by the RNLI in one year (1999), 1,030 lives were saved by lifeboats requiring more than 9,143 hours at sea. The largest lifeboats cost more than $1.5 million (about £1 million) and the smallest about $17,000. All are paid for through volunteer fundraising.

STORM SCENARIO

RNLI Rescue at Sea 1

The following is an account of the rescue of the skipper and four crew from the yacht *Be Happy*, 22 miles off the south coast of England on October 28, 1996 in pitch darkness and driving rain. A lifeboat was launched into the teeth of a Force 9 storm. The account is taken from the official RNLI records.

At 7:33 P.M. on Monday, 28 October, 1996, Portland Coastguard alerted Captain Neil Hardy, honorary secretary of the Swanage lifeboat, that a 29 m (90-foot) yacht, 22 miles from Anvil Point, had lost her sails and one engine, was taking water through a broken window, and was requesting assistance. The honorary secretary authorised the immediate paging of the lifeboat crew.

Twelve minutes later the 11.77 m (38 foot 7 inch) Mersey-class lifeboat *Lifetime Care* (currently on relief duties at Swanage whilst the station lifeboat was undergoing routine maintenance), launched from her slipway. By 7:49 P.M. the lifeboat cleared the shelter provided by Anvil Point and met Force 9–12 winds, heavy squalls, poor visibility and very rough seas with a 6–8 meter (18 to 25 foot) swell. The storm, the remains of Hurricane *Lili*, had devastated parts of the East Coast of America a few days before, and went on to cause havoc in southern England.

A rescue helicopter from Portland arrived over the yacht at 8:04 P.M. The lifeboat coxswain was able to use his VHF/DF set to confirm the course, but at 8:21 the radar went down and at 8:39 the lifeboat lost cooling water to the starboard engine. The engine was shut down while the mechanic investigated the problem. Meanwhile the lifeboat continued at a speed of 8 to 10 knots. At 9:06 P.M. the coxswain requested the helicopter turn on its searchlight, and at 9:12 he reported that he could see its lights.

At 9:20 P.M. Swanage lifeboat arrived on the scene and, while the lifeboat crew refilled the starboard engine fresh-water-coolant tank, Coxswain Haw appraised the situation. Only the yacht's navigation lights were lit, but she was well illuminated by the helicopter. She had a scrap of jib set, only one engine worked and steering was difficult with partial loss of electrical and hydraulic power. A broken window had been shored up. The vessel had been trying to make a course of due north but was rapidly being pushed eastward. The skipper said that he and his four crew wanted to stay onboard, but Coxswain Haw informed him that towing in the prevailing conditions would be impossible.

At 9:37 P.M., having watched the yacht broach twice and get knocked onto her beam ends once, the coxswain told the skipper that once the tide began to ebb, conditions would become even worse and it would then be extremely difficult to evacuate the yacht. At 9:39 P.M. the skipper asked that he and his crew be evacuated.

The yacht rose and fell violently in the very heavy swell. She heeled to starboard, away from the wind (estimated at 60 knots at the time), and was also rolling violently. Driving rain and spray filled the air, reducing visibility to 100 yards. Instructions were passed to the yacht to assemble the crew on deck. The starboard engine was restarted. With five lifeboatmen assembled along the port side, they approached the yacht on her lee side.

The four yacht crew stood at the starboard rail with their skipper at the helm. As the two craft came together, they both rolled with such violence and speed that the lifeboat rails were crushed inboard, giving absolutely no time for the lifeboatmen to jump clear. As a result four lifeboatmen were injured—Chris Coe receiving a broken arm. Despite this, the four yachtsmen jumped aboard and were assisted to the wheelhouse. The skipper had difficulty in freeing his safety harness, but eventually succeeded, and jumped aboard the lifeboat. He clung to the radar support. Only then was the coxswain able to drive the lifeboat astern, clear of the stricken yacht, and shut down the overheating starboard engine, which had worked just long enough to help.

First aid was administered to crew member Chris Coe, who had suffered a severe fracture to his left forearm. Crew members Pond and Aggas had both sustained severe bruises. The Decca Navigator had now failed. At 9:55 P.M. the coxswain informed Portland Coastguard of the situation and the helicopter was tasked with escorting the lifeboat back to Swanage. At ten minutes past midnight, the lifeboat reached Swanage. Returning to the slipway would have been difficult in the circumstances, so the lifeboat was put on a mooring. Survivors were landed ashore and Chris Coe taken to hospital.

In his official report, Leslie Vipond, divisional inspector of lifeboats for the south says:

"Coxswain Haw showed excellent command ability in instructing the yachtsmen of what was expected of them, then considerable courage in placing his lifeboat tight alongside the casualty, in violent sea conditions, knowing that he would have one chance before his starboard engine stopped. That no lives were lost was due to several factors: The coxswain made the best possible speed to the casualty, despite prevailing weather conditions; the Coastguard rescue helicopter was able to guide the lifeboat to the casualty, provide radio communications and illuminated the scene during the evacuation; the crew of the yacht acted in a disciplined manner, responding well to the instructions of coxswain and crew, and Portland Coastguard provided a professional and vital link with the casualty and the rescue elements. Later, this was supplemented by an escort for the lifeboat."

Paul Fryer, the skipper of the yacht, which finally washed up on the Isle of Wight, wrote to RNLI headquarters to express his gratitude:

"In atrocious conditions, with winds exceeding 78 knots, *Be Happy* had broached twice and had taken on water from a storm-shattered window. The hydraulic steering was failing and the electrics short-circuiting. The whole operation was so smoothly executed that my crew remarked on the simplicity of stepping from one boat to another, in amazement—considering the difference in size of the two boats. The bravery of the men who helped us aboard, and the skill of the coxswain in holding the boat in position, could not be surpassed. I was extremely impressed at the professionalism of the whole organisation and feel strongly that some sort of recognition of bravery should be bestowed on the crew of that night. The conditions were appalling, but despite the fact that they were one engine down, they still came to our rescue. Personally I feel that we can never thank these men enough."

Some rescues put these lifeboat crews at considerable risk. And all for little or no pay. When asked why they do it and how they find volunteers to go out in atrocious conditions, RNLI personnel typically give unassuming answers like this one from the former coxswain of *The Mumbles* lifeboat:

> When you are setting off in the blackness of night into a Force 9 gale, into God-only-knows-what, the feeling of unity between a lifeboat crew is inexplicable. No matter how frightened you feel, you know that the crew of the ship who are waiting for you are a great deal more frightened than you.

David Mason, coxswain of the Great Yarmouth and Gorleston Lifeboat, gives further insight into why RNLI volunteers go out in bad weather. "You come off the lifeboat physically wrecked and bruised but you still come back for more, and after a successful rescue you're on cloud nine for days. It really is a hell of a feeling. "

"They were staring death in the face but the satisfaction we felt by saving them was amazing, it's something I'll never forget," says Pat Maclean, coxswain of the Oban lifeboat.

I got the same response from U.S. Coast Guardsmen: "The look on the faces of the people we rescue makes all the training, all the effort and hard work worth it," says HH60 Jayhawk pilot Lt. Brian Washburn.

These trained volunteers in Britain and professionals in America put their lives on the line every time they go out. People get hurt and some get killed, but still they go. As David Chant, ex-coxswain of the St David's lifeboat, puts it, "It's not really fear. You don't have time for that because you've got a job to do. It's more anticipation of what lies ahead."

It is remarkable that in most rescue services, volunteers comprise the backbone of the front line. Finding volunteers isn't easy. "I look for people who fit in. I don't always go for the big hefty blokes. Sometimes a weedy little guy who looks as if he wouldn't say boo to a goose can go out and battle a storm with the best of them," says one lifeboat coxswain on recruiting crew members.

Pay For Rescue?

After some high-profile rescues, including those of solo racers Tony Bullimore and Isabelle Autissier in the Southern Ocean during the 1999 Vendee Globe Around-Alone race, there has been a lot of discussion in the press about whether sailors should pay for their rescues. The same question was asked after the 1979 Fastnet Race disaster and the Sydney-Hobart Race in December 1998.

Interestingly, very little of this comment comes from the people who put their lives on the line. Their attitude seems to be, "We're out there anyway, training for rescues of this nature; however, very few times do we actually have a real event where we can test our equipment and personnel to the limit."

The U.S. Naval Institute held a seminar in 1999 to examine such questions. One participant, Captain Jimmy Ng, made a telling statement: "Risk analysis is my game. In responding to a search-and-rescue case, we don't look at whether the victim is a man, woman, or a child. We don't look at whether they were stupid or smart, rich or poor. We see a life and from there it goes to risk analysis. From an operational perspective, a life cannot be measured in money or resources. I've concluded that one life is worth a life. I don't mean one-for-one. I mean that a life is worth risking to save a life. When we see a life at risk we will put people at risk. Managing that risk is part of the problem."

Another speaker, Lieutenant Colonel Michael Canders of the New York Air National Guard, said, "Human life, of course, is priceless, so that a one-word answer can be given to the panel question. If someone needs help, we go without question. We are ready,

U.S. Coast Guard rescue personnel in an exercise off Ft. Lauderdale. A rescuer descends in harness; guiding a rescue basket aboard (note rotor downwash in background); a "rescuee" is reeled up to the chopper. (Photos by Suki Finnerty)

willing, and able to assist whenever and wherever we can. We are proud of our mission both in peacetime and in combat and consider it a sacred trust that should not be compromised by any financial considerations."

Other comments from well-known people tend to support the work of rescue services. In the online newsletter *Scuttlebutt*, designer Bruce Kirby says,

> [A commentator] has reiterated the often-heard suggestion that those who get into trouble when venturing out into the ocean in racing boats should be responsible for the expenses of

anyone who might be involved in their rescue. The navies and coastal patrols of Australia—where most of the spectacular rescue action has taken place in the past few years—and of other nations as well, are on duty 100 percent of the time. When they are called upon to rescue a yachtsman in difficulty they do not design and build a destroyer and a helicopter and then recruit a crew to man them. These facilities already exist and are constantly on patrol and practice missions. The expenses of the men and equipment involved are fixed costs.

This point has been made in the Australian Parliament on more than one occasion. The percentage difference between fuel costs for a real rescue and the mock rescues they are constantly carrying out would be very small. In many cases an exercise might even be more expensive than the real thing. There is no question that it would be a great tragedy if a serviceman were to lose his life in an effort to rescue a distressed sailor. But again, servicemen are also lost during practice sessions. We have seen exceptional heroism on the part of rescue teams—most of them off the southern coast of Australia—and when everyone is safely ashore and dry there is usually more pride of purpose among the rescuers than among the rescued.

STORM SCENARIO

RNLI Rescue at Sea 2

The following is another account of a dramatic RNLI rescue. The fishing vessel *Hope Crest* got into trouble off the coast of Scotland on February 16, 1997. This account is also taken from RNLI files:

At 6:27 P.M. on Sunday 16 February 1997, Fraserburgh lifeboat station honorary secretary was contacted by MRCC Aberdeen and asked to launch the lifeboat to assist the fishing vessel *Hope Crest*, taking on water some 50 miles to the northeast of Fraserburgh. *Hope Crest* was involved in pair-seining with another vessel, *Olive Ann*, which was standing by.

Aberdeen Coastguard had initially tasked a Sea King helicopter from RAF Lossiemouth to the incident but an attempt by the helicopter trying to lower a pump to the vessel had failed due to the severe weather conditions. The winds were reported to be 40 knots, with the seas reaching 12 m (40 feet) with only 5 seconds between the crests.

At 6:35 P.M. Fraserburgh's 14.3 m (47 foot) Tyne-class lifeboat, *RNLB City of Edinburgh*, launched into the harbour. Immediately prior to launching, Aberdeen Coastguard had requested that one of the lifeboat station's portable pumps be left ashore for the helicopter to collect. However, as the lifeboat cleared the harbour they informed the coxswain that the helicopter was returning to base. Coxswain Sutherland decided to return and collect the second pump before proceeding.

At 6:45 P.M. the lifeboat cleared the harbour and met the full southeasterly gale with wind against an increasing southerly flood tide. As the lifeboat cleared the coast the seas and swell grew all the time and were estimated to be between 10–12 metres (32 to 38 feet). *Hope Crest* was unable to communicate directly with the lifeboat or Aberdeen Coastguard due to loss of electrical power. When the lifeboat was approximately 20 miles from the scene, *Olive Ann* reported that her medium frequency (MF) aerial had been broken by a large sea.

When the lifeboat was within 2 miles, the Coxswain reduced speed to allow the crew to rig the portable pump and get its equipment ready for transfer. The searchlights were manned and the lifeboat approached the casualty, which kept disappearing in the huge swells and breaking seas. At 9:05 P.M. the lifeboat was running alongside and Coxswain Sutherland asked the fishing vessel to turn onto a northerly heading as he considered that this would give the best chance of transferring a pump in the prevailing conditions.

Hope Crest managed to turn to starboard away from the weather and Coxswain Sutherland took up position on her port beam and slowly edged in to attempt the transfer. Both boats were being picked up by the huge swells and being thrown down the face of them. Thus the speed and heading of the lifeboat had to be adjusted constantly in order to avoid collision with the casualty, which was also rolling heavily. A bag containing the suction hoses for the pump were thrown on board as the boats came together, but it was impossible to transfer the pump, as the decks were continuously at different levels, with the lifeboat crew looking down on heads or up at faces on the fishing boat.

Coxswain Sutherland had to bear the lifeboat away sharply at this point, in order to avoid a collision. As the lifeboat closed for a second attempt, Coxswain Sutherland had to go hard astern as the seas and swell threatened to throw the lifeboat onto the casualty as she rolled to port. As the casualty rolled back to starboard, the decks of both vessels came level for a moment and the pump was passed across with the engine running, which enabled the fishing-boat crew to use it immediately.

The *Hope Crest* resumed a southwesterly course towards Fraserburgh at 4.5 knots with the lifeboat in close attendance. This speed was very uncomfortable for the lifeboat crew and one large sea threw her onto her starboard beam resulting in Assistant Mechanic Graeme Campbell sustaining a bruise to his face and the loss of a lifebuoy. At one point the fishing boat disappeared from sight and the skipper reported that he had lost all his navigation and deck lights. Coxswain Sutherland took the lifeboat onto the casualty's starboard quarter as the galley light could be seen from this position. A further heavy sea hit the lifeboat and threw her onto her starboard beam, but there were no injuries or damage, only a fairly shaken crew.

At about 1.00 A.M. the vessels began to see an improvement in the weather and the fishing vessel was able to increase to 7 knots. The vessels arrived in Fraserburgh at 2:30 A.M. and the lifeboat was refueled and ready for service at 2:45 A.M.

In his official report, John Caldwell, Inspector of lifeboats for Scotland says,

> This nine-hour service in extremely adverse weather conditions was exceptionally well executed by Coxswain Sutherland and his crew. That they were able to succeed in transferring a pump in conditions that had defeated the rescue helicopter is testimony to the high standards of seamanship involved. The transfer of the pump, running and ready for use, was described by the skipper and crew of the *Hope Crest* as "unbelievable." I consider that the manner in which Coxswain Sutherland and his crew planned and executed this service is a credit to the RNLI. The decision to have the pump running before transfer saved valuable time and avoided previous difficulties which other casualties have experienced in starting portable pumps. During the return to Fraserburgh he ensured that he was in visual contact with the *Hope Crest* in order that an immediate response could be made in the event of her having further difficulties.

Coxswain Albert Sutherland was presented with a Bronze Medal by Prince Michael of Kent, at the RNLI's Annual Presentation of Awards in London. Medal Service Certificates were presented locally to other crew members.

Towing Services

In 1986 the U.S. Coast Guard started referring non-emergency towing calls to private towing services. There are several towing operators in most areas of the country. Seatow (yellow boats), Towboat/US (red boats), and Vessel Assist (blue boats) have some of the largest fleets around, based in various ports. These three main towing services account for more than 82 percent of the non-life-threatening rescues made off U.S. coasts today. Each service is set up so that members pay monthly or annual dues and get certain services free. Most offer free towing, free jump starts, free delivery of parts, ungrounding when your boat is aground on a soft bottom, and coverage on any boat anywhere in the United States. Costs vary according to the service, and you should shop carefully.

There are many services available to the mariner in distress. Knowing what is available is part of conquering the fear of being out there in the ocean's vastness. With the latest in reliable satellite and electronic technology, rescue services are faster, more precise, and can get there faster. But boatowners need to make sure they have done everything possible to enable rescue services to find them and to get them off the boat safely.

Appendix

U.S. Coast Guard Dewatering Pump Instructions

In an emergency situation, when a dewatering pump is dropped by the Coast Guard, many people tear open the package and in the rush to make something happen, forget to read the instructions. Then they tell the Coast Guard plane that the pump doesn't work. Pumps are checked every 30 days before they are put aboard a plane. The correct procedure, adapted from an original article by HH 60 Jayhawk pilot, Lt. Daniel J. Travers, is outlined here.

These pumps (classified as the CG P1B Salvage pump by the Coast Guard) are capable of discharging 120 gallons (456 L) per minute and will run for about 6–8 hours on the 2 gallons (7.6 L) of gas delivered with the pump. Hopefully, you will never need to use one, but about 10 percent of all SAR missions involve dropping a pump. If you have to use one, here's the expert's way of making it work properly.

The pump is delivered in a water-resistant orange plastic container. First, remove the delivery strap, then remove the orange container lid by unsnapping the locking clips. Do not cut the cord connecting the lid to the box because there is an extra suction hose gasket taped to the inside of the lid. You do not want to damage it. The first thing you will see is a flashlight for night-time delivery and a set of instructions sealed in plastic. Do not discard this package. Open it and *read the instructions.*

There are two double-bagged plastic bags in the container, open the outer one and remove the yellow suction hose. In the inner plastic bag is the pump, a discharge hose, and two 1-gallon (3.8 L) gas cans. Make sure that none of this gear goes over the side in the confusion. Remove the pump from the container by lifting and twisting it slightly to break the seal between the container and the pump. Only now can you activate the pump.

1. Before attaching the yellow suction hose, check the female end of the screw fitting to ensure that the rubber gasket is in place. If it is missing, get the gasket from the container lid and place it inside the female end of the screw fitting. Without this gasket in place, the suction hose will not work properly. Attach the yellow suction hose to the aluminum (or plastic) male end on the pump. Screw it on carefully so that you do not cross the plastic threads. Now put the other end of the hose in the bilge.

2. Unroll the blue discharge hose, leading the red end over the side. Do not cut the red end even though it looks like there is no opening for water to pass through. The red end is designed to keep air and water from back-siphoning into the hose. The force of the discharge water will push the black rubber baffle out of the way.

3. Attach one of the two gas tanks to the pump and couple the loose fuel line to the pump via the coupling nut. Make sure the nut is pushed on properly or you will have a gasoline leak.

4. (VERY IMPORTANT) Prime the pump with the priming handle until water fills the suction hose. Water will discharge from the pump via the grey nozzle when it is primed properly.

5. Even though the instruction card says to choke the pump, do not move the run/choke lever until you have tried two starts. The run/choke lever is set to the middle by Coast Guard mechanics and 95 percent of the time the pump will start as it is set up. To start the pump, pull the starter cord. If the pump does not start within two tries, move the run/choke lever to choke, pull once and move it back to the middle before trying again.

6. Once the pump starts (it sounds just like a lawn mower), move the run/choke lever to run and let it do its job until the boat is empty of water.

7. A step not shown on the instruction card is to reprime the pump with the primer handle until water discharges from the grey nozzle.

If the pump fails to start (and some pumps do because they are shaken up when they are dropped out of planes), call the airplane crew and ask for help. They are trained to use these pumps and can trouble-shoot it for you. They may even drop a second pump and then you'll have to go through the entire procedure again.

Acknowledgements

In the beginning there was an idea, then a proposal, and then came the hard work of putting it all together. Undertaking a book of this nature seemed like a relatively straightforward project until I started to add flesh and muscle to the skeleton outline I had created. As I wrote, it became obvious that although there was a huge amount of information available, a lot of it was only known to a few people. Those people gave freely of their time and often commented on different parts of the manuscript.

There were the specialists like Lt. Brian P. Washburn, Lt. Daniel J. Travers, both U.S. Coast Guard HH60 Jayhawk pilots, and Lt. Craig M. Jaramillo, U.S. Coast Guard, who helped tremendously to give me accurate picture of Coast Guard operations. The RNLI website contained a lot of information which was backed up with help from Shelley Woodroffe of the RNLI. Joseph M. Sienkiewicz, Senior Marine Forecaster, of NOAA read and commented on the weather chapter, and Bob Sweet's *Onboard Weather Forecasting: A Captain's Quick Guide* was a very valuable recource. Dean Clarke, Executive Editor of Sport Fishing magazine, read the manuscript and added many, many, comments. Bill Sisson, Editor of *Soundings* read the manuscript and caught some errors. Robert Adriance, formerly of Boat/U.S. pointed me in the right direction to find various storm anchor studies. J. J. Marie of Zodiac, North America, gave me information on inflatables in heavy seas, and Victor Shane made a pre-publication edition of his *Drag Device Database* available. Henry Little and Mike Toppa, from North Sails, commented on problems and solutions they had experienced in rough weather. Sailmaker Dave Pelissier sent me information on the Jordan Series drogue and put me in touch with Donald Jordan, its inventor. Over many a drink, Rich Worstell introduced me to his friends and owners of Valiant yachts who have sailed around the world. Tom Rodenhouse and Mark Schrader were among the more notable; I picked their brains to the benefit of this book.

Then there are all the marketing and sales managers who know their products well and sent information as I requested it. Many of them, including Jack Dunn and Bert Brodin of Wichard; Dick Rath of Lewmar, Chris Bouzaid, and Steve Armitage of Autoprop; Ron Crowder and Tony Smith of ACR; Mark Mitchell of Comar; Royce Randlett, Jr. of Helix Mooring Systems; Annette Baker of Mustang; David Emmons of Perimeter Industries; and Fred Johnson of Edson International, sent products for me to try.

Others also helped tremendously by providing help and advice about their products and experiences, Skip Raymond of Hathaway Rieser and Raymond; Bob Black and Gordon Houser who provided the Wellcraft pictures and lots of advice; Dave Simmons of UK Sails; and Chip Barber who, on the long trip across the Atlantic, discussed many lifesaving products and the Sea Marshall beacon.

But these were not all the people who gave their help unstintingly. Many members of the U.S. Coast Guard talked freely about their experiences and how they performed their jobs. Jamestown's Harbormaster, Sam Paterson, and the Jamestown Emergency Rescue crew spent time firing flares and "rescuing" me after I jumped off their boat several times wearing various lifejackets. Jeff Going of Zodiac provided the life raft that we used in those "rescues." Sailor friends such as Sheila McCurdy, Bob James, photographer Dan Nerney, and many others related their experiences and gave of their time.

Then there are the books written by people who have experienced survival conditions on the ocean, the Baileys, Steve Calahan, George Sigler, are but a few whose words of wisdom permeate these pages. Others helped in other ways, and while your names may not be listed here, I thank you. Many friends and associates, mentioned in the text, freely gave of their time and expertise. I hope I haven't missed anyone, but in a project that lasts as long as this one did, I may have. Thank you, anyway. Note that while everyone gave their help, the mistakes are mine alone.

For everyone else out there, good luck and sail safely.

Index

Numbers in **bold** refer to pages with illustrations

HICKMANS